Religious Super-diversity and Peacebuilding across Asia and its Diasporas

Religions and Peace Studies

Series Editor: Alessandro Saggioro, Sapienza University, Rome

Peace and religion intertwine and, since they are crucial to all human cultures, they require a more comprehensive analysis to be understood beyond all the clichés that portray religions either as warmongering or peace-promoting factors.

Dealing with peace and religion means navigating the concepts of border and boundary, identity, alterity, and diversity, questioning the role of historical narratives in conflicts and their resolutions.

This book series explores the nexus between peace and religion, providing a reference tool for interdisciplinary, diachronic, and comparative research approaches. Furthermore, it aims to collect and develop scientific analyses dealing with all types of sources, such as sacred texts, literature and art, symbols and musealized objects, official documents about peace issued by governmental and non-governmental institutions, historical records, and many others. Also, a variety of sub-topics are included, all revolving around the peace-religion axis and ranging from ecology to sustainability, from migration to gender issues, and from economy to literature and art.

The interdisciplinary dimension of the book series is grounded in a discursive approach to conflict and (re)conciliation through the languages of history, philosophy, anthropology, sociology, law, literature, and arts. The time span covered is broad and encompasses past civilizations and empires and their legacy, up to the dislocation and crisis of their memory in the present.

Finally, one of the most significant challenges of this book series is to make room for a consistent reflection on the history of the study of religions and peace and the methodological approaches scholars have adopted over the centuries to shape the discipline.

Published

Be Like Adam's Son
Theorising, Writing and Practising Peace in the Arab Region
Edited by Fernanda Fischione and Arturo Monaco

Narratives of Peace in Religious Discourses
Perspectives from Europe and the Mediterranean in the Early Modern Era
Edited by Ludovico Battista, Maria Fallica, and Beatrice Tramontano

Religious Super-diversity and Peacebuilding across Asia and its Diasporas

Edited by
Alessandro Saggioro and Carmelo Russo

SHEFFIELD UK   BRISTOL CT

Published by Equinox Publishing Ltd.

UK: Office 415, The Workstation, 15 Paternoster Row, Sheffield, South Yorkshire, S1 2BX
USA: ISD, 70 Enterprise Drive, Bristol, CT 06010

www.equinoxpub.com

First published 2025

© Alessandro Saggioro, Carmelo Russo and contributors 2025

All rights reserved. No part of this publication may be reproduced or transmitted in any form or by any means, electronic or mechanical, including photocopying, recording or any information storage or retrieval system, without prior permission in writing from the publishers.

British Library Cataloguing-in-Publication Data
A catalogue record for this book is available from the British Library.

ISBN-13 978 1 80050 644 2 (hardback)
         978 1 80050 645 9 (paperback)
         978 1 80050 646 6 (ePDF)
         978 1 80050 708 1 (ePub)

Library of Congress Cataloging-in-Publication Data

Names: Saggioro, Alessandro editor | Russo, Carmelo, 1977- editor
Title: Religious super-diversity and peacebuilding across Asia and its
   diasporas / edited by Alessandro Saggioro and Carmelo Russo.
Description: Sheffield, South Yorkshire ; Bristol, CT : Equinox Publishing
   Ltd, 2025. | Series: Religions and peace studies | Includes
   bibliographical references. | Summary: "This book offers a thorough
   examination of super-diversity, peacebuilding, and dialogue, providing
   valuable insights into the multifaceted nature of contemporary society
   and the complexities involved in fostering peace amidst diversity"--
   Provided by publisher.
Identifiers: LCCN 2025026868 (print) | LCCN 2025026869 (ebook) | ISBN
   9781800506442 hardback | ISBN 9781800506459 paperback | ISBN
   9781800506466 pdf | ISBN 9781800507081 epub
Subjects: LCSH: Religious pluralism--Asia | Religious pluralism--Italy |
   Peacebuilding--Religious aspects | Emigration and
   immigration--Religious aspects | Asian diaspora
Classification: LCC BL1033 .R465 2025 (print) | LCC BL1033 (ebook)
LC record available at https://lccn.loc.gov/2025026868
LC ebook record available at https://lccn.loc.gov/2025026869

Typeset by S.J.I. Services, New Delhi, India

Contents

Introduction   1
    Alessandro Saggioro and Carmelo Russo

1. Religious Diversity, Plurality, and Pluralism: Towards an Analytical Grid   20
    Dionigi Albera and Maria Chiara Giorda

Part 1. Asian Case Studies

2. Nonviolence and Interreligious Dialogue in Islam: The Case of Jawdat Said   57
    Viviana Schiavo

3. From the Hindu Monarchy to the Federal Republic: Some Notes on Religious Pluralism in Nepal   86
    Davide Torri

4. Super-diverse Ancestors: Cemeterial Recollections as Practices of Coexistence in Rural Java   113
    Roberto Rizzo

5. Narrating the Past and the Future: Religious Super-diversity Formation of Catholic Communities in Vietnam   140
    Yuqing Du

Part 2. Asian Diasporas in Italy

6. Migration, Religious Super-diversity, and Cohabitation: Notes from Ethnographic Research on the Sinhala Community in Messina (Sicily)   181
Giovanni Cordova

7. "Out-of-place" Muslims: Public Islam and Youth Activism in Sites of Modernity   211
Andrea Priori

8. The Digital Darśana: Celebrating Durgā Pūjā 2020 During the Pandemic   242
Valeria Giampietri, Randa Khalil, and Ludovica Tozzi

9. Religious "Superconflict": Durgā Pūjā and a Muslim Funeral in a Plural District of Rome, Italy   273
Carmelo Russo

Index of Names   302

Index of Subjects   307

Introduction

Alessandro Saggioro and Carmelo Russo[1]

This book is organised along two main themes: super-diversity – with a particular focus on its acceptance in religious contexts – and the practice of peacebuilding. The editors invited the authors to discuss and analyse the relationship between these two themes. This was achieved both through theoretical discussion and real-world case studies, taking into account both the privileged perspective of anthropological approaches as well as the inherently transdisciplinary nature of peacebuilding.

The volume is the result of a fruitful collaboration between two research projects: the Sapienza University "Negotiating Stories in Cohabitation: Dynamics and Narratives of Peace in the Great Empires of the Past (from Antiquity to Present Times)"[2], and Marie Curie Skłodowska "Relcapetown – Religious Super-Diversity in Cape Town. Dynamics of Leadership and

---

1. The authors shared their reflections on this text. However, the first and the fifth paragraphs should be attributed to Carmelo Russo, and the second, third, and fourth should be attributed to Alessandro Saggioro. The editors of the book would like to thank the readers of the text that offered valuable peer reviews of the final version of many chapters, and specifically Ioan Cozma, Angelica Federici, Eduard Iricinschi, Emma Luise Leahy, and Emily Pierini.
2. Sapienza University Research project RG11916B85F0352C, PI: Alessandro Saggioro; Scientific Board: Sergio Botta, Alberto Camplani, Tessa Canella, Candida Assunta Carella, Serena Di Nepi, Marianna Ferrara, Gaetano Lettieri, Umberto Longo, Mara Matta, Emanuela Prinzivalli; Research Staff: Ludovico Battista, Marinella Ceravolo, Maria Fallica, Arturo Monaco, Carmelo Russo, Fernanda Fischione, Walter Montanari.

Territorialization Through Religious Spaces in the Migration Process"[3]. In this introduction, we will present some of the guidelines that informed our approach while conceiving and editing this book. The book opens with an introductory chapter by Dionigi Albera and Maria Chiara Giorda presenting some opening theoretical and methodological remarks, and eight further chapters, organized into two sections: the first section examines religious super-diversity and its interaction with peacebuilding in Asia; the second part presents research case studies on the Asian diaspora in Italy, with Rome serving as an example of both super-diversity and peacebuilding.

1 Super-diversity, Criticalities, and Religion

In a now famous 2007 article published in the journal *Ethnic and Racial Studies*, Steven Vertovec introduced the analytical concept of super-diversity. It was eloquently entitled: *Super-diversity and its Implication*. According to this notion, the nature of immigration brings with it:

> [...] a transformative "diversification of diversity" not just in terms of bringing more ethnicities and countries of origin, but also with respect to a multiplication of significant variables [that include] differential immigration statuses and their concomitant entitlements and restrictions of rights, divergent labour market experiences, discrete gender and age profiles, patterns of spatial distribution, and mixed local area responses by service providers and residents[4].

Since its introduction, the concept of "super-diversity" has been criticised by scholars who questioned its genuine novelty compared to "simple" diversity, as well as the practical implications of this category. Aneta Pavlenko points out the term's referential indeterminacy that makes it resistant to critique. She also notes its use as a "hot brand name" that enhances market value and distinction to pre-existing research

---

3. Marie Curie Skłodowska Action, Grant Agreement 886578. Researcher: Carmelo Russo; supervisor: Laura Faranda (Sapienza University of Rome), Asonzeh Ukah (University of Cape Town), Marian Burchardt (University of Leipzig).
4. Vertovec 2007, p. 1025.

lines. This branding promotes a new academic hierarchy and elite[5]. Ana Deumert argues that the complexities brought by diversity defy numerical measurement. While super-diversity directs scholars' attention towards complexity and unpredictability, a countermovement focused on a desire for normativity and predictability persists[6]. In terms of numerical data, the work of Mathias Czajka and Hein de Haas challenges the notion that recent decades have seen a global increase in volume, diversity, and geographical scope of migration. Common belief holds that the complexity of international migration has grown. However, their article, which analyses shifts in global migration patterns between 1960 and 2000 through indices that capture changes in the spread, distance, and intensity of migration, demonstrates the decrease in the diversity with recent migrations. These migrations increasingly concentrate in a shrinking pool of destination countries[7]. Sofya Aptekar notes a lack in consideration of power and inequality. Even though social interactions appear without conflict across differences, a consolidated structure of systemic oppressions is still powerfully salient, because of "long histories of unequal distribution of power and resources by race, class, and gender"[8]. Thus, super-diversity can be seen as a byproduct of a border regime, inextricably tied to violence and discrimination[9]. Finex Ndhlovu criticises super-diversity for reinforcing the tendency to regiment cultural and social groups and the uncritical embrace of elitist neoliberal concepts of culture and identity[10]. Sinfree B. Makoni addresses these issues by arguing that the category of super-diversity provides homogenization and fails to acknowledge the significant asymmetries in power[11]. He also notes the tendency to romanticise the diversification of diversity, leading to "a careful concealment of power differences" and "an illusion of equality in a highly asymmetrical world"[12].

5. Pavlenko 2018, p. 143.
6. Deumert 2014.
7. Czajka, de Haas 2014, p. 316.
8. Aptekar 2017, p. 4.
9. Ibid.
10. Ndhlovu 2016.
11. Makoni 2012.
12. Ibid., p. 192.

Despite its wide criticism, the term soon expanded meaning and crossed disciplinary boundaries. It has been subject to a broad interpretation and usage across a wide range of social science literature and disciplines: sociology, anthropology, geography, history, political science, migration, ethnic studies, linguistics, education, law, business studies, management, literature, media studies, public health, social work, urban planning, and landscape studies[13]. It is important to note the geographical expansion alongside the disciplinary broadening of the term. While the 2007 article referred to the United Kingdom, mainly focused on London, the category has since been applied to describe contexts such as Italy, Egypt, Nigeria, French Guiana, Zimbabwe, Cyprus, Hong Kong, Japan, and others. In March 2022, *The Oxford Handbook of Superdiversity*, edited by Fran Meissner, Nando Sigona, and Steven Vertovec was published. This handbook compiles contributions that summarise and build upon research work and the ongoing debate on super-diversity. It offers arguments on how to make sense of diversity considering complex social transformations[14].

In their Introduction to the 2016 special issue "New Diversities", Irene Becci and Marian Burchardt argued that religion was initially not central to the debate around migration-driven super-diversity. They stated that it has radically changed over recent years, affected by three different perspectives: the debate towards secularization and the re-enchantment of the world, the increasing of presence of migrant religions, and that of new religious movements[15].

As Vertovec claimed in his first article, if on the one hand super-diversity could entail patterns of inequality, prejudice, racism, and segregation, on the other it could challenge these negative features in increasingly complex, composite, and stratified societies[16]. Massimo Leone notes that "it is increasingly found that the conceptual framework of 'cultural integration', predominant thus far in social research and policymaking about social cohesion and harmony, is largely unsatisfactory in dealing with the challenges of the so-called super-diverse cities"[17]. Despite certain ambiguities, religious

13. Vertovec 2019, p. 127.
14. Meissner et al. 2022.
15. Becci, Burchardt 2016.
16. Vertovec 2007, p. 1045.
17. Leone 2012, p. 189.

super-diversity could lead to greater interaction, to the development of convivial and cosmopolitan identities, and to contribute to the building of a more concrete peaceful coexistence[18]. Scholars cannot deny conflicts or paternalistic attitudes, yet they have recently debated the role of religion in the peacebuilding process. The statement holds true particularly when considering historical contexts, especially those related to "border area", like the Mediterranean region. Both the Byzantine (4th–15th centuries) and the Ottoman (14th–19th) Empires were more culturally heterogeneous than "Western Europe" and were multireligious political entities. From Anatolia to the Balkans, from the Middle East to Morocco, local societies consisted of different religious communities. In these communities "the other" was a neighbour with whom one interacted, though not always on an egalitarian basis and not always peacefully[19]. Alessandro Saggioro[20] introduced the category of "religious super-diversity's place building" to decode the contemporary superdiverse global cities[21] – not only in "the West". This concept considers that each religious community operates within a territory aware of other communities and interacts with religious diversity and pluralism. These communities engage in a civic dimension, elevating their places of worship to foster a higher level of peaceful interaction within their surroundings[22]. This issue is evident in the rhetoric of religiosity, interreligious dialogue, and volunteer welfare. Dialogue is a fundamental pillar in promoting the peacebuilding process. The risks of engaging in a rhetorical, self-referential dialogue "of the deaf" are real. However, the dialogue is still worthwhile to pursue whether it be a faith-based[23] or a secular dialogue that involves a sense of civic duty.

2 Interreligious Boundaries

Religious pluralism is a crucial aspect of super-diversity that is essential for analysing, describing, and understanding contemporary society. Its

18. Vertovec 2019, pp. 134–136.
19. Albera, Couroucli 2009.
20. Saggioro 2018.
21. Cox 1965; Sassen 1991.
22. Saggioro 2018. See also Cozma, Giorda 2023.
23. Abu-Nimer et al. 2005.

origins are remote and multifocal. One could argue for a form of religious pluralism based on Eurocentric history. The same paradigm of centrality and pluralism, imported to different parts of the world, would not give different outcomes[24]. This applies to quality rather than quantity. In quantitative terms, societies generically referred to as "the West" are based on a structural, long-lasting, albeit variable presence of plural religious perspectives. Any evaluation of the numbers of different religious communities would give a variable outcome over time. If we consider the historical periods of the absolute affirmation of Christianity in European territories, we can identify a variety of theological visions and practices within the Christian horizon. For every historical period, it is also necessary to take into account the presence of Jewish communities in Europe. One must account for the residues of behaviour, aggregative modes, and symbolic affirmation of the polytheistic past, a legacy of pre-Roman and Roman religious practices[25]. Additionally, it is important to recognize the influence of cults and social structures from the eastern Mediterranean that were integrated into European territories. These elements coexisted in various historical developments, sometimes more visibly than others. In the past, as today, migrant communities have carried with them their values and networks of symbolic systems. These have undergone negotiations and changes, emphasising certain elements over others[26].

Throughout Mediterranean history, traces of these movements are evident, along with the ways they reshaped plural religious dimensions. This reshaping occurred through the multiplication of names, titles, spheres of influence, and competence, resulting in a localised and "global" transformation of the networks of religious relations – all carrying different understandings of the "world".

The eternal "global village" is always marked by diversity. At every age, there are comparisons and confrontations between different religious perspectives. In the village, the "aboriginal" communities – considered to be "the autochthons" – and the immigrant communities – regarded as later additions to the "aboriginals" – find themselves coexisting, overcoming the spatial boundaries, and creating a new and original society, melding

---

24. Giordan, Pace 2014.
25. Ginzburg 1991.
26. Hodson, Hewstone 2013; Knott, Vasquez 2014; Williams 1988.

together identity and anti-identity within a univocal and circumscribed space. While quantitative dimensions can vary greatly over time, subject to different factors, qualitative dimensions are markers of time in human history[27]. In other parts of the globe, historical documents, over a long period, involve movement of people and ideas, and therefore of customs and habits, which make it possible to identify the pluralism inherent in human endeavours. We refer here to the great civilisations of the past, the large territories occupied by the most extensive empires in history, or the religions that established themselves in each territory. The central tenet of our theory can be convincingly argued, however, if we reflect on the (fictitious) paradigm of the island. In any dominant religious culture, the inhabitants of every territory consider themselves as being the occupants of an island. But the island *per se* is not "isolated"; it is subject to interaction by sea, commercial contact, war, and exploration[28]. Whether the trade is based on elementary dynamics or is more extensive and invasive, the territory receives raw materials, products of a complex industry, and goods. The need to produce goods is accompanied by the need for sustenance, which requires contacts and relations; hence, exchanges and control of productive areas. This is accompanied by both the breakdown, at every level, of any community's need to isolate itself, and by the human compulsion to relate to each other[29]. Migration could be thus regarded as the effect of this mobilisation; as such, it entails the multiplication of the breaching of original boundaries between religious horizons and philosophical visions of life and human existence[30]. Therefore, every territory is characterised by forms of co-presence and even overlapping which, from a quantitative point of view, may be all encompassing. However, qualitatively this always involves a variety and diversification that invariably leads to a greater pluralist openness[31].

---

27. Stringer 2014.
28. Favole 2010; Sahlins 1985.
29. Hewstone, Voci 2009; Hodson, Hewstone 2013.
30. Hannerz 1992.
31. Levitt 2004, 2007.

3 The Need for Interaction

This observation concerns today's world in which the policies of particular States and constitutional apparatuses imply an idea of religious freedom. Although freedom of religion is not a value affirmed everywhere in the world in an unambiguous and homogeneous manner, it is recognised among universal principles that characterise modern societies. It can be said that even the institutions that practise religious freedom minimally still affirm its right and make an effort to guarantee its implementation. In the contemporary age, religions are increasingly in contact with each other. Representatives are compelled to view boundary lines not as demarcations of their own existence, but as lines along which relational interactions occur. They experience those lines as the surface of their social hold, subject to pushes and pulls that interface with the cohesive force of others[32].

These lines of contact are traversed by different forces, which are affected both by quantity – the numbers of people belonging to a given religious community residing in each territory – and quality – the fact that religious freedom is more or less affirmed, guaranteed, or encouraged, or denied, forbidden, or precluded. In the global world, however, one can imagine this contact as characterised, in each place, by different factors and human modes of management[33].

Dialogue is one of them. Born as an intellectual and educated requirement, today's dialogue means many things, each one different from the other. There is no lack of a top-down, leadership approach, which over the past fifty years has seen a multiplication of initiatives, levels, and perspectives. Alongside the dialogue aimed at theological convergence, or at least to explore the elements of commonality and affinity, a variety of dialogical modes are structured. These operate on levels that are not necessarily religious[34].

The organisation of life, the variety of dress, dietary, regulatory, and in a wider sense, cultural customs, represent a broad field of dialogical confrontation. In other words, religions have established cultural methods for

---

32. Becci et al. 2018.
33. Burchardt, Giorda 2021.
34. Race 2018.

managing human existence, implying a variety of approaches and apparatuses. These alone constitute a complex field of relations. Alongside this plan is that of the respective traditions, sacred stories, rituals, liturgies, and management of time. There are also various social organisations. The dialogue brings with it debates on the relationship between leadership and "ordinary believers" and on the legitimacy of those who are appointed to undertake it. Who dialogues with whom? In what capacity? In what way and to what extent does a dialogue dynamic represent a community? Does it (only) represent the voice of its bearer or leader? How (much) does a dialogue constitute a precedent that can have a duration and impact in history? Can this dialogical dimension constitute a breach of each community's safety net, and thus represent a weakening of it? Or does it constitute a relational reinforcement, a strengthening of the respective networks of meaning, the recognition of one's own limitation that becomes, a point of greater strength and awareness?[35]

True dialogue is not a superficial pretence; it neither conceals secret verbalities, nor is it compelled by a position of lesser strength. Conversely, true dialogue is not imposed by a position of greater strength. All of the above features of true dialogue are likely to generate "interaction". In a pluralistic society, dialogue represents the moment of focus on mutual diversity, indicating the beginning of a phase of work aimed at overcoming one's own and others' criticalities and boundaries. Interaction is the norm.

In everyday life and over time, people constantly interact with others who are different from themselves, within a system of concentric circles that begins with the family and expands outwards. The length of the diameter envelops the local context and expands to a global network. Looking at the world from this enlarged perspective, the need for the particular is not thwarted. Its location is being readapted, as it regards all individual cases and particularities, according to the multiplicity of religious and cultural visions and conceptions. Peaceful interaction constitutes a renunciation of the exclusive assertion of an identity of one's own[36].

If dialogue facilitates reciprocal knowledge and the construction of relational bridges, interaction implies that this knowledge does not lead to

---

35. Celada Ballanti 2020; Ventura 2021.
36. Appleby et al. 2015.

discrimination or prevarication and that the built bridges do not become arenas for opposition. Interaction, therefore, also involves creating spaces for sharing. This means welcoming dialogue projects within one's own institutionalised setting, and overturning stereotypes and negative readings of one's own, and others', realities. It includes conceding spaces and sharing practices that are not necessarily religious but that are oriented towards mutual understanding. One such practice is communal meals, which involve different and "typical" foods prepared for intercultural conviviality.

This scenario also clarifies why interreligious dialogue often shifts true religious perspectives and turns to cultural and specifically inter-cultural issues[37]. The dialogical horizon does not imply a renunciation of one's religious values at all. It does suggest, however, an increased care not to place these religious values in the field of interaction as instruments of differentiation and opposition. Theological interreligious dialogue carries within it structurally unsurpassable limits. While religious phenomenology has indicated a way to overcome them, history emphasises their essence and recognises their distinctiveness. As a result, it is necessary to recognise a different anthropological and sociological horizon of interaction, one in which the multiplication of factors entails the acceptability of the result and not its negation. In other words, mutual knowledge is the instrument of recognition, and it implies understanding the necessity of non-belligerence in the name of religious principles[38].

4 Dialectics of War and Peace

In the analysis of cultural dynamics, applying mathematical formulas of quantity to super-diversity[39] can seem like a stretch, and yet it can be quite effective. Compared to the long history of contacts among different cultures, religions, and civilizations, where cultural relations led to crashes, mergers, aggregations, reshaping, and reformulations as horizons met and confronted, clashed and conflated, the contemporary era is witnessing an accelerated movement of people and things, unprecedented and with no

---

37. Celada Ballanti 2020; Neumaier, Klinkhammer 2020.
38. Becci et al. 2018.
39. Becci, Burchardt 2016; Duyvendak et al. 2021.

signs of slowing down[40]. Indeed, the halt to regular social interactions during the Covid-19 pandemic has been proof of this irrepressible human movement. By triggering crises and famine, impoverishment, and conflict, instead of the expected and utopian solidarity, the pandemic has imposed a slowdown that can be likened to the tension of the elastic band pulled before the relaunch. As a result, the global movement resumed more powerfully and vehemently than before, with all the limitations of the pre-Covid years. The grafting of new conflictual issues confirms that human beings are not overwhelmingly pacifist, or at least the ruling classes are not.

However, pluralism does not always produce peaceful coexistence. The sharing of places and territories, contacts between different life approaches, and the competition and affirmations of values also reveal the other more conflictual face of pluralism[41]. Difference implies a potential respectful acceptance. But it also determines the possibility of structural rejection and unilateral or bilateral rejection. In all kinds of pluralisms, the possibility of total conflict is triggered, articulated in verbal and immaterial forms – contempt, discrimination, and mystification. This is, in a word, stigma, and one which entails – in physical and concrete forms – marginalisation, persecution, and annihilation. Pluralism, therefore, does not necessarily determine peaceful coexistence as one would expect from its most economic implication. Pluralism can increase contrast and thus result in conflict. The difference is not always a constructive factor in a pacifist welfare society, but one which can produce confrontation and induce the destruction of war.

In this sense, the dialectics of pluralism need to be studied and understood according to their multiple meanings and not concealed or obfuscated. Of course, it can be argued that the richness of a plural society is enhanced by diversity and this aspect represents the cardinal principle of its sustainability. A society is regarded as "sustainable" if it preserves the assets of all for future generations. As a result, one could speak of a peaceful society as "sustainable" if said peaceful society puts the well-being of all its members above the needs of just one privileged part of its social body at the expense of another. "Peaceful" is the society that

---

40. Appadurai 1996; Eriksen 2016.
41. Silvestri, Mayall 2015.

overcomes the traditional dichotomies between majorities and minorities[42], that renounces the numerical datum to draw a horizon inclusive of all, in which no one is "lesser" and no one is "greater", no one should be or should feel tolerated, no one is or can be persecuted because of their religious beliefs and practices. "Peaceful" is also the society that fulfils itself by taking into account the migrant dimension, that understands the atavistic sense of migration by understanding its value in its DNA precisely because it finds recorded in it the traces of other ancient migratory movements[43]. A society that includes itself takes an important step of cultural growth by transforming their structures and cultures into something different, something peaceful, something that integrates the pre-existing self with another self that comes from distant lands, with different values and unusual perspectives in the receiving territory. In summary, integration involves not only providing welcoming spaces, creating jobs in response to the market needs, and recognising individuals within the social and economic fabric, but also the interpenetration of diversity, overcoming of mistrust, and designing new citizenship.

The dialectics of sustainability and peacebuilding are part of pluralism and cannot be separated from it. Thus, the construction of citizenship depends on the democratic impossibility of renouncing pluralism. If the identity of a State or nation claims to adhere to democratic principles, it cannot renounce religious freedom or the liberalisation of the religious sphere. Additionally, it cannot avoid engaging with the complexity of the different types of options that coexist and assert their uniqueness in a pluralistic society. Therefore, it cannot shy away from the comprehensive construction of sustainable citizenship, where everyone respects each other, no one is merely tolerated or tolerates others, but is an integral and integrated part of society, with everyone being equal and regarded as an equal citizen.

5 A Path Through the Chapters

This book understands the relation between both these categories as constituted by, and intertwined with, a multiplicity of connections and

---

42. Giorgi 2018.
43. Cavalli-Sforza, et al. 1994.

separations. This approach requires empirical examinations of events and processes across boundaries and the role of historical and anthropological narratives in conflicts and their resolution. The authors' contributions are geographically concentrated in Asian areas – Syria, Indonesia, Nepal, Vietnam – or involve Asian diasporas in Italy – Bangladeshi and young Italian Bangladeshis in Rome, and a Sinhala community in Messina (Sicily). The represented religious contexts vary among Islam, Buddhism, Hinduism, Catholic Christianity, "Traditional Religion", and "Indigenous Religion". The chapters explore the relationship between urban spaces and the public sphere. They examine religious minorities and their (key) roles in peace building, engagement of religious leaders and communities, the involvement and commitment of institutions and political leaders, conflicts, and dynamics of "positive" competition. These matters are often subject to contradictions, illustrating how approaches to religion vary depending on context and broader local or global narratives[44].

Major news items, inter-religious violence and notorious public events often lead to the expression of negative views. The authors highlight that the role of religion in conflict and peacebuilding is complex and cannot be expressed in binary terms[45]. There is no doubt that religion can be both a driver of conflict and a driver of peace. However, it is necessary to reject a static view of religion and instead consider it as a fluid system of variables, influenced by contextual and historical factors[46].

From theological, educational, and pedagogic perspectives, religions encourage their followers to strive for peace and work at peacebuilding. They share several similar concepts such as peace, compassion, and forgiveness. While these concepts are not identical across religions, they may serve as a foundation for dialogue among different faiths for collaborative peacebuilding efforts.

The chapters show that the transformation from religious believers to peacebuilders should concern only a certain number of actors. Various religious actors will never be engaged in active peacebuilding. Some individuals may be indifferent to peacebuilding, at most opposing extremist religious actors and the use of violence in the name of religion.

---

44. Stringer 2014.
45. Ibid.
46. Silvestri, Mayall 2015.

Others, however, may continue to support religious violence in situations of oppression and injustice, opposing peacebuilding efforts[47]. The book seeks to answer to what extent super-diversity leads to either the normalisation of diversity or increased hostility towards individuals in different religious, ethnic, and racial groups[48].

Chapter 1 functions as a theoretical introduction. It presents an analytical grid of the concept of "diversity" in religious dynamics. Dionigi Albera and Maria Chiara Giorda explore the use of the term "super-diversity" in the religious field and discuss the category of "new religious pluralism". Thus, they propose a new typology based on three keywords: diversity, plurality, and pluralism. The aim is to shed light on the different levels and scales of diversity, considering historical, anthropological, and sociological perspectives.

Part 1, *Asian Case Studies*, consists of four chapters. Chapter 2 focuses on Islam. Viviana Schiavo investigates the nonviolent theology of the Syrian thinker Jawdat Said, exploring the relationship between multiple religious identities and peacebuilding. Religious pluralism and religious diversity in modern and contemporary Nepal are the focus of Davide Torri's Chapter 3. He highlights the emergence of two diverse and opposite tendencies: a process towards centralization (1768–1991) followed by a process towards differentiation (1991–ongoing). Chapter 4, by Roberto Rizzo, analyses how recent social and economic issues and religious revivals have complexified and reformulated a Javanese ancestral ritual in a religious super-diverse country. Moving to a northern Vietnamese region, Yuqing Du, in Chapter 5, examines how complex relations between Catholic Church and State histories were reconstructed in local historical narratives, involving religious-political crisis and peaceful coexistence.

Four chapters are included in Part 2, *Asian Diasporas in Italy*. In Chapter 6 Andrea Priori, examines the different expressions of religious activism among young Italian Bangladeshis, exploring the relationship between the public sphere, Islam, and sites of modernity in migratory contexts. Chapter 7 by Giovanni Cordova, investigates the daily interactions between Sri Lankan Catholic and Buddhist communities in the

---

47. Abu-Nimer et al. 2005, p. 13.
48. Duyvendak et al. 2021.

city of Messina (Southern Italy), focusing on their representations and re-shaping of categories of religious and ethnic belonging. In Chapter 8, Valeria Giampietri, Randa Khalil, and Ludovica Tozzi examine one of the main Hindu religious festivals, the Durgā Pūjā, celebrated by the Hindu Bangladeshi and Indian diasporic communities during the pandemic in October 2020 in Tor Pignattara, a semi-peripheral super-diverse district of Rome, Italy. Chapter 9 authored by Carmelo Russo, focuses on Tor Pignattara and the Durgā festival. Russo investigates the ambiguities and conflicts that latently exist in local relational and political practices. He specifically examines the interactions during two distinct events, the Hindu festival (4–8 October 2019) and a Muslim funeral (30 October 2017).

This completes the journey of this book, navigating through the difficult and complex issues of super-diversity, peacebuilding, and dialogue. At the end of this journey, in Chapter 9, Carmelo Russo introduces the term "superconflict". When a super-diverse context becomes an arena for competition among various social and political actors, creating a dispute that removes the religious and peaceful heritage and responsiveness from the debate, we encounter a phenomenon that is the opposite side of the coin. Yet it remains an integral part of the entire complexity of society and human behaviours at large. It is not a pessimistic result of the inquiry about super-diversity and peacebuilding, but a consequence of a deeper understanding of the many layers of reality. Anthropology increasingly offers opportunities for studying contemporary society. Peace is not a common topic for this field of research, but many aspects can be explored: human tension to build peace, the diverse cultural efforts to improve mediation, the understanding of constellations of relationships and contacts between humans. These are only a few potential directions to reflect on current anthropological research and to imagine its future developments. It is a significant task that will undoubtedly require great efforts from people and scholars.

Author's Biographies

Alessandro Saggioro is Full Professor in History of Religions at the Department of History, Anthropology, Religions, Arts, Performing Arts

(SARAS) of Sapienza University, Rome (Italy). He has been the Director of the PhD Course in History and Cultures of Europe of Sapienza University for more than ten years and currently serves as the Director of the Italian National PhD in Peace Studies. He is also an academic delegate of Sapienza University in the Italian network of Universities for Peace and serves as the editor-in-chief of *Studi e Materiali di Storia delle Religioni*, a peer-review journal founded in 1924 by Raffaele Pettazzoni. Saggioro leadsand supervises research and teaching projects related to religious pluralism, mediation, and peaceful coexistence. His interests include: teaching, methodology, and Historiography of the History of Religions; religious conflict and coexistence; religions of the Ancient Mediterranean; religions, law, and politics; religions, identities, and peace studies.

Carmelo Russo is Associate Professor at the Department of History, Anthropology, Religions, Arts, Performing Arts (SARAS) of Sapienza University, Rome (Italy) and has been Marie Skłodowska-Curie Actions Fellow. He teaches Cultural Anthropology, Anthropology of Religion, and Urban Anthropology. Russo has conducted fieldwork in Italy and Tunisia focusing on the migration process, religious dynamics, religious and spiritual minorities, and considering super-diversity theories. He is the author of numerous journal articles and volume chapters. His monograph *Nostra Signora del limite* (*Our Lady of the Boundaries*), concerning the Marian worship in Tunisia, was published in September 2020.

References

Abu-Nimer, M., Bouta, T., Kadayifci-Orellana, S. A. (2005), *Faith-Based Peace-Building: Mapping and Analysis of Christian, Muslim and Multi-Faith Actors*, Clingendael, Netherlands Institute of International Relations, The Hague, and Institute for Peace and Justice, Washington D.C.

Albera, D., Couroucli, M. (2009), *Religions traversées: Lieux saints partagés entre chrétiens, musulmans et juifs en Méditerranée*, Actes Sud, Arles.

Appadurai, A. (1996), *Modernity at Large: Cultural Dimensions of Globalization*, University of Minnesota Press, Minneapolis-Londra.

Appleby, R. S., Little, D., Omer, A. (eds.) (2015), *The Oxford Handbook of Religion, Conflict, and Peacebuilding*, Oxford University Press, Oxford.

Aptekar, S. (2017), *Superdiversity as a Methodological Lens: Re-centring Power and Inequality*, in "Ethnic and Racial Studies", 42, 1, pp. 1–18. https://doi.org/10.1080/01419870.2017.1406124

Becci, I., Burchardt, M. (2016), *Religion and Superdiversity: An Introduction*, in "New Diversities", 18, 1, pp. 1–7.

Becci, I., Monnot, C., Voirol, O. (eds.) (2018), *Pluralisme et reconnaissance: Face à la diversité religieuse*, Presses Universitaires Rennes, Rennes.

Burchardt, M., Giorda, M. C. (eds.) (2021), *Geography of Encounters: The Making and Unmaking Spaces*, Palgrave Macmillan, London.

Cavalli-Sforza, L. L., Menozzi, P., Piazza, A. (1994), *The History and Geography of Human Genes*, Princeton University Press, Princeton.

Celada Ballanti, R. (2020), *Filosofia del dialogo interreligioso*, Morcelliana, Brescia.

Cox, H. (1965), *The Secular City: Secularization and Urbanization in Theological Perspective*, Macmillan, New York.

Cozma, I., Giorda, M. C. (2023), *The "St. Nicholas Greek Orthodox and National Shrine" at Ground Zero: A Supposed Multifaith Place in a Sacred Space*, SMSR 89, 1, pp. 274–297.

Czajka, M., de Haas, H. (2014), *The Globalization of Migration: Has the World Become more Migratory?*, in "International Migration Review", 48, 2, pp. 283–323. https://doi.org/10.1111/imre.12095

Deumert, A. (2014), *Digital Superdiversity: A Commentary*, in "Discourse, Context, and Media", 4–5, pp. 116–120. https://doi.org/10.1016/j.dcm.2014.08.003

Duyvendak, J. W., Foner, N., Kasinitz, P. (eds.) (2021), *Super-diversity and Everyday Life*, Routledge, London.

Eriksen, T. H. (2016), *Overheating: An Anthropology of Accelerated Change*, Pluto Press, London.

Favole, A. (2010), *Oceania: Isole di creatività culturale*, Laterza, Roma-Bari.

Ginzburg, C. (1991), *Ecstasies: Deciphering the Witches' Sabbath*, Hutchinson Radius, New York. (First published in Italian as *Storia notturna: Una decifrazione del Sabba*, Einaudi, Torino, 1989).

Giordan, G., Pace, E. (2014), *Religious Pluralism: Framing Religious Diversity in the Contemporary World*, Springer, New York.

Giorgi, A. (2018), *Religioni di minoranza tra Europa e laicità*, Mimesis, Milano.

Hannerz, U. (1992), *Cultural Complexity: Studies in the Social Organization of Meaning*, Columbia University Press, New York.

Hewstone, M., Voci, A. (2009), *Diversità e integrazione: il ruolo del contatto intergruppi nei processi di riduzione del pregiudizio e risoluzione dei conflitti*, in "Psicologia sociale", 1, pp. 9–28.

Hodson, G., Hewstone, M. (2013), *Advances in Intergroup Contact*, Psychology Press, New York.
Knott, K., Vasquez, M. (2014), *Three Dimensions of Religious Place Making in Diaspora*, in "Global Networks", 14, 3, pp. 326–347. https://doi.org/10.1111/glob.12062
Leone, M. (2012), *Hearing and Belonging: On Sounds, Faiths, and Laws*, in V. K. Bhatia, C. A. Hafner, L. Miller, A. Wagner (eds.), *Transparency, Power and Control: Perspectives on Legal Communication*, Ashgate, Farnham, pp. 183–197.
Levitt, P. (2004), *Redefining the Boundaries of Belonging: The Institutional Character of Transnational Religious Life*, in "Sociology of Religion", 35, 1, pp. 174–196. https://doi.org/10.2307/3712504
Levitt, P. (2007), *God Needs No Passport: Immigrants and the Changing Religious Landscape*, New Press-Norton & Company, New York.
Makoni, S. B. (2012), *A Critique of Language, Languaging, and Supervernacular*, in "Muitas Vozes", 1, 2, pp. 189–199. https://doi.org/10.5212/MuitasVozes.v.1i2.0003
Meissner, F., Sigona, N., Vertovec, S. (eds.) (2022), *The Oxford Handbook of Superdiversity*, Oxford University Press, New York.
Ndhlovu, F. (2016), *A Decolonial Critique of Diaspora Identity Theories and the Notion of Superdiversity*, in "Diaspora Studies", 9, pp. 28–40. https://doi.org/10.1080/09739572.2015.1088612
Neumaier, A., Klinkhammer, G. (2020), *Interreligious Contact and Media: Introduction*, in "Religion", 50, 3, pp. 321–335. https://doi.org/10.1080/0048721X.2020.1756061
Pavlenko, A. (2018), *Superdiversity and Why It Isn't: Reflections on Terminological Innovation and Academic Branding*, in S. Breidbach, L. Küster, B. Schmenk (eds.), *Sloganization in Language Education Discourse: Conceptual Thinking in the Age of Academic Marketization*, Multilingual Matters, Bristol, pp. 142–168.
Race, R. (ed.) (2018), *Advancing Multicultural Dialogues in Education*, Palgrave Macmillan, London.
Saggioro, A. (2018), *Superdiversità religiosa e applicazioni romane: il paradigma plurale*, in A. Saggioro, C. Russo (eds.), *Roma città plurale. Le religioni, il territorio, le ricerche*, Bulzoni, Roma, pp. 151–167.
Sahlins, M. (1985), *Islands of History*, University of Chicago Press, Chicago.
Sassen, S. (1991), *The Global City*, Princeton University Press, Princeton.
Silvestri, S., Mayall, J. (2015), *The Role of Religion in Conflict and Peacebuilding*, British Academy, London.

Stringer, M. D. (2014), *Evidencing Superdiversity in the Census and Beyond*, in "Religion", 44, 3, pp. 453–465. https://doi.org/10.1080/0048721X.2014.903649

Ventura, M. (2021), *Nelle mani di Dio: La super-religione del mondo che verrà*, Il Mulino, Bologna.

Vertovec, S. (2007), *Super-diversity and its Implications*, in "Ethnic and Racial Studies", 30, 6, pp. 1024–1054. https://doi.org/10.1080/01419870701599465

Vertovec, S. (2019), *Talking Around Super-diversity*, in "Ethnic and Racial Studies", 42, 1, pp. 125–139. https://doi.org/10.1080/01419870.2017.1406128

Williams, R. B. (1988), *Religions of Immigrants from India and Pakistan: New Threads in the American Tapestry*, Cambridge University Press, Cambridge.

Chapter 1
Religious Diversity, Plurality, and Pluralism: Towards an Analytical Grid

Dionigi Albera and Maria Chiara Giorda

Abstract

The aim of this chapter is to provide a survey and to suggest an analytical grid concerning the issue of diversity in religious dynamics. We start with a discussion of a terminological genealogy linked to the concept of "super-diversity". Then we explore the transfer of this idea in religious domains, through the concept of religious super-diversity. Following, we examine another terminological stream, namely the use of the concept of "new religious pluralism" and, more generally, the semantic sphere covered by the term pluralism. Subsequently, we tentatively propose a new typology based on three key terms: diversity, plurality, and pluralism. After briefly testing its possible relevance on some historical fields, we offer a slightly modified version of the grid in order to capture the main dynamics in the contemporary religious field, mobilising the prefix "hyper" to stress the enormous and multi-layered amount of religious diversity, and the complexity of the mechanisms trying to channel it. In addition to offering a possible tool for linguistic and conceptual scrutiny, this tripartite typology can be useful for analysing – from historical, anthropological, and sociological points of view – the different levels and scales of diversity, focusing on both inter and intra religious relationships.

Keywords: super-diversity, anthropology of religions, history of religions, interdisciplinarity, urban religion, religious diversity

1   Sociological Super-diversity

The concept of "super-diversity" was proposed by Vertovec and adopted by a great number of scholars from different fields, who have approached it with a variegated range of attitudes, from an automatic acceptance to severe criticism[1].

Almost fifteen years ago, the journal *Ethnic and Racial Studies* published a seminal article by Steven Vertovec, *Super-diversity and its Implications*[2]; an article which, as it has been remarked, "has turned out to be the most highly cited article in the journal's forty-year history"[3]. Since then, the concept of super-diversity has become widely popular among many scholars: mainly, but not only, in the field of migration studies. Some criticisms addressed to super-diversity have not been a significant obstacle to this massive success[4]. If it is true that, from a chronological point of view, this concept is still in its infancy[5], or perhaps in its adolescence, one may add that thousands of references in academic literature (and elsewhere[6]) already gave it a somewhat premature adulthood.

In the 2007 article, the scope of this conceptual invention was well delimited. The idea of super-diversity "was intended to give a name to changing patterns observed in British migration data", with growing movements of people involving many ethnicities, languages, and religions[7]. The concept of super-diversity aimed at capturing a number of shifts linked to these transformations. It pointed the attention towards the dynamic interaction of several crucial variables, such as "differential

---

1. We are grateful to our colleagues who have read and commented on previous versions of this text: their remarks were useful for our work in progress. We want to thank, in particular, Irene Becci, Peter Brown, Marian Burchardt, Giovanni Filoramo, Nimrod Luz, and Luca Patrizi.
2. Vertovec 2007.
3. Duyvendak et al. 2019, p. 1. The term appeared for the first time in 2005, see Vertovec, Steven, "Opinion: Super Diversity revealed", BBC News, 20 September 2005: http://news.bbc.co.uk/2/hi/uk_news/4266102.stm (last accessed 23 September 2025).
4. Boccagni 2015; Makoni 2012; Ndhlovu 2016; Pavlenko 2019.
5. Duyvendak et al. 2019, p. 2.
6. See, for example: https://www.linkedin.com/pulse/how-could-super-diversity-benefit-organisations-atena-hensch (last accessed 23 September 2025).
7. Vertovec 2019, p. 126.

legal statuses and their concomitant conditions, divergent labour market experiences, discrete configurations of gender and age, patterns of spatial distribution, and mixed local area responses by service providers and residents"[8]. The combinations of these variables produced "new patterns of inequality and prejudice including emergent forms of racism, new patterns of segregation, new experiences of space and 'contact', new forms of cosmopolitanism and creolization (including what's more recently discussed in terms of conviviality and multicultural), and more"[9].

The tremendous expansion of this concept has involved its application to extremely varied fields. This entailed a semantic and theoretical enrichment, but at times it also somewhat obfuscated the substance expressed by the original article. Reflecting more than ten years later about the astonishing success of his concept, Vertovec himself pointed out the huge variety of meanings and interpretations that have accompanied its triumphal reception:

> Across a range of social scientific terrains, the concept of super-diversity is variably invoked, referenced, concocted or criticized as an idea, setting, condition, theory or approach. Sometimes such talking is really about the concept; that is, discussions ensue with reference to its original meaning or intention. Other times, super-diversity is just a cue around which something else is talked about, a springboard to present a set of related research findings, a segue to another topic, or indeed a false starting point, misnomer or sheer strawman[10].

Paradoxically, one could say that, like in a mirror-play, a super-diversity of significance is attributed to the concept of super-diversity itself. As a matter of fact, this is not entirely surprising. In some respects, it is the price to pay for success. This often happens to concepts that circulate widely in the scholarly world, like coins that pass from one hand to the other for a long time, ending up losing the clarity of the lines they were engraved with. What is surprising is the speed of this process, which probably corresponds to the increasingly rapid pace of scientific production in

---

8. Vertovec 2007, p. 1025.
9. Vertovec 2019, p. 126.
10. Ibid., p. 125.

a globalised academic world. Another mirror effect, after all, between the reality and its representation, one could insinuate.

Reviewing 325 publications that, between 2008 and 2014, made reference to his concept, Vertovec has critically commented on several uses of super-diversity, and outlined a typology of the various ways in which scholars have understood the reference[11]. He dismisses some basic interpretations, in which the term has simply the meaning of "very much diversity"[12], or of "more ethnicity", with the presence of a growing number of ethnic groups in a nation or in a city[13]. Moreover, Vertovec does not seem completely persuaded by the researchers who use the concept just as a "backdrop to a study". In this case, "scholars invoke super-diversity as a new condition or setting and then carry on with describing whatever set of research findings they wish to present (that more often than not do not really have much directly to do with super-diversity)"[14]. A somewhat peripheral use is that he refers to super-diversity like a background canvas in order to propose a *methodological reassessment* of a field or discipline, through a conceptual re-tooling[15]. Finally, Vertovec indicates, in the scientific literature examined, some uses that he considers more fruitful and more faithful to the original inspiration of his article. From this point of view, he identifies three main directions in which the concept has been productively taken up and developed. Some works have elaborated "descriptions and analyses of a *multi-dimensional reconfiguration* of various social forms"[16]. Other scholars "have drawn upon the multidimensionality of super-diversity to augment their desire to move *beyond a focus on ethnicity* as the sole or optimal category of analysis surrounding migrants"[17]. Finally, there are a number of studies that, "although invoking the concept of super-diversity, actually draw attention to something rather different (though often not wholly unrelated) to what was originally intended: *new or other complexities*"[18].

11. Ibid.
12. Ibid., pp. 127–128.
13. Ibid., p. 130.
14. Ibid., p. 128.
15. Ibid., pp. 128–130.
16. Ibid., p. 130.
17. Ibid., p. 131.
18. Ibid.

This authoritative reading is a useful caveat in order to avoid the pitfalls of hasty and simplistic renderings of the concept of super-diversity. Following Vertovec's suggestions, scholars should be aware of the need of talking *about* super-diversity, not just *around* it[19]. Adopting the perspective of super-diversity means to conceive of it primarily as a tool for grasping the new complexities of phenomena linked to *a diversification of diversity*, as Ulrich Beck[20] aptly resumed the core of this concept[21]. This idea was previously proposed by Hollinger[22], in a book in which he developed a post-ethnic perspective. In the United States, he argued, the articulation of difference had accelerated, and the usual ethno-racial grid was unable to contain this diversification of difference[23]. From the point of view of urban anthropology, the concept of super-diversity is less an analytical device than "a lens to describe an exceptional demographic situation characterised by the multiplication of social categories within specific localities"[24]. In this perspective, the concept represents a stimulus towards the experimentation of new approaches in order to capture the proliferation of difference at a local scale. But, as Vertovec himself has made clear, the concept of super-diversity is not in itself a theory[25]. Instead, it is a first step for orienting the analysis towards the study of new complexities in contemporary societies. A huge quantity of work is necessary to draw a fresh cartography of globalisation. Ulrich Beck has eloquently indicated the necessity of such an *aggiornamento*: "over the last decades the cultural, social and political landscapes of diversity are changing radically, but we still use old maps to orient ourselves". And then he put in italics his main point: "we do not even have the language through which contemporary super-diversity in the world can be described, conceptualised, understood, explained and researched"[26].

19. Ibid., p. 136.
20. Beck 2011, p. 55.
21. Duyvendak et al. 2019, pp. 3, 7, 13.
22. Hollinger 1995, p. 12.
23. Hollinger 1995.
24. Wessendorf 2014, Introduction.
25. Vertovec 2019, p. 126.
26. Beck 2011, p. 53.

2 Religious Super-diversity

In several works, including Vertovec's, the main dimension associated with the concept of super-diversity was ethnicity[27]. Yet the prospect of building a bridge with the religious sphere too was in any case clearly in the air, in a millennium that opened with the attack on the Twin Towers and in which the prophecies of a clash of civilizations seemed gradually to materialise in various conflicts with a religious background. In this period a shift from race to religion has become increasingly visible in debates concerning difference in Europe[28]. Religion has emerged as an important variable in immigration studies[29]. Significantly, Vertovec himself has founded and directed the Max Planck Institute for the Study of Religious and Ethnic Diversity. This label is clearly enlightening the relevance of religious issues, along the ethnic ones, in relation to diversity and super-diversity.

The richest attempt to articulate super-diversity with religion has been, precisely, a special issue of the Max Planck Institute's journal "New Diversities", directed by Irene Becci and Marian Burchardt[30]. In the introduction these two scholars offer a clear theoretical statement concerning the elaboration of the relationships between religion and super-diversity. They propose two distinct ways to do so. In the first perspective, religion is seen as one of the fields in which urban super-diversity appears in contexts of strong migration. In the second perspective, they define a relatively autonomous religious super-diversity, conceived as the cumulative result of the intersection of several religious diversities:

> First, there are important questions about "religion in the context of super-diversity," which address the relationships between religion and other status categories in contexts of migration-driven

---

27. Oke et al. 2016.
28. Eade 2011, p. 155. Eade observes that, in Britain, there has previously been a shift in the opposite direction: "The arrival of labour migrants from the (former) colonies from the late 1940s moved debates concerning difference, discrimination and inequality away from religion towards race". Therefore, the contemporary transformation is paradoxically reproducing an older situation in which religion was the central issue.
29. Levitt 2007; Connor 2014; Kivisto 2014.
30. Becci, Burchardt 2016.

diversification such as race, ethnicity, legal status, age, and gender. Second, we emphasise the emergence, parallel development and mutual constitution of different kinds of religious differences, in other words: the interactions of different religious diversities, which give rise to what we call religious super-diversity[31].

In their discussion of the concept of religious super-diversity, Becci and Burchardt try to extricate it from an indispensable link with migration. They propose a larger acceptance of it by defining "religious super-diversity as a more encompassing and complex cultural formation involving variables and dynamics such as religious innovation (e.g., scientology or transcendental meditation) that are not directly related to migration and much more connected actually to normative and symbolic dimensions"[32].

No doubt, this distinction is relevant. Nevertheless, the two perspectives singled out by Becci and Burchardt are interconnected. It is not easy to disentangle them on an empirical terrain, as the case studies that make up the issue largely show. Furthermore, Becci and Burchardt's characterization of religious super-diversity seems to be influenced by some traits more generally associated with the wider sociological idea of super-diversity. The latter is neither an analytic concept nor the chart of a theory. Rather, it is a signal, a lens that warns of mixing a series of factors that generate growing diversification in contemporary urban contexts.

Similarly, the concept of religious super-diversity defined by Becci and Burchardt manifests an outbreak of meanings, a bundling of variables, ranging from the diversity of individual conceptions and practices to the distinctions between groups and denominations, to their internal complexification, to individual and collective forms of spirituality, to spatial and political strategies from religious groups to affirm their religious identity and to obtain official recognition. Such a general exploration is a necessary step to grasp the growing complexity of religious phenomena and to create a descriptive framework. We suggest it could be integrated by an analytical approach which can offer more tools for discriminating and identifying processes inside this framework.

31. Ibid, pp. 1–2.
32. Ibid., p. 4.

3 The New Religious Pluralism

We turn now to another terminological genealogy that often covers similar phenomena. To describe the spectacular changes in the religious field that the immigration has induced during the last decades on both Atlantic shores[33], several authors have popularised the concept of "new religious pluralism"[34]. This definition has also been adopted by some Italian scholars[35]. This concept has the merit of highlighting the fact that contemporary transformations are inscribed on a history. For instance, Italy, despite a long-lasting overflowing Catholic hegemony, also saw other religious presences, even if extremely reduced in numerical terms (Jews, Waldensians, other Protestant groups).

Yet this idea also presents some epistemological and methodological problems. The designation of these phenomena as "new" may induce some anachronisms. In the context of American sociology, the concept of "new religious pluralism" has been used to define the variety of religious groups that had settled in the US after the relative opening of the borders in 1965. Therefore, the adjective "new" risks being imprecise and transitory in a comparative perspective, ending by referring to divergent chronologies. Some problems remain, moreover, if we focus only on the Italian case. Until when can the term "new" be used to define phenomena that began to manifest themselves later than in the United States, but still more than thirty years ago?[36]

In addition to these specific problems, there are some difficulties more widely linked to the very concept of "religious pluralism". In its uses in academic literature, this expression is often characterised by an overlapping of meanings, which often generates a certain ambiguity. Beckford has warned of the dangers of the phrase "religious pluralism"[37]. His

---

33. Ebaugh, Saltzman Chafetz 2000; Eck 2001; Lippy 2000; Warner, Wittner 1998. See also Pluralism Project of Harvard University, in particular the section "Mission", available at: https://pluralism.org/mission-and-history (last accessed 23 September 2025).
34. Machacek 2003; Banchoff 2007; Wuthnow 2008.
35. Ballabio 2001; Di Sciullo, Paravati 2020; Naso 2015, 2020.
36. Doubts about this have been recently expressed by Di Sciullo, Paravati 2020, p. 232. They suggest that the word "new" should be updated.
37. See especially Beckford 2003.

recommendation "has been either to avoid it or to attribute an unambiguous meaning to it"[38]. Not without a sense of humour, Beckford has compared his long-lasting struggle to the labours of Sisyphus:

> So, my form of rebellion for the last 10 years has been to keep struggling to convince sociologists that some conceptual hygiene is desirable concerning use of the term "pluralism". It is a highly ambiguous and slippery term with at least three fundamentally different meanings. The first meaning of the term is "diversity". Diversity clearly identifies situations in which differences occur. Second, "pluralism" refers to institutional arrangements that promote or protect diversity for normative and legal reasons. In this sense, it implies approval for, and recognition of, diversity. Third, "pluralism" refers to sets of intellectual ideas that place a high value on diversity and on the social arrangements for sustaining it[39].

His central suggestion is that "it is preferable to associate 'pluralism' with ideological and normative positions"[40], using instead the term diversity to qualify the situations in which religious difference occurs. In spite of Beckford's lucid auto-ironical posture, it appears that his efforts have not certainly been fruitless, never-ending Sisyphean labours. His suggestions have been recognized and espoused by several other scholars[41]. The contributions collected in Giuseppe Giordan and Enzo Pace (2014) have adopted the perspective proposed by Beckford. This viewpoint is clearly stated in the introduction:

> Pluralism is a key concept toward understanding what is happening in our world, even if the risk, as with all the words that suddenly become popular and fashionable, is that it becomes an umbrella under which we put together quite different and heterogeneous phenomena, sometimes hardly consistent with each other. This error, which still often occurs in much sociological literature, is to superimpose the meaning of pluralism onto that of diversity, as if they were synonyms. Actually, [...] we must not confuse the normative-regulatory

---

38. Beckford 2010, p. 217.
39. Ibid., p. 218.
40. Beckford 2003, p. 79.
41. See, e.g., Frigerio, Wynarczik 2008 in relation to Latin America.

level, namely that of pluralism, with the descriptive level of empirical diversity[42].

Giordan makes clear that religious diversity is managed and regulated by the State and other authorities. Therefore, pluralism emerges as legitimization of religious diversity:

> ...the transition from "religious diversity" to "religious pluralism" [...] consists precisely in the "institutional arrangements", especially of legal nature, that regulate diversity, and in the ideas of political and philosophical nature that tend to consider cultural and religious diversity as a high value[43].

Moreover, this author argues that such a process of legitimization becomes more and more complex in the contemporary world, especially due to the huge growth of migratory flows. Some areas, like several gigantic towns in all the continents, are confronted with an unprecedented social and cultural diversity, including a crucial religious issue, that "will be among the most relevant ones in the agenda of the governors of the major global cities"[44]. In this respect, Giordan mentions the notion of super-diversity, but only in the descriptive meaning of "very much diversity"[45].

Another interesting attempt to disentangle the conundrums of the concept of religious pluralism runs quite parallel to that which we have just examined. It consists of an effort to establish an analytical distinction between plurality and pluralism. This perspective is clearly exposed in collective research published under the auspices of the European University Institute of Florence[46]. The aim of the book is to show that

---

42. Giordan 2014, p. 1.
43. Ibid., pp. 8–9.
44. Ibid., p. 8.
45. He is referring to a research program entitled "Super-diversity" inspired by Vertovec's essay and launched by the City Council and the University of Birmingham "to understand the challenges and the opportunities offered by the presence in the same urban space of an unusual variety of languages, ethnic groups, faiths, and traditions that make the daily interaction of the citizens more and more variegated and complex" (Giordan 2014, p. 8). The University of Birmingham created the Institute for Research into Super-diversity (IRiS): https://www.birmingham.ac.uk/research/super-diversity-institute/index.aspx (last accessed 23 September 2025).
46. Bardon et al. 2015.

"a clear distinction between pluralism and plurality can advance both the academic and public debate on religious diversity". Therefore, the chapters collected in this volume are aimed at exploring and illustrating "the complicated dynamics between pluralism and plurality"[47]. From this point of view, plurality is conceived as "an entirely descriptive term": it simply expresses the existence of religious differences and disagreements[48]. The idea of pluralism is clearly distinct from it and has a normative dimension. In the framework of the classical theory of political liberalism, normative pluralism "refers to the commitment to respect certain disagreements"[49], without imposing a single view, but defining instead the conditions surrounding the exercise of freedom. In an introductory chapter, Elise Rouméas delineates a map of different meanings of religious pluralism. A first meaning is theological: "pluralism assumes that other religious paths are true". Another meaning sees pluralism as a philosophical school, "what is known as value-pluralism in which values are irreducibly plural". Still another conception of religious pluralism "refers to a political ideal of peaceful interaction among individuals and groups of different religious faiths, as well as non-believers". Quite apart from these meanings, there is a sociological sense, in which "pluralism simply means religious plurality or diversity"[50].

We cannot continue further a discussion of the extremely complex issue of pluralism, with all its theological, philosophical, ethical, and political ramifications. The literature is immense, and the space we have is restricted. We will limit ourselves to draw a few tentative conclusions from this narrow exploration.

As a whole, like the idea of religious super-diversity, a new religious pluralism implies an inflation of meanings. It provides a descriptive tool that conflates different levels, while what seems to be missing is an analytical perspective that would allow discriminating dimensions, arrangements, and idioms. The studies we have considered convincingly indicate the need to restrain the concept of religious pluralism to a more specialised denotation, of a normative and ideological sort. However, they end

47. Ibid., p. 1.
48. Ibid.
49. Ibid., p. 2.
50. Rouméas 2015, p. 11.

up providing a rather vague meaning of the sociological field that they detach from the specialised meaning of religious pluralism, by incorporating it under the label of "diversity" or "plurality".

Yet, Vertovec's work, together with that of other scholars, alerts us to the necessity of developing a greater analytical focus on the dimension of diversity. From this point of view, not only should pluralism not be seen as synonymous with diversity or plurality, but we could gain in clarity by maintaining that diversity too is not synonymous with plurality. It therefore seems useful to go beyond not only the use of a single, all-embracing descriptive concept, like super-diversity or new religious pluralism, but also of a binary logic, which often ends up obscuring one segment of reality to illuminate another. In light of the above, we will suggest a new typology based on three terms: diversity, plurality, pluralism. We will also refer it to the past and to the contemporary scenarios.

4 Towards an Analytical Grid

Becci has formulated some perceptive reflections on the distinction between diversity and plurality in the religious field. She remarks that in its etymology the term *diversus* indicates a divergence. It is the result of a movement that has taken an opposite direction. Becci relies on an insightful definition formulated by an important French Dictionary, which observes that "in modern language, the words diverse and diversity always imply that terms or objects have an intrinsic and qualitative difference (as opposed to simple numerical multiplicity)"[51]. As for the term plurality, Becci suggests that "its etymological connotation, *pluralis*, refers to a quantitative dimension, to number"[52]. According to the same dictionary, what it designates is "the fact of existing in large numbers, of not being unique"[53]. Becci rightly concludes that the term diversity "emphasizes a difference and a singularity", while the term plurality "indicates rather the opposite of diversity", since it stresses the quantity and considers the different elements "as comparable and forming part of the same category"[54].

---

51. Robert et al. 1991, p. 560, quoted by Becci 2018, p. 77.
52. Becci 2018, p. 77.
53. Robert et al. 1991, p. 1463, quoted by Becci 2018, p. 77.
54. Ibid.

Drawing on these suggestions, we propose a provisional tripartite taxonomy based on a distinction between diversity, plurality, and pluralism.

With the expression of *religious diversity*, we mean the multifaceted set of beliefs, practices, conceptions, prohibitions, taboos, and spatializations which characterise religious behaviours and ideas in each context. Religious diversity is magmatic, disorganised, and anonymous and it evades any formal identification. It is a constant of religious behaviour and derives from human diversity itself. It is the result of the variety of individual dispositions (starting from the "religious unmusicality" of which Max Weber spoke). The assortment of religious experiences intersects with the influence of external variables, such as gender, age, class, education, membership in social networks, adherence to social or political groups and values, and cultural orientations.

With the expression *religious plurality*, we designate the sphere in which collective agents operate. These are generally more or less coherently organised religious groups that possess, even if sometimes only informally, a particular collective identity. These groups acquire at least partial visibility in the public sphere. Significantly, they designate themselves with a name, and this designation is taken up externally (sometimes however the process can go the other way round: an externally attributed label may be adopted by the group). This also implies an identification at the individual level, as members of a group.

Through the expression *religious pluralism*, we indicate a more formal field of relations, including the institutional arrangements and the social mechanisms (with political and juridical implications) through which the presence of different religious groups is officially recognized and legitimised. This implies a series of duties, but also of tangible and intangible advantages for each of them. The participation in this arena also entails a confrontation with a more abstract debate on the meaning and place of religious plurality inside the society. The representatives of the religious groups that are officially involved in a context of religious pluralism should be able to develop significant discourses and actions, in which the theological differences with other groups are somewhat negotiated, the holders of political authority are recognized in their legitimacy, and the religious coexistence is presented to some extent as a religious, ethical, or philosophical ideal.

The concepts of religious diversity, religious plurality and religious pluralism are not to be understood as the description of three irrevocably distinct situations. Instead, they constitute salient points in an ever-changing continuum. They draw attention to intermediate situations and on the processes that allow for transitions.

The aim of this grid is to offer a processual tool that encourages us to see how, within a variegated diversity of religious conceptions and practices, some positions coalesce in order to acquire a common coherence and aspire to be recognized as a clearly defined collective identity in the field of a religious plurality. Moreover, we aim to understand how a religious group, present in each territory only in an informal way, can work to acquire formal recognition within a framework of religious pluralism. Obviously, all this generates feedback effects on the other levels. The formal recognition in a pluralistic religious field involves the acknowledgment of a series of general principles of behaviour and entails a number of retroactive consequences on the structure of the group and on the acceptance of diversity of religious expressions inside. Or again, the three concepts of *religious diversity*, *plurality*, and *pluralism* lead us to analyse to what extent a religious group can admit a diversity of ideas, beliefs, and rituals within it, without experiencing a schism (which could create a new aspirant in the field of religious plurality, and perhaps also in that of religious pluralism).

Having used the idea of recognition, we need to take a stand on the ideas expressed. In his influential philosophical work, Axel Honneth has rescued this notion from its rather remote origins in Hegel, and, grounding also his view in Fichte, has transformed it into a crucial tool for reflecting on social and moral dilemmas of contemporary society. The prevailing meaning of this term, in Honneth's work – and in that of many of its interpreters and followers – is rather positive. It tends to indicate a benevolent attitude. This literature offers a generous and insightful attempt to indicate solutions for several intricated conundrums in contemporary societies. Referring to a well-known definition formulated by Clifford Geertz[55], it is both a *model of* reality – intended to know it – and a *model for* acting within reality and positively transforming society. However, the word

---

55. Geertz (1973 [1966]). See above all Chapter 4, *Religion as a Cultural System*, pp. 87–125.

"recognition" may have different meanings. At a first level, "to recognize" means to identify, and more precisely to reidentify: to know again, to perceive that a thing or a person is "something or someone previously known". At a second level, it means "to admit" or "to acknowledge": for instance, "to admit as being of a particular status" or "to acknowledge the de facto existence or the independence of" something[56]. In this meaning, the verb may be used, for example, to admit the truthfulness of a statement or to acknowledge the legitimacy of a government. A third sense corresponds to the philosophical meaning introduced by Honneth. Recognition for him refers to an active engagement with other people and with nature[57]. As it has been neatly stated by Raymond Geuss:

> Recognition, in [Honneth's] theory, is supposed to satisfy *two* distinct conditions at the same time: on the one hand, the recognition in question is supposed to be something which is a strict precondition for any form of human cognition, and, on the other, this recognition is supposed to provide the foundation for a non moralizing analysis of social pathologies, and thus for radical criticism of societies[58].

For Honneth recognition comes before cognition, in the meaning that "empathetic engagement precedes a neutral grasping of reality"[59]. This engagement is based on affective relations with a positive tonality, such as concern and care. It is only due to a process of reification that this "genuine, involved human perspective is neutralised to such a degree that it ultimately transforms into objectifying thought"[60]. This opens the doors to distanced observation and instrumentalization of the others.

Some authors have criticised Honneth's conception, charging it with a reliance on a too optimistic anthropology. From this point of view, Judith Butler's remarks appear particularly relevant[61]. Contrary to Honneth, she insists on the ambivalent nature of human drives, and argues that an active and affective engagement may also stem from negative pulsion.

---

56. See the entry "recognize" in the Merriam-Webster online dictionary, https://www.merriam-webster.com/dictionary/recognize (last accessed 23 January 2024).
57. For a discussion of these different meanings, see Geuss 2008, pp. 125–126.
58. Ibid., p. 126.
59. Honneth 2008, p. 40.
60. Ibid., p. 54.
61. Butler 2008.

The recognition is not necessarily aimed at affirming the existence of the other, but it may be directed at injuring it and even at eradicating it. Moreover, she affirms that an approach that tends to be normative – "an unfair normative burden"[62] – risks confusing if not nullifying the difference that exists between the conditions that influence the possibility of recognition and the varied forms that recognition can assume. Put simply, recognition should not obscure the possibility of acknowledging the otherness of the other and the presence of socio-cultural boundaries.

It is not our intention to engage here in a discussion of these wide issues. When recognizing the multiple stimuli of Honneth's approach, in our grid – which represents an infinitely more modest attempt to grasp a fragment of reality – we are distancing ourselves from the mainstream of the literature on recognition and use the term in a broader sense. By "recognition" we indicate a stance that may be positive or negative (or both at the same time). In other words, we put the accent, more than Honneth and other authors tend to do, on the multivocal and ambivalent nature of recognition. Adopting this perspective, it is possible to identify several dynamics of religious recognition, embedded in the processes that stem from the transition between the different positions in our grid.

At the religious diversity pole, it prevails an intuitive recognition of the individual alterity. By this we mean an occasional and spontaneous attribution of a religious character to some of other people's conceptions and practices. This means that these items are identified as belonging to an already known field qualified as "religious". At this stage, recognition remains partial and occurs in a fluid and unorganised state. The attitude linked to this kind of recognition may span from benign stance to indifference, criticism, repulsion, and condemnation.

Moving towards the religious plurality position, a more tangible, social recognition increasingly identifies other human beings as members of religious groups and categorises the existence of these groups. This means that another religious group is recognized in its organisation and in its visibility, as a unit inside a multiplicity. Its de facto existence is acknowledged. The group's members are seen as carriers of some emblematic characteristics and are referred through a common name. This recognition is the result of the actions and the negotiations engaged by the

---

62. Butler 2008, p. 119.

members and the leaders of the group. The actors of this recognition are people without specific religious qualifications, as well as members or leaders of other religious groups. Even in this case, the affective content of recognition is ambivalent. It may imply an acceptance of others' views and practices or a neutral indifference, as well as disapproval, censure, denunciation, or pugnacious criticism, until the attempt to annihilate the other group and to kill its members. The recognition of a particular religious position as an open player in the religious field is not a guarantee of success and longevity. It may often generate stigma and humiliation.

Finally, near the pole of religious pluralism, it is possible to observe institutional and normative recognition. In this case the positive – or at least not belligerent – attitude is dominant. The independence and the legitimacy of a religious movement is acknowledged. Among the crucial actors of this kind of recognition are the representatives of political power. Yet, even in this case, the acquisition of an official and legitimate status inside a religious field, under the umbrella of political authorities and with the assistance of legal specialists, may involve manifest or elusive forms of domination and is not devoid of manifestations of physical or symbolic violence. Moreover, the position acquired in a pluralistic field is not guaranteed, and it may easily be revoked, depending on the evolution of the socio-political context.

A last issue concerns the religious borders. In several cases, the channelling of diversity through the recognition of a number of religious units may operate inside what, for the sake of brevity, we may identify as a "religion". In other cases, vice versa, this process may intersect these boundaries. To describe these situations, we may speak of *intra-religious* plurality and pluralism, and of *inter-religious* plurality and pluralism.

5   Historical Perspectives

The analytical grid that we have sketched in the former paragraph composes a generative model[63] that, we hope, may be activated in relation to religious dynamics inside the modern State. Moreover, this taxonomy may contribute to interpreting historical processes of religious transformation

---

63. This perspective is mainly inspired by Friedrich Barth's work (1987; 1993).

that activate the endless interchange between diversity, plurality, and pluralism in other historical periods. We suggest that this model could be a tool for deciphering situations at different historical moments inside the monotheistic tradition[64], and could help to describe the variegated relationships among individuals and religious groups, and between them and the society in the past.

There is some amount of "chronocentrism" that shapes many studies on religious dynamics, which tend to focus on contemporary situations. With regard to diversity, plurality, and pluralism, it may, on the contrary, be important to take into account the past, even a fairly remote one. In other words, a perspective based on a historical comparison may be greatly productive[65]. Moreover, it is vital to go beyond Eurocentrism. This tendency is quite pervasive and implicitly generalises the situation of a relative religious monochromia that has characterised the countries of Western Europe during the past centuries. For instance, various parts of the Mediterranean area were far more polychrome from a religious point of view in modern times.

The first centuries of Christianity could offer a first laboratory to verify the dynamism of our tripartite taxonomy. The movement was born within a miscellaneous Jewish panorama, including several groups and tendencies. Christian identity boundaries were defined over a few centuries, both in terms of practice and doctrine. Contacts, disputes, and the Judaeo-Christian hybrid forms were the necessary steps that, from the group of the followers of Jesus Christ, went on to define a way of belonging to a religion, which named itself as such and was recognized as such: the Christians. The centrality of Jesus, religious leader, prophet, and thaumaturge, united the Gentiles and the Jews, bound people of different

---

64. The limitation of the references to monotheisms in this paragraph is dictated by the choice of observing religious dynamics from a historical perspective. Historically, monotheistic religions have a comparable organisation, boundaries, and sense of belonging and inclusion. In order to include the historical trajectory of other religions, we should probably modify the grid presented in this article.
65. A first attempt in this direction has been made by the research group coordinated by Alessandro Saggioro (Botta et al. 2017; Saggioro, Battista 2020), whose objective is to identify the ways of reflecting on "pluralism", from Religious Studies' disciplines, to compare them, to explore how a lexicon is used in a specialised way in different historical and geographical contexts.

languages and cultures, and varied Mediterranean geographies and different social classes.

Among those who followed Jesus (and at the same time other local charismatic figures), debates focused on practices, such as feeding or circumcision, and only later became theological, as the first ecumenical councils on the Trinity or the nature of Jesus attest. A magmatic space testified to a multifaceted *diversity*, especially in the early centuries, during which Christianity was not a *religio licita*. Unity in diversity was tantamount to survival and was defined above all by conformity to the apostolic *paradosis (traditio)* – considered of divine origin (from God to Christ, apostles, and followers: The Church) – a notion that in the times of the formation of Christian terminology (3rd–4th centuries) extended to doctrine, morals, liturgy, discipline, and catechesis.

Since the 2nd century, this diversity started to coalesce in a plurality of better-defined groups, often designated with the name of the founder (e.g., Marcion, Sabellius, Apollinaris, Arius, Nestorius, Eutyches, Macedonius, etc.). These groups were often the protagonists of fierce sectarian battles. Such a differentiation based on internal fragmentation led to a sort of plurality inside of Christianity. The boundaries between coexistence and conflict were expressed by instances and dynamics (socio-spatial and political) which framed the sphere of religious plurality. Religious groups – who designated and communicated to "the others" their identities – interacted in different forms of dialogue and struggle. However, in the first centuries, the Christian religion, even though prohibited, was functioned inside of a juridically framed religious *plurality*, using the State legal instruments (for example, one of the legal forms of legal existence of Christian communities were the so-called *collegia funeralia* and *collegia tenuiorum*).

In the post-Constantinian era, this situation was progressively impacted by the centralisation of a religion that considered itself as "catholic" and universal. Above all, however, this was made possible by the support of political power that, during the 4th century, legitimised and then made it the only accepted religion. The conflicts were increasingly regulated by a central authority that included or excluded.

This was the period of the so-called Christological heresies, such as that of Arius, defeated in a council convened by the emperor in 325 CE (Council of Nicaea), or those of the Manichaeans, Montanists, Docetists,

Marcionists, and Sabbellians, groups that could not be accepted due to incompatibility of doctrinal positioning, but often also for social and political reasons. That was the end of movements, currents, heterogeneous groups, and the beginning of schisms and fractures, such as the one that led in 431 CE (Council of Ephesus) to the creation of the Syriac Church (Nestorian or Chaldean) or that which led in 451 CE (Council of Chalcedon) to the establishment of the non-Chalcedonian Orthodox Church in Egypt (known latter as the Coptic Church). This multiple and deep fragmentation contributed to the expansion of the Christianity, while its complex and solid hierarchization, based on a pyramidal organisation, was pivotal for its survival and its progressive success[66].

In the Weberian perspective, the transition between charisma and institution is evident and was expressed in terms of legitimation and recognition of authority. A sub-species of the Christian religion was the monastic movement born in and dispersed across a vast area between Egypt, Palestine, and Syria. It structured itself for quite different reasons (spiritual, but also economic and social), and it organised itself in a few decades so that the initial disorder, challenging to manage even from a juridical point of view, was transformed into an almost perfect institution. It suffices to think of the crystallisation since the 4th century in the normative tripartition between cenobite, anchorite, and wanderer monks, the last ones often stigmatised and proscribed.

Since the juridical and political powers shared the policies of acceptance or expulsion of Christian currents (including the monastic groups), we can state that during the 4th century a regulated and controlled (and admittedly uneven) Christian *pluralism* was emerging. These are the centuries of Late Antiquity in which the passage of Christianity from persecuted to persecutor/tolerant takes place, both internally and externally. Tolerance and intolerance were calibrated on factors that could threaten the religious community's security and the social and political order.

In terms of intra-religious pluralism, minorities and majorities asserted themselves on a local basis, as the aforementioned Nestorians and non-Chalcedonians, with alternating dynamics of conflict, separation, dialogue, and reconciliation (but not fusion) that persisted over the

---

66. We are indebted to Peter Brown for these remarks on fragmentation and hierarchy that he shared by email in July 2021.

centuries, through the Great Schism of 1054 CE, the Reformation, up to the present day with the continual budding of movements and currents, like those of Pentecostals and Baptists, accepted nowadays as Christians or, like Mormons, now at close to inclusion.

Interreligious pluralism was undoubtedly structured starting from Constantine's edict of 313 CE, when the conventional tolerance for every religion slowly shifted toward a substantial intolerance of non-Christian religions. The religious uniformity of the state characterised by the participation of all religions to the emperor-worship definitively changed with the Theodosian decree of 380 CE that made Christianity the "religion of the State". From then on, a political strategy of substitution favoured the dominant Christian group. In the following centuries, the concept of religious tolerance was rather seen as a tool for securing the political and religious unity of the Holy Roman Empire.

If during the greater part of the 4th century the acceptance of the "others" was still chiefly inspired by the strategies of integration or assimilation pursued by the Graeco-Roman world, there was a significant change in the following period, with a growing struggle, even a violent one, against residual forms of paganism, which was defeated, expelled, and even physically destroyed. The relationship with the Jews, which can be traced primarily in the polemic against the Christ-killers with which proto-Christian literature is replete, also evolves according to social contexts. Jews were recognized and tolerated while remaining without political or civil privileges. They were often marginalised and ostracised, as evidenced by the destruction of synagogues, the prohibition of mixed marriages, and the limitation of certain rights.

The situation was considerably different in the Islamic world. Here religious *diversity* had a right of citizenship over the centuries. In the absence of a central regulatory authority comparable to the Church in the Christian world, a diversity of opinions and practices has been able to find hospitable ground, without the risk of being systematically repressed.

Legal decisions (*fatwas*) have always had the character of a personal position expressed by a jurist and were always susceptible to being contradicted by other decisions or challenged by another law school. Sharia law distinguishes five categories of human actions. At one end stand the prescribed actions, at the other end those that are prohibited. Between the two, there are three intermediate gradations, which indicate what is recommended, indifferent, or condemnable. Only the positions of prescription and prohibition imply mandatory adhesion, while the wide area between them remains largely grey and free of a compelling norm. As a consequence, many practices judged condemnable by Sharia law have been able to perpetuate freely through the centuries, without being uprooted.

Moreover, and differently from the hierarchization of Christianity, the lack of a central authority has also favoured the organisation of religious diversity in a substantial inclusive *plurality* of currents, movements, and schools. This is true on a general level for the Sunni and Shiite branches, but also for the multiple segmentations of these groups into different legal and theological schools. This also entailed a kind of *intra-religious proto-pluralism*, through interaction with political authority. In the same way, many mystical currents have flourished, also determining in this case a substantial plurality of religious options, and a proto-pluralistic regulation with the support of political authority.

Inter-religious pluralism has also existed in Islamic societies. The State has always granted other monotheistic religious groups a substantial freedom to practise their own worship. It would naturally be misleading to look for the modern standard of "tolerance". The rights accorded to the dhimmis were, however, mixed with several uncomfortable impositions: for example, the payment of a tax, certain clothing restrictions, and the prohibition (not always respected) to build new places of worship.

We should add that the characterization of a plural or pluralistic field as intra-religious and inter-religious may be shifting in time and much depends on the historical context. To mention some well-known historical examples, we may make reference to the gnostic groups in the first centuries' CE Christianism that heresiologists assimilated sometimes to pagans. A similar ambiguity stems from the uncertain position of the Manicheans with respect to the Christian field. During its first centuries, Islam was sometimes perceived as a heretical Christian movement by Christian authors. Since the Middle Ages, the Druses had a liminal position in the societies of the Middle East: they were not inside Islam but not completely outside it either. This situation still exists today. Somewhat similar considerations may be made concerning the position of groups like the Alevis in Turkey.

6 Exploring Contemporary Super-diversity

As we have already observed, it would be wrong to exaggerate the novelties introduced by globalisation in relation to religious diversity. From this point of view, some continuities should not be underestimated. Migration studies indicate, for example, that the levels of transnational mobility were often high in the past. In other words, transnationalism is not necessarily linked to the development of modern means of transport and telecommunication. Deidre Menteil has showed:

> [...] how transportation and communication between Cape Verde and New England were far more developed in the sailing era than for much of the twentieth century, and that there were many Cape Verdeans who were living authentically transnational lifestyles before the restrictive American immigration policies of the early 1920s[67].

The early development of transnational lifestyles undoubtedly also induced phenomena of contact and mixing on the religious level. A reputed scholar as José Casanova does not hesitate, for example, to speak of the "vibrant religious super-diversity" of eighteenth century American colonial towns[68].

To add another example, the societies located on the southern and eastern shores of the Mediterranean basin have experienced for many centuries, starting from the Middle Ages, a situation of close coexistence between many religious groups. These societies have been affected by a pervasive diversity of practices and conceptions which have produced innumerable forms of sharing, accommodation, and hybridization across religious borders[69].

While all of this is undoubtedly true, it does not mean that the present-day transformations in the circulation of people, goods, and information do not induce a crucial shift. They generate a change of scale in the intensity of diversity and do amplify the stakes that this situation poses to the establishment of religious plurality and pluralism. The analytical grid we have

---

67. Meintel 2016, p. 24; see also Meintel 2002.
68. Casanova 2013, p. 115.
69. Albera, Couroucli 2009; Barkan, Barkey 2014.

proposed may offer some hints for pursuing the discussion of the issue we started with. We propose that the intricate situation often designated under the labels of "super-diversity" or "new religious pluralism" that characterises some sectors of our increasingly globalised world may be analytically understood through a modified version of our general taxonomy.

In some areas, the enormous amount of religious diversity that is generally present generates a condition of *religious hyper-diversity*. This condition represents the refraction, in the religious field, of the wider processes of Vertovec's sociological super-diversity which, besides religion, also touches other entrenched fields like culture and especially ethnicity. In order to avoid confusion with the wider and descriptive category of "super-diversity", we maintain a slightly different phrasing, distinguishing between sociological super-diversity and religious hyper-diversity. The huge expansion, in this context, of more or less recognizable religious sets produces a situation that we propose to call *religious hyper-plurality*. The number of identified religious groups – the players in the local or national religious field – is growing dramatically. It is now quite recurrent for European or American cities, also of middle range, to host hundreds of different religious groups, which are working to acquire autonomy and an operational space. Moreover, these groups are distributed along a broad spectrum of characteristics. This creates very heterogeneous collections, which often refuse the qualification of religion, favouring a label referring to the dimension of spirituality. In its turn, this situation engenders the dilemma of what we may call *religious hyper-pluralism*, readapting a concept that has been proposed, in a wider framework, by Alessandro Ferrara in 2014.

It is possible to identify some main factors that influence contemporary religious hyper-diversity in some Western countries. Besides the usual variables that generate different religious behaviours, there are new factors that complexify the situation. We may mention the growing number of options in the religious repertoire, due to the intercontinental flows of people and their concentration in limited zones; the internal differentiation between and inside ethnic groups; the impact of global connections that create multi-layered religious-scapes; the growth of the so-called majority-minority cities or neighbourhoods; the patterns of spatial distribution of immigrants, generating both segregation and contact with other segments (more or less sedentary) of the population in a kaleidoscopic arrangement.

The impact of transnational migratory movements, with the establishment of diasporas connected to the motherland through a series of telematic channels and the circulation of people, has created a fertile ground for the proliferation of religious difference. Foreign religions like Islam, Hinduism, or Buddhism (with all their huge internal variety and nuances) have been widely imported. New styles of religiosity have made their way inside established religious traditions like Catholicism or Protestantism, with the affirmation of new forms of liturgy and style of worship; new forms of spirituality have changed the relationship between the care of the spirit and the care of the body, and have modified the relationship between tradition and innovation, often breaking the boundaries between belief, faith, superstition, and magic. The process of relative secularisation which occurred in many Western countries – both in Europe and in the US[70] – since the second half of the twentieth century, has generated a loss of consensus and influence of traditional religious organisations, and has liberated several spaces in the religious market, which are visible in terms of free access and competition[71]. These spaces can be partially filled by an offer that generates conversion or simply adhesion. This offer comes from new religions brought by immigrants, and even more from the movements that are inscribed in the galaxy of spirituality and often take advantage of the new digital technologies as instruments of recruitment and propaganda.

The magmatic whole of diversity secretes a series of paths that determine the formation of a plurality of movements. These movements often arise from the action of religious entrepreneurs who import a religious current from their homeland or inscribe their action in the horizon of new spiritualities, activating a whole series of hybridizations with more traditional – external or local – movements. Many faithful thus find a factor of identification and solidarity, at least temporarily, in a collective whole, especially thanks to gatherings and common celebrations.

Nowadays plurality is unable to contain the proliferation of diversity, which overflows abundantly from the corridors that attempt to channel it.

70. Berger et al. 2008.
71. Berger 1967.

Individuals often create hybrid spiritualities, for instance participating in various groups offering Hindu-inspired meditation techniques or adhering to groups related to Spiritualism, Neoshamanism, or Wicca without renouncing their Catholic identity[72]. Liza Steele has drawn attention to what appears to be an increasingly widespread phenomenon of individuals having ties to multiple faiths, through the effects of globalisation, migration, intermarriage, and greater individual freedom and mobility in superdiverse societies[73]. Furthermore, people of different religious affiliation may attend the same religious space, practising what has been defined as religious "butinage"[74].

This scenario is complicated by the "hyperconnected" dimension that creates new forms of fruition and belonging. These rarely impact only the virtual dimension, but often have links and changes with the offline, in that hybrid dimension of "onlife"[75]. Onlife refers to the contemporary lack of distinction between being online or being offline due to the persistent presence of technologies in our everyday life which can be observed in meditations, spiritual retreats, liturgies, and prayers that go beyond the local and physical dimension and pervade the space both on and off.

The establishment of a plurality implies a social recognition of the de facto existence of a multiplicity of entities which share some basic qualities. From the point of view of identification, the situation of hyperplurality has a somewhat fuzzy character. A number of collective agents that may be recognized as religious from an etic point of view, have a fluctuating position from an emic perspective. In particular, the groups that belong to the spirituality constellation have an ambiguous status and may play on different grounds. According to the convenience or the context, they may stress or obliterate the religious character of their orientation.

From the point of view of the affective engagement in the recognition, it is possible to detect a number of possible configurations, ranging from a positive or relative neutral appreciation (often this seems to happen for instance in relation to Buddhist movements), to a stigmatising and dehumanising vision, like in the case of Islam. In this case a stereotyping

---

72. Meintel, Mossière 2013, p. 64; Palmisano, Pannofino 2021.
73. Steele 2016, p. 47.
74. Soares 2011; Droz et al. 2016.
75. Floridi 2015.

stance seems frequently dominant, also generating what, in Honneth's terms, we could define as reification and instrumentalization. An even worse fate occurs to movements pertaining to the spiritual galaxy, when they are labelled as sects.

Even if one expects a somewhat physiological concurrence between religious movements, it is often possible to see a certain extent of reciprocal acceptance and collaboration. Obviously, conflicts do often exist, and cleavages may intersect quarrelling ethnic boundaries. Yet a great number of forms of conviviality have been described, with the elaboration of common rituals and various types of formal and informal exchanges. This attitude also concerns one of the strategic terrains for the acquisition of a position in the field of the plurality, namely the acquisition of a place where the faithful may gather. Even in this case, there exist several forms of sharing or mutualization of spaces. Some projects with a wide mediatic resonance, like the House of One in Berlin, are only the visible top of a mountain made of subterranean efforts to build a common religious environment.

The shift between plurality and pluralism involves a formal recognition, which is cast in juridical terms. This implies a complex work concerning the relations between formally represented religious groups and the secular, cultural, political, and social institutions, both local and national, that establish and regulate their relations. An important role is, at this stage, that of decision makers who are concerned with pluralism and integration.

At this level, the regulative action promoted by the State, or the local political authorities is hindered by the number and the variety of the collective actors that struggle for obtaining an official position inside the religious field, as well as by the concurrence and the antagonism between some of them. The shifting positions at the level of public opinion, media, ideological movements, political parties, and so on, are a further factor that heavily conditions the decisions. Moreover, a situation of hyper-pluralism implies the risk that a minimum consensus on some essential principles that allows the functioning of religious pluralism (generating a situation that, with the terms of John Rawls, one can define as "reasonable pluralism") is lacking. Without this minimum common denominator, an "overlapping consensus" between different and antagonist positions becomes problematic. In fact, the dynamics of formal recognition are double-edged. In order to find their space *in the* common framework of a juridically and politically sanctioned pluralism, the collective actors should also show an acceptation *of the* common framework[76].

7 Conclusion

In this contribution we have discussed some methodological and epistemological difficulties that characterise the study of religious diversity, of its organisation in collective frames and of the institutionalisation of these frames on a political and legal level. We suggested, from this point of view, the need to avoid both single all-embracing concepts – so encompassing that they end up being scarcely operational – and dichotomous approaches that are too schematic.

The tripartite typology – (hyper)diversity, plurality, and pluralism – we have proposed seems to us to be a first tool for trying to get out of the impasse. This terminology may be useful for tracing forms of continuity between different historical and cultural contexts, while at the same time highlighting historical fractures. The unprecedented characteristics that the contemporary context presents are in fact emphasised through the prefix "hyper" applied to the three proposed concepts. We have offered this systematisation as a modest contribution to the effort of conceptual hygiene advocated by Beckford. In the very summary discussion of the possible fields of application of our analytical grid, we have identified, naturally in a very preliminary way, various areas which seems to confirm its plausibility. Of course, a more compelling evaluation of its usefulness can only come from a broader discussion as well as from more complex attempts to measure it with empirical reality.

We suggest, finally, that our model may contribute to a critical discussion of the conceptualization of the relationship between religious groups in terms of majorities and minorities[77]. As Giorgi points out, in Italy, but also in Europe – speaking broadly – traditional religions are no longer practised by the majority of the population, even though they remain the religions of the majority in the collective imagery[78]. Catholicism, in this

---

76. Becci et al. 2018.
77. Giorgi 2018; Giorda, Mastromarino 2020; Kymlicka 1995; Obadia, Zwilling 2016.
78. Giorgi 2018, p. 23.

respect, is an influential majority in the domain of a mythological collective imagery, thus remaining the reference model and dominating on a symbolic level.

The relations between religious groups, and between them and the institutions that hold the power of recognition, is fundamental in defining a minority. The struggle for recognition and legitimization is characterised by different forms of conflict, opposition, compromise, and camouflage between major and minor religious groups[79]. Investigating these relations, both quantitatively and qualitatively – in terms of political, economic, cultural, and social as well as religious power – and on different scalar perspectives, but also re-thinking the way we use categories and terms (such as minority and majority) is a fruitful approach for analysing the competition (and also the exclusion from it), in the possibilities of access to resources, such as space, money, or visibility.

Author's Biographies

Dionigi Albera (PhD Anthropology, University Aix-Marseille, 1995) is Research Director at the CNRS (Institut d'Ethnologie et d'Anthropologie Sociale, University Aix-Marseille, France). His main topics of research are pilgrimage, ritual, interfaith practices, kinship, domestic organization, migration, museography, Alps, and the Mediterranean. His recent publications on religion include *Sharing Sacred Spaces in the Mediterranean: Christians, Muslims and Jews at Shrines and Sanctuaries*, edited with Maria Couroucli (Indiana University Press, 2012), *Dieu, une enquête. Judaïsme, christianisme, islam: ce qui les distingue, ce qui les rapproche*, edited with Katell Berthelot (Flammarion, 2013), *International Perspectives on Pilgrimage Studies: Itineraries, Gaps and Obstacles*, edited with John Eade (Routledge, 2015), and *New Pathways in Pilgrimage Studies*, edited with John Eade (Routledge, 2017).

Maria Chiara Giorda (PhD Paris, EPHE 2007) is Full Professor of History of Religions at the Department of Humanities at the University of Roma Tre in Rome, Italy. She is coordinator of the international SHARP Lab Project and her research activity focuses on the following topics: history

---

79. Giorda, Vanolo 2019, p. 223.

of religions, geography of religions, religion and urban spaces, and history of monasticism. Her most recent publications include the co-curatorship of the volume *Geography of Encounters: The Making and Unmaking of Multi-Religious Spaces* with Marian Burchardt (Palgrave, 2021) and *La Chiesa Ortodossa romena in Italia: Per una geografia storico-religiosa* (Viella, 2023).

References

Albera, D., Couroucli, M. (2009), *Religions traversées: Lieux saints partagés entre chrétiens, musulmans et juifs en Méditerranée*, Actes Sud, Arles.
Ballabio, F. (2001), *Il nuovo pluralismo religioso*, EMI, Brescia.
Banchoff, T. (2007), *Democracy and the New Religious Pluralism*, Oxford University Press, Oxford.
Bardon, A., Stoeckl, K., Birnbaum, M., Lee, L. (eds.) (2015), *Religious Pluralism: A Resource Book*. European University Institute, Florence.
Barkan, E., Barkey, K. (eds.) (2014), *Choreographies of Shared Sacred Sites: Religion, Politics, and Conflict Resolution*, Columbia University Press, New York.
Barth, F. (1987), *Cosmologies in the Making: A Generative Approach to Cultural Variation in Inner New Guinea*, Cambridge University Press, Cambridge.
Barth, F. (1993), *Balinese Worlds*, The University of Chicago Press, Chicago.
Becci, I. (2018), *Vers la superdiversité religieuse: diversité, pluralité, pluralisme et reconnaissance*, in *Pluralisme et reconnaissance: Face à la diversité religieuse*, in I. Becci, C. Monnot, O. Voirol (eds.), Presses Universitaires de Rennes, Rennes, pp. 73–92.
Becci, I., Burchardt, M. (2016), *Religion and Super-diversity: An Introduction*, in "New Diversities", 18, 1, pp. 1–7.
Becci, I., Monnot, C., Voirol, O. (eds.) (2018), *Pluralisme et reconnaissance: Face à la diversité religieuse*, Presses Universitaires Rennes, Rennes.
Beck, U. (2011), *Multiculturalism or Cosmopolitanism: How Can We Describe and Understand the Diversity of the World?*, in "Social Sciences in China", 32, 4, pp. 52–58. https://doi.org/10.1080/02529203.2011.625169
Beckford, J. A. (2003), *Social Theory and Religion*, Cambridge University Press, Cambridge.
Beckford, J. A. (2010), *The Return of Public Religion? A Critical Assessment of a Popular Claim*, in "Nordic Journal of Religion and Society", 23, 2, pp. 121–136. https://doi.org/10.18261/ISSN1890-7008-2010-02-02

Berger, P. L. (1967), *The Sacred Canopy: Elements of a Sociological Theory of Religion*, Doubleday and Company, Garden City (NY).

Berger, P. L., Fokas, E., Davie, G. (2008), *Religious America, Secular Europe?* Ashgate, Burlington (VT).

Boccagni, P. (2015), *(Super)Diversity and the Migration-Social Work Nexus: A New Lens on the Field of Access and Inclusion?*, in "Ethnic and Racial Studies", 38, 4, pp. 608–620. https://doi.org/10.1080/01419870.2015.980291

Botta, S., Ferrara, M., Saggioro, A. (eds.) (2017), *La storia delle religioni e la sfida dei pluralismi*, Quaderni di Studi e Materiali di Storia delle religioni, 18, Morcelliana, Brescia.

Butler, J. (2008), *Taking Another's View: Ambivalent Implications*, in A. Honneth (ed.), *Reification: A New Look at an Old Idea*, Oxford University Press, Oxford, pp. 97–119.

Casanova, J. (2013), *Religious Associations, Religious Innovations and Denominational Identities in Contemporary Global Cities*, in I. Becci, M. Burchardt, J. Casanova (eds.), *Topographies of Faith: Religion in Urban Spaces*, Brill, Leiden, pp. 113–127.

Connor, P. (2014), *Immigrant Faith: Patterns of Immigrant Religion in the United States, Canada, and Western Europe*, New York University Press, New York.

Di Sciullo, L., Paravati, C. (2020), *Il panorama multireligioso dell'Italia e la sua difficile gestione*, in *Dossier Statistico Immigrazione*, Centro Studi e Ricerche IDOS-Centro Studi Confronti, Rome, pp. 230–233.

Droz, Y., Soares, E., Gez, Y. N., Rey, J. (2016), *La mobilité religieuse à l'aune du "butinage"*, in "Social Compass", 63, pp. 251–267. https://doi.org/10.1177/0037768616629305

Duyvendak, J. W., Foner, N., Kasinitz, P. (2019), *Introduction: Super-diversity in Everyday Life*, in "Ethnic and Racial Studies", 42, 1, Special Issue: Super-diversity in Everyday Life, pp. 1–16. https://doi.org/10.1080/01419870.2017.1406969

Eade, J. (2011), *From Race to Religion: Multiculturalism and Contested Urban Space*, in J. Beaumont, C., Baker (eds.), *Postsecular Cities: Space, Theory and Practice*, Continuum, London, pp. 154–167.

Ebaugh, H. R., Saltzman Chafetz, J. (2000), *Religion and the New Immigrants: Continuities and Adaptations in Immigrant Congregations*, AltaMira Press, Walnut Creek (CA).

Eck, D. L. (2001), *A New Religious America: How a 'Christian Country' Has Become the World's Most Religiously Diverse Nation*, Harper, San Francisco.

Ferrara, A. (2014), *The Democratic Horizon: Hyperpluralism and the Renewal of Political Liberalism*, Cambridge University Press, Cambridge.

Floridi, L. (2015), *The Onlife Manifesto: Being Human in a Hyperconnected Era*, Springer International Publishing, New York.

Frigerio, A., Wynarczyk, H. (2008), *Diversidad no es lo mismo que pluralismo: cambios en el campo religioso argentino (1985–2000) y lucha de los evangélicos por sus derechos religiosos*, in "Sociedade e Estado", 23, 2, pp. 227–260. https://doi.org/10.1590/S0102-69922008000200003

Geertz, C. (1973 [1966]), *The Interpretation of Cultures*, Basic Books, New York, pp. 87–125.

Geuss, R. (2008), *Philosophical Anthropology and Social Criticism*, in A. Honneth (ed.), *Reification: A New Look at an Old Idea*, Oxford University Press, Oxford, pp. 120–130.

Giorda, M., Mastromarino, A. (2020), *Maggioranze e minoranze: andare oltre? Le mense degli ospedali come laboratorio di analisi*, in B. Bertarini, C. Drigo (eds.), *Diversità culturale come cura, cura della diversità culturale*, Giappichelli, Turin, pp. 95–122.

Giorda, M., Vanolo, A. (2019), *Religious Diversity and Inter-faith Competition: The Politics of Camouflage in Italian Cities*, in "Territory, Politics, Governance", 5, pp. 220–240. https://doi.org/10.1080/21622671.2019.1702894

Giordan, G. (2014), *Pluralism as Legitimization of Diversity*, in G. Giordan, E. Pace (eds.), *Religious Pluralism. Framing Religious Diversity in the Contemporary World*, Springer, New York, pp. 1–12.

Giorgi, A. (2018), *Religioni di minoranza tra Europa e laicità*, Mimesis, Milan.

Hollinger, D. A. (1995), *Postethnic America*, BasicBooks, New York.

Honneth, A. (ed.) (2008), *Reification: A New Look at an Old Idea*, Oxford University Press, Oxford.

Kivisto, P. (2014), *Religion and Immigration: Migrant Faiths in North America and Western Europe*, Polity Press, Cambridge.

Kymlicka, W. (1995), *Multicultural Citizenship: A Liberal Theory of Minority Rights*, Clarendon Press, Oxford.

Levitt, P. (2007), *God Needs No Passport: Immigrants and the Changing Religious Landscape*, W. W. Norton & Company, New York.

Lippy, C. H. (2000), *Pluralism Comes of Age: American Religious Culture in the Twentieth Century*, M. E. Sharpe, Armonk (NY).

Machacek, D. W. (2003), *The Problem of Pluralism*, in "Sociology of Religion", 64, 2, pp. 145–161. https://doi.org/10.2307/3712368

Makoni, S. B. (2012), *A Critique of Language, Languaging, and Supervernacular*, in "Muitas Vozes", 1, 2, pp. 189–199. https://doi.org/10.5212/MuitasVozes.v.1i2.0003

Meintel, D. (2002), *Transmitting Pluralism: Mixed Unions in Montreal*, in "Canadian Ethnic Studies", 34, 3, pp. 99–120.

Meintel, D. (2016), *Religion, Conviviality and Complex Diversity*, in "New Diversities", 18, 1, pp. 23–36.

Meintel, D., Mossière, G. (2013), *Sulla scia della rivoluzione silenziosa: dalla secolarizzazione al cosmopolitismo religioso*, in "Antropologica", Numéro spécial "Montrealology", 55, 1, pp. 57–71.

Naso, P. (2015), *L'incognita post-secolare. Pluralismo religioso, fondamentalismi, laicità*, Guida Editori, Napoli.

Naso, P. (2020), *Il Nuovo Pluralismo Religioso (PNR), un patrimonio sociale che si disperde*, in *Dossier Statistico Immigrazione*, Centro Studi e Ricerche IDOS-Centro Studi Confronti, Roma, pp. 234–237.

Ndhlovu, F. (2016), *A Decolonial Critique of Diaspora Identity Theories and the Notion of Super-diversity*, in "Diaspora Studies", 9, pp. 28–40. https://doi.org/10.1080/09739572.2015.1088612

Obadia, L., Zwilling, A. L. (eds.) (2016), *Minorité et communauté en religion*, Presses Universitaires de Strasbourg, Société, droit et religion en Europe, Strasbourg.

Oke, N., Sonn, C. C., McConville, C. (2016), *Making a Place in Footscray: Everyday Multiculturalism, Ethnic Hubs and Segmented Geography*, in "Identities", pp. 1–19. https://doi.org/10.1080/1070289X.2016.1233880

Palmisano, S., Pannofino, N. (2021), *Religioni sotto spirito: Viaggio nelle nuove spiritualità*, Mondadori, Milano.

Pavlenko, A. (2019), *Super-diversity and Why It Isn't: Reflections on Terminological Innovation and Academic Branding*, in S. Breidbach, L. Küster, B. Schmenk (eds.), *Sloganization in Language Education Discourse: Conceptual Thinking in the Age of Academic Marketization*, Multilingual Matters, Bristol, pp. 142–168.

Robert, P., Rey, A., Rey-Debove, J. (eds.) (1991), *Le petit Robert: Dictionnaire alphabétique et analogique de la langue française*, Le Robert, Paris.

Rouméas, E. (2015), *What is Religious Pluralism?*, in A. Bardon, K. Stoeckl, M. Birnbaum, L. Lee (eds.), *Religious Pluralism: A Resource Book*, European University Institute, Florence, pp. 11–17.

Saggioro, A., Battista, L. (2020), *Come definire il pluralismo religioso? Riflessioni su un lessico interdisciplinare*, in A. Saggioro, *Definire il pluralismo religioso*, Quaderni di Studi e materiali di Storia delle religioni, 26, pp. 287–311.

Soares, E. (2011), *Religious 'Butinage': Looking at Paranaguá-Mirim (Brazil)*, in "Social Compass", 58, 2, pp. 223–234.

Steele, L. (2016), *Muli-Religiosity: Expanding Research on Ties to Multiple Faiths in the 21st Century*, in "New Diversities", 18, 1, pp. 37–52.

Vertovec, S. (2007), *Super-diversity and its Implications*, in "Ethnic and Racial Studies", 30, 6, pp. 1024–1054. https://doi.org/10.1080/01419870701599465

Vertovec, S. (2019), *Talking Around Super-diversity*, in "Ethnic and Racial Studies", 42, 1, pp. 125–139. https://doi.org/10.1080/01419870.2017.1406128

Warner, R. S., Wittner, J. G. (eds.) (1998), *Gatherings in Diaspora: Religious Continuities and the New Immigration*, Temple University Press, Philadelphia.

Wessendorf, S. (2014), *Commonplace Diversity: Social Relations in a Super-diverse Context*, Palgrave Macmillan, Basingstoke.

Wuthnow, R. (2008), *Responding to the New Religious Pluralism*, in "CrossCurrents", 58, 1, pp. 43–50. https://doi.org/10.1353/cro.2008.a782407

Part 1
Asian Case Studies

Chapter 2

Nonviolence and Interreligious Dialogue in Islam: The Case of Jawdat Said

Viviana Schiavo

Abstract

Studies on nonviolence are numerous, but only a small number of them have considered this concept in relation to the Islamic world. On the contrary, recent years have seen an increase in analysis about the interrelationship between religion and violence, with a specific focus on Islam since the 2001 terrorist attacks. This chapter explores the relationship between religious diversity and peacebuilding in the Islamic context, by analysing the nonviolent theology of the late Syrian thinker Jawdat Said (1931–2022). The multiple religious identities he encountered during his lifetime influenced his considerable scholarly output, much of which has yet to be translated into English. The importance of diversity, seen as a mechanism for social progress, is a pillar of Said's nonviolent thought.

Keywords: interreligious dialogue, nonviolence, Syria, Islamic theology, Islamic reformism

1 Introduction

Contrary to what positivist sociologists predicted, religion has not disappeared from the contemporary public sphere but continues to play an essential role[1]. This is particularly true in the Islamic world, where the

---

1. Pace 2007.

link between religion and society is notably present. As the philosopher Jahanbegloo underlines[2], public and academic interest in recent decades, especially since the 2001 terrorist attacks, has mainly focused on the interrelationship between violence and religion. On the contrary, less attention has been paid to the nonviolent theories indigenous to the Islamic context. Although scholarly studies on nonviolence are numerous, those concerning the Islamic world are few in number.

This chapter aims to explore the role religious super-diversity[3] and interreligious dialogue could play in nonviolent action and peacebuilding processes in the Muslim world, from a practical and a theoretical point of view. The issue will be addressed through the theological and experiential case study of the Syrian intellectual Jawdat Said (Ğawdat Sa'īd, d. 30 January 2022), advocate of a theory of radical nonviolence based on Quranic exegesis, Islamic tradition, and historical phenomena analysis. His innovative theoretical and exegetical approach seeks to stay anchored to the Muslim tradition whilst opening to new interpretations. The distinctive feature of his writings lies in his application of the philosophical concept of nonviolence to the Islamic context[4]: he presents the nonviolent method as the only efficient tool to achieve social change. It is important to highlight that he is little known in Europe and only somewhat more recognised even in the Arab-Muslim context, despite the importance of his contributions. Only a few of his many books are

2. Jahanbegloo 2014.
3. When speaking about religious super-diversity, I refer to a diversity resulting from several variables, namely the coexistence of multiple religions and of their various internal ramifications and currents, their interconnectedness, and the way they are managed on a political level. See Becci, Burchardt 2016, pp. 2–6.
4. He employs the Arabic term *lā-'unf* to render the English word "nonviolence". This last one has been created in 1919 by Mohandas Karamchand Gandhi to translate the Hindu concept *ahiṃsā* (*a-*, no, and *-hiṃsā*, violence), which Gandhi defined as "the complete absence of ill-will", and in his active form, as "good-will towards all life" (M. Gandhi 1924, p. 286). In the political sphere, it represents a fighting method, rejecting violence as an opposition tool and preferring to employ other means, such as non-collaboration, boycotts, pacific protests, etc. Likewise, Jawdat Said's nonviolence does not mean a passive attitude, as often believed and criticised in the Muslim world, nor the simple refusal of violence. It refers to an active approach, seeking for social and political change through peaceful tools. That is why, in books, newspapers and research, Said is frequently described as the "Arab Gandhi" (Pierret 2011) or the "herald of nonviolence" (Said 1995).

accessible to international readers in English translation; in Italy, a short volume entitled *Vie islamiche alla nonviolenza*, published by Zikkaron publishing house, brings together some excerpts from his works and provides an initial introduction to his thought. That is why the translation of additional writings by Said from Arabic is a central part of my research[5].

With his cultural background and his theoretical writings, Said offers an important contribution to international reflection on the possible connection between religious super-diversity and peacebuilding. Said's relevance is primarily because of his theoretical reflections on the relationship between diversity and peacebuilding, rather than because of the eventual influence on his intellectual development of Syrian and, above all, Muslim multiple religious identities. It is precisely the importance he gives to the otherness in his religious conception that constitutes one of the pillars of his non-violent thought. What follows is an overview of Said's evolution as a scholar, placing particular emphasis on his historical and cultural context. Discussion of the religious diversity with which Said came into contact will allow the reader to understand the impact these encounters could have had on his intellectual development. Analysis of Said's theology will highlight the importance of human relationships to his theoretical framework, which identifies diversity as a source of growth. The chapter will also explore the role of interreligious dialogue as a tool for nonviolent change.

2 Between Religious Super-diversity and Nonviolence

2.1 Jawdat Said and Syrian Religious Multiple Identities

Jawdat Said's story began on 9 February 1931, in Beer Ajam, a small village in the Syrian Golan. Like most locals, he was of Circassian ethnicity, one of the many groups making up the multifaceted Syrian identity mosaic. Created from the ruins of the Ottoman Empire and the French mandate, contemporary Syria is a crossroads of civilizations

---

5. This chapter is the result of research I carried out thanks to a grant appointed by the CUC (University Catholic Centre at CEI – Communication and Culture Foundation), under the supervision of Ida Zilio Grandi. Throughout the text, I will refer to Said's different books. I chose to present the author by topics and not by single books, because he deals with the same subject within several of his writings.

and a meeting point for religious identities[6]. Jawdat Said was imbued with this religious super-diversity; although, according to his son Bišr, it was not a major factor in the development of his ideas, Said's reflections about the truth were partially inspired by the variety of confessional identities with which he interacted. Typical of the Syrian experience, he was exposed to different religions from early childhood. He reported to his son that "one day, he heard that a disbeliever, namely a non-Muslim, was visiting the village". When the young Said ran to see how this man looked, he discovered that the man was normal, like everybody else: "he started wondering what made this exact person a disbeliever: he didn't pray, but lots of people in the village didn't pray either, like the Muslims should do"[7]. In second grade, Said noticed that there were slightly different Muslim ways of praying according to the *maḏhab* (Sunni school of jurisprudence)[8]. Through these formative experiences, Said realized that each of these currents believed their religious school to be more authentic than the others, so he started wondering what brings human beings nearer to the truth, regardless of whether they are Shafi'is or Hanafis, Sunnis or Shias, believers or disbelievers[9].

The specific type of diversity which most directly affected Said's intellectual training was internal to the Sunni world. Indeed, Said's non-violent theology resulted from the influence of different discursive traditions[10], a

6. The majority ethnic group is the Arab one (50%), flanked by a constellation of minorities, such as the Kurds, the Druzes, the Turkomans, the Armenians, the Assyrians, the Circassians, and others. The Syrian confessional mosaic is made up of various religious communities (87% Muslims, 10% Christians, 3% Druzes, and a small Jewish presence) and of their internal differences and ramifications, specifically Sunnis (74%), Alawis, Ismailis, and Shites (13%) in Islam and Orthodox, Nestorians, and Uniates among the Christians. All population data is taken from *Syria*, The World Factbook 2021. Syria's current situation, in terms of ethnic and religious percentages, may have changed following forced migration flows due to the country internal conflict after the 2011 uprisings.
7. Interview with Bišr Said, 16 November 2021.
8. The Sunni schools of jurisprudence are four, designated by the name of their founders: Hanafi (Abū Ḥanīfa, 699–767), Maliki (Malik Ibn Anas, 711–796), Shafi'i (Muḥammad Ibn Idrīs al-Šāfi'ī, 767–820), and Hanbali (Aḥmad Ibn Ḥanbal, 780–855). The most widespread in Syria is the Shafi'i.
9. Said 1998b, p. 3.
10. "An Islamic discursive tradition is simply a tradition of Muslim discourse that addresses itself to conceptions of the Islamic past and future, with reference to a particular Islamic practice in the present" (Asad 1986, p.14).

feature that makes him difficult to categorise as an author. In the 1995 text *Immigration to Islam*, which sets forth his answers to the fourteen questions of the Syrian writer Ibrāhīm Maḥmūd, Said described himself as someone who is seeking to speak two languages: "that of modernity and that of 'back to our origins'"[11]. As he later clarified in an interview for the Iranian magazine "Qaḍāyā Islāmiyya Muʿāṣira" (Current Islamic Issues), Said was initially a follower of the Salafist current, having been attracted to Ǧamāl al-Dīn al-Afġānī[12] and Muḥammad ʿAbduh[13] and their efforts to reconcile modernity and Islam, going back to the Quranic religion's origins and giving pre-eminence to reason. Later, the Pakistani poet and philosopher Muḥammad Iqbāl[14] drew Said's interest with his particular attention to the exterior and interior of human experience and its constant variation, ideas that played an important role in Said's conception of world knowledge. In particular, Said appreciated Iqbal's emphasis on the Quran's scientific approach. Said also drew on Iqbāl's ideas in finding a way to distinguish deeper truth underlying different currents, ideologies, and religions: by looking to their fruits and the kind of men they produce[15].

11. Said 1995, p. 16.
12. Ǧamāl al-Dīn al-Afġānī (b. 1839) is considered one of the founders of Islamic Modernism, the movement that sought to renew Islam, especially from a political point of view, by reconciling the values of Western modernity with the Muslim tradition. More specifically, al-Afġānī argued that this renewal should not be achieved by imitating the West, but through a return to the *salaf*, "the ancestors", the first Muslim generation. That's why, his movement is also known as *salafiyya* (Campanini 2005, pp. 27–28).
13. A disciple of al-Afġānī, Muḥammad ʿAbduh (b. 1849) inherited from his teacher the ideology of the return to the *salaf* and the belonging to the Islamic Modernism current, also defined as neo-Mutazilite, due to the emphasis placed on reason. Indeed, ʿAbduh defined Islam as the first religion merging reason and revelation (Ibid., pp. 28–30).
14. Muḥammad Iqbāl (b. 1877) was aligned with ʿAbduh's Islamic modernism. Like him, the Indian philosopher and poet was engaged in politics: he is actually considered one of Pakistan's spiritual fathers. He suffered the influence of some Western philosophers, including Nietzsche and Bergson, and of the sufi Jalāl ad-Dīn Muḥammad Rūmī (Ibid., pp. 30–33).
15. Said 1998b, pp. 8–9.

In the early 1970s, Said discovered the thought of Mohammed Arkoun (Muḥammad Arkūn)[16] which he found to be free from the tendency to sharply classify reality into what is perfect and what has no value, instead recognising that reality is dynamically changing[17]. Arkoun's vision particularly affected Said's approach to the West, balanced on a golden mean that neither idealizes nor demonizes but recognizes the positive fruits while discarding the negative ones. Arkoun's most known concept is that of the "unthinkable" of Islam, referring to all the issues that Islamic orthodoxy does not consider as objects of analysis, such as historicity, secularism, or sexuality. Said applied this concept to nonviolence: "It is at this moment unthinkable that one refrains from killing if commanded to kill"[18].

Finally, the most fundamental moment in Said's intellectual formation was his reading of the Algerian philosopher Malek Bennabi (Malik b. Nabī), whom he discovered as a student in Egypt. Bennabi's theory of "colonizability" led Said to focus on the primacy of individual responsibility. When writing about colonialism, Bennabi described the characteristics of the colonizer, but his attention was focused on the internal situation, specifically a nation's permeability to colonialism, for which he developed the term *colonisabilité*. Bennabi argued that the apparent permeability of Arabs was due to their backwardness, caused by both external and internal factors, mainly the Arab-Islamic world's need for intellectual development[19]. This idea struck Said as radically different from the familiar notions of al-Afġānī, 'Abduh and Iqbāl; "it was such a jolt [...] when he refrained from blaming the enemies, the colonizer,

---

16. Mohammed Arkoun was born in 1928 in Algeria. In his opinion, Islamic revival needs a historical-critical analysis of the Quran. Moreover, according to Arkoun, it is necessary to consider the symbolic dimension of the Islamic sacred text and of reality, that are both divine signs. As we will see later, this approach is very similar to Jawdat Said's view of the sacred text and the world as proofs and signs of divine truth (Campanini 2005, pp. 112–116).
17. Said 1998b, p. 8.
18. Ibid., p. 13.
19. In addition to the need for an Islamic renewal, Malek Bennabi, an Algerian thinker born in 1905, stressed the necessity to criticize the Islamic world, pointing out its backwardness. As a solution, he proposed a rapprochement between science and conscience through the application of the Western theoretical approach to the Muslim spiritual content (Campanini 2005, pp. 35–39; Halverson 2012, p. 68).

the imperialist, the crusader, the Zionist, the freemason, and all the other foes. [...] It was such a giant step to turn our attention to our own responsibility"[20].

2.2 Said's Positioning in the Syrian Context

The multiplicity of influences which Said incorporated into his writing gave him an ambiguous status within the Muslim intellectual context. On the one hand, secularists accuse him of being too close to Islamist thought, while Islamists evaluate his positions as excessively liberal and removed from tradition[21]. At the same time, he influenced some Islamist thinkers, such as 'Umar al-Tilmisānī, the third supreme guide of the Egyptian Muslim Brothers[22]. For his part, Said criticizes both the Islamists and the Secularists, declaring that they are similar "in their blind allegiances to a past that we have not brought under analysis, or to foreign systems that we do not comprehend"[23]. According to him, the Muslim world is like a set of branches that are detached from the trunk: everyone is against each other, and no one tries to understand the other[24].

In Syria, Said "is not rejected and not welcomed; he is used, when they need someone speaking about Islam in an open way"[25]. According to his son Bišr, in the 1960s, Said was one of the most prominent names in the country: even today, he is primarily known for being one of the main scholars who stood against the Ba'athist coup[26]. Said's intellectual activity often brought him into conflict with the Syrian government, which initially tried to stop the spread of his ideas by forcibly transferring him

---

20. Said 1998b, pp. 7–8. As seen, Said's main focus is on internal problems, although, he does not hold back from criticizing the Western world. According to him, the major powers, such as the US, and international relations are still driven by the logic of power and force (which he believes is in opposition to democracy). In his opinion, the same goes for the UN, where the veto right contradicts the principles of equality and democracy. Said considers the veto as a form of racism (Sa'īd 1997, pp. 155–156; Sa'īd 1998a, pp. 135–147).
21. Said 2017, pp. xx–xxii.
22. Halverson 2012, p. 77.
23. Said 1998b, p. 16.
24. Said 1995, p. 16.
25. Interview with Bišr Said, 16 November 2021.
26. Ibid.

several times. He was arrested on five different occasions, culminating in an official ban from the profession of teaching at the end of the 1960s[27]. After the 1979–1982 Islamist uprising[28], the concept of nonviolence began to gain a foothold in Syria. In this context, according to Thomas Pierret, Said seduced "a relatively large audience" because he was different from "the dominant religious rhetoric saturated with identity reactions"[29]. Even if Said was on the sidelines of the Syrian religious landscape, the mainstream traditional establishment did not consider him an enemy, although this was the case for most Islamists[30]. Indeed, Said never took a polemical approach towards the traditional ulema. For example, in the 1990s, in response to the Oslo Accords and to the nonviolent creation of the European Union, he started affirming that the priority of the MENA region should be "Peace among us" (namely peace among the Arabs and the Muslims)[31]. To put that exhortation into practice, Said decided to visit these religious scholars, despite his ideological differences with them[32].

The Syrian Muslim landscape was broadly characterized by the historical opposition between the traditionalist ulema orthodoxy and the Salafists[33]. However, the Syrian religious debate was not limited to the Salafist-Traditionalist binary. The last decades witnessed the emergence of Sunni independent currents, a third way of contemporary reformists with ambiguous and complex relationships to the Sunni orthodoxy[34]. Among these is the "Independent Islamic Democratic Current", a liberal Islamist movement independent from the Muslim Brotherhood and headed by Syrian lawyer Haitham al-Maleh (Haytam al-Māliḥ); Jawdat

---

27. Said 2017, p. xix.
28. The 1979–1982 Islamist uprising, which included the Syrian Muslim Brothers, and which led to the arrest, the killing and the exile of hundreds of Islamists by the Syrian security forces. Pierret 2011a, pp. 86–87.
29. Pierret 2011a, p. 171, my translation.
30. Ibid., p. 172.
31. Said 1998b, pp. 18–19.
32. Interview with Bišr Said, 16 November 2021.
33. While the traditionalist ulema strongly opposed the ideas of Ǧamāl al-Dīn al-Afġānī and Muḥammad 'Abduh, on the contrary, Sufism, as an integral part of Syrian Sunni orthodoxy, became the main target of the Salafist attacks on tradition. See Pierret 2011a, pp. 127–148.
34. Ibid., p. 166.

Said is its spiritual guide[35]. It consists of a liberal current, a social structure which, since the 2000s, has been looking for freedom and for a democratic State in an Islamic perspective[36]. Besides Said and al-Maleh, the Current encompasses a range of Government opponents characterized by religious sensitivity, such as "liberal-conservative" intellectuals and reformist ulema. It also includes the nonviolent movement of the *Šabāb Dārayyā* (the youth of *Dārayyā*, a city near Damascus), led by the Imam 'Abd al-Akram al-Saqqā, likewise inspired by Jawdat Said[37]. One of Said's former students, al-Saqqā quickly attracted the hostility of the government when in the 2000s he declined to invoke God on behalf of the new President and later organized with his students a number of protests against the Iraqi invasion and public corruption, calling on the public to boycott cigarettes. Many participants in these actions, including al-Saqqā, were arrested[38]. Moreover, unlike Said, he was opposed by the mainstream ulema because of some of his positions, mainly on women: in his classes, men and women could study together and he argued that the study was more important than the veil. That is why no religious figure supported him when he was victimized by the regime[39]. He was arrested in 2011[40].

Said's political engagement was also visible during the 2011 revolution when he took part in public meetings, notably delivering speeches at the funeral of some opponents of the regime[41]. On various occasions, he publicly criticized the government's reaction to popular protests[42].

2.3 The Egyptian Experience and the Role of History

The influence of diversity on Said's theological evolution further developed during his travels[43], first in Egypt, where he moved in 1946. There,

35. Filiu 2013, p. 167.
36. Al-Jazeera 2013.
37. Pierret 2011b, p. 883; Filiu 2013, p. 130. Jawdat Said's influence on the *Dārayyā* group should still be investigated as part of my PhD research.
38. Hakim 2016.
39. Pierret 2011a, p. 172.
40. Filiu 2013, p. 150.
41. Said 2017, pp. 65–66.
42. Filiu 2013, p. 145.
43. Becci, Burchardt 2016, p. 6.

he studied at al-Azhar in Cairo, the most important mosque-university of the Sunni Islamic world, and obtained a degree in Arabic language and a diploma in pedagogy[44]. During the ten years he spent in Cairo, Said began the theoretical progression which eventually led him to articulating his ideas of nonviolence. Through his closeness to the Muslim Brotherhood, he participated in changes affecting the country's political and social life. At that time, he started criticizing those Brothers who considered the use of violence acceptable, taking issue with the position advanced by the writings of Sayyid Quṭb, one of the Brotherhood's main theorists. According to Quṭb, the Quran legitimates the use of violence in the name of God, to achieve an ideal form of society[45]. On the contrary, Said's thought is founded on the rejection of violence as an instrument of social and political change. His first book, *Maḏhab Ibn Adam al-Awwal. Muškila al-'unf fī al-'amal al-islāmī* (*The Doctrine of the First Son of Adam: The Problem of Violence in the Islamic Action*) was published the same year as Sayyid Quṭb's death by hanging, in 1966, and was conceived as a genuine response to Quṭb's reflections. According to Said, Qutb's thought represented "an inversion of the truth"[46] because the way to restore a deviant society was through nonviolence, rather than coercion.

More broadly, Said's experiences during his Egyptian period made him focus on the importance of history. While he was in Cairo, Maḥmūd al-Nuqrāšī, a former Egyptian minister, was killed by a Muslim Brother. Upon hearing the news, many of his university colleagues evinced satisfaction. Said on the other hand claimed to have felt a sense of sadness, realizing this was not the way to solve problems. That killing was followed by the assassination of Ḥassan al-Bannā, the founder of the Muslim Brotherhood. Shortly afterwards, the 1952 coup against King Fārūq took place, with the Free Officers' rise to power in Egypt, headed by Colonel 'Abd al-Nāṣir. This moment inspired Said to embark upon an analysis of historical events which led him towards his doctrine of nonviolence[47].

In fact, in the interview for "Current Islamic Issues", Said explicitly contrasted the model of using violence to impose one's ideas with Quranic

---

44. Said 2017, p. xviii.
45. Muller 2009, p. 562.
46. Halverson 2012, p. 71.
47. Said 2017, pp. 3–6, 69–70.

precepts. He played with the dual meaning of the Arabic word *aya*, "sign/verse", referring both to God's signs in the world, as well as to the ones revealed by the Quran. Trying to explain the relationship between human history and the Quran, he argued that the signs and verses of the Quran are connected to the signs of the outside world: "the right approach is to view history and the revealed text as inseparable partners"[48]. In this view, the influence of Iqbāl's poetry becomes apparent: "it was Iqbāl who alerted us to the importance of the facts of the real world and human experience" and who stressed that "the Quran takes the observable world, and man's inner world, as sources of knowledge"[49]. It is in this sense that Said appreciated Iqbāl's understanding of the "seal of the prophethood", the Islamic concept considering Muhammad the last prophet of God. Indeed, according to the Pakistani poet, the prophethood can come to an end because "the signs of the world and the signs in our souls have become a source of learning the truth"[50].

In 1998, Said published the book *al-Dīn wa al-qānūn* (Religion and Law), which aimed to explore the relationship between law, religion, and violence. To understand the origins of historical and religious violence, Said tried to deepen his knowledge of humankind. In the first chapter, he wrote that humans can understand reality simply through their perception. He argued that, considering the numerous cases throughout history of errors in human perception, we can distinguish between the real world we live in and the world we create in our minds. However, at the same time, Said highlighted human beings' particular skill: they can learn, thanks to their nervous systems, and through social relations. This ability has grown in accuracy throughout history, as attested by the last centuries' scientific achievements. Moreover, Said stressed that objective reality does not change according to erroneous interpretations of human beings: the sun was fixed in its central position while the earth continued to orbit it, even when humans thought the opposite was happening. Therefore, in his opinion, humanity should always turn our gaze towards objective reality, as our perception of it changes over time while the expansion of our knowledge brings us closer to the truth[51].

48. Said 1998b, pp. 22–25.
49. Ibid., pp. 8–9.
50. Ibid.
51. Saʿīd 1998a, pp. 9–21.

This perspective illustrates the essential role that history came to occupy in Said's thought: history provides the purpose, because humanity can learn through history. The laws of history tend to affirm what is positive for the majority of people: as Iqbāl already pointed out, by examining the fruits of human actions over time, humans can get closer to the truth. The Quran itself, Said wrote, bases its regime of permissions and prohibitions on the benefits or risks that arise from human behaviour[52]. In his works, Said emphasized that analysis of the signs of time and the Quran confirms the uselessness of violence in solving problems, since the cost is always higher than the benefit. Said wrote: "What is the meaning of the atomic bomb, what is the meaning of the fall of the Soviet Union, which possessed so many atomic bombs so that it could have destroyed the world thirty times? And what is the meaning of Japan's rebirth without an atomic bomb?"[53]. According to Said, these events are all signs to be interpreted. Like the subsequent creation of the European Union on a peaceful basis, in contrast to Hitler's attempted violent occupation, which failed: "Europe combined into a single word, without any war […], its peoples overcame nationalism and languages"[54]. In Said's opinion, the EU experience represents an alternative method of safeguarding the interests of all parties, the method which Adam's first son Abel initially exemplified.

2.4 The Quranic Foundation of Nonviolence

In his first book, *Maḏhab Ibn Adam al-Awwal*, trying to reflect on the issue of violence in the Islamic context, Jawdat Said introduced the foundation of his nonviolent thought. He invited his readers to follow the example of Adam's first son, who in the Quran claims that he would never kill his brother despite the latter's declaration of violent intent. Verses 27–29 of the *sūra al-Mā'ida* (5) state:

> Tell them the truth about the story of Adam's two sons: each of them offered a sacrifice, and it was accepted from one and not the other. One said, "I will kill you", but the other said, "God only accepts the sacrifice of those who are mindful of Him. If you raise your hand to

---

52. Ibid., pp. 67–77.
53. Said 2017, p. 56.
54. Saʿīd in A. Al-Ḥūrī 2008, pp. 50–51, my translation.

kill me, I will not raise mine to kill you. I fear God, the Lord of all worlds"[55].

Said highlights these verses as the foundations of the Muslim theology which preaches nonviolence. In his opinion, the Quran presents the human being with an existential choice between two possible options: Cain's violence or Abel's nonviolence. To further support his thesis, Said referred to the Sunna of the Prophet, in particular a *hadīṯ* reported by Abū Mūsā in which the messenger of God commands men to follow the example of Adam's first son in case someone would threaten to kill them[56]. Ultimately, as Said pointed out, the Quranic words appeal to humans' rationality and to their capacity for discernment, through which human beings can rise above the law of the jungle to values of knowledge and dialogue. The emphasis is therefore placed on the responsibility of the individual to choose one way or the other. Abel thus assumes an attitude akin to Socrates, who accepts the risk of death, refusing to revert to corporal violence[57].

3 Knowledge and Dialogue as Nonviolent Strategies

3.1 Knowledge as a Nonviolent Tool

Why, over time, did Cain's violent method become preeminent over Abel's rational one? Said wrote that the main reason is humanity's ignorance of the laws of change. In his assessment, people change their ideas and perspectives only when they are persuaded through evidence. For this reason, Said considered violence a useless tool to achieve the goal of persuasion. Use of violence, consequently, attests to the incapacity of humans to assert their reasoning with the mere force of dialectic. In Said's opinion, the desire to impose one's will through violence, as the simplest way to solve problems and assert one's opinions, results from a lack of

---

55. Qur. V: 27–30. All Qur'anic citations in this article refer to the following edition: Abdel Haleem (trans.) 2005.
56. Said refers to the *hadīṯ* reported by Abū Dāwūd 1952, Kitāb al-Fitan wa-l-Malāḥim, II, 416.
57. Saʿīd 1993, pp. 75, 93, 183–192; Saʿīd 1998a, pp. 100–103.

complete confidence in the potential of one's ideas and, at the same time, from an absence of respect for the diversity of the other.

The Syrian philosopher describes this intellectual ignorance as a virus leading to the disease of violence, which he compares to an epidemic. The spread of epidemic diseases is made possible by a lack of knowledge of their causes; on the other hand, thanks to scientific discoveries societies can prevent this spread. Likewise, Said believes that insufficient awareness of intellectual viruses infects societies with hate, driving them to ferocity[58]. However, as seen before, humans have a strong inclination to learn. Returning to the Quran, the human cognitive potential becomes evident in the ability to name things, to give them a symbolic name. Even angels are forced to admit their ignorance in front of humanity's particular skill. The angels actually complained to God for having chosen the human being rather than them as vicar (ḥalīfa)[59] on earth, foreseeing that humans would bring corruption and bloodshed, to which God replied: "I know things you do not"[60]. In Said's view, the following verses explain the meaning of this sentence:

> He taught Adam all the names (of things), then He showed them to the angels and said, "Tell me the names of these if you truly (think you can)". They said, "May you be glorified! We have knowledge only of what You have taught us. You are the All Knowing and All Wise". Then He said, "Adam, tell them the names of these". When he told them their names, God said, "Did I not tell you that I know what is hidden in the heavens and the earth, and that I know what you reveal and what you conceal"[61]?

---

58. Muller 2009, p. 566.
59. The etymological root of the word ḥalīfa refers to the idea of representing, succeeding. It is found twice in the Quran, related to Adam and to David, as vicars of God on earth. After Muḥammad's death, it started being employed referring to the prophet's successors, ḥalīfa rasūl Allāh (the delegate of God's messenger), namely the temporal leader of the Islamic community: it's the beginning of the historical caliphate (Lewis 2005, pp. 51–59; Lambton 1997). During the 18th and 19th centuries, the Ottoman sultans started presenting themselves as the Muslims' caliphs, meaning the defenders of Islam in front of the European threat. An attitude that was also inspired by al-Afġānī's ideal of pan-Islamic unity (Sourdel 1997).
60. Qur. II: 30.
61. Qur. II: 31–33.

Thanks to this skill humans can learn things, especially in matters of good and evil, and become aware of the consequences of their actions. God gives humans viceroyalty precisely by virtue of their ability to distinguish good from evil and to choose whether to obey or not. Although the angels' prediction proved to be true and men did in fact shed blood and bring corruption onto the earth, Said wrote that God has another wisdom towards which human beings are moving. Even though they are still in the violent phase predicted by the angels, thanks to their unique ability, humanity will be able to fix its mistakes and to move towards the wisdom of God. Said pointed out that human beings are slowly learning to solve problems by appealing to reason rather than to the law of the jungle: it is a scientific evolution.

Therefore, change in Said's opinion occurs through knowledge. In his book *al-Dīn wa al-qānūn*, but also in many other texts, the author reemphasises that the primary sources of knowledge are always in the words of God, in the Quran and in the world, showing men the good and evil so that they can do good and reject evil[62]. The greatest responsibility, Said pointed out, lies in the hands of intellectuals: "the time of the prophets has ended and the responsibility has been transferred to the people of knowledge to bring people out of darkness and into light, from injustice to justice, from slavery to freedom"[63]. However, to make this possible they must return to the example of the prophets, which has regrettably been abandoned.

3.2 The Pluralistic Vision of the Prophetic Model

In support of his ideas, Jawdat Said references the Quranic prophets as models. According to him, they had Abel's attitude, that is to refuse to do evil, even when faced with an imminent threat. However, in his book *Lā ikrāha fī al-dīn: dirāsāt wa-abḥāt fī al-fikr al-islāmī* (*There is No Compulsion in Religion: Studies and Research in the Islamic Thought*), he highlighted that the prophets' refusal to do evil did not imply remaining silent in the face of evil: "They didn't ask for their freedom of expression […], but they have fulfilled their duty to transmit (the message) and

---

62. Saʿīd 1998a, pp. 79–85.
63. Said 1995.

to preach and have suffered the consequence of their action"[64]. The author stressed the prophets' intellectual integrity, arguing that they steadfastly refused to repay evil with evil, preferring the law of dialogue and reason to the mechanism of violence. Human beings, especially Muslims, have a similar obligation to refuse any complicity with evil: responding to violence with violence can lead to confusion between victim and perpetrator, and to the legitimization of killing. On the contrary, he wrote that when victims do not defend themselves, assassination can only be a crime, an aberrant act, because "success in battle can be interpreted with honour and heroism [...] but killing those who do not even defend themselves [...] can only be considered a repugnant crime"[65].

According to Said, all prophets share common traits. They represent a single model, and they have the same message, that is, "not killing people, and not killing the despot or the oppressor: it is rather to disobey the tyrant if he commands you to kill"[66]. In Said's thought, the expression "all the prophets" also encompasses those of other religions: "no matter how we brand Christianity or Judaism as polytheistic or chauvinistic, the essence of all the divine religions is one and the same: they all revolve on monotheism"[67]. Indeed, his writings stress the Quran's openness to recognising divine messengers not specifically included in the sacred text[68]. In his opinion, openness creates possibilities for a pluralistic perspective which shuns ethnocentrism as the quality of prophecy is not limited to Muslims but encompasses all those possessing the qualities of a messenger:

> We are prevented from denying the possibility of prophecy to other religious and cultural figures. This method eliminates racism and

64. The title of the book, published in 1997, is referred to the Quranic verse II: 256. This quotation is part of a chapter regarding human rights in Islam. In order to indicate the right and the duty, Said employs the same word *ḥaqq*, playing with its double meaning in Arabic (*ḥaqq li* is the right; *ḥaqq 'lā* is the duty). Sa'īd 1997, p. 145, my translation.
65. Sa'īd 1998a, p. 118, my translation. This one and some of the remaining quotations of this paragraph are part of a chapter devoted to the prophets, included in Said's book *al-Dīn wa al-qānūn*.
66. Said 1998b, p. 13.
67. Ibid., p. 11.
68. The author refers to Qur. XL:78: "We have sent other messengers before you – some We have mentioned to you and some We have not – and no messenger could bring about a sign except with God's permission".

recognises all those inviting to and defending justice and charity. [...] It enables us to acknowledge the messengers of other cultures, whether in the Far East, Africa, or among the indigenous peoples of the new continents[69].

Besides citing classical prophets, Said often cites Socrates too, contending that the Greek philosopher could match the prophetic criteria through the integrity of his ideas, his determination to defend them and the sense of duty he felt in spreading them. Said concludes that a pluralistic approach, allowing for the identification of ethical convergences even beyond the monotheistic religions, reinforces mutual understanding and enhances intercultural and interreligious relations[70].

3.3 The Importance of Respecting Others' Diversity

Said strongly emphasizes the contribution that every human being can make towards positive change. However, he states that change must begin from within by healing the heart from violence, including the violence of thoughts and words; this is the change that leads to joy[71]. These concepts are most fully discussed in his book *Ḥatta yuġayyiru ma bi-anfusihim* (*Unless They Change What is in Themselves*)[72], published in 1972 and dealing with the rule of change and with intellectuals' role in the crisis of the Islamic world. Nevertheless, from the beginning of the book, Said was clear that the principles included in the text, namely the rules of social change, as many other Quranic principles, applied to everyone, not just to Muslims[73]. In particular, he highlighted the responsibility all individuals have towards themselves and the whole world. According to Said, human destiny does not rely on others but on all individuals, who have to take the lead in their own destiny in order to change their souls. Before stressing other people's mistakes, he wrote, it is thus essential to begin by analysing one's own. In this regard, the author explained that Cain's violence originated from

69. Saʿīd 1998a, p. 35, my translation.
70. Ibid., pp. 34–39.
71. Said 2017, p. 23.
72. It refers to the Quranic verse "God does not change the condition of a people unless they change what is in themselves". Qur XIII:11. Throughout the book, Said presented his interpretation of this verse.
73. Saʿīd 1972, p. 27.

his inability to take responsibility for his mistakes: rather than pondering why his offer had not been accepted, Cain preferred to blame his brother, taking out his anger on him. In this perspective, God's actions follow those of humans. Indeed, Said recalled that in Qur. XIII:11, God declares that he will not change the situation of humans, be it positive or negative, if they do not change themselves first: this is the task and the responsibility God assigned to human beings by choosing them as earthly viceroys[74]. This is not a completely new idea: we can find it in many Islamic reformists' thoughts, especially in Bennabi, who wrote the foreword to Said's book. Indeed, according to the Algerian writer, the main problem is not external tyranny, but what is inside the human being. Bennabi therefore argues that it is impossible to realize political democracy if it is not first impressed upon the interior self of the individual. Indeed, he considers democracy as a mental operation of affirmation in contrast with two negations: first, the slave's denial of self-worth, and second the despot's denial of the other's worth. In order to achieve democracy, it is thus essential for all involved individuals to assign value both to their own conscience and to the dignity of the other, recognising themselves as God's favourite creatures[75].

In a similar way, Said deals with the idea of acknowledging otherness as a liberating possibility founded upon mutual tolerance of error. In the author's view, "living with the error" means understanding that if an individual does not let others have their own ideas – however wrong they may be, that individual will likewise not have the right to their own ideas. This also means realizing that errors cannot be remedied through violence:

> Your certitude of being right and that others are wrong is not enough to make change happen. Therefore, you need to realize another certitude, namely that the one erring has the right to live in his/her error and that s/he can change only if […] you change what you have in your heart, by persuading yourself that s/he has the right to remain his/herself[76].

---

74. Ibid., pp. 45–47, 57, 63–68. More and more often, contemporary Muslim intellectuals and activists stress human being's individual responsibility as God's vicegerent on earth. For a detailed discussion see Bin Saud 1990.
75. Bennabi 2016, pp. 25–40.
76. Said 2017, p. 47, my translation.

Indeed, as seen before, Said believes that the law of history tends to affirm what is fruitful. Consequently, according to him, mistakes can only be fixed by showing what is good: that is, living by one's own principles and letting the error die of a natural death. From this perspective, diversity becomes something to protect. As he already stated in his first book, the act of building relationships while maintaining diversity gives humans the opportunity to discover what is right and to get closer to the truth[77].

Said goes even further, affirming that meaningful transformation is only possible if individuals can learn to love diversity. By opening one's inner self to love, he argues, individuals will thus cultivate the possibility to spread love, achieving real change, because "you will not solve the problem if you do not love who diverges from you"[78]. How can this be achieved? In Said's opinion, it is essential to separate the mistake from the person who makes it, the disease from the sick, and to consider the diseases of the soul as akin to physical ones. As is true for physical illnesses, we must avoid fighting the disease with violence, because this would mean killing the sick, rather than healing them:

> Do we not love the sick person and hate the disease and strive with all our effort to kill the second and to save the first? [...] is not a person with sick ideas comparable to a physically sick person? and is it not possible to love this person while hating his or her ideas? A sick person needs love and compassion. Ignorance and hatred are the diseases of an intellectually sick, therefore he needs love and knowledge. When will we realize that knowledge is love and love is knowledge?[79]

3.4 Ğihād Against Compulsion

Even Said's interpretation of ğihād[80] takes into account the relationship with diversity and the importance of respecting others' opinions. In this

---

77. Sa'īd 1993, pp. 45–52.
78. Said 2017, p. 47, my translation.
79. Sa'īd 1998a, p. 120, my translation.
80. From an etymological point of view, the word ğihād denotes firstly an "effort towards a specific goal". More broadly, in the Quran, the expression "holy war" does not exist and the term ğihād never has this meaning. The Islamic tradition distinguishes between the big and the small ğihād: the first one indicates the interior effort towards

regard, he offers a historical perspective on the conception of war in Islam. According to him, Muḥammad only began employing violence in the so-called Medinese period (from *madīnat al-nabī*, "the city of the Prophet" where he moved after Mecca), as a political leader, not as a prophet. During the early Meccan phase, Muḥammad refused leadership roles, wanting instead to spread his ideas through persuasion. Moreover, he forbade self-defence, exhorting his followers to patience with the persecutions carried out by his tribe of origin, the *Qurayš*, who were hostile to the new faith. When in 622 CE the Prophet and his followers moved to the city of Yaṯrib, later called Medina, the first Islamic State was founded. Said reminds his readers that this new State observed Quranic teachings and included members of other religions according to a specific agreement. At this precise moment, he asserts, the first verses concerning the war began to descend, permitting Muslim people to use violence to defend themselves from oppression. In order to back this interpretation, Said mainly refers to the following Quranic verse: "Those who have been attacked are permitted to take up arms because they have been wronged – God has the power to help them – those who have been driven unjustly from their homes only for saying, 'Our Lord is God'"[81].

In Said's opinion, war is therefore linked to a political function exercised by the State and not by the individual: "the fight was prescribed after the messenger of God came to power with no other force than those of persuasion and thought"[82]. Furthermore, according to Said's interpretation of the verse, the purpose of war is human liberation from any constriction, especially in terms of belief: indeed, resistance is permissible for those who are subjected to tyranny and those who have been thrown out from their homeland for having said "Our Lord is God", that is, for having confessed their faith[83]. Said underscores that this verse does not specifically mention a particular faith, nor does it explicitly restrict recourse to armed resistance to Muslims alone. Instead, for him, the

---

God; the second one points out to the exterior effort, the armed struggle, which is the most discussed in Islamic classical literature, especially in law manuals (Cook 2007, pp. xi, xvi, xix; Lewis 2005, pp. 85–99). The concept received many interpretations over the time. In this respect, see Afsaruddin 2013, pp. 35–43, 61–76.

81. Qur. XXII:39–40.
82. Saʿīd 1993, p. 41, my translation.
83. Saʿīd 1997, p. 154.

Quranic verses refer to everyone: any person, of any creed and culture, has the right to fight anyone who oppresses their freedom of opinion and belief, as long as the defensive war is not instigated by the individual but by the legitimate authority.

In Said's interpretation of war, there is a clear reference to verse 256 of the *sūra al-Baqara* (2), which he investigated in some of his writings: "There is no compulsion in religion: true guidance (*rušd*) has become distinct from error (ġayy), so whoever rejects *ṭāġūt*[84] and believes in God has grasped the firmest handhold, one that will never break"[85]. Indeed, one of Said's main ideas is the opposition between *rušd* (true guidance, discernment, spiritual maturity) and ġayy (error, temptation, evilness). He interprets the quoted verse as equating religious compulsion with error and wickedness, counterposing these to righteousness (*rušd*), which is itself inseparable from tolerance: "The third sentence further explains that anyone who rejects *ṭāġūt* (such as by resisting the temptation to impose his or her religion by force upon others), and believes in God, will have grasped the most secure handhold of all that never breaks loose"[86]. Furthermore, in Said's view, the prohibition of compulsion does not concern only religious matters but encompasses all fields of life, starting with society and politics. That is why, in his interpretation, a believer is a person who stands against *ṭāġūt*, or "tyranny". The rejection of coercion is therefore total and departs from an awareness that society can only change through persuasion.

The refusal of religious compulsion leads Said to proclaim the inadmissibility of killing the apostate. According to him, this is a clear prohibition in the quoted verse, which is reiterated in other Quranic passages. Indeed, as he highlights, the Islamic sacred text never orders believers to kill those who leave the faith, but rather states: "Let those who wish

---

84. It is a pre-Islamic pagan deity, but it can be also used as a collective word, indicating the "demons". The root of the word is frequent in the Quran, with a connotation of immeasurable pride and rebellion against God. In the Muslim sacred text, it is used pointing to the Pharaoh, who defied the law of God, and to the rulers whose legitimacy was not recognized (Lewis 2005, p. 112). That is why the term can also be translated as "tyranny", as interpreted by Said.
85. Qur. II:256.
86. Sa'īd 1998a, p. 63, my translation.

to believe in it to do so and let those who wish to reject it to do so"[87]. Moreover, the author recalls that six years after *hiǧra* (the transfer from Mecca to Medina), Muḥammad himself signed the *Ḥudaybiyya* agreement, allowing Muslims to return to Mecca and to get back into the *Qurayš* tribe[88].

Jawdat Said's thinking has been continuously evolving over time, especially in the last twenty years, towards a radical nonviolence and a final conception of war as a non-functional tool, even from a defensive perspective[89]. By reviewing his books, it becomes apparent that the seeds of Said's intellectual evolution[90] are driven not by a single event, but by his interpretation of history, leading him to the conclusion that weapons stocks do not determine the success of contemporary nations. Indeed, Said states that the major powers have developed such a massive capacity for violence that they could destroy the entire world, while smaller powers when entering war are manipulated by bigger ones: in the end, no one really wins. According to his interpretation, the first nuclear explosion proclaimed "the death of war"[91].

3.5 The Practice: The Interreligious Dialogue

As shown in Said's texts, the theme of nonviolence is closely linked to respect for others' opinions and for cultural and religious diversity. This link is further reinforced by his personal commitment to interreligious dialogue. Said actively participated in a number of interfaith dialogue meetings in Syria and around the world. Nevertheless, as his son Bišr explains, Said's attention during the early stage of his life was mainly drawn to problems within the Muslim world: it was only later in life

---

87. Qur. XVIII:29.
88. Said 2017, pp. xlviii–xlix.
89. Said 2017, p. 52.
90. For instance, an intermediate position is represented by the book *Lā ikrāha fī al-dīn: dirāsāt wa-abḥāt fī al-fikr al-islāmī*. In the text, referring to the conditions for the use of violence, he distinguished between the relation with Muslim or non-Muslim people. He argued that in the first case, a Muslim person should always act in a non-violent way. Meanwhile, in the second case, if the non-Muslims first embrace arms and if the war conditions are met, it is possible to fight them (Saʿīd 1997, p. 158).
91. Said 2009–2010, p. 18.

that he started encountering people of other cultures and religions, when he was invited to conferences in the US and in Canada in the 1980s. According to Bišr Said, the collapse of the Soviet Union could have been a turning point in his father's commitment to interreligious dialogue. At that point, some Syrian communist militants gravitated toward civil society activism: some of them were Christians and "maybe at that time, for his way of thinking, they began to invite him to international conferences"[92]. Furthermore, his son relates that when Jawdat Said started speaking about "peace among us" in the 1990s, besides visiting Muslim scholars as previously reported, he also visited Christian leaders: "at that time, he started having relationships with other religions inside Syria. During that period, he often visited Mar Musa"[93].

Notably, Said took part in Islamic-Christian dialogue sessions along with the Jesuit priest Paolo Dall'Oglio[94], a close friend of his. An example is the interreligious meeting held in 2002 at *Dayr Mār Mūsa*, a monastery near the Syrian city of Nabk, 80 kilometres from Damascus. The dialogue consisted of four sessions and saw the participation of *al-Ḫalīl* community monks together with Muslim pious men, such as the sheikhs Ṣalāḥ al-Dīn Kiftārū, Maḥmūd Abū al-Hadā al-Ḥusaynī, Muḥammad Dayb, Yāsir Ḥāfiẓ and others. Interventions at the meeting, whose theme was the impact of spiritual experiences on society, were collected into a book entitled *al-Ḫibra al-rūḥiyya wa taṭawwur al-muǧtamaʿ* (*The Spiritual Experience and the Development of Society*). As father Dall'Oglio explained at the beginning of the meeting, "the first question we propose [...] is: do human beings have spiritual senses, different from the five physical senses [...]? Does spiritual life represent a different life? Is the spiritual dimension another world?"[95]. The Jesuit priest affirmed that the spiritual life is a single whole, although people and religions have talked

---

92. Interview with Bišr Said, 16 November 2021.
93. Ibid.
94. Paolo Dall'Oglio is a Roman Jesuit who founded in Syria the monastic community *al-Ḫalīl*, "the intimate friend", that is the attribute given to Abraham in the Quran. It is a Syro-Catholic rite ecumenical community, particularly committed to Islamic-Christian dialogue.
95. Dall'Oglio in A. Al-Ḫūrī (ed.) 2008, p. 9, my translation.

about it in different ways, since "to enter a single world, as it is indeed only one, there are many gateways"[96].

The particular relevance of Jawdat Said's contribution to the discussion was recognised by the book editor, Adīb Al-Ḫūrī. Indeed, in the introduction, Al-Ḫūrī highlighted the spontaneous intervention of the nonviolent thinker, who told delegates his life story with simplicity, innocence, and wisdom[97]. Jawdat Said fully engaged in the meeting presenting his ideas, listening to others' interventions, and answering questions. The dialogue was also an occasion to better clarify some of his own thoughts. In order to further explain his ideas, the Syrian thinker employed some examples from the Gospels, a methodological innovation[98]. For instance, while explaining his interpretation of the Quranic verse "there is no compulsion in religion"[99], he stated that "with compulsion the human being gives you as little as possible, while with benevolence he gives you his most valuable things"[100]. He illustrated this by referring to Jesus' call to forgive one's brother's sins seventy-seven times[101]: "When we are patient with someone offending us and we don't pay him back, we change his heart"[102].

Actually, Said frequently employed Gospel quotations to explain his ideas. In particular, he often referred to the Christian concept of love towards one's enemies, as demonstrated by the first speech he gave during the 2002 dialogue session. When describing a previous meeting with a Mormon community in Canada, he said that, even though he did

96. Ibid., my translation.
97. A. Al-Ḫūrī (ed.) 2008, p. 20.
98. Muslim thinkers rarely use the Christian synoptic Gospels as an authoritative source. Actually, it is often believed that the canonical Gospels are a falsification of the original one, transmitted by God to Jesus (considered a prophet in Islam). Said's son narrates that at an early stage of his life, unlike other Muslim scholars, his father read the Bible, as well as other holy books and Confucius' and Gandhi's writings. Indeed, according to Bišr, in his father's opinion "the traditional Islamic interpretation draws a line at reading other sacred texts, but the Quran does not. Instead, the Quran clearly says that God sent these books to the prophets and that they are full of light. Even if some changes had taken place, the light and the wisdom of these books wouldn't have disappeared" (Interview with Bišr Said, 16 November 2021).
99. Qur. II:256.
100. Saʿīd in Al-Ḫūrī (ed.) 2008, p. 50, my translation.
101. Matthew 18:21–22.
102. Saʿīd in Al-Ḫūrī (ed.) 2008, p. 52, my translation.

not deepen the theology and the sacred texts, he learnt by heart a sentence from the Gospels, that is: "Love your enemies, do good to those who hate you"[103]. According to Said, love towards our enemies is something foolish, that we cannot rationally understand, but "he who can carry out this commandment is a follower of Christ, Moses, Muhammad, Abraham, Confucius and Buddha.... And he who cannot, does not follow any of them. [...] We talk a lot about dogmas and look for things distinguishing us, but we are not able to enter the world of love"[104].

On other occasions, Said argued that love towards our enemies elevates us to a higher level, as verse 34 of the *sūra al-fuṣṣilat* recalls: "Good and evil cannot be equal. (Prophet) repel evil with what is better, and your enemy will become as close as a close friend"[105]. According to Said, this is the attitude that "makes people love Islam"[106]. The exhortation to reject evil with good is often found in the Quran, especially in the verses corresponding to the Meccan period[107], sometimes interpreted in harmony with the evangelical concept of love towards one's enemies. In Said's opinion, this concept is confirmed by God's words: "You love them, but they don't love you"[108]. According to him, it is therefore by spreading good and love that you can change the world, making the enemy a close friend.

4 Conclusion: Between Nonviolence and Dialogue

Jawdat Said's life and theoretical contributions offer us indications to deepen the relationship between peacebuilding and religious superdiversity within the Islamic context. The concept of religious superdiversity is a process of "diversification of diversity"[109] resulting from the dynamic interplay of different variables linked to religious phenomena. This concept is directly applicable to the complexity of the Syrian religious landscape, namely the forms and patterns that the Syrian religious dimensions can take and the impact they can have on the politi-

103. Luke 6:27.
104. Saʿīd in Al-Ḥūrī (ed.) 2008, pp. 29–30, my translation.
105. Qur. XLI:34.
106. Saʿīd 1997, p. 159, my translation.
107. For example, Qur. XIII:22 and Qur. XXIII:96.
108. Qur. III:119.
109. Vertovec 2007, p. 1025.

cal space and social dynamics[110]. Syrian super-diversity is not a recent phenomenon: like most countries of the area, Syria has always dealt with multiple religious identities. The country's religious complexity does not only depend on migration flows but is generated by a multiplicity of historical and indigenous variables: the simultaneous presence of multiple religions, the internal diversification of confessional practices and identities and their interaction with one another, the heterogeneity of State policies towards local religious realities and the domestic and international political dynamics[111] (e.g., the political exploitation of the faith-based community separation or the role of colonialism in the emergence of new Islamic currents). It is also important to mention factors of public perceptions, conflicts, mobility of persons, and processes of globalization. Moreover, in the present study, the concept of super-diversity also refers to the internal diversification of the broader Muslim community.

Said is an integral part of this religious super-diversity: not only did he live within it and directly experience it, but through his scholarly reflections he also personally contributed to the diversification of the country's confessional context. Said's intellectual life was most directly connected to the diversity within the Sunni world, as he occupied a position midway between its different discursive traditions. Indeed, his intellectual development was firstly influenced by al-Afġānī's and 'Abduh's Islamic modernism, while at the same time the impact of critical reformism is also visible through his fascination for Arkoun and Bennabi. These multiple influences made Said an author criticized by various Muslim currents, although within his country he was never totally marginalized and had an enduring social and political impact.

Nevertheless, for the purposes of this volume, Said's most remarkable feature is the special relevance that diversity has had to his scholarly and biographical trajectory. According to him, violence stems from humans' inability to accept otherness and from their ignorance of the laws of change: people and society cannot be changed by compulsion, only by persuasion. Therefore, in Said's opinion, a wrong idea cannot be eradicated by killing it, but by showing what is right, creating a space where diversities can communicate. Thereby, in his experience, interreligious

---

110. Becci, Burchardt 2016, p. 1.
111. Ibid. pp. 6–7.

dialogue becomes a useful tool for non-violent change at the interpersonal and societal levels: diversity is a richness and through personal relationships, it can elucidate the truth and facilitate the spread of what is morally right. In this sense, Said is not the only example in the Islamic world: other Muslim thinkers similarly recognise the essential role of interreligious dialogue in enhancing nonviolent conflict resolution and democratic paths.

Among others, a similar approach can be found in the American Palestinian scholar Abu Nimer, who holds the function of senior councillor of KAICIID, an international organization working for intercultural and interreligious dialogue. He deals with the subject both as a Muslim who attempts to promote nonviolent methods based on a renewed understanding of Islam, and as an expert in conflict resolution who considers nonviolence a synonym of peacebuilding. According to Abu Nimer, pluralism and diversity figure among the traditional Islamic values that can be the basis for an Islamic theology of nonviolence:

> In peacebuilding, diversity and tolerance of differences are core principles of practices. [...] For Muslims, diversity and tolerance of difference are God's wish, because if God had wished, he could have created all humans alike. Instead, he created a pluralist world with different humans[112].

Author Biography

Viviana Schiavo graduated in International Relations (Inter-Mediterranean curriculum) at Ca' Foscari University and subsequently obtained a licence from the Pontifical Institute for Arab and Islamic Studies (PISAI). Her academic training and her professional and research experiences have been mainly dedicated to the themes of intercultural and interreligious dialogue, focusing particularly on Islamic theology. Since 2021, she is a PhD candidate at the University of Naples "L'Orientale" with a research project on Nonviolence in Islam.

---

112. Abu Nimer 2000–2001, p. 263. It refers to the Quranic verse: "If Your Lord had pleased, He would have made all people a single community, but they continue to have their differences" (Qur. XI:118).

References

Abdel Haleem, M. A. S. (ed.) (2005), *The Qur'an*, Oxford University Press, Oxford.
Abū Dāwūd (1952), *Sunan*, Širka Maktaba wa Maṭbaʿa Muṣṭafā al-Bābī al-Ḥalbī wa Awlāduhu, Miṣr, II.
Abu-Nimer, M. (2000–2001), *A Framework for Nonviolence and Peacebuilding in Islam*, in "Journal of Law and Religion", 15, 1–2, pp. 217–265. https://doi.org/10.2307/1051519
Afsaruddin, A. (2013), *Striving in the Path of God. Jihād and Martyrdom in Islamic Thought*, Oxford University Press, New York.
Al-Ḫūrī, A. (ed.) (2008), *Al-ḥibra al-rūḥiyya wa taṭawwur al-muǧtamaʿ*, Dār al-Ḫalīl lil-našr, Nabk.
Al-Jazeera. (2013), *al-Tayyār al-islāmī al-dīmuqrāṭī al-mustaqill*, in "al-Jazeera", available at https://www.aljazeera.net/ (last accessed 22 November 2021).
Asad, T. (1986), *The Idea of an Anthropology of Islam*, Center for Contemporary Arab Studies, Washington.
Becci, I., Burchardt, M. (2016), *Religion and Superdiversity: An Introduction*, in "New Diversities", 18, 1, pp. 1–7.
Bennabi, M. (2016), *La démocratie en Islam*, Alem El Afkar.
Bin Saud, M. (1990), *Is Man the Viceregent of God?*, in "Journal of Islamic Studies", 1, pp. 99–110. https://doi.org/10.1093/jis/1.1.99
Campanini, M. (2005), *Il pensiero islamico contemporaneo*, Il Mulino, Bologna.
Cook, D. (2007), *Storia del jihad. Da Maometto ai giorni nostri*, Piccola Biblioteca Einaudi Storia, Torino.
Filiu, J. P. (2013), *Le nouveau Moyen-Orient. Les peuples à l'heure de la Révolution syrienne*, Fayard, Paris.
Gandhi, M. (1924), *Young India, 1919–1922*, S. Ganesan Publisher, Madras.
Hakim, Y. (2016), *Histoire(s) de Daraya: 2001–2016 (1)*, in "Un oeil sur la Syrie", Le Monde, available at https://www.lemonde.fr/blog/syrie/2016/01/08/histoires-de-darayya-2001-2016-1/ (last accessed 11 December 2021).
Halverson, J. R. (2012), *Searching for a King: Muslim Nonviolence and the Future of Islam*, Potomack Books, Washington.
Jahanbegloo, R. (2014), *Introduction to Nonviolence*, Palgrave Macmillan, New York.
Lambton, A. K. S. (1997), *s.v.* "Ḵhalīfa, (ii) In Political Theory", in *The Encyclopaedia of Islam*, 3rd ed., vol. IV, Brill-Luzac&Co, Leiden-London, pp. 947–950.
Lewis, B. (2005), *Il linguaggio politico dell'Islam*, Editori Laterza, Roma-Bari.
Muller, J.-M. (2009), *Désarmer les Dieux. Le christianisme et l'islam face à la non-violence*, Les Éditions du Relié, Gordes.

Pace, E. (2007), *Introduzione alla sociologia delle religioni*, Carocci editore, Roma.
Pierret, T. (2011a), *Baas et Islam en Syrie. La dynastie Assad face aux oulémas*, PUF, Paris.
Pierret, T. (2011b), *Syrie: l'Islam dans la Révolution*, in "Politique étrangère", 4 Hiver, pp. 879–891. https://doi.org/10.3917/pe.114.0879
Saʿīd, Ǧ. (1972), *Ḥatta yuġayyiru ma bi-anfusihim*, Matbʿaa ziad bin ṯābit al-anṣārī, Dimašq.
Saʿīd, Ǧ. (1993), *Maḏhab Ibn Adam al-Awwal. Muškila al-ʿunf fī al-ʿamal al-islāmī* (5° ed.), Dār al-fikr al-muʿāṣir, Bayrūt.
Said, J. (1995), *Immigration to Islam. Answers to Fourteen Questions Posed by Ibrahim Mahmoud*, AlKhaiat, A. (trans.), available at https://www.jawdatsaid.net/en/images/6/6f/IMMIGRATION_TO_ISLAM.pdf (last accessed 23 November 2021).
Saʿīd, Ǧ. (1997), *Lā ikrāha fī al-dīn: dirāsāt wa-abḥāt fī al-fikr al-islāmī*, Markaz al-ʿilm wa-l-salām lil-dirāsāt wa-l-našr, Dimašq.
Saʿīd, Ǧ. (1998a), *Al-dīn wa-l-qanūn*, Dār al-fikr al-muʿāṣir.
Said, J. (1998b), *Jawdat Saʾeed Answers Twelve Questions*, "Current Islamic Issues", available at: https://www.jawdatsaid.net/en/index.php/Current_Islamic_Issues (last accessed 23 November 2021).
Said, J. (2017), *Vie islamiche alla non violenza*, Edizioni Zikkaron, Marzabotto.
Sourdel, D. (1997), *s.v.* "Kẖalīfa. (i) The History of the Institution of the Caliphate", in *The Encyclopaedia of Islam*, 3rd ed., vol. IV, Brill-Luzac&Co, Leiden-London, pp. 937–947.
Syria. (2021), *Syria*, in "The World Factbook", available at https://www.cia.gov/the-world-factbook/countries/syria/ (last accessed 10 April 2021).
Vertovec, S. (2007), *Super-diversity and its Implications*, in "Ethnic and Racial Studies", 30, 6, pp. 1024–1054. https://doi.org/10.1080/01419870701599465

Chapter 3
From the Hindu Monarchy to the Federal Republic: Some Notes on Religious Pluralism in Nepal

Davide Torri

Abstract

    In the religious narrative of Nepal's modern and contemporary history, two contrasting trends emerge: centralization and differentiation. The centripetal phase, spanning from 1768 to 1991, reflects a drive towards unity under the Shah kings and Rana family, emphasizing a shared identity based on language, religion, and customs. However, this unity was often hierarchical, with power and identity centered around the monarchy and high-caste practices. The centrifugal phase, starting with the 1991 "people's movement" and its consequences, witnessed challenges to monarchy, leading to democratization, secularism, and multiculturalism. This phase saw a resurgence of marginalized religious practices against state-sponsored Hinduism, highlighting a push for diversity and recognition of ethnic identities.

Keywords: Nepal, secularism, religion, Hinduism, Maoism

1 Introduction

From a religious perspective, the modern and contemporary history of Nepal can be characterized by two diverse and opposite tendencies. I am going to summarize these two tendencies, broadly speaking, with a process towards centralization in the first, centripetal phase, and a process towards differentiation in the second, centrifugal phase. The first phase I am referring to is constituted by the religious dynamics accompanying, following, and sustaining the process of political and cultural unification of the country under the royal dynasty of the Shah[1] kings, including the one-hundred-year hereditary premiership of the Rana[2] family, *de facto* holding power from 1846 to 1951. This process continued after the Rana demise, when the Shah kings regained full power and pursued a policy of modernization grounded and on the creation of a shared sense of identity. In Nepal, as practically elsewhere in the world, national identity is predicated upon the sharing of a set of traits usually including language and literature, religion, customs, and beliefs. Here, language is the basis and medium of a common narrative and literature is the space where communities imagine and create themselves[3]. Religion constitutes the basis of a shared cosmology and worldview while customs and beliefs construct and reinforce, reifying the sense of belonging. But proximity to or distance from fluency, orthodoxy, orthopraxis, high caste customs, dietary prescriptions, and geographical seats of political and symbolic power determine, and *ipso facto* create, hierarchy and marginality. In Nepal, this process could be visualized, quite literally, like a mandala model, where people, deities, landscapes, and practices are arrayed and oriented towards the centre (the king, the capital, etc.) and yet are unequally distributed along the radiuses.

What I would call the centripetal phase of Nepalese history spans between 1768 and 1991. That is, it spans from the conquest of Kathmandu Valley by the king of Gorkha Prithvi Narayan Shah, an event leading to the unification and the creation of the Kingdom of Nepal (1768–2008), to the 1991 *jana andolan* ("people's movement"), when the struggle for democracy vigorously challenged the monarchic institutions and took important steps not only towards multi-party democracy but also towards the assertion of secularism and multiculturalism, implying the

---

1. For a general introduction to the history of Nepal and the Shah dynasty, see Whelpton 2005.
2. Ibid., pp. 61–85.
3. Anderson 1983.

recognition of diverse languages, religions, and customs. It is true that the monarchy survived fifteen more years after the first *jana andolan*, but these years saw an increase in activism and repression, including a full-fledged civil war (1996–2006), before finally crumbling after a second *jana andolan* (April 2006), when civil society, democratic forces, and Maoist rebels joined hands and efforts[4] for the final push. For these reasons I consider 1991 as the starting point of what I call the centrifugal phase of Nepalese history: a phase characterized by ethnic revivals, bitter rivalries, and marked moves towards differentiation. From a religious point of view, it is interesting to notice that opposition to the monarchic institutions entailed a revival, a resurgence, and a politicization of marginalized religious practices *versus* a certain real or perceived state-sponsored Hinduism.

2 First Phase: Centralization (1769–1990)

The beginning of modern Nepal has a precise event at its core: the conquest of Kathmandu valley. The creation of the modern kingdom of Nepal was the culmination of a vast effort of military expansion of the king of Gorkha. Before the unification, the word Nepal was used only to indicate the Kathmandu valley and its three kingdoms (Kantipur, Patan, and Bhatgaon), while the rest of the Himalayan region comprised several other polities of various origin. While not being a religious conflict, the war led by Prithvi Narayan Shah against his neighbours decidedly involved different religious expressions. The Himalayan region, now divided between India and Nepal, was the home of several small political units tracing their origins, allegedly, to a wave of migration of Rajput clans from the plains to the hills to avoid muslim incursions. These Islamic incursions between the 12th and 16th centuries culminated with the establishment of the Delhi

---

4. The Seven Party Alliance (SPA) was a coalition of political parties which held meetings with the Communist Party of Nepal (Maoist) with the aim to end the autocratic rule of the monarchy and resolve the conflict with the Maoist rebels. The full text of the agreement between the SPA and the Maoists to end the civil war and dismiss the Monarchy is available at https://peacemaker.un.org/nepal-12pointunderstanding2005 (last accessed 28 May 2021).

Sultanate first and, later on, of the Mughal empire[5]. These small polities, collectively known as the twenty-two and twenty-four small kingdoms, constituted a bastion of Hinduism in the hill region. They were ideally built in opposition to the Islamic potentates of the plains, and, at the time of the unification, of the Mughal court. It is probably in reference to this concept that, after the unification of Nepal, Prithvi Narayan Shah proclaimed it "*asal Hindustan*": the true land of the Hindus.

But Hinduism was certainly not the only religion thriving among the hill people of this part of the Himalayan region: Buddhism was flourishing in the Nepal mandala among the Newar people, and several indigenous religions, centred on animism and revolving around shamanic religious specialists, were popular among the many groups inhabiting the hills. The upper fringe of the southern slopes of the Himalaya, in addition, was exposed to the influence of Tibetan culture, and many Tibetan enclaves cherished religious traditions belonging to the different schools of Tibetan Buddhism, or of Bön. Religious differences were paired also by linguistic diversities, with several languages, dialects and idioms spoken in the area, and belonging to the two distinct and overarching groups of the Indo-Aryan and Tibeto-Burman linguistic families.

The religious, cultural, and linguistic heterogeneity of the people subdued must have appeared in all its bewildering and faceted variety to the new administrators of the newly created kingdom, as Prithvi Narayan Shah himself declared in his well-known description of Nepal as a magnificent garden of four *varna* and thirty-six *jat*:

> This is a garden of all Castes, everybody should acknowledge it. Everybody from all the four Jat (Castes) and Thirty Six Barna (creeds) should protect and promote (Sambhar) this garden. This is the real Hindusthan (place of Hinuds [*sic*]). Do not give-up your Kul-dharma (religions inherited by the dynasty). Abide by the order of the Khwamit (King)[6].

---

5. Regmi 1961; Todd 1950.
6. Full text available at www.lawcommission.gov.np (last accessed 20 May 2021). Apparently, the official English translation inverts the word of *jat* and *varna* and is marred by misspelling.

It was nothing more and nothing less than the simple appreciation of a general diversity, unified and subsumed into the overarching framework of the caste system, as indicated by the reference to the notions of *varna* and *jati*, literally "colour" and "birth", indicating the classes and castes of the orthodox Hindu social system. The creation of the "asal Hindustan" probably implied the incorporation of the existing social structures into the folder of Hinduism, together with the absorption of their religious expressions in a subordinate position vis-à-vis the deities associated with the ruling powers. Religious pluralism was thus tolerated, to a certain extent, but we cannot avoid noticing that this tolerance was limited insofar mainly to Buddhism and indigenous religions. Catholic missionaries active in the Kathmandu valley were threatened, their networks dismantled, and, together with their small community of converts, they had to leave the country[7]. Christianity was thus banned from Nepal at least until 1951, when missionaries could again enter the country for humanitarian purposes, but proselytization and conversion were still prohibited.

Hinduism benefitted from its close association with the royalty and the hegemonic segments of the society and, as it ideologically supported the caste system, it became one of the main pillars sustaining the Khas establishment. Adoption of Hindu deities and customs also widely influenced all those groups interacting on a regular basis with the state apparatuses or seeking closer links with the ruling powers. However, this process was not unilineal. Local deities and their ritual places and clergy were incorporated too, according to the hierarchized framework I mentioned earlier. This mutual recognition of diverse religious practices is more than the mere superimposition of a thin veneer of Hinduism on something radically different, or, on the other hand, the simple acceptance of the supremacy of the Hindu pantheon over one's own. It was a more complex process of mutual recognitions, leading to the creation of a unified system: where we see religious pluralism, there was in fact a system of ritual exchanges across blurred or overlapping boundaries, with a certain amount of religious freedom insofar as the main tenets, emissaries, and stakeholders of power were not directly challenged.

Centralization patterns were confirmed during the Ranarchy (1846–1951), with the promulgation of the *muluki ain*, the legal code compiled

---

7. Perceval 1928, p. 66.

during the 19th century to provide a legal framework for the kingdom. The social structure sanctioned by this legal code confirmed the hegemonic predominance of the Hindu high castes, indicated as *taghadhari* and *dvija*, i.e., wearers of the holy cordon and twice-borns. Both expressions refer to the members of the Brahmin and Kshatriya classes, known in Nepal respectively as Bahun and Chetri, plus the Vaishya (merchants). Those familiar with Hinduism, will recognize in the terms Bahun and Chetri the traditional classes of the religious specialists and the warriors. As a norm, a king belongs to the warrior class, but he can rule only in a close association with ritual experts ensuring, through the proper rituals, the smooth functioning of the kingdom, in its daily routine as well as in its cosmic significance. The other groups are equally positioned according to their proximity to the ritual standards of the upper segments of the social pyramid. The *adivasi* groups are described as alcohol-drinkers (*matwali*), of which two kinds exist: those that can be enslaved and those who cannot. The menial castes are equally divided into two groups: those from whom it is possible to accept water, and those from whom water cannot be accepted. It goes without saying that the criteria for these groups, *adivasi* and menial castes, derive from the distance from the ritual purity, and the consequent intrinsic pollution, idealized, practiced, and modelled upon the customs and the dietary habits of the twice-born castes.

Even though this model seemed to take into account, and thus acknowledge, the formidable variety of the composition of the Nepalese society, its structure remained strongly unbalanced in favour of a hierarchic arrangement privileging Hindu high castes. This bias was to become, in the subsequent phase, one of the main targets for the democratic forces, the ethnic minorities, and the *maobadi*[8] rebel forces. In such a system, what we can envision as recognition of cultural and religious pluralism is

8. The story of the communist movement in Nepal is a long and complicated one, and a footnote is certainly not the place for properly addressing it. To clarify, I am using the word *Maobadi* to indicate here the Communist Party of Nepal-Maoist of the civil war (1996–2006). Due to the following process of splitting and merging, the CPN-Maoist (1994–2009) became the Unified Communist Party of Nepal-Maoist (2009–2016). In 2016, breakaway factions rejoined the main party, which was renamed Communist Party of Nepal (Maoist Centre). In 2018, the CPN-Maoist Centre merged with Communist Party of Nepal (Unified Marxist-Leninist) to give birth to the Communist Party of Nepal, *sic et simpliciter*. The Nepal Communist Party was dissolved on 8 March 2021, splitting again into the two former parties

actually an assemblage of hierarchically arranged units, arrayed following the tenets of caste-ideology, and thus heavily influenced by Hindu values and beliefs. It should be noted at this point that what we define as Hinduism is in fact a more or less fluid configuration of diverse elements, embracing different schools of thought and ritual traditions, drawing from the vast corpus of Vedic and post-Vedic literature, up to its most recent declinations. While some scholars think it is more appropriate to talk about Hinduisms[9], it is certain that the loose ensemble we call Hinduism, or *sanatana dharma*, is perceived as inclusive. According to a popular perception in Nepal, this inclusiveness was extended to embrace all the religious expressions employing the sacred syllable *om*, which were then addressed collectively through the expression "the *omkar* family"[10]. The *omkar* family grouped all the religious expressions of Indic origin, i.e., Hinduism, Buddhism, Jainism, and Sikhism, but certainly excluded "foreign" ones, namely Christianity (in all its denominations) and Islam. In this regard, it is worth noting that, following the conquest of the Kathmandu Valley, one of the first actions of the King Prithvi Narayan Shah was to decree the expulsion of the Italian Capuchin missionaries together with the small community of local converts, which were forced to leave the country and resettle across the border, in India[11]. As a matter of fact, it should be worth adding that the aforementioned Capuchin missionaries, having successfully established a small network of hospices and raised a small community of followers, were also sometimes engaging in activities which included serious provocations, like the desecration of "idols" in the active search for martyrdom "among the infidels".

The end of the Ranarchy in 1951 brought back to power the Shah Kings. Even though the leaders of the anti-Rana revolt were essentially struggling for a democratic state, their hopes were short-lived.

The 1951 anti-Rana revolt was inspired by the struggles for Indian Independence. The *Praja Parishad*, a revolutionary movement plotting to assassinate key-functionaries and top officials of the Rana was formed in 1936 and was disbanded in 1941 after its members were arrested and

---

from which it originated before the merging. For an overview of the Maoist insurgency, see Hutt 2004; Lawoti, Pahari 2009.
9. Lipner 2004.
10. Bhattachan 2006; Gellner et al. 2016.
11. Petech 1952.

executed. Its founder, Tanka Prasad Acharya, was sentenced to death. However, because the killing of a Brahmin was prohibited by the religiously influenced legal code, his sentence was commuted to imprisonment for life. Many other Nepalese activists were involved in the struggle for the independence of India. In addition, it was in India that the anti-Rana activists formed and strengthened their political organizations: the Nepali National Congress, one of the main forces of the revolt, was founded in India in 1947 and active in the organization of *satyagraha* campaigns against the regime. The dismissal of the Rana regime restored the power of the kings and the monarch. King Tribhuvan promulgated the interim constitution of 1951 as a first step towards modernization and relevant reforms of the state apparatuses. His successor, King Mahendra Bir Bikram Shah Deva, promulgated the 1959 Constitution, whose preamble is worth quoting as it states quite clearly the Hindu foundations of the monarchy and the state:

> Whereas His late majesty King Tribhuvan Bir Bikram Shah Dev, Father of the Nation and revered descendant of the illustrious King Prithvi Narayan Shah, adherent of Aryan Culture and Hindu religion, having led a Great revolution for the rights and welfare of His subject, earned immortal fame in the history of the world and was firmly resolved to establish real democracy in Nepal by giving fundamental rights to the people; [...] And Whereas for the said purpose it is desirable to enact and promulgate a Constitution for the Sovereign Kingdom of Nepal, I, King Mahendra Bir Bikram Shah Deva in the exercise of the sovereign powers pf the Kingdom of Nepal and prerogatives vesting in US in accordance with the traditions and customs of our country and which devolved on US from Our August and Respected forefathers, do hereby enact and promulgate this fundamental law entitled. (The Constitution of the Kingdom of Nepal)[12]

The words and expression employed, namely Aryan culture, Hindu religion, traditions, and customs inherited from the ancestors, embedded the Constitution in the cultural milieu and conceptual horizon of Hinduism, trying to conciliate the Hindu monarchic institution and

---

12. The full text of the 1959 Constitution, in English translation, can be found here: https://constitutionnet.org/sites/default/files/1959_constitution_english.pdf (last accessed 12 May 2021).

the democratic aspirations of the Nepalese people. Regarding religion, specifically, Art. 5 (Religion) of the Constitution stated: "Every citizen having regard to the current traditions, may practice and profess his own religion as handed down from ancient times. Provided that no person shall be entitled to convert another person to his religion"[13]. In practice, while religious pluralism was acknowledged and tolerated, it was granted insofar the religious expression in question was in fact "handed down from ancient times", underlying the fact that proselytizing and trying to convert other people was a crime, punishable according to the law. As mentioned before, the experiment with democracy was short-lived: the first elections, in February 1959, saw the Nepali Congress, led by B. P. Koirala, securing the two-thirds of the parliamentary seats, but the following months of unfruitful political debate and civil unrest in the western regions of the country constituted the pretext for King Mahendra to dismiss the elected government. The Army moved in quickly to arrest Koirala and several other prominent politicians, in what is remembered as the Royal Coup of December 1960[14]. Mahendra never hid his scepticism towards parliamentary democracy, and his ideas about it shaped Nepalese politics for almost three decades. In 1962, in fact, King Mahendra promulgated another Constitution. Regarding religious matters, the contents of the relevant articles were basically the same as the 1959 Constitution, but the whole state structure was reformed with the suppression of political parties. As stated in Article 11(2a): "no political party or any other organization, union or association motivated by party politics shall be formed or caused to be formed or run".

From 1960 to 1990, the country was to be ruled according to the so-called *panchayat* system[15]. Whereas the term *panchayat* refers to the traditional village assembly (literally, "a council of five") of the elders and the wise, its Nepalese version of the second half of the 20th century consisted of a multi-tiered system of councils ranging from village to national level, whose apex was the king himself. In the same years, the country experienced a prolonged effort at the creation of a national identity in the modern sense of the word, supported by the increase of

---

13. Constitution of Nepal (1959), Art. 5.
14. Mishra 1982.
15. Hachhethu, Gellner 2010; Whelpton 2005.

literacy in *Nepali* language, the building of infrastructures, and substantial reforms. The *panchayat* system and ideology appeared to be Mahendra's way to development, balancing the push towards modernization with the more conservative elements of the social structure[16]. The modernization of Nepal was grounded in a national identity centred on the idea of the Hindu Kingdom, as clearly stated by Art. 3(1): "Nepal is an independent, indivisible and sovereign monarchical Hindu State". Alphabetization of the population increased in an effort to increase literacy[17] in *Nepali bhasa*, Hindu religious festivals and festivities became national holidays, and a popular slogan summarized the mood of the times: *ek raja, ek desh, ek bhasa* ("one king, one dress, one language")[18]. Modernization, as is often the case in the creation of national identities, stems from cultural homogenization and standardization. In between the two gigantic neighbours of Nehru's India and Mao's China, Mahendra envisioned his own way to develop and modernize the country[19].

The crisis of the *panchayat* system began during the reign of Mahendra's heir, King Birendra, who ascended to the throne in 1975. Despite a referendum in 1980[20] that confirmed that the preferred political system for the Nepalese was still the *panchayat*, it was during the 1980s[21] that pro-democracy, leftist, and ethnic activists increased their activities and started to challenge the status quo once again. The consequences of the 1988 earthquake sparked ample protests across the country and the year after, in the wake of the news coming from Eastern Europe, where a political earthquake shocked the Soviet system and called for democracy, the pro-democracy movement of Nepal launched a mass campaign for the restoration of multi-party democracy. The MRD (Movement for the Restoration of Democracy) entered a phase of direct confrontation with the state apparatuses in the first months of 1990. On 18 February, the *jana*

---

16. Hayes 1975.
17. For an interesting analysis of the education program during panchayat times see Onta 1996.
18. Pradhan 2019.
19. For an overview of the Nepalese political relations with India and China see Chaturvedy, Malone 2012.
20. Heck 1981.
21. Davis 2009.

andolan (people's movement)[22] took to the streets, and after weeks of clashes with the security forces and many civilian casualties, on 8 April 1990, Birendra released a public statement removing the ban established by Mahendra on political parties.

A new Constitution was promulgated in November 1990[23], thus marking a new phase in the political history of Nepal. Despite setbacks and a bitter civil war, as we will see in the following paragraphs, we could consider 1990 as the turning point, from the centripetal phase to the centrifugal one. It is in this phase, in fact, that we find centrifugal forces at work, leading to the emergence not only of a multi-party political system, but also of a variegated and vociferous civil society. This society, as we will see, claims, or reclaims, dignity, space, and visibility and brandishes diversity and specificity across ethnic, cultural, linguistic, and religious boundaries in a prolonged effort to create an inclusive, multicultural, secular, and federal new Nepal.

3   Second Phase: Differentiation (1991–2021)

The Constitution promulgated at the end of 1990 declared that Nepal was a multiethnic and multilingual Constitutional Monarchy, yet it retained its Hindu denomination. In fact, Art. 4(1) declared: "Nepal is a multiethnic multilingual, democratic, independent, indivisible, sovereign, Hindu and Constitutional Monarchical Kingdom"[24]. While granting equal rights to each citizen and condemning ethnic, religious, or caste-based discriminations, the fact that the state was still defined as Hindu, and that Nepali was its official language, disappointed many of those who struggled to create a pluralistic society. Yet, it was from those effervescent times and in the new, more open, and conducive environment, that the stage was set for the events that followed. In the spring of 1990, the country was on the brink of a civil war. A few years later, it plunged into it.

---

22. For a detailed chronicle of the events, see Hachhethu 1990; Raeper, Hoftun 1992.
23. Hutt 1991.
24. The complete text of the Constitution of the Kingdom of Nepal 2047 (1990) is available at https://www.refworld.org/docid/3ae6b4fa10.html (last accessed 18 May 2021).

For the time being, the months between 1990 and 1991 saw the formations of several organizations and groups whose aim was to revive the social identities marginalized during the previous decades. While diverse communities formed cultural groups, several of them decided to join in an umbrella-organization for the promotion of the adivasi minorities. It was called *Nepal Adivasi Janajati Mahasangh*, known in English as the Nepal Federation of Indigenous Nationalities (NEFIN). At the beginning, it represented fifteen groups only (the Kirant Yakthung Chumlung, the Kiran Rai Yayokkha, the Chantyal Pariwas Sangh, the Nepal Magar Sangh, the Tamu Boudha Sewa Samiti, the Nepal Bhasa Manka Khala, the Thakali Sewa Samiti, the Yahmbu Sherpa Chi-Chhog, the Meche Samaj Sudhar Samiti, the Nepal Hyolmo Samaj Sewa Sangh, the Nepal Tamang Ghedung sangh, the Dhimal Jatiya Utthan Kendra, the Rajbhansi Bhasha Prachar Samiti, the Niko Thami Sewa Samiti, the Kirat Dharma Tatha Sahitya Utthan Sangh[25]), while now it comprises fifty-six minorities and it is one of the major pressure-groups in the country.

The indigenous ethnic organizations were at the forefront of the mobilization for democracy and, in the following years, they began agitating against marginalization for a substantial and formal recognition of multiculturalism, and for secularism[26]. To the ethnic activists, the multi-party political environment, which emerged from the spring upheavals of 1990, was perceived as insufficient to foster a real inclusive society. In the very same years, the multi-party democratic environment and the Constitutional Monarchy were denounced by another coalition of discontented. Several ultra-leftist groups were merging and forging alliances to launch an assault against the "feudal system" controlling the country, in order to create a *new democracy*[27]. In 1996, these elements, grouped under the leadership of the Communist Party of Nepal-Maoist (CPN-M), declared a war of liberation against the State, thus starting a civil war[28] that raged until 2006. The civil war engulfed the country with the flames

25. Fisher 1993; Subba 1999.
26. See also Torri 2019.
27. In Maoist jargon, the *new democracy* is a political phase in between feudalism and socialism. In this phase, according to Mao's vision, the working class forms an alliance with elements of the bourgeois system in order to relinquish the remnants of the feudal system's social structure. See Mao 1940; Karunakaran 1952.
28. On the Maoist movement and the civil war, see Hutt 2004; Lawoti, Pahari 2009.

of guerrilla actions, extra-judicial killings, kidnappings, and bombings for a full decade. Together with the loss of many lives and the destruction of several infrastructures, the years between 1996 and 2006 also saw the almost total annihilation of the civil society, especially after the 2001 massacre of the royal family. According to the official version, during a family dinner the crown-prince Dipendra killed several members of his family, including Birendra, before taking his own life. The massacre paved the way for the king's brother, Gyanendra, to the throne. In 2005, Gyanendra dissolved, once again, the parliament in an autocratic experiment before facing mounting protests which eventually lead to a second *jana andolan* in April 2006. The second people's movement brought together the democratic parties and the Maoist rebels, intellectuals, students from across the country, workers, and peasants in a mass protest protracted until Gyanendra had to resign and cede the power to the parliament once again. Two years later, the April elections for the Constituent Assembly (CA) saw the Maoists emerge as the first political party of the country and one month after, on 8 May 2008, the first meeting of the CA abolished the Monarchy and declared the country a federal democratic republic.

What was the role of religion in the fifteen years between 1990 and 2008? Broadly speaking, the attacks towards the monarchy and its institutions targeted Hinduism insofar as it constituted one of the pillars of the state, promoting an image of society modelled after Hindu values and caste ideology. It goes without saying that when the Maoist ideologues attacked "feudalism", they had in mind also the system of privileges which was deeply ingrained in the state machinery, but also diffused in the society at large. In doing this, they banked on the discrimination produced by the caste system and successfully rallied the underprivileged, the marginalized, and the oppressed. Part of the success of the Nepalese Maoists derived from the appeal exerted on the indigenous groups, on the Dalits[29] and on the low castes. Maoists targeted village[30] Hinduism[31] insofar as it was perceived as an instrument for class and gender based exploitation.

---

29. Bownas 2015.
30. For an ethnographic description of Maoist-controlled areas, see de Sales 2010, 2013; Pettigrew 2013; Shrestha-Schipper 2013.
31. Lecomte-Tilouine 2017.

The village described by Marie Lecomte-Tilouine constitutes an example of the Nepalese version of the cultural revolution waged by a zealot local leader in order to eradicate "backward" religious practices from what was described as a model Maoist community: in Deorali, it was forbidden to perform or attend collective rituals related to agricultural cycle, animal sacrifices, the *tij* festival (in which women fast and worship their husbands), and ancestor worshipping; the ritual offerings to the dead were shortened, and caste-rules regarding the sharing of food and drinks and access to places[32] were disregarded. In addition, the revolutionary movement saw the participation of female activists at every level, including combat units, and it empowered women in unprecedented ways[33].

Beside Maoist militants in rebel-controlled rural areas, Hinduism was targeted also by movements of the civil society in the struggle for democracy, secularism, and inclusivism. The already mentioned Nepal Federation of Indigenous Groups was very active in campaigning for the specific rights of the ethnic minorities, and the ensuing so-called ethnic revival of Nepal engaged what was perceived as state-sponsored Hinduism at every level. The indigenous groups, or *janajati adivasi*, claimed historical precedence and cultural specificities obfuscated by the Hinduization of the state and its apparatuses promoted by the monarchic state throughout its history. It is certainly true that several groups absorbed elements taken from Sanskritic culture, due to the combined effects of acculturation and enculturation processes, yet, it is equally true that each and every group tried to maintain and cultivate its own specificity vs. the state in terms of language or idiom, cultural heritage, attachment to specific territories described as ancestral, and the worshipping of vernacular deities belonging to indigenous pantheons.

Several of these groups, beside a formal adherence to Hinduism and Buddhism, continued often to rely on indigenous religious specialists, in charge of clan-deities, ancestors and local gods, goddesses, and spirits. A certain homogeneity characterizes these belief-systems, despite their local manifestations. In the context of Nepal, scholars have defined these

32. In Hinduism, the partaking of food and drinks, as well as the access to temples and the use of fountains and wells, in strictly regulated by concepts of purity and pollution, with the effect to discriminate members of the low castes, the Dalits, menstruating women, strangers, etc.
33. Pettigrew 2012.

religious practices and beliefs as animism or shamanism, while the 2011 census defines them as *prakriti*, in the sense of "nature worship". As stated above, many groups inhabiting the northern regions of the country embrace Tibetan Buddhism, all the while maintaining a parallel ritual practice rooted in vernacular traditions akin to the aforementioned forms of animism and shamanism. Regarding Buddhism, it should be added that it is present in Nepal with its numerous traditions, including the various schools of Tibetan Buddhism, the indigenous Newari Buddhism, and the Theravada tradition recently embraced by some among the Tharu and the Magar *adivasi* groups[34]. The rise and revival of ethnic minorities in Nepal contributed to pushing the country towards federalism and secularism. These two trends exemplify what I defined, at the beginning of this chapter, as the centrifugal, differentiation phase. While federalism[35] aimed at the decentralization of administration in favor of a regional approach, secularism aimed at displacing Hinduism from the centre of the cultural and religious stage it occupied since the establishment of the monarchy. In the context of Nepal, secularism goes hand in hand with religious pluralism.

Bridging the gap time between the end of the autocratic regime and the April 2006 elections of the Constituent Assembly (CA), the Interim Constitution of 2007, Art. 4 defined the country in the following terms: "4. State of Nepal: (1) Nepal is an independent, indivisible, sovereign, secular, inclusive and a fully democratic State"[36]. This formally recognized the country as a secular one for the first time in history. This definition was confirmed by the first meeting of the CA in May 2008, when Nepal was officially declared a secular republic, a *dharma nirapeksha rajya*, i.e., a "State autonomous from religion"[37]. We could say that this was the outcome of decades of agitations for democracy, religious freedom, minorities' rights, and last, but not least, socialism: diverse groups, parties, and communities had finally identified in the Hindu monarchic institutions their target and, with the fall of the monarchy, Hinduism also came under scrutiny. Reformation or dismantlement of the Hindu

---

34. On Buddhism among the Tharu and the Magar, see Letizia 2014; Krauskopff 2009.
35. Lecours 2014.
36. The full text of the Interim Constitution is available at http://www.ilo.org/wcmsp5/groups/public/---ed_protect/---protrav/---ilo_aids/documents/legaldocument/wcms_126113.pdf (last accessed 20 May 2021).
37. Letizia 2016, p. 36.

Kingdom, the ethnic revival or the struggle for religious pluralism in some ways were also directed against Hinduism as the culture and ideology of the hegemonic groups allied with the monarchic powers. Because of this, the clause "state autonomous from religion" meant, primarily, non-Hindu.

Discourses about secularism surfaced in Nepalese society during the 1990s, when Theravada monks and *janajati adivasi* activists started to campaign for the equal recognition of diverse religions[38], beyond the pervasive fold of Hinduism. Since Hinduism appeared to be ingrained into the state-machine, the struggle for secularism was at once political and religious, bringing together clergy, believers, intellectuals, and minorities' activists. In a system characterized by a social structure assigning status, power, access to resources, and privileges on the basis of Hindu caste ideology, secularism provided the occasion to rally diverse groups with different agendas in order to mobilize for "minority inclusion in all these spheres and for recognition of the multi-ethnic and multi-religious composition of the country"[39]. Public display of cultural or religious diversity, in terms of clothing, dances, songs, and rituals[40] became a primary modality of representation of a distinct identity[41]. The campaigns for recognition of religious pluralism entailed the performance of socio-religio-political display of specificities, in which it was not possible anymore to disentangle the ethnic or religious from the political. During my intermittent fieldwork between 2008 and 2015, I witnessed many demonstrations for secularism and religious freedom. As the people marched around the city and towards the Government buildings, the most striking feature concerning the *adivasi* segment was that each indigenous group tried to march as a bounded entity, led by its religious representatives. A clear sign that, despite the intended aim to foster secularism and religious pluralism, the march was the result of the convergence of each and every marginalized community towards a common aim.

The revival of marginalized groups led to effervescent times in terms of activism and the process of asserting and making visible one's own

38. Ibid., p. 42.
39. Ibid., p. 43.
40. As pointed out by Sarah Shneiderman, ethnicity itself is produced *through* ritual activities (Shneiderman 2015, p. 58).
41. Berg 2003; Holmberg 2016; Torri 2017.

heritage projected different religions onto the public space in unprecedented ways. A first, tangible effect of this was the proliferation or appropriation of sacred places, which dotted the landscape and from which, in turn, specific identities could articulate themselves, thus emerging to visibility. Appropriation of material and symbolic space increased with the growing awareness and confidence of the once marginalized communities[42]. The growing number of worship places constitute a relevant feature of the revitalization movement of the marginalized communities, together with the increase of ethno-cultural-religious festivals fulfilling at the same time the needs for self-representation and the demands of cultural recognition[43]. In this regard, we could say that the de-Hinduization of Nepal coincides with the emergence and visibility of differences in the legal arena (epitomized by the Constitution's clauses on secularism), in the democratic institutions (the parliament), the physical landscape (temples, shrines, cemeteries, sacred places), in the discursive formations and intangible heritage (indigenization, songs, dances, and dress). The religious pluralism emerging and gaining space in Nepal is visible at a glance by looking at the calendar of public holidays, which still include Hindu festivities (Shivaratri, Krishna Janmasthami, Dashain, etc.), together with Buddha Jayanti, the birthday of Muhammad and the end of the Ramadan, Christmas Day, and properly secular holidays like International Labor Day, Democracy Day, Constitution Day and Martyrs' Day, plus various New Year's days.

4 Conclusions: Secularism and Religious Pluralism

As previously mentioned, the 2015 Constitution of Nepal refers to the state as *dharma nirapeksa*, "autonomous from/neutral to religion", and that expression is usually equated to a declaration of secularism. The debate over secularism in the Indian sub-continent has quite a long history, grounded in the struggle for Indian independence, and generations of militants and activists had speculated over it and over its application[44].

---

42. Gaenszle 2016; Holmberg 2016; Torri 2017, 2019.
43. Holmberg 2016, p. 302.
44. For a general overview of secularism and its crisis in India, see Smith 1963; Needham, Rajan 2008.

While Nepal was quite unique insofar as it was a Hindu Kingdom, the debate over secularism and the relations between religions and the state has been running deep among the country's politicians and thinkers, and the analytical categories involved bear some resemblance with the Indian discourses on secularism. In Indian history, secularism found a champion in Jawaharlal Nehru[45] who had, during the Karachi Congress Resolution of 1931, envisioned a state neutral to all religions[46]. According to Nehru, a humanist and an agnostic, the free India should have been a secular democracy, enabling each and every community to live together in peace, whereas instead he saw communalism as a direct threat to the creation of a democratic state. Different from his views were those of Mohandas Karamchand Gandhi, who had a more positive attitude towards religions, and who understood secularism more as equal respect and tolerance towards diverse religious traditions, an attitude exemplified by the expression *sarva dharma sama bhava*[47]. While I avoid a detailed account of the two Indian understandings of the concept of secularism (exemplified above as Nehru's and Gandhi's approaches), it should be worth mentioning here that the debate over secularism was crucial for the Indian independence movement in order to bridge the gap between the Hindu majority of the population and the other religious minorities. Political events like the partition of Bengal of 1905 and the creation of the All-India Muslim League in 1906 prefigured the rise of communalism and the creation of Pakistan as a Muslim state, and the separate births of India, Pakistan, and Bangladesh[48] was the direct outcome of the failed dialogue over secularism and religious pluralism.

It should not be forgotten that Bhimrao Ramji Ambedkar criticized Gandhi's position, arguing that some religious expressions were keeping people in a subaltern position, as in the case of Dalit people in the fold of Hinduism. The *dharma nirapeksha* view, promoted by Nehru, was grounded instead on the values of modernity and rationalism, aiming at the separation of religion and state, and ideally relegating religious ideas

---

45. Ghouse 1978.
46. Rajasekhariah 1987, p. 218.
47. Joseph 2012.
48. Bangladesh was formerly known as East Bengal (after the Partition of 1905) and East Pakistan (after 1947). The current name was adopted after the 1971 Liberation War. See Van Schendel 2020.

to the private sphere with science replacing it in the public one. In the Indian Constitution, fundamental religious rights are granted in articles 25, 26, 27, 28, 29, and 30, which establish religious freedom for all citizens, the right to form religious institutions, exclude religious education from the state-founded education system, and protect the "interests of minorities" and especially their rights to preserve "a distinct language, script or culture of its own"[49], which is particularly relevant to the *adivasi* situation. In a similar way, in drafting the new constitution, the members of the Nepalese CA were striving to produce an advanced democratic system, firmly centered on secular values, as reflected already by articles of the Interim Constitution.

The 2007 Nepal's interim Constitution, in fact, defined the state as secular, a feature later confirmed also in the 2015 Constitution: "Art 4. State of Nepal: (1) Nepal is an independent, indivisible, sovereign, secular, inclusive, democratic, socialism oriented, federal democratic republican state". An explicative note follows: "For the purposes of this Article, "secular" means religious, cultural freedoms, including protection of religion, culture handed down from the time immemorial"[50].

While this passage seems to grant religious freedom and equality to all the religious expressions of marginalized groups, according to Letizia, it also "evokes the notion of sanatan dharma"[51], the eternal religion of the Hindus. In the end, while the initial ideas of secularism were mainly and openly anti-Hindu, the final version of the process seems more reconciling. Undoubtedly, even the staunch view of the Maoist delegates were pragmatically mitigated by taking into account the ideas of their Hindu fellow members of the parliament. The ban on proselytism and conversion (Art. 26.3)[52] seems a relic from the monarchy days, although it was

---

49. Constitution of India, Art. 29.
50. Text available at http://extwprlegs1.fao.org/docs/pdf/nep155698b.pdf (last accessed 15 May 2021).
51. Letizia 2016, p. 69.
52. "Art. 26. Right to religious freedom:
    (1) Each person shall be free to profess, practice, and preserve his/her religion according to his/her faith.
    (2) Every religious denomination shall, maintaining its independent existence, have the right to manage and protect its religious places and religious trusts in accordance with law. Provided that it shall not be deemed to have hindered

explained as a measure[53] to contrast the aggressive conversion campaigns launched by Evangelical Christians after the fall of the monarchy. Conversion campaigns increased especially after the 2015 earthquake. The 2015 Constitution of Nepal declared the cow the national animal of Nepal[54], and the Criminal Code of 2017 explicitly prohibits the killing or beating of cows and oxen[55]. It should be noted that slaughtering cows and oxen in order to consume beef was a very sensitive issue in the past. Occasional consumption of cow meat by members of the *adivasi* communities was perceived as a heinous criminal act, and many Hindus

---

to make law to operate and protect a religious place or religious trust and to manage trust property and regulate land management.

(3) While exercising the right as provided by this Article, no person shall act or make others act in a manner which is contrary to public health, decency and morality, or behave or act or make others act to disturb public law and order situation, or convert a person of one religion to another religion, or disturb the religion of other people. Such an act shall be punishable by law". Available at: http://extwprlegs1.fao.org/docs/pdf/nep155698b.pdf (last accessed 27 May 2021).

53. See for example the Criminal Code Art. 158:
"158. Prohibition of proselytizing:
(1) No person shall convert any one from one religion to another or make attempt to or abet such conversion.
(2) No person shall do any act or conduct which undermines the religion, opinion or faith of any caste, race, community or convert any one into another religion, whether by inducement or not, in a manner to so undermine or propagate such religion or opinion with the intention of making such conversion". Available at: https://www.ilo.org/dyn/natlex/docs/ELECTRONIC/106060/137998/F-1544911756/NPL106060.pdf (last accessed 21 May 2021).

54. According to Art. 9(3) "The *Rhododendron Arboreum* is the national flower, Crimson is the national color, the cow is the national animal and the *Lophophorus* is the national bird of Nepal". Full text of the 2015 Constitution available at: http://extwprlegs1.fao.org/docs/pdf/nep155698b.pdf (last accessed 20 May 2021).

55. See also Criminal Code Art. 289: Prohibition of killing or beating cows or oxen: (1) No person shall do, or cause to be done, any act with the intention of killing, or causing hurt to, any cow or ox. (2) Where any act referred to in sub-section (1) causes the death of any cow or ox, the offender of such offence shall be liable to a sentence of imprisonment for a term not exceeding three years". An English version of the Criminal Code is available at: https://www.ilo.org/dyn/natlex/docs/ELECTRONIC/106060/137998/F1544911756/NPL106060.pdf (last accessed 25 May 2021).

feared that with the advent of secularism a beef diet would be encouraged by Maoists, Muslims, and Christians[56]. Because dietary customs are an integral part of religious behaviour, the killing of cows and consumption of beef could spark communal violence, as has happened in India[57]. Yet, while these measures seem, in a sense, to safeguard the place of Hinduism in the legal framework, it should be noted that other articles from the 2015 Constitution[58] and the 2017 Criminal Code safeguard and guarantee religious pluralism. For example, the Criminal Code Articles 155 and 156 state:

Offences Relating to Religion:

> 155. Prohibition of injuring shrines or places held sacred: (1) No person shall damage or injure or, in any way, defile, destroy or pollute any place of religious worship, pray or function or place, object held sacred or burial place or place of sepulture or do similar other act with intent to outrage or insult the religion or religious feelings of any caste, race, community or class or with the knowledge that such outrage or insult is likely to occur.
>
> 156. Prohibition of outraging religious feelings: (1) No person shall outrage the religious feelings of any caste, race, community or class by words, either spoken or written, by visible representation or signs or otherwise[59].

In the context of the Nepalese process towards a secular state and a secular society, the religious field is one of the main arenas where different groups meet and forge alliances or compete with each other. As a rule, it seems that non-Hindu groups try to disentangle themselves from the Hindu arch-narratives which played a pivotal role during the Monarchic era by enhancing and displaying their non-Hindu heritage in terms of

---

56. Letizia 2016, p. 81.
57. Recently, the rise of vigilante groups devoted to protecting the cows has gained resonance after the killings of Muslims accused of slaughtering cows and eating beef, as documented by several news sources and by Human Rights Watch. See, for example: https://www.hrw.org/news/2017/04/27/india-cow-protection-spurs-vigilante-violence (last accessed 24 May 2021).
58. Such as the already mentioned Art. 26.
59. https://www.ilo.org/dyn/natlex/docs/ELECTRONIC/106060/137998/F-1544911756/NPL106060.pdf (last accessed 25 May 2021).

cultural expressions, from the revival of indigenous languages as mother tongues, to customs, food habits, dancing styles, as well as artistic performance and embodiment of a specific culture. Even more interesting is the process of intensification affecting non-Hindu religious expressions. As a matter of fact, in every public event where ethnicity and cultures are displayed, the religious element vehemently appears, as a clear marker of specific collective identities that, while rejecting the state-sponsored Hinduism, try to forge a new and more inclusive sense of Nepali-ness, based on the recognition of diversities.

Several scholars have studied the more recent developments in terms of religious pluralism, in its manifold expressions in the framework of the federal republic of Nepal[60]. Religious pluralism in Nepal was already self-evident from the religio-scape of the Kathmandu valley, where the ancient three cities of Bhaktapur, Patan, and Kathmandu were built as real *mandala*, whose centres, peripheries and gates were marked, guarded, and protected by deities localized into specific physical focal points of the terrain. In addition, crossroads as well as courtyards are teeming with shrines of various sizes, where the many deities of various pantheons receive constant offerings and worship. To the vast numbers of Hindu and Buddhist holy places, the various ethnically related worship places are now added. The religio-scape has a parallel in the flourishing of religious festivals. This flourishing seems to be tied not only to the ethnic revival, but also more specifically to the de-construction of state Hinduism. As aptly noted by David Holmberg, the religious festivals are serving the double purpose of portraying the correct identity of the group to its members, and show the internal cohesion to outsiders[61]. Competition between groups can also be seen in the process of constant enriching of public performances, growing more elaborate year after year. Yet, the process is far from over and the dust from previous conflict has not settled yet, as new tensions also arise. It seems, in fact, that the de-Hinduization of the state is moving on at a slower pace than expected, as shown by the extremely

---

60. See, for example Gellner et al. 2016. In this edited volume a vast array of case studies from the Himalayan country gives an idea of the religious dynamics at work and depicts the vibrant and effervescent pluri-religious milieu intersecting politics and identities from individual to community and state level.
61. Holmberg 2016.

slow process of Constitution writing, and by the political changes taking place in the parliament.

According to the 2011 Census, there are actually ten religions in Nepal:

> Religion: There are ten types of religion categories reported in the census. Hindu is followed by 81.3 percent (21,551,492) of the population followed by Buddhism (9%; 2,396,099), Islam (4.4%; 1,162,370), Kirat (3.1%; 807,169), Christianity (1.4%; 375,699), Prakriti (0.5%; 121,982), Bon (13,006), Jainism (3,214), Bahai (1,283) and Sikhism (609)[62].

The new Census, which should have been completed in June 2021[63], will reveal the current trends of democratic Nepal, where the positioning of each individual and community in terms of religion is also indicative of their social and political standing. The data collection operations for the Census revealed some of the fault lines mentioned above: the data-collectors were criticized for using pencils instead of pens, for omitting questions about religion, or deliberately ignoring answers about spoken languages, as documented by several newspapers and denounced by the Nepal Federation of Indigenous Nationalities in an official statement[64]. Is it a sign that the idea of a Hindu state is still residing inside the state apparatuses, and popular among state functionaries? In the last Census, more than 80% of the population declared its allegiance to Hindu religion. Some politicians, and even some left-wing parties, have tried to bank on Nepalese Hindu voters, as when the then Prime Minister, K. P. Sharma Oli, declared that the birthplace of Ram was not in Ayodhya (India) but in Madi (Nepal)[65]. It should come as no surprise, then, that some political movements are overtly campaigning for a return to the Hindu state. In

---

62. See *National Population and Housing Census* 2011, p. 4. Full text available at https://unstats.un.org/unsd/demographic/sources/census/wphc/Nepal/Nepal-Census-2011-Vol1.pdf (last accessed 15 May 2021).
63. Originally scheduled for the summer 2021, the Census was postponed to November 2021 due a surge in Covid cases. Data collection took place from 11–25 November 2021.
64. See https://www.onlinekhabar.com/2021/11/1039515 (last accessed 19 December 2021).
65. See https://thehimalayantimes.com/kathmandu/pm-oli-tells-madi-delegation-to-promote-ayodhyapuri-as-rams-place-of-birth (last accessed 19 December 2021).

August 2021, former Nepal Army General Rukmandag Katuwal launched the *Hindu Rastra Swabhiman Jagran Abhiyan* ("movement for the dignity and awareness of the Hindu State")[66], with the support of Hindu religious leaders. This movement is, undoubtedly, closer to the Hindutva[67] ideology than to the republican ideals of the second *jana andolan*.

Author Biography

Davide Torri is Associate Professor of Himalayan Religions at the Department of History, Anthropology, Religions, and Performing Arts, Sapienza University of Rome. He completed his PhD at the University of Napoli "L'Orientale" in 2009, and he has been teaching and researching at the Universities of Chester (UK), Heidelberg, and Bochum (Germany). Vice-President of the International Society for Academic Research on Shamanism (ISARS), he has been carrying out research mainly in Nepal and the Himalayas. Among his works, several publications deal with indigenous religions like the monograph *Landscape, Ritual and Identity among the Hyolmo of Nepal* (Routledge, 2020) and the edited volume (with Sophie Roche) *The Shamaness in Asia. Gender, Religion and the State* (Routledge, 2021).

References

Anderson, B. (1983), *Imagined Communities: Reflections on the Origin and Spread of Nationalism*, Verso, London and New York.

Berg, E. (2003), *On Local Festival Performance: The Sherpa Dumji in a World of Dramatically Increasing Uncertainties*, in "European Bulletin of Himalayan Research", 25–26, pp. 168–204.

---

66. See https://english.khabarhub.com/2021/19/204041/ (last accessed 22 December 2021).
67. Hindutva, as a term and a political concept, refers to modern forms of Hindu nationalism. Originally employed by Indian nationalists, i.e., Chandranath Basu (1844–1910) and Vinayak Damodar Savarkar (1883–1966), it has become the main ideology of certain political groups advocating for an essentially Hindu-oriented state and society. As such, it has been interpreted as a form of fundamentalism or integralism. See, for example, Frykenberg 2008.

Bhattachan, K. B. (2006), *Nepalese Buddhists' View of Hinduism*, in J. D. Gort, H. M. Vroom, H. Jansen (eds.), *Religions View Religions: Explorations in Pursuit of Understanding*, Rodopi, New York and Amsterdam, pp. 227–239.

Bownas, R. A. (2015), *Dalits and Maoists in Nepal's Civil War: Between Synergy and Co-optation*, in "Contemporary South Asia", 23, 4, pp. 409–425. https://doi.org/10.1080/09584935.2015.1090952

Chaturvedy, R. R., Malone, D. M. (2012), *A Yam between Two Boulders: Nepal's Foreign Policy Caught between India and China*, in S. von Einsiedl (ed.), *Nepal in Transition: From People's War to Fragile Peace*, Cambridge University Press, New York, pp. 287–312.

Davis, C. (2009), *Decade of Dreams: Democracy and the Birth of Nepal's Engaged Stage, 1980–1990*, in "Asian Theatre Journal", 26, 1, pp. 94–110. https://doi.org/10.1353/atj.0.0027

de Sales, A. (2010), *Pride and Prejudice: An Encounter between Shamans and Maoists in Western Nepal*, in P. Manandhar, D. Seddon (eds.), *Hope and in Fear: Living Through the People's War in Nepal*, Adroit, New Delhi, pp. 123–134.

de Sales, A. (2013), *Thabang: The Crucible of Revolution*, in M. Lecomte-Tilouine (ed.), *Revolution in Nepal: An Anthropological and Historical Approach to the People's War*, Oxford University Press, London, pp. 164–212.

Fisher, W. (1993), *Nationalism and the Janajati*, in "Himal", 6, 2, pp. 11–14.

Frykenberg, R. E. (2008), *Hindutva as a Political Religion: An Historical Perspective*, in R. Griffin, R. Mallett, J. Tortorice (eds.), *The Sacred in Twentieth-Century Politics*, Palgrave Macmillan, London, pp. 178–220.

Gaenszle, M. (2016), *Redefining Kiranti Religion in Contemporary Nepal*, in D. N. Gellner, S. L. Hausner, C. Letizia (eds.), *Religion, Secularism and Ethnicity in Contemporary Nepal*, Oxford University Press, Delhi, pp. 150–191.

Gellner, D. N., Hausner, S. L., Letizia, C. (eds.) (2016), *Religion, Secularism, and Ethnicity in Contemporary Nepal*, Oxford University Press, Delhi.

Ghouse, M. (1978), *Nehru and Secularism*, in "Journal of the Indian Law Institute", 20, 1, pp. 103–116.

Hachhethu, K. (1990), *Mass Movement 1990*, in "Contributions to Nepalese Studies", 17, 2, pp. 177–201.

Hachhethu, K., Gellner, D. N. (2010), *Nepal: Trajectories of Democracy and Restructuring of the State*, in P. Brass (ed.), *Routledge Handbook of South Asian Politics*, Routledge, London and New York, pp. 131–146.

Hayes, L. D. (1975), *The Monarchy and Modernization in Nepal*, in "Asian Survey", 15, 7, pp. 616–628. https://doi.org/10.2307/2643344

Heck, D. (1981), *Nepal in 1980: The Year of the Referendum*, in "Asian Survey", 21, 2, pp. 181–187. https://doi.org/10.2307/2643763

Holmberg, D. (2016), *Tamang Lhochhar and the New Nepal*, in D. N. Gellner, S. L. Hausner, C. Letizia (eds.), *Religion, Secularism and Ethnicity in Contemporary Nepal*, Oxford University Press, Delhi, pp. 302–325.

Hutt, M. (1991), *Drafting the Nepal Constitution, 1990*, in "Asian Survey", 31, 11, pp. 1020–1039. https://doi.org/10.2307/2645305

Hutt, M. (2004), *Himalayan People's War: Nepal's Maoist Rebellion*, Indiana University Press, Bloomington.

Joseph, S. K. (2012), *Gandhi, Religion and Multiculturalism: An Appraisal*, in "Gandhi Marg", 33, 4, pp. 409–425.

Karunakaran, K. (1952), *"New Democracy" – The Chinese Communist Concept*, in "The Australian Quarterly", 24, 3, pp. 33–42.

Krauskopff, G. (ed.) (2009), *Les Faiseurs d'histoires: politique de l'origine et écrits sur le passé*, Nanterre, Société d'ethnologie.

Lawoti, M., Pahari, A. K. (eds.) (2009), *The Maoist Insurgency in Nepal: Revolution in the Twenty-First Century*, Routledge, London and New York.

Lecomte-Tilouine, M. (2017), *Terror in a Maoist Model Village in Midwestern Nepal*, in A. Shah, J. Pettigrew (eds.), *Windows into a Revolution: Ethnographies of Maoism in India and Nepal*, Routledge, London, pp. 207–232.

Lecours, A. (2014), *The Question of Federalism in Nepal*, in "Publius: The Journal of Federalism", 44, 4, pp. 609–632. https://doi.org/10.1093/publius/pjt030

Letizia, C. (2014), *Buddhist Activism, New Sanghas, and the Politics of Belonging among some Tharu and Magar Communities of Southern Nepal*, in J. Pfaff-Czarnecka, G. Toffin (eds.), *Facing Globalization in the Himalayas: Belonging and the Politics of the Self*, Sage, Delhi, pp. 286–322.

Letizia, C. (2016), *Ideas of Secularism in Contemporary Nepal*, in D. N. Gellner, S. L. Hausner, C. Letizia (eds.), *Religion, Secularism, and Ethnicity in Contemporary Nepal*, Oxford University Press, Delhi, pp. 35–76.

Lipner, J. (2004), *On Hinduism and Hinduisms: The Way of the Banyan*, in S. Mittal, G. Thursby (eds.), *The Hindu World*, Routledge, London, pp. 21–46.

Mao, Z. (1940), *On New Democracy*, Foreign Language Press, Beijing.

Mishra, S. (1982), *Royal Coup 1960 in Nepal*, in "Proceedings of the Indian History Congress", 43, pp. 754–765. https://doi.org/10.1093/jaoac/43.3.754

Needham, A. D., Rajan, R. S. (eds.) (2008), *The Crisis of Secularism in India*, Duke University Press, Durham.

Onta, P. (1996), *Ambivalence Denied: The Making of Rastriya Itihas in Panchayat Era Textbooks*, in "Contributions to Nepalese Studies", 23, 1, pp. 213–254.

Perceval, L. (1928), *Nepal*, Constable & Company, London.

Petech, L. (1952), *I missionari Italiani nel Tibet e nel Nepal*, part 1 and 2, Libreria dello Stato, Roma.

Pettigrew, J. (2012), *Unexpected Consequences of Everyday Life during the Maoist Insurgency in Nepal*, in "Journal of International Women's Studies", 13, 4, pp. 100–112.
Pettigrew, J. (2013), *Maoists at the Hearth: Everyday Life in Nepal's Civil War*, University of Pennsylvania Press, Philadelphia.
Pradhan, U. (2019), *Simultaneous Identities: Ethnicity and Nationalism in Mother Tongue Education in Nepal*, in "Nations and Nationalism", 25, 2, pp. 718–738. https://doi.org/10.1111/nana.12463
Raeper, W., Hoftun, M. (1992), *Spring Awakening: An Account of the 1990 Revolution in Nepal*, Viking, New Delhi.
Rajasekhariah, A. (1987), *Jawaharlal Nehru's Contribution to Secularism in India – Am Estimate*, in "The Indian Journal of Political Science", 48, 2, pp. 212–224.
Regmi, D. R. (1961), *Modern Nepal*, K. L. Mukhopadhyay, Calcutta.
Shneiderman, S. (2015), *Rituals of Ethnicity: Thangmi Identities between Nepal and India*, University of Pennsylvania Press, Philadelphia.
Shrestha-Schipper, S. (2013), *The Political Context and the Influence of the People's War in Jumla*, in M. Lecomte-Tilouine (ed.), *Revolution in Nepal: An Anthropological and Historical Approach to the Peoples' War*, Oxford University Press, New Delhi, pp. 258–301.
Smith, D. E. (1963), *India as a Secular State*, Princeton University Press, Princeton.
Subba, T. B. (1999), *Politics of Culture: A Study of Three Kirata Communities in the Eastern Himalayas*, Orient Blackswan, Chennai.
Todd, J. (1950), *Annals and Antiquities of Rajasthan*, Routledge and Kegan Paul, London.
Torri, D. (2017), *Caring for Ancestral Heritage Away from Home: The Hyolmo Adivasi (Indigenous People) of Helambu in Kathmandu*, in "Material Religion", 13, 3, pp. 385–386. https://doi.org/10.1080/17432200.2017.1335087
Torri, D. (2019), *Religious Identities and the Struggle for Secularism: The Revival of Buddhism and Religions of Marginalized Groups in Nepal*, in "Entangled Religions", 8. https://doi.org/10.13154/er.8.2019.8355
Van Schendel, W. (2020), *A History of Bangladesh*, Cambridge University Press, Cambridge.
Whelpton, J. (2005), *A History of Nepal*, Cambridge University Press, Cambridge.

Chapter 4

Super-diverse Ancestors: Cemeterial Recollections as Practices of Coexistence in Rural Java

Roberto Rizzo

Abstract

In the present contribution, I propose to extend the working notion of super-diversity originally devised by Steven Vertovec to encompass socio-religious configurations which are typically at the analytical margins of super-diversity discussions. Existing research into phenomena of super-diversity has tended to limit itself to its manifestations within urban polities, most often in the frame of Euro-Atlantic nation-states or in emergent "global cities". By drawing on ethnographic examples from rural Java, namely the social and economic dynamics surrounding the revitalisation of *nyadran* cemetery rituals of communal ancestor remembrance, I suggest a different application of the super-diversity concept. Influenced by Buddhist return migrants from urban areas, revamped *nyadran* practices have brought about new ritual platforms in the countryside that not only converse with a complex religious landscape but make religious cohabitation (re)conceivable in a province increasingly burdened by interfaith frictions.

Keywords: super-diversity, Indonesia, Buddhism, inter-religiosity, ancestors

1 Introduction: (Religious) Super-diversity and its Other

Surjosari[1] is a village extending over a mountain slope in the craggy volcanic inland of Central Java. Equidistant from the province's two major cities, Yogyakarta to the south and Semarang on the north coast, the village is within the province breadbasket of Temanggung and agriculture constitutes the main occupation for virtually all its residents. A single unpaved east-west street divides two rows of houses built from brick and bamboo, while to the south a large field with a wooden pavilion opens up by way of a town square, and to the north cultivated plots of land dissolve imperceptibly into a thick forest inside which a rocky waterfall serves as the village's ceremonial water spring. When I first visited the area in 2016, the village lacked reliable mobile phone service and only one household owned a car. A family shop selling essentials (detergents, snacks, and cigarettes) was the only commercial establishment; other services, including schooling beyond the elementary level, were located at a distance of nearly one hour ride by motorbike.

At first glance, Surjosari and its surroundings appear to reflect essentialising tropes of a static, backward, and traditional "remote area"[2], at odds with the urban cosmopolitan framework in which processes of super-diversity are commonly understood to unfold. Nonetheless, Surjosari and Temanggung at large interact with patterns of contemporary globalised neoliberalism, sometimes at the margins, sometimes at the core, confronting quandaries of multi-directional mobility patterns and events that resonate with global religious flows. Such processes coalesce in emergent religious practices and are particularly evident in how residents approach an old-new local ritual tradition like *nyadran*. The re-valorisation of rituals of communal ancestor remembrance, along with the multiple motivations and symbolic associations brought by a diverse pool of participants, exemplifies religious super-diversity. Such innovation in the ritual sphere shows how religious super-diversity constitutes a pervasive sociocultural dynamic that also manifests in contexts typically underrepresented in academic discussions engaging the

---

1. The names of the smallest administrative units (villages and hamlets) have been anonymised, like the given names of the participants.
2. Ardener 2012.

concept, that is, contexts that are not immediately associated with processes of (sub)urbanisation or with emerging global cities.

When Steven Vertovec[3] coined the term super-diversity, he envisioned it as a working notion that could overcome the problems intrinsic to the concept of "diversity". In scholarly and political discourse, diversity is essentialised as ethnic and class divisions, a static interpretation which obscures dynamic processes by which identities and sociocultural formations shifted, mingled, and were negotiated. To advance a novel perspective on cultural complexity, Vertovec stipulated a thorough consideration of multiple "variables"[4] that must be accounted for when situating sociocultural phenomena. Intersecting positionalities of individuals and communities within power hierarchies of labour markets, age, and gender stratifications, patterns of sociospatial distribution – along with the nature of local legislative and policy responses – were significant variables that influenced specific super-diverse formations, according to how they intersected with one another. Though Vertovec's analysis concerned primarily migratory patterns in contemporary Britain, it has gained recognition as a salient framework applicable to a number of contexts and social dynamics[5].

Although Vertovec did not explore religion as a major "variable" in his seminal work, other scholars have expanded on his contribution to inquire into specifically religious phenomena[6]. Becci and Burchardt[7] identified two levels at which religion enters the frame of super-diversity. First, religion as a variable, in the meaning of Steven Vertovec, intersects and interacts with other variables such as status, occupation, ethnicity, age group, and gender, to produce super-diverse milieus. Second, the interaction and mutual constitution of different religious diversities (as discrete, reified units) are processes themselves giving rise to super-diversities. These two levels are obviously co-present and, more often than not, require simultaneous attention. As D'Amato[8] indicate, moreover, the interaction of religion and religious diversities with other ideological constructs is ever

3. Vertovec 2007, 2010.
4. See also Vertovec 2019.
5. Foner et al. 2019; Flores 2016.
6. Becci et al. 2017; Casanova 2016; Kivisto 2014.
7. Becci, Burchardt 2016.
8. D'Amato 2015.

more significant with religion becoming an increasingly fraught territory in many contexts worldwide.

The inclusion of religion in reflections over super-diversity is pivotal. However, many authors have concentrated predominantly on Euro-American host societies as the logical centre stage where the qualities that make religious super-diversity a distinct dimension (crossed with large-scale migration, complex identities, and questions of policy and power) could possibly come together[9]. Even those studies that have endeavoured to shift attention from the post-colonial West have nonetheless tended to situate super-diversity in its closest resemblance, the neoliberal global city[10]. These broad tendencies in super-diversity studies unwittingly reproduce polarities of the urban/rural, centre/periphery type[11] and assume complexity to unfold at the heart of production modes, policymaking, or corporate governance. The non-urban and non-Western are often relegated to the role of the "other" in discourses of super-diversity, in terms that engender closely a new incarnation of the nature/culture dichotomy[12].

Given the diffuse contemporary networks of neoliberal practices, multidirectional mobility patterns, and mediated imaginaries, it is helpful to extend our gaze to contexts that typically appear at the geographical and figurative margins of super-diversity studies. In this way, we may be able not only to better appreciate the fuller breadth of the super-diverse condition but also to inquire into the multiscalar processes of production of religious super-diversity. The rural Javanese context was famously described in Geertz's ethnography on Mojokuto[13] as a site in which diverse views were held around the subject of religious practice. Javanese villagers' religion resided in a tension between orthodox Islamic positions (*santri*) and various forms of intersection between Islam and Javanese traditional religion (*abangan*). These tensions further intersected with the religious orientation of the Javanese aristocracy (*priyayi*). Geertz's archetypal account might not be considered an instance of super-diversity proper, to the extent that he failed to acknowledge the concurrent emergence of alternative forms

9. Knowles 2013; van Dijk 2011.
10. As in the work of Van der Veer 2013 on Singapore and Mumbai.
11. See Agnew 2005 for a vivisection of these concepts; Giorda 2020 for a recent debate on these notions.
12. Vasantkumar 2017.
13. Geertz 1960.

of modern religious manifestations in rural areas (Buddhism, Christianity, Hinduism)[14], and that his narration lacked the historical specificities that should comprise a super-diverse dimension – large-scale economic and mobility flows, in other words, the "multiplication of social categories"[15]. Nevertheless, Geertz's ethnography remains a vivid illustration of the backdrop against which contemporary super-diverse dynamics are articulated in contexts like Temanggung.

My ethnographic case study (2017–2019) was undertaken in the central Javanese highland villages of Temanggung, with a special focus on *nyadran* rituals of communal ancestor remembrance. The data was collected as part of a larger study on the revival of Indonesian Buddhism in the Muslim-majority country. Although the area appears peripheral from the economic, social, and religious developments underway on the island, the relationships and the cultural dynamics that are engendered on the ground reveal an intense degree of interdependence. In some cases, Temanggung itself is the site in which sociocultural initiatives are produced that have an impact and media diffusion elsewhere. Religious initiatives like *nyadran* exemplify this phenomenon. At the same time, the idea of remoteness and seclusion functions for some subjects as a discursive device supporting a narrative of ethnocultural authenticity, with reference to Javanese lore and some dynamics of the Buddhist revival at large. After situating Temanggung as interacting with multi-levelled social and economic dynamics, I frame the reemergence of *nyadran* not as a linear cultural revival but as a super-diverse religious instance.

2 Mobility, Agro-politics, Religion: Temanggung's Super-diversity

In spite of being located in the geographical centre of Java, the administrative and cultural hub of contemporary Indonesia, the Temanggung highland regency has been largely unaffected by the intensive processes of industrialisation and infrastructural upgrades which have concerned the island in the past few decades. The regency is also one of the least

---

14. See Johnson 1961.
15. Wessendorf 2014.

densely populated[16] in an island that has been long singled out by policy planners as especially burdened with overpopulation[17].

The question of local demographic balance is significant given that the controversial *transmigrasi* program resulted in the relocation of entire segments of local populations across the archipelago, both within Java and from the island to the outer provinces[18]. Practices engineered by late-colonial and early post-colonial administrations further complexified and diversified local everyday sociocultural configurations in a region where internal migration had already been commonplace and thick with narratives for centuries[19]. Moreover, the choice of resettlement zones has been held responsible for interethnic violence in the host regions, frictions that were frequently triggered by religious discourses[20].

Temanggung was no stranger to these processes. A few valleys and slopes became abruptly depopulated when entire families were relocated to allotted farming districts in Sumatra or Borneo. Conversely, Temanggung was at other times a host region for resettlement of families from other areas of Java,[21] resulting in a highly diverse socio-religious makeup in the highland regency. Practices of government-instigated relocation constituted clear instances of internal migratory patterns that not only blurred boundaries between centres and peripheries but also formed the basis upon which more recent forms of multi-directional mobility started to overlap – for traditional forms of agricultural labour or new spheres of income, such as the development of leisure infrastructure in the frame of culture economy and ecotourism.

Additional threads embed Temanggung into the political and economic fabric of the country. From an economic and agricultural perspective, Temanggung is a crucial hub for two of the most important products of the national agro economy, the farming of coffee and tobacco. Tobacco is an especially vital good in the domestic industry, for the production of *kretek*

---

16. National centre for statistics (BPS) data for 2020: https://jateng.bps.go.id/indicator/12/766/1/jumlah-penduduk-menurut-kabupaten-kota-di-jawa-tengah.html (last accessed 24 March 2021).
17. Otten 1986.
18. Hoey 2003; Hardjono 1988.
19. Salazar 2016.
20. Recall König 2016; Barter, Côté 2015 for case studies.
21. Yuli Setyaningtyas 2008.

cigarette varieties, and Temanggung has been its primary source since it was identified as a particularly suitable area for large tobacco plantations in colonial times. The largest local industry in the sector, Sampoerna, has been acquired, moreover, by US-based Philip Morris International[22], which also runs the Sampoerna Museum opened in 2003 in the city of Surabaya. The area came to media visibility between 2012 and 2014 when local farmers and unions organised mass demonstrations against the low rates negotiated by Philip Morris corporation[23]. Demonstrations intensified in response to a bill proposed by the central government for curbing tobacco consumption in the country[24]. The protests effectively neutralised the bill, but tensions remained among unions, farmers, and the corporation.

Temanggung also made headlines for reasons more closely related to religion. On two occasions, in 2009 and 2018, the regency's administrative seat was the objective of terrorist acts attributed to religious radicalism. In the first case, members of the Jemaah Islamiyah group, a radical organisation formed in the late 1990s[25] and notorious for the deadly Bali bombings of 2002, were caught in the process of planning the assassination of then-president Susilo Bambang. More recently, in 2018, the anti-terror governmental body "Densus 88" raided a house in Temanggung in which three men allegedly affiliated with the transnational Islamic State, were suspected of planning to bomb the local police headquarters. All three men were arrested and were subsequently found to be linked to suicide attacks in Surabaya churches in the same year[26].

In 2011, Temanggung was the epicentre of another episode of social-religious friction. This occurred when controversial Protestant pastor Antonius Bawengan was reported to the police on the accusation of having disseminated booklets that alleged resemblances between the Kaaba's black stone and female genitalia, and between the three pillars of

---

22. Sampoerna's website: https://www.sampoerna.com/sampoerna/id/overview (last accessed 24 March 2021).
23. Sobary 2016.
24. Astuti, Freeman 2017.
25. Osman 2010.
26. *Tempo* report (in Indonesian): https://nasional.tempo.co/read/1056310/densus-88-tangkap-tiga-terduga-teroris-di-temanggung/full&view=ok (last accessed 24 March 2021).

Mina and male sexual organs. When in August the pastor was issued a five-year blasphemy sentence, mobs and riots flared up around Temanggung's administrative seat, organised by radical Muslim factions who had called for the death penalty[27]. Three churches were burned in the regency and police vans were set afire.

These episodes and wider social-economic processes convey a sense of the degree to which a region that is ostensibly secluded and externally constructed as a quintessentially timeless rural Java is in fact directly involved in dynamics that encompass it at the core of broad national and transnational trajectories. Temanggung is entrenched in the web of variables that produce a religious super-diverse condition. The next section explores how these dynamics manifest in the religious context of Surjosari village. The organisation of *nyadran* provides both a prism for the manifestation of religious super-diversity, and an instantiation of super-diversity as an opportunity for weaving peacebuilding and coexistence.

3   Religionisation and its Aftermath in Surjosari

Like other locations in Java, the demographic profile of Surjosari and the surrounding hamlets is a reflection of the specific events that over the course of the last century have produced religiously diverse locations on the island. Before the trend towards sectarianism was set nationwide, the religious life of Surjosari and of the region at large used to be characterised by a fluid combination of Islamic notions, dharmic references and a vast pool of localised Javanist traditional practices[28]. When the New

---

27. Human Rights Watch (in Indonesian): https://www.hrw.org/id/report/2013/02/28/256410 (last accessed 24 March 2021). Parts of the episode were also reported on international media, see New York Times: https://www.nytimes.com/2011/02/09/world/asia/09indonesia.html (last accessed 24 March 2021).
28. I refer to religious "Javanism" throughout this contribution in the sense of Hefner (1987). The term is used to identify the less articulate local religious tradition of Javanese communities in respect to both the official state religions and the movement known as *kejawen*. The latter is a religious orientation which, although stemming from the same ritual and cosmological premises as Javanism, is a more self-defined and consciously syncretic phenomenon in relation to other religious traditions such as Islam.

Order policy of mandatory religious affiliation was put in place in 1966[29], the choice of one distinct religion over another was perceived by many as a matter of mere bureaucracy and was largely left to the judgement of chiefs and local intellectuals. While scattered villages like Surjosari opted overwhelmingly for Buddhism due to the proximity of the then village head with spiritualist-revivalist groups[30], many others on the highlands "converted" to Islam or Christianity as their formal orientation. Diversity was thus produced and celebrated as a defining feature of national life. However, on all the sides of formal affiliation, Buddhist, Muslim, or Christian, actual adherence to a single religious orientation was extremely patchy.

The attunement towards a more or less orthodox understanding of a given national religion grew increasingly uneven as education, mobility, and status contributed multiple factors in super-diversifying religious practice "from within" given religious identities. In the case of Surjosari, at the time of my first visits to the village, the residents held very different orientations. Many villagers subscribed to the Buddhayana movement, a local ecumenic Buddhist school particularly active in the 1960s and 1970s that acknowledged a theistic rendering of Buddhism through the figure of *Adibuddha*[31], while others practised and affiliated exclusively in reference to global Theravada Buddhism. Linked to Thai and Burmese monastic lineages, the school had become popular in Indonesia after the 1980s and surged arguably as the largest denomination in the country ever since. In recent years, individual Theravada monks began to reside occasionally in Buddhist villages like Surjosari for stints such as the period of *vassa*[32].

29. The policy was intended to suppress atheism, which was thought to be the outpost of communism, by imposing a clear religious affiliation on all Indonesian citizens. The regime introduced the policy in the wake of the tragic 1965–1966 anti-communist killings.
30. Rizzo 2022.
31. See Brown 1987 for an early commentary on Buddhayana and Chia 2018 for a recent biographical work on its charismatic founder, Ven. Ashin Jinarakkhita.
32. A period of several weeks, traditionally occurring during the rainy season, in which monks are expected to retire in contemplation. According to the Pali canon, the practice was established by the Buddha Sakyamuni himself. To this day, in Theravada-majority countries the advancement of a monk is measured in number of vassa practiced during his ordained life.

However, many still would only loosely attend formal Buddhist devotional activities and were mostly concerned with the adherence to Javanist religious practices, such as the ritual offerings and individual meditations performed on given days of the lunisolar cycles of the Javanese calendar as well as the officiation of Javanist rites of passage. Such practices were not exclusive to Buddhists but formed a common pool of religious life that used to bring together residents from throughout the wider region irrespective of formal religious affiliation. However, according to the older villagers, such instances had become extremely rare nowadays, as there were different perspectives held on the perpetuation of Javanist forms of religiosity, especially as to whether they could be conciliated with religions such as Islam or Christianity but also in respect to more doctrinal forms of Buddhism.

The various orientations towards the conciliation of Buddhist devotion and affiliation with the practice of Javanism issued an extremely heterogeneous religious profile in the village of Surjosari. The biographies of Subagyo and Sura condense this form of super-diversity "from within". They are also crucial in conducting a variety of social-religious activism that led to the reformulation of *nyadran* rituals as religiously convivial situations. Subagyo and Sura were two young adults in their early thirties of fairly different backgrounds. They were both university graduates and had decided for distinct reasons to move back to the village after a period spent in major urban settings on the island.

Subagyo was not originally a Surjosari resident as he was born and raised in a province on the north coast. Although a Buddhist from birth, he attended a Christian school and later moved on to a college for Buddhist Studies in Jakarta, a branch of the larger educational network of Indonesian Theravada. After a short period in the touristic town and cultural hub of Yogyakarta, he relocated to the Surjosari countryside after marrying Metta, the daughter of a Surjosari-born farmer. Subagyo yearned for a career as a journalist and his main occupation over my stay in the village was to write for a country-wide Buddhist magazine. His house in the village had also become his office and a library, both of which gave him some degree of reputation as a knowledgeable person in Buddhist affairs. He actively worked for organising social events in the village, involving in differentiated ways the youth and the elderly, with a set of activities that ranged from outdoor Sunday excursions to informal evening gatherings.

In all cases, Subagyo tried to constantly draw in elements of Buddhist devotion in the sociality thus created. Excursions with adolescents revolved around getting to know the region's Buddhist temples or visiting sites that were perceived as crucial in the foundation of contemporary Buddhism in the mid-20th century, while home gatherings were accompanied by sessions of communal Buddhist worship or meditation. With a rich network of contacts in religious and lay environments established along with his mobility, Subagyo managed to forge the *Pemuda Buddhis* organisation (the "Buddhist youth") and make it visible via mutual visits with youth organisations based elsewhere and chains of social media posting.

A couple of years younger, Sura was born in a hamlet right outside of the confines of Surjosari to a family of tobacco farmers. While his parents' household was still the place where he ordinarily lived, he had meanwhile completed undergraduate studies in Economy in the city Semarang, the provincial capital, to which he still commonly commuted whenever there was a small job or an event in which he wished to partake. Recently, Sura had also spent a few months as a *samanera*, a temporary monk, and resided for a while in a monastery near Yogyakarta. With his father's help, he had begun not long before I met him to invest time and energy in the emerging coffee industry. Over the time of my stay in the area, the business around coffee beans was a buzz-topic in the Temanggung regency, as coffee had become a booming domestic industry nationwide[33].

Aside from being already the regency with the highest rate of land allocated to coffee plantations in Java[34], in 2016 the region acquired from the General Directorate for Intellectual Property a certificate of Geographical Indication for the local varieties of the bean, the Temanggung Robusta crop and the Sindoro-Sumbing Arabica coffee, with all the economic

---

33. 2018 Ministerial report: https://www.bps.go.id/publication/2019/12/06/b5e163624c20870bb3d6443a/statistik-kopi-indonesia-2018.html (last accessed 24 March 2021).
34. Table of land allotment in the province of Central Java, 2018 data (see also Febriharjati 2015): https://jateng.bps.go.id/statictable/2019/10/16/1768/produksi-tanaman-perkebunan-menurut-kabupaten-kota-dan-jenis-tanaman-di-provinsi-jawa-tengah-ton-2018.html (last accessed 24 March 2021).

benefits that would come with it, once a set of requirements was met on the farming site. When I visited Sura at home, transactions of bags of both green and roasted coffee beans seemed to be constantly going on in the living room and piles of transparent plastic bags of unsorted beans dotted the entire house. One of the reasons why he decided to be based again in the village, confessed Sura, was precisely the strategic position of the area for the island-wide "coffee scene". Not only was he trying to implement the know-how necessary to upgrade his crop with the view of meeting the certification standards, but he intended also to open in the village a café of the trendy and leafy kind that have mushroomed all over the country in the previous years[35].

Subagyo and Sura had been religiously socialised in distinct ways. Sura had been widely exposed to the Javanist religious tradition, via his family and neighbourhood, but also through the traditional music ensemble in which he occasionally played[36]. His involvement in projects relating to Javanese ethnocultural revitalisation was of a pragmatic nature: he intended to hunt for possibly relevant heritage sites buried or neglected in the region for enhancing the tourist potential of the area. However, he was also consistently exposed to Theravada Buddhism. He routinely attended meditation initiatives in Semarang, his period as a temporary *samanera* was undertaken under the supervision of a Theravada monastery and he often guided meditation sessions at the temple in Surjosari. Subagyo had instead a more erudite approach towards Buddhism and was discontinuously acquainted with local Javanism, although his views related to Javanese ethnocultural stances were of a larger breadth. He was a firm believer in prophecies according to which Java was about to return to its former truer cultural-religious self after a 500-year hiatus[37] and he took on the task of preserving Javanese culture as a personal ethical exercise, starting from his everyday attire. His activism through the *Pemuda Buddhis* youth organisation was also in the frame of "preserving and advancing" Buddhism as an expression of a truer Javanese identity.

35. In late 2020, in the mid of the Covid pandemic, the café of Sura had become reality, a couple of kilometres south from the village.
36. Gamelan or *karawitan* music groups are often artistic environment in which young people become acquainted with Javanist notions and practices (Rizzo 2020; Weiss 2006).
37. Pemberton 1994.

The organisation of communal *nyadran* ceremonies coordinated by the Buddhist youth organisation, through the particular activism of Subagyo and Sura, stems from the combination of visions around Javanism as a religious and ethnocultural facet that served a multiplicity of purposes. *Nyadran* was an especially fecund ritual field to mobilise for it was at once a renowned practice and a symbolically indeterminate religious platform for the ambiguity of the cosmologies that participants could draw in.

4   *Nyadran* Ancestor Remembrance: The Reformulation of a Waning Tradition

Rituals of ancestor remembrance have been present in Java for centuries and have crisscrossed formal religious affiliations. Collectively known by the umbrella term *nyadran* (or *sadran*[38]), these ritual traditions are only loosely related to one another. Substantial differences are there not only in terms of their outward scope or supposed historical genealogy but also in the calendrical and cosmological connections they establish, as well as in the choice of the location deemed appropriate for their performance. Broadly speaking, *nyadran* might be used to refer to a short individual prayer in Javanese uttered over a relative's grave, after a Qur'anic recitation, as well as a large communal feast performed in the memory of a more general class of "deceased" or "ancestors" often formulated through village founding myths that involve the deeds of one or more ancestors (*nenek moyang*). Conversely, collective ritual acts rich in offerings could also be dedicated to a specific departed, just like single individuals could claim to perform prayers or meditations invoking more abstracted interlocutors. A private home, cemeteries, uninhabited slopes or the southern shore of the island are all possible settings found across the *nyadran* spectrum in Java. In this broader frame, *nyadran* might be simply understood to describe all forms of funerary rituals that do not fall directly into the eschatological repertoire of the formal national religions and stand in varying relationships with these. In the Temanggung regency alone, *nyadran* rituals could manifest in very different ceremonies, occurring at

---

38. See Zoetmulder (1974) for an etymology of the term and Nugroho (2015) for an ethnograhy in East Java.

different time intervals and more or less tied, in morphology and calendar, to a formal religion – predominantly Islam.

The organisation of a collective *nyadran* ceremony is overall rather complex as it needs to intersect the two main calendrical cycles (Gregorian and Javanese), to which the Islamic one is typically added, but it also takes into account the astronomical prediction of the approximate start and conclusion of the yearly rainy season. The diversity in calculations between villages or clusters of villages makes it possible to participate in multiple communal *nyadrans*. This is done oftentimes, not only because the farmers of the area establish forms of kinship and other kinds of intra-regional connections, but also because the ancestors conjured in the ritual could refer to various sociological and territorial units – a family, a village, a slope or the entire regency. In my visit to the village in 2017, I counted five *nyadran* organised on the slope around Surjosari in the period between March and early May alone.

Overall, the sequence of an average *nyadran* in the Surjosari area maintains major resemblances to a regular Javanese ritual feast performed for various rites of passage, from circumcisions to home inaugurations and anniversaries[39]. The feast is loaded with symbols and numerologies, with particular attention to the number and types of food items involved. For *nyadran*, the culinary requirements are less fixed than they are for other types of feasts. A white cone of steamed rice laid on banana leaves is the minimum that every participating household is expected to bring along. In addition, the participants can bring various baskets of cooked meats and tofu and one of coconut sweets and fresh fruit. All food other than rice is supposed to be shared with fellow participants. Like other types of ritual feasts, food is never eaten in its entirety, but considerable quantities are intentionally left, repacked and consumed later at home or, less frequently, offered to the spirits of the ancestors in individualised fashions. Before and after the feast the participants engage in prayers and meditations which can be uttered in unison or performed in small groups.

Like other forms of Javanist rituality, however, communal cemetery *nyadrans* were waning. Several domestic currents of Islam have been vocal in warning Muslims against the danger of performing rituals and

---

39. Both Geertz (1960) and Beatty (1999) have paid extensive attention to the history and symbolisms of communal feasts, known as slametan.

customary traditions of dubious provenance. Debates over the appropriateness and the extent to which embracing (upon careful theological examination) or abandoning a given ritual have become common currency in recent decades and have touched upon funerary rituals too[40]. While in some cases communities have continued to carry out the practice under the banner of "culture" and not religion, communal events that included fellow residents or neighbours who were known to affiliate with religions other than Islam had become extremely rare.

In the wider Surjosari area, cemetery *nyadran*s had never completely disappeared, but their attendance had considerably shrunk according to the accounts of one of the village elders with whom I interacted the most, Rahayu (72). The first time I witnessed a communal *nyadran* in 2017 in the area's graveyard, located a couple of kilometres downhill from the village, the ritual was attended by about seventy people, which gave the impression of a "large enough" event, especially by the standards of a relatively small village. However, according to Rahayu, only a small number of the participants were of non-Buddhist background. This was sharply different from the kind of *nyadran*s he was used to as a young man, when rituals of this scale were even larger and, most importantly, attended by residents from the surrounding hamlets regardless of their formal affiliation. Beginning from the 1970s, Rahayu expressed a feeling of overall decline, not only in the relevance of *nyadran*s, but in the sociality of village life in general. He recollected how the different religions crystallised around the area had resulted in several episodes of friction. Some of them were obvious, from the terrorist cells to the mobs and riots against the region's Christian churches. Other forms of friction were more subtle, such as the province's taxation system on land ownership, calculated in differing proportions for Muslims and non-Muslims. The implementation of these policies depended oftentimes on the individual orientation of the appointed regional chiefs, but they had triggered over the years various episodes of "economic conversion" into Islam, especially among the poorer farmers. In a similar vein, obtaining a permit for building places of worship other than mosques had become increasingly

---

40. See Burhanuddin, van Dijk (2013). Cfr. a discussion over *nyadran* on a Qur'anic platform (in Indonesian): https://konsultasisyariah.com/18762-tradisi-nyadran-dan-bersih-desa-sebelum-ramadhan.html (last accessed 24 March 2021).

complicated, since a nationwide bill was passed that made it obligatory, before constructing a worship house, to obtain express agreements to the construction of all the surrounding households. For Rahayu, this was detrimental to all the minority faiths in a given region and raised underlying tensions along religious lines among the residents.

The perception of religious-cultural decline, suggested by the accounts of Rahayu but that resonated also in the activities of *Pemuda Buddhis* youth militants, formed the backdrop of the expectations surrounding the 2019 edition of communal *nyadran*. Although organised as a positive instance of interreligious communion, the revamping of social *nyadran* could not be abstracted from the intent of the youth militants to enhance their visibility and attractiveness towards the area's minority Buddhist community. That is, the motives of participants were themselves super-diverse from the start.

5 "Nyadran Perdamaian": Religious Super-diversity through the Lens of Culture

Subagyo prepared the ground for the launching of *nyadran* as a social, cultural and interreligious event already the previous year, upon the regular occurrence of the ancestor remembrance gathering in the cemetery of the Surjosari slope. On that occasion, he equipped himself with state-of-the-art cameras and, together with a couple of other activists, he captured the sequences of the ritual for Facebook and Instagram posts and content in the form of online articles and blog entries. When the calendrical calculations for the 2019 ritual were completed, the *Pemuda Buddhis* group began to put together ideas and side-events for what was essentially devised as a cultural festival. Although the main *nyadran* ceremony was to be held on a Friday, the activists decided to organise an extended three-day festival, filled with side events, lectures, and concerts.

Thanks to thick networks of personal acquaintances, Subagyo and Sura managed to reach out to people and organisations well outside the Temanggung region, ranging from Buddhist religious associations to academics and personalities from the entertainment industry. The format of the festival allowed for a live-in option, for a fee of 100.000 IDR (approximately 6 Euros), which would enable the participant to experience authentic "local culture" from the inside. However, sensing that the main event of the festival, the actual *nyadran*, might turn out locally to continue the trend established in previous years – that is, to be attended predominantly by the Buddhist minority of the district, Subagyo made sure to actively involve the local Muslim population. Weeks before the festival, he paid visits to his Muslim acquaintances and friends in the villages around the slope to personally notify them about the initiative and sensitise them about the relevance of reviving traditional practices in general.

Figure 4.1: Digital poster advertising *nyadran* 2019 (Photo by Author).

Attended by a few hundred participants, some overnighting in the area and others joining only for individual events, the broader festival was indeed a showcase of Javanese aesthetic and performative features.

Nevertheless, Buddhism always lay just below the surface of the ethno-cultural vocabulary. A group of Buddhist monks joined the event from the city of Semarang, while one of the main workshops was a lesson in Theravadin meditation open to all, arranged on a wooden platform in the forest uphill from Surjosari. References to Buddhism linked to the perceived authenticity of the area's lifestyle dotted all the speeches. An archaeologist from Yogyakarta University lectured on temple epigraphy, while a French writer residing in Java recounted her interest in classical Hindu-Buddhist court literature and praised the farmers' lifestyle of the area as an example of a "living Borobudur", referring to the large tenth-century Buddhist heritage complex in Central Java.

Despite the ubiquitous references to Buddhism as a form of "authentic" religious identity inherently closer to tradition, the format of the festival was designed as patently interfaith and devoted to the coexistence between the different religious affiliations of the district. The name itself was *Nyadran Perdamaian* (the *nyadran* of "peace" or "reconciliation") and all of the advertising material was prepared in such a way so as to underscore these values over references to single religions.

The sequence of the *nyadran* ritual on that Friday was remarkably successful in balancing out the different religious orientations of the participants. Animated by a cheerful atmosphere, with *dangdut* music[41] from loudspeakers and children playing with balloons of cartoon characters, the ceremony proper was held as usual by the cemetery outside of Surjosari. The event was inaugurated by a speech at the microphone from one of Surjosari's elders, who happened to be also Subagyo's father-in-law, while the participants aligned on the ground in two rows facing each other. Between them, a few blue plastic runners were positioned, for the opening of the food baskets later in the ceremonial feast. Farther from the "centre", that is, where the microphone station was set, the crowd grew less orderly and as the runner reached the gates of the graveyard the participants would simply stand and look on. During the speech, the sitting crowd took out the first set of dishes carried from home, consisting of snacks and fruit, although they were left untouched.

---

41. A popular pan-Indonesian music genre that fuses Western-style pop-rock with Bollywood and Arabic influences (Weintraub 2010).

After the introductory speech, a discourse in mixed Indonesian and Javanese on the values of community and solidarity, a different resident came to the microphone to recite the *tahlil* in Arabic. The audience fell silent and all those present undertook the actual act of recollection, which was thoroughly interiorised and individual. Many murmured the *tahlil* while taking on the characteristic Javanist posture for meditation, cross-legged and arms crossed inward. After a few moments of absolute silence, the atmosphere returned festive and the feast began, following the typical progression: the first portion of the food was quickly consumed, offered to the neighbouring participant, and the rest immediately repacked. After that, banana leaves were laid on the runner and the second set of food was taken out of the basket and laid on top of it. A line of cones of white rice now appeared between the two rows of the audience, each surrounded by a few plates with meats, tofu and vegetables brought by the individual households. Before the second part of the feast, another moment of prayer and introspection was introduced from the microphone. This time the Pali-Buddhist *namaskara* recitation[42] was declaimed, whispered not only by the Buddhist portion of the audience but also by some of the people who a few minutes before had chanted the Islamic *tahlil*. The feast was once again frugal and the leftovers repacked for later consumption at home. The ritual process at the cemetery was therefore concluded, although the crowd lingered a while longer for group photos, mutual greetings, and casual chats.

The cross-religious recitations during the core of the *nyadran* ceremony, in some cases overlapping in the same individuals, were telling of the sheer set of connections that were articulated through the public instauration of the ancestors, as well as of the different representations and intentions that individuals brought to their inward recollections. According to the opening speech, the ceremony was meant to remind those assembled of the spiritual and social significance of *nyadran* at large and to address the importance of establishing a tight community regardless of formal religious affiliation through respect and homage towards Javanese tradition. The ritual was dedicated therefore officially to "our ancestors" (*leluhur*), in an intentionally abstracted fashion. Actual

---

42. The recitation involves taking the refuge in the Buddha, the dharma, and the *sangha* (the community).

individual commemorations, however, went into more specific tracks. Several of the participating residents recognised the occasion as an offering to the *nenek moyang* of the administrative unit – Surjosari or a neighbouring village, depending on their place of residence. For Sura, instead, this was an opportunity to reconnect with the "founding forefathers" of Java at large. Some others still invested *nenek moyang* with a more immediate kind of relation, such as the recollection of Agus.

Agus was a man in his fifties, and he had come all the way from the southern city of Yogyakarta to take part in the ceremony. Although he was aware that the practice of *nyadran* was formally still carried out in the area, he had decided to participate this year for the first time only after he heard about it through a social media page. A Muslim, Agus was born in the hamlet closest to Surjosari and had moved to the Yogyakarta region in his late teens, before taking a job in the state bureaucracy. Although his parents had already passed away and he only rarely came back to his birthplace, he never lost the awareness of "where his *nenek moyang* was set". The point of the event, he informed me right after the feast, was to pay homage to one's family members who were in some way also perceived to be genealogically connected to the ancestors of the village. He acknowledged the existence of a strong continuing "glue" that subsisted through physical distance and even in ontological distance, after death. "Many believe that with bodily death that relationship is cut forever, but 'we' recognise that the lymph (*getah*) between us and our ancestors keeps flowing after death". The moment of the recollection during the ceremony was so emotional for him, that he couldn't help but shed a few tears upon drifting back to the following stages of the ritual.

Like Agus, Sumarsono had family roots in the Surjosari countryside, although that very *nyadran* ceremony was the first occasion he had to visit the area. He was a Buddhist and lived in a city in West Java, where he also occasionally volunteered as a *manggalia*, a trained lay minister in temple service. Sumarsono was not sure of the pragmatic requirements of ritual feasts since he spent his entire life in a region where such practices were only seldom seen and therefore decided to participate at the fringes of the congregation, without food offerings. He nonetheless followed the recollection earnestly and he meditated on the *nenek moyang* as "spiritual beings" to which he sent energies of loving-kindness, framing it as an ethical practice of bodhicitta, the dedication of one's (Buddhist) moral discipline for the benefit of all sentient beings, including to invisible and less defined manifestations like *nenek moyang*.

Those who had joined the festival without personal or familial connections to the Surjosari area, many of whom were university students from Java's main cities, did not participate in the feast but tried nonetheless to commune with some understanding of ancestry. Acts of remembrance were in these cases of the most varied sort and ranged from Catholic prayers in Indonesian, to one's deceased relatives, to whispered mantras in Javanese, uttered as offerings in themselves to the forefather of the region. Fadil, a B. A. student from Jakarta, was instead one of the few who knowingly decided not to participate to the moment of recollection, as he feared the danger of communicating or, possibly, miscommunicating with the *djinn*s, the generic Islamic referent for spiritual beings.

The *nyadran* festival turned out overall successfully according to the expectations of the *Pemuda Buddhis* activists. Those who participated in the live-in format were invited by Subagyo to submit a short text to him on their experience and he exhorted them to share social media visual content about the festival – something that Subagyo himself did extensively in the following days. The festival managed to mobilise an unprecedented number of both locals and visitors and could be considered in many respects a showcase of the religious, aesthetic, and environmental life of the Surjosari country, something that also worked indirectly in the direction of establishing a strand of local eco- and cultural tourism in the area. This was a tacit side of the organisation of the festival that would recur more intensively in the months to come. The festival in fact triggered a sense of optimism among the residents so that Subagyo and the activists did not hesitate to propose the organisation of two additional cultural events revolving around the Surjosari area within the same year. The trend increased the mediatic appeal of the village and was only restrained by the spread of the Covid pandemic of 2020, a situation that nevertheless did not prevent the activists and residents from organising a new edition of *Nyadran Perdamaian*.

6 Ancestors, Peacebuilding, and the Super-diverse Countryside

The account of the 2019 *Nyadran Perdamaian* and the perspectives of some of the participants emphasise the formation of a religious super-diverse platform. As I have suggested, this form of super-diversity is produced by a multiplicity of variables that coalesce in the reformulation of the ritual of ancestor remembrance in a distinctly super-diverse direction. The village in which the initiative originated, Surjosari, displayed upstream the characteristics of super-diversity. Albeit overwhelmingly Buddhist in its formal affiliations, the villagers held a multiplicity of orientations within Buddhism and in respect to local Javanist devotional traditions. This variety was produced by the workings and the crossings of several variables, in the sense of Vertovec[43]. Such variables were instantiated in the case of Surjosari and the Temanggung regency at large by the positioning of individuals and communities on the grid of the labour market, agro-politics, and macro-economic processes. Exposure to higher educational institutions and, especially, the shifting dynamics of internal mobility contribute additional components of complexity.

The experiences of Sura and Subagyo show how the countryside is not only the site from which individuals are drawn univocally to the benefits of urbanisation. Instead, their perspectives underscore an angle of internal migration which is rather overlooked when it comes to Asian patterns of mobility, which are often understood as occurring unidirectionally and irreversibly[44]. The diffused nature of neoliberal modes of production and the appeal of new forms of profit, including the surge of leisure economy based on cultural or ecological principles blur any definite divide in internal migratory patterns. In Indonesia, this process is also driven by specific mass-mediatic constructions of attractive village lore and lifestyles[45] and the impact of welfare policies and ageing, as underscored by a growing body of regional literature on ageing[46].

Both a cultural festival in its extended frame and a specific religious occurrence, *Nyadran Perdamaian* highlighted the establishment of a

---

43. Ibid., p. 2.
44. Goebel 2017; Hugo 1982, 2015; Suryadinata et al. 2003; Vidyattama 2016.
45. Farré, Fasani 2013.
46. Kreager, Schröder-Butterfill 2015.

distinct super-diverse dimension in the Javanese countryside on multiple levels. Remembrance of the ancestors as a shared religious space was joined by individuals and families with multiple religious and sociological configurations. These included mostly men and women from the wider area around Surjosari who subscribed to different formal religions (Islam, Buddhism, Christianity) and various degrees of engagement towards traditional Javanism, but also individuals who participated in the ritual from other regions, either for kinship connections or out of sheer culturalist sentiments or curiosity.

The super-diversity arising from the multiple demographic and religious profiles of those who participated in the *nyadran* recollection generated also a multifaceted makeup in the ontology attributed to the summoned ancestors. While many approached *nenek moyang* as the specific genealogical ancestor of one's family or one's wider community, others brought it to the pool of more abstracted spiritual agencies, including that of *djinn*s, or approached it as simple repository of "Javaneseness". Regardless of these different understandings, the recollection of ancestors constituted an instance of religious coexistence and reconciliation in a region marked with overt and underlying patterns of friction mobilised on religious grounds. In this sense, it is one of the possible dimensions through which reified religious thresholds can be "crossed"[47].

From the perspective of religious super-diversity, Surjosari's *nyadran* signals the productivity of the concept, once it is dissected in the traits that compose its complexity, as indicated by Burchardt and Becci[48]. Phenomena of religious super-diversity may reveal in this way the processes of mutual reverberation that subsist with special intensity in the current neo-liberal landscape between rurality and urbanity, within and beyond Western-metropolitan scenes. Like in major world cities, the countryside is not immune to super-diversity induced instances of religious conflict, nor is it indifferent to positive efforts of peacebuilding and religious coexistence.

---

47. Albera, Couroucli 2009.
48. Ibid., p. 3.

Author Biography

Roberto Rizzo is a Robert H. N. Ho fellow at the American Council of Learned Societies. He obtained his PhD from the University of Milan – Bicocca and has collaborated with various institutions in Europe and in Southeast Asia. His research focuses predominantly on Buddhist revivalism in Indonesia and broader inter-religious dynamics in Java and Sulawesi.

References

Agnew, J. (2005), *Space: Place*, in P. Cloke, R. Johnston (eds.), *Spaces of Geographical Thought: Deconstructing Human Geography's Binaries*, Sage, New York, pp. 81–96.

Albera, D., Couroucli, M. (2009), *Religions traversées: Lieux saints partagés entre chrétiens, musulmans et juifs en Méditerranée*, Actes Sud, Arles.

Ardener, E. (2012), *"Remote Areas": Some Theoretical Considerations*, in "HAU: Journal of Ethnographic Theory", 2, 1, pp. 519–533. https://doi.org/10.14318/hau2.1.023

Astuti, P. A. S., Freeman, B. (2017), *"It is Merely a Paper Tiger": Battle for Increased Tobacco Advertising Regulation in Indonesia: Content Analysis of News Articles*, in "BMJ Open", 7, 9, pp. 1–9. https://doi.org/10.1136/bmjopen-2017-016975

Barter, S. J., Côté, I. (2015), *Strife of the Soil? Unsettling Transmigrant Conflicts in Indonesia*, in "Journal of Southeast Asian Studies", 46, 1, pp. 60–85. https://doi.org/10.1017/S0022463414000617

Beatty, A. (1999), *Varieties of Javanese Religion: An Anthropological Account*, Cambridge University Press, Cambridge.

Becci, I., Burchardt, M., (2016), *Religion and Superdiversity: An Introduction*, in "New Diversities", 18, 1, pp. 1–7.

Becci, I., Burchardt, M., Giorda, M. (2017), *Religious Super-diversity and Spatial Strategies in two European Cities*, in "Current Sociology", 65, 1, pp. 73–91. https://doi.org/10.1177/0011392116632030

Brown, I. (1987), *Contemporary Indonesian Buddhism and Monotheism*, in "Journal of Southeast Asian Studies", 18, 1, pp. 108–117. https://doi.org/10.1017/S0022463400001284

Burhanuddin, J., Dijk, C. van (eds.) (2013), *Islam in Indonesia: Contrasting Images and Interpretations*, Amsterdam University Press, Amsterdam.

Casanova, J. (2016), *Religious Associations, Religious Innovations and Denominational Identities in Contemporary Global Cities*, in I. Becci, M.

Burchardt, J. Casanova, *Topographies of Faith: Religion in Urban Spaces*, Brill, Leiden-Boston, pp. 113–127.

Chia, J. M.-T. (2018), *Neither Mahāyāna nor Theravāda: Ashin Jinarakkhita and the Indonesian Buddhayāna Movement*, in "History of Religions", 58, 1, pp. 24–63. https://doi.org/10.1086/697932

D'Amato, G. (2015), *How Foreigners Became Muslims: Switzerland's Path to Accommodating Islam as a New Religion*, in M. Burchardt, I. Michalowski (eds.), *After Integration*, Springer Fachmedien, Wiesbaden, pp. 285–301.

Farré, L., Fasani, F. (2013), *Media Exposure and Internal Migration: Evidence from Indonesia*, in "Journal of Development Economics", 102, pp. 48–61. https://doi.org/10.1016/j.jdeveco.2012.11.001

Febriharjati, S. (2015), *Keberlanjutan Penghidupan Petani Kopi Desa Tlahab, Kecamatan Kledung, Kabupaten Temanggung*, in "Jurnal Teknik PWK", 4, pp. 4–17.

Flores, N. (2016), *Introduction: US Perspectives on Superdiversity and Schooling*, in "International Journal of the Sociology of Language", 241, pp. 1–7. https://doi.org/10.1515/ijsl-2016-0020

Geertz, C. (1960), *The Religion of Java*, University of Chicago Press, Chicago.

Giorda, M. (2020), *Territories, Spaces and Religious Places*, in "Metamorfosi – Quaderni Di Architettura", 8, pp. 20–27.

Goebel, Z. (2017), *Superdiversity from Within: The Case of Ethnicity in Indonesia*, in K. Arnaut, J. Blommaert, M. S. Karrebk, M. Spotti (eds.), *Engaging Superdiversity: Recombining Spaces, Times and Language Practices*, Multilingual Matters, Bristol, pp. 251–276.

Foner, N., Duyvendak, J. W., Kasinitz, P. (2019), *Introduction: Super-diversity in Everyday Life*, in "Ethnic and Racial Studies", 42, 1, pp. 1–16.

Hardjono, J. (1988), *The Indonesian Transmigration Program in Historical Perspective*, in "International Migration", 26, 4, pp. 427–439. https://doi.org/10.1111/j.1468-2435.1988.tb00662.x

Hefner, R. W. (1987), *Islamizing Java? Religion and Politics in Rural East Java*, in "Journal of Asian Studies", 46, 3, pp. 533–554. https://doi.org/10.2307/2056898

Hoey, B. A. (2003), *Nationalism in Indonesia: Building Imagined and Intentional Communities through Transmigration*, in "Ethnology", 42, 2, pp. 109–126. https://doi.org/10.2307/3773777

Hugo, G. (2015), *Demography of Race and Ethnicity in Indonesia*, in R. Sáenz, D. G. Embrick, N. P. Rodríguez (eds.), *The International Handbook of the Demography of Race and Ethnicity*, Springer, Heidelberg, pp. 259–280.

Hugo, G. J. (1982), *Circular Migration in Indonesia* in "Population and Development Review", 8, pp. 1–59. https://doi.org/10.2307/1972690

Johnson, H. (1961), *Review: The Religion of Java, by Clifford Geertz*, in "Journal for the Scientific Study of Religion", 1, 1, pp. 138–140. https://doi.org/10.2307/1385195

Kivisto, P. (2014), *Religion and Immigration: Migrant Faiths in North America and Western Europe*, Polity Press, Cambridge.

Knowles, C. (2013), *Nigerian London: Re-mapping Space and Ethnicity in Superdiverse Cities*, in "Ethnic and Racial Studies", 36, 4, pp. 651–669. https://doi.org/10.1080/01419870.2012.678874

König, A. (2016), *Identity Constructions and Dayak Ethnic Strife in West Kalimantan, Indonesia*, in "The Asia Pacific Journal of Anthropology", 17, 2, pp. 121–137. https://doi.org/10.1080/14442213.2016.1146917

Kreager, P., Schröder-Butterfill, E. (2015), *Differential Impacts of Migration on the Family Networks of Older People in Indonesia: A Comparative Analysis*, in L. A. Hoang, B. S. A. Yeoh (eds.), *Transnational Labour Migration, Remittances and the Changing Family in Asia*, Palgrave Macmillan, London, pp. 165–193.

Nugroho, B. S. (2015), *Tradisi upacara nyadran di desa Sonoageng, Kecamatan Prambon, Kabupaten Nganjuk tahun 1994–2014*, Universitas Jember, Jember.

Osman, S. (2010), *Jemaah Islamiyah: Of Kin and Kind*, in "Journal of Current Southeast Asian Affairs", 29, 2, pp. 157–175. https://doi.org/10.1177/186810341002900205

Otten, M. (1986), *Transmigrasi: Indonesian Resettlement Policy, 1965–1985*, International Work Group for Indigenous Affairs.

Pemberton, J. (1994), *On the Subject of "Java"*, Cornell University Press, Ithaca (NY).

Rizzo, R. (2020), *Knowledge Transmission in Javanese Karawitan: Is It Time for an Ontological Turn?*, in "Asian Music", 51, 1, pp. 94–117. https://doi.org/10.1353/amu.2020.0004

Rizzo, R. (2022), *Lithic Devotionality and other Aesthetic Strata: Buddhist Garden Shrines in Rural Java*, in "Asian Anthropology", 21, 4, pp. 283–300. https://doi.org/10.1080/1683478X.2022.2122686

Salazar, N. (2016), *The (Im)Mobility of Merantau as a Sociocultural Practice in Indonesia*, in N. G. Bon, J. Repič (eds.), *Moving Places: Relations, Return and Belonging*, Berghahn Books, Oxford and New York, pp. 21–42.

Sobary, M. (2016), *Perlawanan politik & puitik petani tembakau Temanggung*, Kepustakaan Populer Gramedia, Jakarta.

Suryadinata, L., Nurvidya Arifin, E., Ananta, A. (2003), *Indonesia's Population: Ethnicity and Religion in a Changing Political Landscape*, ISEAS Publishing, Singapore.

van der Veer, P. (2013), *Urban Aspirations in Mumbai and Singapore*, in I. Becci, M. Burchardt, J. Casanova, *Topographies of Faith: Religion in Urban Spaces*, Brill, Leiden-Boston, pp. 61–71.

van Dijk, R. (2011), *Cities and the Social Construction of Hot Spots: Rescaling, Ghanaian Migrants, and the Fragmentation of Urban Spaces*, in N. Glick Schiller, A. Çağlar (eds.), *Locating Migration*, Cornell University Press, Ithaca, pp. 104–122.

Vasantkumar, C. (2017), *From World Cities to World Sites: Strategic Ruralism and the Case for an Anthropology of Actually Existing Connectivity*, in "Critique of Anthropology", 37, 4, pp. 364–382. https://doi.org/10.1177/0308275X17735370

Vertovec, S. (2007), *Super-diversity and its Implications*, in "Ethnic and Racial Studies", 30, 6, pp. 1024–1054. https://doi.org/10.1080/01419870701599465

Vertovec, S. (2010), *Towards Post-multiculturalism? Changing Communities, Conditions and Contexts of Diversity: Towards Post-multiculturalism*, in "International Social Science Journal", 61, 199, pp. 83–95. https://doi.org/10.1111/j.1468-2451.2010.01749.x

Vertovec, S. (2019), *Talking around Super-diversity*, in "Ethnic and Racial Studies", 42, 1, pp. 125–139. https://doi.org/10.1080/01419870.2017.1406128

Vidyattama, Y. (2016), *Inter-provincial Migration and 1975–2005 Regional Growth in Indonesia: Vidyattama Internal Migration and Growth in Indonesia*, in "Papers in Regional Science", 95, pp. 87–105.

Weintraub, A. N. (2010), *Dangdut Stories: A Social and Musical History of Indonesia's Most Popular Music*, Oxford University Press, Oxford.

Weiss, S. (2006), *Listening to an Earlier Java: Aesthetics, Gender, and the Music of Wayang in Central Java*. KITLV Press, Netherlands.

Wessendorf, S. (2014), *Commonplace Diversity: Social Relations in a Super-diverse Context*, Palgrave Macmillan, Basingstoke.

Yuli Setyaningtyas, B. (2008), *Evaluasi Pelaksanaan Program Transmigrasi Melalui Model Kerjasama Antar Daerah*, Universitas Diponegoro, Semarang.

Zoetmulder, P. J. (1974), *Kalangwan: A Survey of Old Javanese Literature*, Martinus Nijoff Press, The Hague.

Chapter 5

Narrating the Past and the Future: Religious Super-diversity Formation of Catholic Communities in Vietnam

Yuqing Du

Abstract

In contemporary Vietnam, religious diversities arise in the context of the postcolonial urban social landscape, illuminating the historical nuances of mutual integration and religious conflicts. While many scholars have examined religious super-diversity attributed to transnational migration and globalization, this chapter posits that religious super-diversity is cultivated within the context of an ethnic homogeneity, where various religions were incorporated in local political and social structure, thus enabling the process of diversifications of local religious forms and expressions. Based on 12 months of fieldwork in a northern Catholic community, a resettled community of 1954 *bắc di cư*, this chapter explains the manner in which complex church/state histories and religious-political crises were reconstructed in local historical narratives, and how these developments shaped the future aspirations of local parishioners and forms of peaceful coexistence in Vietnam. In particular, the chapter considers a local Catholic community's perspective in order to illustrate the formation of religious super-diversity. Local histories and particular social/ cultural preoccupations are found to account for the country's multidimensional religious diversities.

Keywords: religious super-diversity, Vietnam, Catholic community, 1954 *bắc di cư* migration

1 Introduction: Locating the Catholic Communities in Contemporary Vietnam

In Ho Chi Minh City, along the *Nhiêu Lộc* Canel, a famous Khmer Pagoda is quietly seated at the edge of District 3. Looking west, the homely church buildings of northern refugees are scattered in the neighbouring *Tân Bình* district, expounding the historical narrative of the 1954 great migration. The scene is a common phenomenon among cosmopolitan cities but narrates distinctive religious diversity in the postcolonial Saigon. Seven decades after their migration, northern Catholic refugees have integrated into Vietnam's modern urban social life. However, their social, spiritual, and political attributes were contested against the backdrop of the historical trajectory of Vietnam nation-building. Revisiting Vietnam's Catholic Church of the bygone era, official historiographies recorded conflicts, some violent in the past, between different religious groups in pre-and postcolonial Vietnam,[1] especially involving Catholicism and various Buddhist denominations.[2] In addition to the beleaguered colonial histories, about half a million northern Vietnamese Catholics migrated to South Vietnam in 1954[3] following the Geneva Accords, which was one of the results of the Indochina War. After the French army was defeated in 1954, Vietnam was divided into two regimes at 17 degrees north latitude, with Ho Chi Minh's communist Viet Minh in control of the north and the State of Vietnam[4] in the South. The Geneva Accords allowed for 300 days of free movement between the two Vietnams. The political motivation and accompanying ramifications of the migration were extensively studied by historians, who related the migration to US foreign policies imbued with anti-Communist sentiments.[5] The massive migration of northern Catholics into south Vietnam had a profound effect on the social, political, and religious dynamics in Vietnam. These northern Catholic migrants

---

1. Taylor 2013, pp. 415–425; Goscha 2016, p. 58.
2. Topmiller 2002, pp. 63–96.
3. The migration in 1954 is referred to as *Cuộc di cư Nam 1954* in Vietnam. Operation Passage to Freedom was a term used by the US government. *Bắc di cư* refers to the northern migrants who moved to southern Vietnam in 1954.
4. In 1955, the state was reformed as the Republic of Vietnam. The US-backed prime minister of the State of Vietnam, Ngô Đình Diệm, was elected as the president.
5. Frankum 2007.

played an important role in the elections of pro-Catholic politician *Ngô Đình Diệm* and subsequent political-religious crisis.[6] Nevertheless, the resettlement and integration campaign intensified the political-religious conflicts in southern Vietnam.

The historical trajectory of Vietnamese nation-building exemplifies an intricate intertwinement with domestic politics as well as religious categories. This is evidenced in the fact that numerous religious groups have actively participated in the anti-colonial movement, absorbing their group interests and distinct religious-political aspirations. In the aftermath of the second Indochina war, the partition of Vietnam and the ensuing political cauldron unfolded in South Vietnam, exacerbating interreligious hostilities. In the 1950s, *Cao Đài* sect initially supported but then opposed South Vietnam. In 1955, the then President *Ngô Đình Diệm* disbanded the *Cao Đài* army, seized power, and forced the religious leader into exile. This inexorably resulted in the repression of other religious groups, including those who supported South Vietnam.[7] In 1963, several monks publicly self-immolated to protest the extreme pro-Catholic policies in South Vietnam, resulting in further conflicts between Catholics and other religious groups.[8] After 1954, *Hảo Hảo* began armed opposition to challenge the U.S.-backed government. By the time *Diem* died in 1963, *Hảo Hảo* had taken control of many western and southern provinces of South Vietnam, emerging as a powerful independent force in the region's politics until the communists' final victory in 1975.

The conflicting past has been camouflaged in the urban landscape of religious diversity in today's Ho Chi Minh City. Decades of peaceful coexistence, unification and social development reassembled the political-religious dynamics in Vietnam and nurtured a distinct religious environment in today's post-revolution Vietnam.[9]

During my fieldwork in Ho Chi Minh City from 2016 to 2017, I was struck by the prosperity and diversity of religious environments. The religious buildings and spectacular events challenged the assumptions of alleged conflicting, suppressive religious dynamics in the socialist

6. Jacobs 2004, pp. 1–25.
7. Blagov 2001, pp. 107–109.
8. Jacobs 2005, pp. 25–59.
9. Taylor 2007, pp. 1–56.

regimes. What struck me more was when I discovered that the Catholic community I studied was a northern Catholic resettled community. With the end of the French Indochina War in 1954, millions of Catholics living in northern Vietnam moved to the South, resulting in the establishment of the pro-Catholic southern regime and interreligious conflicts. For the parishioners of the northern Catholic resettled communities, the passing of time did not deprive them of the memories of migration. Rather, the collective memories of moving and resettlement became an essential part of their religious identification, shaping their everyday lives and social networks. The "refugee camps" that had been set up by the northern migrants were changing into new parish communities, embodying the religious traditions of "Catholic villages". During my fieldwork, I gradually acquired the parish history from narratives of the parishioners, life stories, and parish everyday lives. The narration of the past revealed that they were not the passive victims and the marginalized as described in the historiographies. Rather, they were the creators of their own lives and traditions, who strived for peace and prosperity.

This chapter investigates how historical knowledge impacted their religious identifications and interreligious dynamics, and how it informs the diversification of religious forms and expressions. Previous literature on Vietnamese Catholicism tended to investigate the political dimension of religious domains, highlighting the church/state opposition and conflicting interreligious dynamics in the Vietnamese anti-colonial nationalist movement. These matters of concern were represented in the Vietnamese national historiographies, whereas many of the historical studies argued for the meta-narrative of state/church position,[10] suggesting that Catholicism was substantially incompatible with Vietnamese culture. However, this view on religion overlooked the agency of individual religious communities, diversified religious expressions and capacities for changes manifested. The concept of "super-diversity" provided a "flattened ontology" for combining both the political and lived religion, stressing the "process of formation" instead of beginning with an assumption of *a priori* religious categories. In this contribution, I considered super-diversity, not as a mixed research lens that explores the phenomenon of intersectional diversities in urban space but as a research

---

10. Chu 2008, pp. 151–192.

paradigm that investigated the complexity of religious domains. From the perspective of "super-diversity", the conflicting past of Vietnamese Catholicism can be reconstructed as a work of a set of variables, such as intersections of religion with politics, mission, nationalist movement, and the great migration in a historical specific context, through which the Vietnamese Catholic assemblage emerged as a significant part of the local society.

The anthropological research in an urban northern Catholic resettled community provided a concrete case of how the changes happened and how they impacted people's everyday lives. From a perspective of political religion, the great migration of 1954 has been associated with domestic and international politics and ideological oppositions. However, in the everyday lives dimension, the religious identifications were more related to local historical knowledge, narratives, and collective memories of individual communities. Based on one year of fieldwork experiences in a northern Catholic resettled community and oral history interviews, this article will analyse the impact of immigration on their religious community identities and interreligious relationships. This chapter argues that the history of migration and resettlement is an integral part of religious identities, embodied in the northern social networks, community organisational structure, regional religious customs, and everyday lives.

2 Understanding Religious Super-diversity Formation

The concept of "super-diversity" is a relatively new idea. Initially, the concept of super-diversity was developed by elucidating the changing patterns of global migration flows observed over the past few decades. Steven Vertovec[11] suggested that the term was intended to fill the gap of "conventional migration studies" and examine the "diversification of diversities" caused by high levels of immigration and population mobility. Focusing on the phenomenon of "diversification of diversities" that emerged in the context of globalization and increasing transnational migrations, the concept was dedicated to the methodological and theoretical innovations that allow scholars to move beyond the conventional

---

11. Vertovec 2007, p. 1025.

focal point, such as ethnicity, race, religious categories, analyzing "a changed set of condition and social configurations" in the increasingly complex world.[12]

While the term helps articulate the multidimensional diversities capable of being observed elsewhere, its primary focus on European countries and prevailing phenomena have overlooked the preoccupation of historical and cultural context and its parallels with the past. Foner[13] problematized the notion of super-diversity, asking whether super-diversity is a new phenomenon in the 21st century. Secondly, he asked whether it can be applied to non-Western/non-European contexts?[14] Certainly, to respond to these questions requires more empirical studies and interdisciplinary dialogues. As the concept of "super-diversity" has grasped the diversified dynamics and complexity behind the constructed social categories, restricting the application scenarios in the transnational migration in the 21st century has limited its theoretical connotations.

One can easily find the parallels of diversifications in histories or non-European contexts. Foner[15] presented the case of super-diversity in the context of urban areas of the United States. She argued that race played an important role in shaping the intergroup dynamics in the urban areas due to the contentious history of slavery trade and segregation. More outlying, the port cities emerged in maritime trade, such as Macau Manila, since the 17th century, and more generally, the diversification of the population in some Southeast Asian countries, such as the Philippines, Malaysia, Indonesia, can also be examined from the perspective of "super-diversity". For these port cities and countries, regional immigration can be considered one of the formative factors: the arrival of Western traders, corporations, immigrants, together with the moving of the overseas Chinese and Japanese merchants, intensified the religious, ethnic, and cultural diversities in the region. The histories might entail different bases of divarication. In the context of Southeast Asian countries, the intersections of global trade, colonialization, and independent nationalist movement generally shaped how the diversified group related to each other and how they reassembled the social worlds of complexity.

12. Vertovec 2014, p. 87.
13. Foner 2017, p. 51.
14. Foner et al. 2019.
15. Foner 2017, pp. 49–57.

The religion domain opens new conceptual spaces for revisiting the super-diversity and its concomitant theoretical and practical implications. With the growing presence and importance of migrations, many scholars have focused on the religious aspects of diversities and how they have impacted the migrants' social worlds and everyday lives[16]. These studies were proved to be fruitful in revealing the diversified religious dynamics, expressions, and identifications while stressing the complexity of religious domains[17]. Repstad[18] argued that there are two dimensions of the understanding of religion in sociological research – the political one and the everyday one. While the former focused on the role religion played in the macro-political, economic, and social institutions, religion as lived by people was fragmented, fluid, and blurred boundaries[19]. In addition to calling for a mixed approach that binds the micro and macro dimensions of the realities, we can specify the constructed macro social, religious domain into a tangible assemblage. In this regard, I concur with Becci and Burchardt's definition that religious super-diversity is "a more encompassing and complex cultural formation that involves variables and dynamics"[20]. By tracing the formation process, it is possible to extend the scope of research from the static and observable phenomenon to the varied mechanism of social structures and the myriad possibilities of lifeways. Through the lens of "super-diversity", the historical trajectories of the Vietnamese Catholic community reflected the complex intersection of politics and religion and its impact on everyday religious lives.

Moreover, as the notion of super-diversity makes its way across the continent, we might be able to identify what has been taken for granted in these new paradigms and how the variables work to shape the formation process. While the presence of immigration communities played a dominant role in constituting the super-diversity in modern society, other factors, such as the local spiritual infrastructures, the demographic composition of religious categories, and historical and cultural contexts, have also influenced how diversities are formed and manifested. In order to explore the historical trajectory of formation, it is important to delve deep

16. Bouma et al. 2021, pp. 7–25; Becci, Burchardt 2016, pp. 1–7.
17. Becci, Burchardt 2016, pp. 1–7, Hüwelmeier 2016, pp. 9–22.
18. Repstad 2019, pp. 55–66.
19. Ammerman 2006, pp. 219–238.
20. Becci, Burchardt 2016, p. 4.

to understand the indigenous knowledge on religion and its intersection with other social structures. The intersection of politics and religion is one of the crucial points for the base of diversification. With its contentious history of French colonialism, the Catholic Church was regarded as a cultural and political entity in Vietnam that was perennially incompatible with Vietnamese nation-building. However, the historical conflicts do not necessarily imply that the Catholics in Vietnam were excluded from the local culture arena. Rather, it denoted a complex intersection between political orientation and religious belongings in Vietnamese domestic politics, making the status of the Catholic minority in Vietnam and its relation to the dominant groups.

3 Reconstructing the Conflicting Past

Since its inception in the sixteenth century, Catholicism has been a minor but significant religion in Vietnam, constituting about six percent of the total population[21]. The historiographical studies on Vietnamese Catholicism have been focused on the role of Catholicism in politics and the economy. On the one hand, the incorporation of Vietnamese states in the maritime trading networks opened up spaces for missionary activities. As early as the 17th century, numerous catholic churches and communities emerged in both northern and southern Vietnam. On the other hand, due to the increasingly strict anti-Catholic policies, the missionary activities were limited to the coastal areas, leaving room for the syncretical development of local religious communities. The emergence of Catholic communities with extensive foreign networks was regarded as a threat for the local rulers, who denounced Catholicism as a "heterodox religion" (đạo tả) and possible sources for division[22].

The intersectionality of trading, military expansion, and mission impacted the place of Catholicism in Vietnam. As suggested by Ngo, in the 17th and 18th centuries, Catholic communities became a prominent force in domestic politics because of the increasingly rigid anti-Catholic policies and the lack of significant presence of foreign missionaries[23]. In the time

---

21. Vietnam General Statistics Office 2019, p. 21.
22. Ramsay 2007, pp. 371–398.
23. Ngô 2016, p. 30.

of military tension between the Annam and Cochichina, the established Catholic minorities became a potential political resource, not only in the sense of the political intervention of some missionaries in the domestic politics but also the presence of the cohesive communities in Confucian dominated society. The political forces of Catholic communities contributed to the founding of the last empire of Vietnam. With the help of MEP bishop, Adraa Pigneau de Behaine (1762–1799) and the support of Catholic mandarins, generals, and soldiers, the King managed to defeat the *Tây Sơn* army. The building of the last dynasty of Vietnam reflected the intensification of the intersection of religion and politics. The tolerance of Catholicism faded as soon as Vietnam began its "empire project", while Catholic mandarins and intellectuals were eliminated after a failed political revolt and more strict anti-Catholic policies. Massive persecution against Catholics had taken place in 1833, leading to further political and military intervention of France in 1840, which was marked as the beginning of French colonialization. These historical episodes shaped the status and experiences of Catholic communities in Vietnam. Throughout recent modern history, the Vietnamese Catholic communities have suffered from extensive communitarian violence for being the ally of the invaders and colonizers. The social positions of the Catholic communities were not defined by their relation to God or the Holy See, but by their connection to the suspicious foreign empires. In the following centuries, the tensions between the Vietnamese Catholics and non-Catholics were scaled up to a national ideological level, actualized in the nationalist movements in the late 19th and early 20th centuries[24].

In the historiographies, the Vietnamese Catholic Church was constructed as a passive victim of communitarian violence and a by-product of Western colonial ambition[25]. However, this view on Vietnamese Catholics was primarily based on the political dimension of the institutional religions. The agency of indigenous minority communities was overlooked or reduced to its resistance against the dominant discourses. The process of diversification of local Catholic tradition revealed the subjectivities of local believers and religious communities. They were not only the practitioners but also the creators of local religious tradition, as opposed to passive recipients

24. Keith 2012, pp. 1–17.
25. Ibid., pp. 1–17.

of teachings of orthodoxy. Based on the local social-cultural conditions, they actively reflect the social and political realities, imparting embodied knowledge and new forms of diversity. As suggested by Keith[26], Catholic minorities were an integral part of the Vietnamese nationalist movement, manifested in the rise in the number of well-educated local priests and intellectuals. After ruminating on the highly constrained circumstances, many Catholic elites engaged with different political actions, such as revolution, reform, empire restoration, cultural renovation, and more. Religious belongings do not necessarily inform the political affiliations. Instead, the religious institution became an arena for contesting the existing power structure. Personal experiences, class privileges, educational backgrounds, and regionality also shaped the political ideas and actions of Catholic elites. In Tonkin, the centre of communitarian violence, many Catholic elites showed empathy towards Nguyễn's regime to establish a strong Vietnamese sovereign by political reform. On the other hand, the political realities also shaped the social worlds of Vietnamese Catholics. To insulate themselves from the extensive communitarian violence and military intervention, they formed a regional political-religious community in resisting the exterior threats. Culturally, Vietnamese Catholic traditions were an integrated part of constructing cultural and religious diversities of Vietnamese societies.

From the perspective of super-diversity, the inception of Catholicism intensified the process of diversification in Vietnam, generating new forms of religious expression. Tran's research on Catholic apologetics revealed the interreligious dynamics between Buddhism, Confucianism, and Catholicism in the 18th century of Vietnam. As suggested by Tran, despite the state restriction on Catholics, there existed various forms of interreligious communications and mutual integration[27]. The indigenous spiritual structures open up possibilities for generating new forms of religious expression and integration[28]. The theological invention was later joined by Christianity, which went on to assume a significant presence. For example: "our Lady La Vang" (Đức Mẹ Lá Vàng) pilgrimage reflected a combination of goddess worship with Catholicism,

---

26. Ibid., pp. 101–102.
27. Tran 2017.
28. Do 2003.

illuminating the historical sufferings of Vietnamese Catholic communities[29]; the *Cao Đài* movement in the early 20th century represented a combination of Confucian ethical principles, Buddhist karmic concepts, and the hierarchical organisation of Catholicism; the ideological innovation of *chủ nghĩa nhân vị* (personalism) introduced in the 1930s resonated with labour union activists (including Buddhists), intellectuals, students, and lay Catholics[30]. In social realities, the presence of Catholic minority groups has not only been a source of tension and conflicts, but it formed new interreligious dynamics, allowing for the differentiation of religious forms and expressions.

The religious communities were the major sites for the cultural formation of religious super-diversity. In addition to the intertwinement in the political domain, regional differences, missionaries' activities, and religious orders served as a base for diversification of Vietnamese Catholic traditions. By the time Catholicism was first introduced to Vietnam in the 16th century, Vietnam was divided into two parts, northern Vietnam, which relied on the Confucian legitimacy of the former dynasty, and southern Vietnam, which relied more on maritime trade. There were three major missionary groups in Vietnam serving different regions of Vietnam. The divergences of missionary strategies, number of missionaries, and form of missionary mechanism resulted in the diversified form of the indigenous Catholic community and religious tradition.

The Society of Jesus was among the first missionary groups that arrived in Vietnam and established a base for missionary activities. By virtue of Portuguese maritime trading networks and the Padroado system, missionary activities achieved great success in both northern and southern Vietnam at the end of the 17th century. The Jesuits who arrived in Vietnam used various methods to attract new converts, including trade, technology, and cultural adaptation strategies[31]. While these methods proved to be effective, their legitimacy was challenged by other missionary groups, who opposed the expanding power of the Portuguese and its tolerances of "ancestor worship". In the 17th century, two major historical events changed the landscape of Vietnamese Catholicism. First

---

29. Nguyen 2017, pp. 180–190.
30. Nguyen 2018, pp. 741–771.
31. Hsia 2018, p. 287.

is the rite controversy (1645–1702) which raised the contradictions of Vietnamese Catholicism to the ideological level, leading to more violence. The influences of the contradictions between various religious groups were distributed unevenly in the northern and southern territory, engendering diversified interreligious encounters. In northern Vietnam, where the influences of Confucian ideology dominated, the Catholic ban on Confucian rites resulted in more communitarian violence and state persecution[32]. In the more diverse southern Vietnam, Catholic activities were tolerated and integrated with the local belief system[33]. Second is the founding of MEP by the French to retrieve the ecclesiastical power of the Portuguese and the Spanish in the Far East. By the end of the 17th century, all the Jesuit-overseen communities were replaced by MEP missionaries. The region from the Red River delta to the coastal area of northern Vietnam was distributed to the Spanish Dominican Group, while the Paris Foreign Mission Church in France governs the rest of Vietnam.

Regional differences resulted in the differences in the scales, organisational structures, and traditions among local Catholic communities. Tonkin, the northern Vietnam, had always been the "heartland" of Catholicism in Vietnam before the 1954 migration. As one of the earliest places to receive the gospel, local Catholic communities have confronted various challenges in expanding their influences. After the Spanish Dominican group claimed its authority over the Eastern Tonkin Vicariate during the late 17th century, the ban on ancestor worship and Confucian rites further intensified the interreligious conflicts, resulting in persisted communitarian violence and anti-Catholic edicts. In this case, rural areas in the Red River Delta became a significant growth point. In the absence of foreign missionaries, many self-sufficient Catholic villages (*làng đạo*) were formed in the northern rural areas to achieve religious security and autonomy. Influenced by the Spanish Dominican group, people who lived in the self-contained "Catholic villages" (*làng đạo*) showed little sympathy towards French colonial rule. Their political loyalty remained to the Vietnamese courts, who they believed represented the Vietnamese ethnicity. By the late 19th century, in the time of political crisis, most Catholics lived in the "Catholic villages" (*làng đạo*) and formed a community

---

32. Keith 2012, pp. 52–62.
33. Do 2003, p. 9.

defence to protect cluster Catholics in the region[34]. While in the Cochin-China (southern Vietnam) and Mekong delta, Catholics and non-Catholics co-existed in port cities and rural areas, forming the spectrum of religious diversity in the southern region[35]. As for Catholics living in southern Vietnam, they were more exposed to Western thoughts and colonial rule. Some urban Catholic elites emerged as bourgeoisie class, working for the French-sponsored industries and colonial state[36]. They wish to improve the conditions of Vietnamese society through modernised thoughts, techniques, and industries.

4 Revisiting the History of 1954

One of the key events to have impacted the religious landscape in Vietnam was the migration in 1954, also known as Operation Passage to Freedom. Under the terms of the Geneva Conference, Vietnam was temporarily divided at the 17th parallel north. Following this division, people from both areas began the migration with the help of military forces and foreign political organisations. According to the statistics, in 1954, around 860,000 people moved to the South[37], and approximately 70% of the northern Catholic population moved south to the southern Republic of Vietnam (RVN) in the mass exodus. This led to a drastic change in the distribution of Catholics in Vietnam. Prior to 1954, northern Vietnam was the centre of Vietnamese Catholicism. By 1954, there were nearly 1.9 million Catholics in Vietnam, of which 27.4% resided in the South, with the majority of Catholics living in northern Vietnam. After the 1954 migration, around 600,000 northern Catholics moved to the South. Consequently, South Vietnam emerged as the Vietnamese Catholic Church, with approximately 1.1 million Catholic residents below the 17th parallel[38].

34. Keith 2012, p. 26.
35. Do 2003, p. 190.
36. Keith 2012, pp. 219–226.
37. According to the archive document *"Phủ tổng ủy di cư tỵ nạn gửi Phủ Tổng thống"* (The Office of the General Committee for Migration and Refugees sent to the Presidential Palace), there were 860,206 northern migrants moved into southern Vietnam, cited in Hansen 2009, p. 204.
38. Bùi 1998, p. 214; Trần 1978.

It is not surprising that the history of 1954 and the great migration has elicited widespread attention. This is not only due to the scale of immigration but also because of the participation of many international forces during the process of migration and resettlement. Given the high percentage of Catholics in *bắc di cư*, the political and social status of these northern Catholic migrants was assessed primarily by reference to their relationship with *Ngô Đình Diệm*, a Catholic politician who later became the president of South Vietnam. Some scholars associated migration with US foreign strategies and approached the movement from a Cold War perspective[39]. They interpreted this migration as a result of a well-calibrated propaganda campaign aimed at the Catholic population in North Vietnam and strove to weaken the forces of *Việt Minh*. The propaganda campaign is suggested to have been operated by the Central Intelligence Agency (CIA) of the US government, which appointed Edward Lansdale to lead the psychological warfare against the Northern Communist Party[40]. Propaganda campaigns previously mainly targeted northern Catholics. Over time, slogans such as "Christ has gone South" and "the Virgin Mary has departed from the North" were widespread.

While most academic attention has been devoted to the political dimension of migration and the role of Catholicism shaping the event[41], little attention has been given to the northern Catholic migrants themselves. In the narrative of political studies, northern Catholics were constructed as a passive community that exerted little agency in their decision of moving. Their political, social, or religious agendas were abjectly predicated on the will of others, such as the US, Pope, and *Ngô Đình Diệm*. To what extent was the migration imposed by external factors, such as US foreign strategies and the Vatican's opposition to communism? How did the Catholic belief affect the decision-making process and the experiences of moving and resettlement? Hansen's[42] interviews with northern Catholics revealed the heterogeneity of the motives in the migration. According to his interviews, some northern Catholics revealed that they had not received any propaganda messages from outside their parish. In their nar-

---

39. Tran 2005, pp. 427–449.
40. Jacobs 2004; Frankum 2007.
41. Hansen 2009, pp. 173–211.
42. Ibid.

ratives, they listed various reasons to explain their decisions to depart. In parallel to the concerns over religious freedom and potential threats posed by the new Communist government, regionality, economic status, and security concerns were also mentioned as the driving forces. It reflected a more comprehensive context in northern Vietnam, from the disruption of economic activities and food shortages in some regions[43], to communities and neighbourhoods destroyed by the Indochina war. Hansen suggested that the motivation of northern Catholic migrants was complex and informed by various sources of information and aspirations[44].

The diversification of Vietnamese Catholicism has manifested in the divergences of the migration rate of northern Catholic dioceses. Statistics from the Vietnamese Church indicate that approximately 150,000 Catholics and 150 clergy from Bùi Chu, along with 80,000 Catholics and clergy from another northern diocese, moved south, accounting for over 70% of the total population in these areas[45]. This migration rate was much higher than in other northern rural dioceses and exceeded that of urban centers, such as Hà Nội, a port and the capital city (33.4%), and the major port city Hải Phòng (52.3%)[46]. As in the case of the two northern dioceses of Bùi Chu and Phát Diệm, the northern hometown of the Catholic communities where I did my fieldwork, merit attention. While the demographic statistics revealed the significant roles of the two dioceses in the great migration, in what particular contexts the decisions were made? And, how do the religious organisations of these communities intersect with domestic politics?

To answer these questions, first, we shall explore the demographic contexts of the region. Situated in the Red River Delta, the majority of Catholics from these two dioceses were farmers. To avoid the communitarian violence against Catholics and political upheavals, by the time of the late 19th century, the majority of the Catholics in the region were living in so-called "Catholic villages" (làng đạo), set apart from other non-Catholic villages (làng lương). Catholic villages had their roots in the powerfully corporate nature of villages in these regions, which facilitated

43. Gunn 2014, pp. 1–9.
44. Hansen 2009, pp. 173–211
45. Hansen 2009, p. 180.
46. Ibid.

the conversion of extended social networks. Due to the absence of foreign missionaries in the region, local priests served as the head of the village, managing both religious and non-religious affairs. Influenced by Spanish missionaries and nationalist sentiments, the villagers developed strong anti-colonial sentiments and sympathized with the nationalist movements in Vietnam[47]. In times of intensified violence and political crisis, these villages also built community defensive forces, protecting the Catholic communities.

At the end of the 19th century, these cohesive religious communities grew into an emerging political force in northern Vietnam under the leadership of local Vietnamese priests. The French colonial invasion of Tonkin could not ameliorate the dangers of northern Catholic communities and exposed them to the danger of further communitarian violence and stigma. As a result, the French invasion and colonisation had been unfavoured by these northern dioceses, who had historically been managed by Spanish missionaries and expected a peaceful life. Under this circumstance, the traditional isolated "Catholic villages" had to equip themselves with self-defence armies. Under the leadership of Vietnamese priests, the group of people with the same regional belongings, beliefs, and sufferings had become a distinct religious-political force, forming an "autonomy safety zone". The local priest, as the leader of the community, served as an empire intermediator between the foreign colonizers and local states, wishing to end the wars.

In the meantime, the Vietnamese Church also underwent a national transformation. Inspired by the nationalist movement, local Catholic clergies and laities were eager to eliminate the shadow of the colonial Church and establish an independent national church[48]. The revolutionist spirit also impacted the Catholic communities in the Red River Delta. While the urban elite Catholics who lived in the French-ruled Cochichina sought to reform Vietnamese society with Western modernity, the Red River Delta with anti-French sentiments developed a cooperative relationship with the northern revolutionary parties. During the second Indochina war, the *Bùi Chu* and *Phát Diệm* dioceses were developed into an autonomous "safety zoom" (safety room), independent of the Vietnamese Socialist

---

47. Keith 2012, pp. 72–73.
48. Keith 2012, p. 181.

government and French colonial regime. The bishops of *Bùi Chu* and *Phát Diệm*, Father *Lê Hữu Từ* were the representatives of the Vietnamese national Church and were opposed to the colonial Church supported by the French. Being the absolute spiritual and secular leader of the region, he publicly condemned the French invasion and demonstrated his support of Ho Chi Minh. However, the cooperation between the revolutionary party and *Phát Diệm* and *Bùi Chu* was broken off when the French army took over the region. In order to maintain the status of the autonomous zoom, Father *Lê Hữu Từ* hadto make compromises that stopped public rebellions against France. France incorporated the Catholic Self-Defense Force, which was used to resist the Revolutionary Army of Ho Chi Minh. These historical details were recorded in the memoirs "*Thập Giá Và Lưỡi Gươm*" (The Cross and the Sword) written by a northern priest *Trần Tam Tỉnh* and provided an alternative narrative to the political studies[49].

The great migration of 1954 can be seen as an extensive result of the intersectionality of religions and politics in the time of the anti-colonial war. Vietnamese priests became the religious and political leaders of the believers, whose influences were channelled through clerical order and the vision of building the national Church. Their motivation for leaving cannot be reduced to ideological differences and foreign interference. Rather, it involved complex political and religious dynamics within which the decisions were made, reflecting the agency of Catholics in the political chaos and diversified ways of the expressions. In the migration process, the local clergy played a vital role in leading and organizing the departure of their fellow parishioners. According to the historical records, the decision to migrate *Bui Chu* dioceses was made on 15 June 1954 by the Vietnamese bishop *Lê Hữu Từ* and *Phạm Ngọc Chi*, ten days before the end of the Geneva Conference. On 30 June 1954, many northern Catholic villages started moving with their parish priests and were resettled in the outskirts of Saigon. The Vietnamese Catholic Church, particularly the clergies from northern Vietnam, played a significant role in this resettlement. *Phạm Ngọc Chi*, the bishop of the *Bùi Chu* diocese was appointed as the Bishop in Charge of Laity Migrants (*Giám Mục Phụ Trách Giáo Dân Di Cư*). The ten northern dioceses also co-founded *Ủy ban Hỗ trợ Định Cư* (Immigration Assistance Committee), worked

---

49. Trần 1978.

with Catholic international charity organisations and the US government in resettlement and resource distributions, whereas the local churches in Saigon were not directly involved in the refugee resettlement.

5 Remaking the Parish History

This part of conflicting, multidimensional political history may interest researchers or political commentators: why did the northern Catholics move? The expected answers were political ones – the US, the Pope, or the Republic of Vietnam. This seemingly reasonable causal link overlooked the subjectivities of the individual Catholics and the community, who made up their minds in hesitance, packed their belongings, and onboarded the ships that were going to take them to the places that they had never been to. For them, the priority was not to look back and rethink why the decision had been made. Rather, they were busy with moving on and surviving in this national political-religious crisis together with their village fellows.

Their perceptions on migration were reflected in the local parish historiographies, which highlighted the process of community-making. Catholics in *Phát Diệm* and *Bùi Chu* were the first to arrive at Saigon under the leadership of clerics. Bishop *Lê Hữu Từ* had chosen some vacant places around Saigon to resettle these Catholic, including *Gia Kiệm, Bình Thành, Tân Bình*, and *Gò Vóp*. However, the process was not that well-regulated. As most of the northern Catholics in these two areas were moving together with their village fellows and clergy, they were resettled in the same refugee camps and built their resettled communities in the land they chose. As Hansen[50] noted, the resettlement was determined by circumstance and by the choices made by individual *bắc di cư* communities. This was also recorded in the historical record of *Bùi Phát* parish:

> [...] Trần Vinh Quang and Trần Đức Điềm found a place that can accommodate the entire community – the garbage dump on Trương Minh Giang Road. This place was originally a wasteland, which was used by the Saigon authority to store and process garbage in

---

50. Hansen 2009, p. 199.

Saigon-Gia Dinh urban area. In May 1955, Father Gioan Baotixita Ngô Xuân Hảo formally took charge of the migrant community and established Bùi Phát parish in this area[51].

The resettlement in Saigon marked the start of a new phase of life for northern Catholic migrants. In the parish historical narrative, the refugee camp set up in 1954 was the origin of the new parish and duly recorded in the parish history document:

> At that time, the Tân Bình – Gia Long district three big migrant camps: Tan Viet 1 Camp, guided by Father Daminh Vũ Đức Triêm, Tan Viet 2 Camps, guided by Father Bartolomeo Nguyễn Quang Ân, and Tan Viet camp, that guided by Father Daminh Vũ Phụng Thiên. The primary purpose of the camp was to manage and distribute the supplements. Then, under the guidance of Father Daminh Vũ Phụng Thiên, the Camp Tan Viet 3 settled at Ong ta Market. The camp members are from Tan Nhan parish, Hung yen province. [...] In the year of 1957, the Father Simon-Hoà Nguyễn Văn Hiền Announced the establishment of the parish and the Church, with the name of Tân Linh[52].

Parish records and interviews with parishioners indicate that what was most relevant to the making of the northern Catholic resettled community was the local priests and the parishioners that shared the same religious belief and place of origins. A church building was one of the first buildings built by the northern migrants. As recalled by journalists in the 1950s, the northern migrant churches sprung up around Saigon. As one journalist described, "it was like a competition"[53]. Building a church meant more than their devotion to the faith. Rather, it meant reconfirming the sense of belonging to the refugee camps based on the same place of origin and the common experiences of migration. These newly built churches were renamed by the northern migrants and clergies themselves,

---

51. *Giáo Xứ Bùi Phát* (*Bùi Phát* Parish) n.d.
52. *Giáo Xứ Tân Linh* (*Tân Linh* Parish) 2015. In order to maintain anonymity, safeguard privacy, and mitigate any potential risk, I have adopted pseudonyms for the parish *Tân Linh* and my informants. I avoided using pseudonym for the names of the other parishes because they are all based on publicly accessible information and have names related to the history of migration.
53. Luce, Summer 1969, p. 111.

usually in Vietnamese, which recalled their northern parishes. For example, *Bùi Phát* were named after their northern origin in *Bùi Chu* dioceses. In several cases, the character "*Tân*" was common among the batches of new Churches, such as *Tân Linh, Tân Việt*, and *Tân Sa Châu*, as it refers to "the new" in Sino-Vietnamese vocabulary.

The building of *Tân Linh* church was marked as an important starting point for the Catholic refugees living in the *Tân Việt* refugee camps. The local historical recorded the commemorative moments: "In 1956, the first parish church was built. It was made of iron frame, bricks and cement rooftop, which was bought at a low price by parishioners who worked for a French Shipping company". The building of the Church exhausted all the human resources of the parish, including the parish priest himself who was self-appointed as the project manager. It was built with the best construction materials, located in the refugee compounds of temporal shelters. The church became the pride of the newly built community, as at the time, "most of the other churches (in the refugee camps) were built by light, temporary material"[54]. The church building was one of the tallest buildings in the area at the edge of Saigon city, looking down at the refugee camps and temporary shelter spread out. Surrounding the Church were the single-story temporary shelters and farmland they reclaimed from the wasteland at the outskirts of Saigon. The region naturally bonded by the canal had become the basis for the making of the resettlement community. Under the leadership of the priests, the migrants resumed their village lives.

As recorded in the local parish history, the time between 1962 to 2002 was summarized as the "developmental period" (*giai đoạn phát triển*). It was during this period that the population of the parish multiplied. Originally, the parish only consisted of three residences along the main road by the side of the canal. To cater for the growing populations, new residential areas were built in 1957 and in 1962. In 1968, a new church of 1000 square meters was built at the base of the old Church, together with a two-story seminary building and a church primary school. In 1973, a sub-parish affiliated with *Tân Linh* parish was detached from its mother parish to create a new *Vĩnh Sơn* parish. Initially, this place was only a small praying room set by the believers of *Tân Linh* parish in honour

54. *Giáo Xứ Tân Linh* (*Tân Linh* Parish) 2015.

of Saint Vicent in 1960. In 1973 when the new parish was founded, it became home to around 2500 believers. Although the previous prayer room for Saint Vincent was reconstructed into a building of three stories, the floor space remained limited. Most parishioners in *Vinh Sơn* parish would still choose to attend Mass at the *Tân Linh* church.

The parish community was the basic unit for producing local historiographies and making collective memories. Many parishioners' did not remember clearly the historical trajectories of the modern Ho Chi Minh City and the social-economic changes. What they have remembered is how their parish expanded and integrated into the city centre. The senior members of the parish were the primary sources for my understanding of the parish histories. In my fieldwork, Uncle Tran, the senior member of the Church, was the primary source for me to learn the histories of the parish. The narratives were fragmented, intertwined with the family history of his and his neighbours, in terms of how they made a living and how the living conditions were raised:

> It was tough. I remembered sharing one room with seven siblings and our neighbours' children. The household includes my parents, my parents' siblings. It was until, when I turned 20, my parents and my siblings moved about afforded our places. To feed us, my parents did a lot of labour work, as we didn't have the land to farm. As a child, I helped to tend pigs and took care of my younger sisters and brothers. My aunts and uncles made petty trades in the market nearby; sometimes, I take care of my cousins too. […] One of my cousins opened a small food stall, selling bánh canh cua (a kind of crab rice noodle) in the parish, and his son inherits the place now.

Tran did not remember much of the migration process, as he was a little kid that was "carried on the back of his father", nor did he know much about the wars or unification. He held a generally critical view towards politicians in recent Vietnamese history, including his co-religious politician, who claimed to protect their interests. What counted as the most important thing for him was that "life in the parish was improving gradually", as he stated.

Instead of elaborating on the brutality of the Vietnam War and the unification of Vietnam, Tran's narration expounded the improving living conditions. "Life was improving gradually", he said. The unification of

Vietnam brought peace to the war-torn nation. By the time of unification, Tran was transformed from a northern Catholic peasant to an urban citizen. He managed to find a job through his relationship with northern Catholic networks. Although his life was still fraught with challenges, the salary enabled him to support his wife and two children. According to him, several parishioners started doing business, while the temporary farmland in the parish was turned into houses to cater to the growing population.

The urban lifestyle placed the traditional self-contained "Catholic village" in a multi-religious urban setting. Their collective identities as northern Catholic migrants shaped their cultural experiences. Teacher Phu, one of my interlocutors that worked for the church catechism school, described the big parade they held for Easter weeks before the unification. All the churches would carry their distinct palanquins and troop to the Notre-Dame Cathedral Basilica of Saigon. People would assemble in front of the sculpture of Saint Mary and have a great mass at the plaza in the city centre: "We were the country that was dedicated to the Virgin Mary". This, of course, was not his first-hand experience. Born in the 1980s, the glorious past of Catholic Saigon was remembered, while the miracle "crying" Virgin Mary Status had become a city legend.

The urban landscape brought the migrants into the context of urban religious diversities. They were aware of religious sects in their neighbourhoods, such as pagodas, temples, and prayer houses. Some parishioners also recalled their trip to the Mekong Delta, where they visited the *Cao Đại* temple, a famous tourist spot in southern Vietnam. When the temporary farmland of the parish was converted into houses, the local parishioners engaged with various types of communications with non-Catholics in the workplace and schools, established friendships, and even got married.

In the aforementioned process of social integration, the northern migrants confronted social discrimination. The language was the most obvious reflection of the social prejudices facing the migrants. They were referred to as "*Bắc 54*" by southerners, which has a negative connotation of regional discrimination. Although most of the "*Bắc 54*" were Catholics, the term was used to target the people from "*Bắc Kỳ*" (Tonkin), which pinpointed migrants as a distinct social category in southern Vietnamese society. After seven decades of integration, the social construction of the stigma gradually became a cultural symbol representing the northern migrants' cultural experiences. The social category of "*Bắc 54*" represented a cultural process of northern migrants, that they have "followed the calling of God and headed south" (*Đi theo tiếng gọi của Chúa để vào nam*) and integrated their northern heritage with experiences of displacement. While they acknowledged the original negative connotation of "*Bắc 54*", many local parishioners valued their northern cultural heritage and regarded it as a source of pride. One of the interlocutors proudly told me about many famous singers and writers among "*Bắc 54*". "If people enjoy the music of *Anh Bằng, Trịnh Công Sơn*, they appreciated the culture of '*Bắc 54*'".

The arrival of "*Bắc 75*" indicates how different categories of the migrant community were constructed in particular historical and political contexts. After the 1975 unification, Saigon welcomed another exodus of migrants from North Vietnam. Unlike the northern Catholic migrants in 1954 who were from a relatively poor background, the new migrants enjoyed a superior social status. The local parishioners stated that some of the migrants in 1975 were indeed privileged because they participated in the war and had proven their loyalty to the socialist government. These migrants were more likely to work in higher positions within the state-owned companies and public sectors, which enjoyed a coveted status in Vietnam of that era. According to him, "*Bắc 54*" kept 80% of authentic *Bắc Kỳ* culture, while those "*Người 75*", who had gone through socialist collectivism and thus cannot represent authentic northern traditions.

6   Remaking the Hidden Northern Catholic Villages in Ho Chi Minh City

How was the northern Catholic resettled community constructed and sustained in the urban setting? While religion had a comprehensive impact on migration, these Catholic communities often replicated organisation patterns, leadership modes, and village sociality. When I entered this community, I felt an atmosphere different from that of the city. This was not so much about the religion – you cannot tell the religious affiliation from the outside but in relation to the everyday lives. It didn't take long for me to realize the residential areas surrounding the Church was a closely knit community that consisted of about 900 Catholic households. Almost everyone living there knew one another other. They were woven in social networks that covered all the residential areas in this compound, including shops, restaurants, coffee stalls, and even printing shops in the community. They all have the same beliefs, the same place of origin, and similar life trajectories.

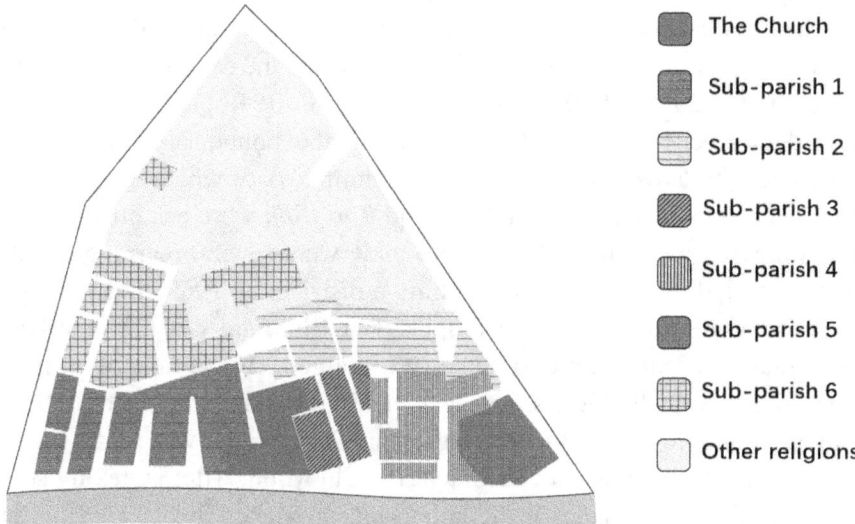

Figure 5.1: Map of Tan Linh Parish[55].

As shown on the map, the Catholic parish has well-defined geographic boundaries between it and its non-Catholic neighbours. The three main roads served as "natural boarders" of the residential compound. The part in light blue is marked as "tôn giáo khác" (other religions). In that area, there is a Buddhist temple at the end of the north boundary. Situated in the rather bucolic residential area near the historic *Nêu Lộc* channel, this Catholic community was inconspicuous in comparison to the Gothic church architecture in the city centre. Away from the tourist attractions and modern infrastructure, the parish life was well organized and peaceful.

The church building is situated in the centre of the parish. It provides almost all the religions and social functions, such as holding Mass, sermons, and group praying sessions. The church yard offers the space for

55. Giáo Xứ Tân Linh (*Tân Linh Parish*) 2015.

hosting the Easter parade, Christmas gala, and even reunion activities for northern fellow villagers from other places. Next to the church building is the five-story, multi-functional administration building. The administration building contains the living space for the priests and male clergies, offices, and a meeting room for the Church Council, classrooms for Catechism school, marriage preparation classes, a prayer room for group praying sessions, and a spacious lecture hall for organizing special events.

The urbanization of Ho Chi Minh City has long included the parish in the urban area. In 1956, *Saigon-Chợ Lớn* became the capital city of South Vietnam. On 29 April 1957, the government of the Republic of Vietnam issued Decree 138-BNV/HC/ND defining the boundary of Gia Dinh province with 6 districts (10 totals, 61 communes), of which 2 new urban administrative districts *Bình Chánh* and *Tân Bình* were established[56]. In the following years, the urban spaces underwent several rearrangements and expanded to 11 urban administrative districts by 1969. The resettlement communities, located in today's Tân Binh and *Gò Vấp* districts, were included in the metropolitan area of Saigon. By the time of unification, Saigon was the biggest city in Vietnam, covering an area of 1295.5 square kilometres. After the unification in 1975, Saigon was renamed Ho Chi Minh City in honour of President Ho Chi Minh. After annexing several counties and villages in neighbouring provinces, by 1997, Ho Chi Minh City had 17 urban administrative districts and 5 rural districts, covering over 2000 square kilometres.

The migration flow to Saigon did not cease during wartime. From 1954 to 1975, people from the southern provinces continued to move to Saigon. In South Vietnam, Dang et al. reported that the population in urban places rose from 20% to 40% between 1960 and 1975. Despite the restriction on migration since 1975 and the state-planned population relocation program, from 1981 to 1991, the urban population grew at a much faster rate (40.6%) than the rural population (16.7%)[57]. According to the 1999 national census, the urban population rose to over 20%, while Ho Chi Minh City accounted for 23% of the total urban population, much higher than the northern capital city Ha Noi (8%)[58].

56. *Ban Tuyên Giáo Quận Ủy* (Propaganda Department of The District Party Committee) 2008.
57. Dang et al. 1997, pp. 317–321.
58. Cu 2005, p. 120.

The descendants of migrants have also accepted their urban citizenship. For those who moved to Ho Chi Minh City after 1954 or 1975, the northern Catholic migrants were more of a native, as they were granted citizenship, houses, and land. Especially for those who were born after 1975, they had no problems calling themselves Saigonese and took it as a source of pride. After the farmland was transformed into residential areas to cater to the growing population, their lives depended on the urban industries. Many of the parishioners have also taken the initiative to introduce reforms to improve their economic, social status, and living standards. Their everyday lives were no longer confined to the isolated refugee resettled communities on the outskirts of Saigon, as they became increasingly integrated into the urban lives. However, their social and spiritual lives were confined mainly to the parish community, through which they kept the village sociality and religious tradition.

In addition to the aforementioned collective memories and shared places of origin, the parish also recreated the village church councils based on the northern social networks. Most of the parishioners were the descendants of the northern Catholic migrants who originally belonged to the same Catholic village in *Bùi Chu* diocese. After several generations of being village fellows and living in the same community after the migration, the kinship relations within the community turned rather complicated. Although some of the families are not related by blood, they might know each other as neighbours, acquaintances, or members of the same church group. Inexorably, the close-knit community ties recreated an "acquaintance society" in the urban space. The familiar social network gave the parishioners a sense of belonging and security. Except for the houses facing the main street, some of the residents would open their doors in the daytime or just leave their properties from the side. My participants opined that the parish community was a relatively safer place where "everyone knows each other", and "there were no bad people or strange people in the parish".

The parish was managed by the church council, which is similar to the council of notables operated in the rural areas in pre-revolution Vietnam. To better manage the parish and organize religious life, the parish was divided into six sub-parishes in accordance with their location. These sub-parishes were not built at the same time but gradually developed with the expansion of the parish. Each sub-parish has its leader groups responsible for organizing activities and reporting to the local church council committee. All sub-parishes are subservient to the leadership of the parish priest as well as the chairman of the church council, who are elected from among the parishioners. The parish priest is the spiritual leader of the parish, whose contribution to the parish and leadership was highly respected by parishioners. The authority of the parish priest comes from his religious order and also from the fact that he participated in the great migration in 1954 and shared a northern origin identity with the parishioners. Members with higher socio-economic status became members of the new church committee. In addition to their successful and stable career, they also have a strong network of relationships and enjoy a good family reputation in the parish.

Most of the parishioners were the descendants of the northern Catholic migrants who originally belonged to the same Catholic village in *Bùi Chu* diocese. After several generations of being village fellows and living in the same community after the migration, the kinship relations within the community turned rather complicated. Although some of the families are not related by blood, they might know each other as neighbours, acquaintances, or members of the same church group. Some residents left their homes or properties accessible from the side, reflecting the everyday trust and familiarity within the community.

This intersection of the social and religious domain in everyday life facilitated my inquiries about parish history. Through investigating social relations and attending on-site religious activities, I managed to grasp the traces of the past. What struck me the most was when my young friend Anh disclosed that he had 80 cousins in the parish. The answer to a common question revealed the past tradition of intermarriage within the communities and the reproduction of the close-knit socialites. Anh talked about the marriage between his parents, whose parents were village fellows and resettled here. A combination like this was common during those days when the parish was still a relatively isolated minority away from the city centre. Being a descendant of *bắc di cư*, Anh's religious lives were closely related to the family tradition and the parish's history. He was well aware of the parish's history, though he had not directly experienced it. The influences of migration and the following years of resettlement penetrated his everyday life and social relations. For him, believing in God was more about attending Mass and penance with his family, participating in youth activities in the community with his friends, and assisting the works of priests and church council members. In the future, he would, like many other parishioners, have a matrimony ceremony at his home church and even become a member of the church council like his father. The religiosity did not solely denote one's relation to God but also included one's association with family, friends, and the entire community, through which they have acquired the knowledge of religion.

In the parish, religious activities are not only an expression of individual devotion but also an expression of collective social and religious affiliations. Religious ceremonies have been the major activities that bind people together. The Mass, festival celebration, and catechism are the major activities that require the participation of the whole parish. A successful mass does require not only the liturgical service of priests but also the efforts of council members in arranging the choirs and homely speakers and the attendance of the congregation. Attending Mass at least once a week has been the routine for the whole parish community, which gives the mass attendance social bonding functions. Attending Mass is more like a family activity or a chance to meet up with friends once a week at Church. The close-knit social networks in the parish guaranteed the attendance rate. As one of my young friends told me, he never skipped a week, as his absence would be easily made known to his parents and friends.

The village sociality nurtured the "participatory culture" of the community, where everyone felt obliged to be devoted to the collective activities. As a community that hosted more than 3000 people, three clergies were certainly not enough. The festival events, such as the Christmas Gala and Eastern dinner reception, required the participation of the entire community. After the church council members planned the festival agenda, the works were distributed to each sub-parish and families. To host a meaningful event, people would invest money, time, ideas, and manpower. The celebration of Easter week was the biggest event of the parish. Aside from the preparation of the traditional Vietnamese rite of *"kiệu rước lễ"* (palanquin rite), dinner receptions and gala were also prepared for marking shared joyful experiences. Participants enjoyed the wonderful shows that were presented, including singing, dancing, and comedy.

While the Church witnessed the major life stages of a parishioner from his birth time, through the marriage stage, and until the death, religious education served as an important institution in perpetuating the cohesiveness of the northern Catholic resettled community. Providing solid religious education was the shared responsibility of the entire community, especially for the senior members of the Church who wished to carry on the traditions. In addition to stressing the importance of family education, the Church opened its catechism school in 1990, providing religious education for children and prospective Catholic couples. The teachers were selected from among the parishioners. They were the parish priests, nuns, and senior church council members who invested their spare time in nurturing the younger generations. Education in the form of formal schooling made religious education more of a serious preparation for the sacraments. Children who grew up in the parish were expected to attend the parish catechism school and finish the three-year course before they were qualified to have their own sacrament of Confirmation. These kids were learning together with their peers and nurturing friendship while enhancing their relationship with God. To be a grown member of the Church, they were expected to recite the scripts of Catholic prayers, learn the biblical stories, and most importantly, study the Catholic morality that would distinguish them from other non-believers. After passing the exam, the group Confirmation ceremony would also be their graduation ceremony. This event would have the biggest congregation, including hundreds of pupils, families, and friends, in formal suits and *áo dài* (traditional Vietnamese dress). The most outstanding students would become the young homely speaker for the ceremony and would present themselves in front of the entire congregation.

7 Modern Religious Aspirations and Peacemaking

The economic reforms in 1986 resulted in drastic changes in the religious sphere of Vietnam. The resurgence of major religious sects and various innovations in ritual practices challenged many worrying predictions in the modern world[59]. It also requires us to look beyond the theological differences and major institutional conflicts and examine the embodied practices and experiences in an ever-changing political and economic context.

---

59. Taylor 2007, p. 15.

The economic reforms not only improved the overall living conditions of the parishioners but also facilitated the pursuit of modernity and development agendas and created diverse ways of meaning-making. As Keane[60] suggested, the overarching effects of Christian imaginaries across the postcolonial world can be ascribed to their coupling of religion with certain concepts of modernity and vice versa. In a similar vein, Ngô[61] argues that the conversion of the Hmong people in Vietnam reflected their active pursuit of modernity as a response to their marginalized and backward state in society. According to Ngô, identifying themselves as Christian was a technology of the self so that they could project themselves as modern subjects and make them exempt from the social stigma of being "backward" and "uncivilized". For Vietnamese Catholics, the modernist imaginaries have contested the public perceptions as an alien religious group and eased their social stigma as hostile political forces who are perpetually opposed to the Vietnamese state. The demographic changes following the economic reform subsumed the "old", "indigenous" Catholic faith with a new meaning of "modernity" and "morality".

Although the Catholics in Vietnam never labelled themselves as "modern" or "enlightened", Catholic morality was exemplified in their religious beliefs and practices, which distinguish the faithful from the non-believers. The local parishioners are no longer represented by their political orientations and the stigma of *Bắc 54*. In the time of peace, the religious domain has been increasingly intersected with the moral domain. While the market reform in 1986 caused the moral crisis in the Vietnamese societies, Catholic morality and value, which highlighted spiritual devotion to God, family, and Church, provided a remedy. The Catholic morality and the spiritual devotion were embodied in the everyday religious practices, such as penance, praying, and donation, conforming to the standard of a moral citizen. Rather than myopically focusing on political expressions and aspirations, they tend to engage with moral subjectification in the private sphere. What distinguishes the Catholics from the non-believers and other religious people was their faith in God, practises of sacraments, and marital and reproductive ethics.

60. Keane 2007.
61. Ngô 2016.

Moral cultivation was an important part of religious education in the parish community. In addition to stressing the importance of sacraments prayers to communicate with God, the teachers also highlighted the general traditional virtues, such as filial piety to parents and elders, self-sacrifice as opposed to the self-interest in the market economy, and chastity in any pre-marital relationships. As stressed by the parish priests, this content was the basic moral element that constituted the humanness of a person. Moral knowledge was a source of pride for the younger generation that encouraged them to participate in more religious activities. By promulgating Catholic morality, parishioners embrace their religious identity as a source of pride and, equally importantly, avert their former adverse position. Most young people firmly believe in the moral superiority of Catholicism over non-believers and actively participate in the Church organisation and Catechist work. Many young people will consider priesthood their vocation, while their decisions will be welcomed and respected by their family and parish.

Catholic morality has become an arena contesting the boundary of religious communities. In addition to the widening interreligious connections, the urban spaces also paved the way for more frequent interfaith communications. Catholics who lived in the parish community developed broader social connections with non-believers as they attended schools, made friends, and looked for jobs. With the increasing interfaith connections, Catholic marriage has become the institution that mediates the boundaries between Catholics and non-Catholics. On the one hand, the Catholic marriage was the key institution perpetuating the closeness of the parish community because the Catholic doctrine of indissolubility was strictly adhered to by local Catholics and distinguished them from non-believers. The family became the primary institution for attracting new converts and passing on religious heritage. To address the increasing rate of interfaith marriage and divorces, all the prospective Catholic couples are expected to go through a four to six month marriage preparation course and pass the final exams before they hold matrimony. Non-Catholic partners will also receive catechism education within these months and receive baptism at the end of the programme. Becoming a Catholic through marriage meant the prospective couples would conform to the indissolubility of marriage, not use any contraceptive methods, and raise their children in a Catholic way. While disparity of cult (*phép chuẩn*) requires special permission from the level of bishop, most of the non-Catholic partners will choose to change their beliefs for the sake of marriage. While moral rules of a religious minority do not have legal effects, the individual community has become the major site nurturing, leading, and governing the moral domain of the believers. In the parish community, the social authority of individuals is closely related to individuals' moral quality and their devotion to parish affairs. Although the parish priests are usually the most respectful individuals, members of the church council are selected based on moral rectitude and their devotion to the community. Those who are guilty of moral misconduct will be marginalized by the community.

Interreligious conflicts have always been one of the major social issues in the history of the Vietnamese nationalist movement[62]. In the politico-religious crisis unfolding in the past century, political orientations have become an essential aspect in defining the boundaries between different religious groups. Apart from the political representations of Catholics, several religious sects were also involved in the intricate entanglement between religion and demographic politics. For example, Hue-Tam Ho Tai[63] explored the history of millenarian tradition and the emergence of *Hòa Hảo* sects in anti-colonial peasant politics. In a similar vein, Werner[64] examined the social and political context of *Cao Đài* movement in the 1930s and how local peasants incorporated political expressions with religious expressions. The combination of religious aspirations and revolutionist mission in the time of crisis created a particular religious-political-military community through which they deliver their collective political pursuits.

In times of peaceful coexistence, moral and spiritual devotion has become the arena for reassembling the interreligious dynamics. As the conflicting pasts were faded away together with the memories of wars and violence, they were occupied with renewed civic agenda of the society. The shared experiences of religious restriction since the unification and resurgences of ritual practises and religion in the 1990s have shaped their common vision of the society, including how to pursue spirituality

62. McLeod 1991.
63. Tai 1983.
64. Werner 1976.

and how to nurture a moral society? The content was included in the religious education programme of the Vietnamese Church, manifested in the Catholic sermons, public lectures, catechist classroom, and publications. Also, the devotion to spiritual and moral cultivation bound different religious groups together in forming new interreligious relationships based on mutual respect and sharing. The new positive interreligious dynamics were embodied in the everyday interactions, while religious belief did not invoke any misunderstandings and misconceptions. The marriage preparation courses brought more grown adults to the Catholic value. During the courses of education, teachers showed great respect towards those of other faiths, highlighting the common ground of different religious beliefs in cultivating the moral values of the human race. This understanding of interreligious dynamics was more than a personal reflection. The discussion of the differences between major religions and the common agenda of different religious groups were common topics in the public domain. The knowledge of religious diversity, religious differences, interreligious dialogues were spread through various online/off-line religious media, such as sermons, lectures, and various religious media and channels. At the official level, a great variety of activities were organized to enhance interreligious relationships. For instance, the Catholic seminary organized a day trip for priests and nuns of *Cao Đài* sects, inviting them to themed seminars. Vietnamese Church also invited monks from *Hảo Hảo* sects to attend their special Mass. Furthermore, it was not uncommon for Catholic priests to attend the special occasion of other religious sects. These events were even recorded on the Church-sponsored website, thereby indicating a peaceful coexistence of different religious sects. The cooperative relationship between the religious groups, however, is forged by the possibilities afforded by the historical and cultural preoccupations and the state modernist agenda.

8 Conclusion

The rich histories and socio-cultural contexts of Ho Chi Minh City provides a fertile group for the formation of religious super-diversity. The long-term, rural-urban, regional, and cross-regional migration draw different groups into the cities infusing the urban spaces with diversified buildings, traditions, and lifeways. In the meantime, the interactive dynamics of different groups further diversified the urban diversities, not only because of the changes of living environments for the residences but for the perpetuation of the past in everyday lives.

This chapter mainly discusses the impact of history on religious super-diversity in Vietnamese Catholic communities. While the majority of scholarly attention has focused on the political dimension of the religious domain, it has overlooked the spiritual and moral dimensions of a religion that manifested in everyday lives. Re-examining the conflicting past of the Vietnamese Catholic church, the intersection of political and religious served as the major variables that shaped the diversification of Catholic communities and the political subjectivities of local Catholics. At the community level, factors such as missionary organisations and regional differences also shaped the forms of local Catholic communities, constituting diverse community organisation structures and interreligious dynamics. In the diocese of eastern Tonkin run by Dominican missionary groups, there were many self-contained Catholic villages. In parallel to the nationalist movement, these villages were transformed into an "autonomous safety zone" with independent religious and political vision.

These histories are important premises for the 1954 great migration and inform our understanding of the everyday lives and changes of religious communities after migration. Although most of the historical studies focused on the political implication of the historical event, migration also changed the lives of the northern Catholic migrants, displacing them in an alien urban environment. An anthropological study on the historical narratives of an urban northern Catholic resettled community suggests that the histories constituted an important part of their religious identification. It was not only reflected in their collective memories on migration and resettlement, but also in their everyday lives. While the shared beliefs, place of origin, collective memories of resettlement bound them together, the intersection of religious activities with sociality further enhanced the cohesiveness of the religious communities and senses of belongings. They have reconstructed the northern "Catholic villages" and perpetrated the northern Catholic networks in contemporary Ho Chi Minh City.

The profound social-political transformation after the economic reform in 1986 also renovated their religious expression in moral and spiritual domains. Morality and spiritual devotion have become a feature point of the contested boundaries between religious groups. By promoting Catholic morality through religious education programs, public lectures, and media outlet, the Catholic Church is increasingly engaged in dialogue with other religious and non-religious groups, forming a peaceful, mutually respected interreligious relationship.

Author Biography

Yuqing Du is an Assistant Professor in the Institution of Humanities at ShanghaiTech University. She received a doctoral degree in anthropology from SOAS, University of London. From 2020 to 2022, she worked as a post-doctoral fellow at Sun Yat-Sen University. Her research interests include anthropology of Christianity, Vietnamese Catholicism, and gender.

References

Ammerman, N. T. (2006), *Studying Everyday Religion: Challenges for the Future*, in N. T. Ammerman (ed.), *Everyday Religion: Observing Modern Religious Lives*, Oxford University Press, Oxford, pp. 219–238.

Ban Tuyên Giáo Quận Ủy (Propaganda Department Of The District Party Committee) (2008), *Địa Danh Tân Bình – Tân Phú (Tan Binh-Tan Phu Location)*, in *Trang Thông Tinh Điện Tử (Electronic Portal Of Tan Phu District)*, available at: http://www.Tanphu.Hochiminhcity.Gov.Vn/Gioi-Thieu-Chung/Dia-Danh-Tan-Binh-Tan-Phu-C267-1.Aspx (last accessed 26 March 2021).

Becci, I., Burchardt M. (2016), *Religion and Superdiversity: An Introduction*, in "New Diversities", 18, 1, pp. 1–7.

Blagov, S. A. (2001), *Caodaism: Vietnamese Traditionalism and Its Leap into Modernity*, Nova Publishers, New York.

Bouma et al. (2021), *Religious Diversity Through a Super-Diversity Lens: National, Sub-Regional and Socio-Economic Religious Diversities in Melbourne*, in "Journal of Sociology", 58, 1, pp. 7–25. https://doi.org/10.1177/14407833211011256

Bùi, Đ. S. (1998), *Giáo Hội Công Giáo ở Việt Nam* (Catholic Church in Vietnam), Veritas Press, Calgary.

Chu, L. T. (2008), *Catholicism vs. Communism, Continued: The Catholic Church in Vietnam*, in "Journal of Vietnamese Studies", 3, 1, pp. 151–192. https://doi.org/10.1525/vs.2008.3.1.151

Cu, C. L. (2005), *Rural to Urban Migration in Vietnam*, in T. H. Ha, S. Sakata (eds.), *Impact of Socio-Economic Changes on the Livelihoods of People Living in Poverty in Vietnam*, Institute of Developing Economies, Japan External Trade Organisation, pp. 115–143.

Dang, A. et al. (1997), *Internal Migration and Development in Vietnam*, in "The International Migration Review", 31, 2, pp. 312–337. https://doi.org/10.1177/019791839703100203

Do, T. (2003), *Vietnamese Supernaturalism: Views from the Southern Region*, Routledge, New York.

Foner, N. (2017), *A Research Comment: What's New about Super-Diversity?*, in "Journal of American Ethnic History", 36, 4, pp. 49–57. https://doi.org/10.5406/jamerethnhist.36.4.0049

Foner, N., et al. (2019), *Introduction: Super-diversity in Everyday Life*, in "Ethnic and Racial Studies", 42, 1, pp. 1–16. https://doi.org/10.1080/01419870.2017.1406969

Frankum, R. B. (2007), *Operation Passage to Freedom: The United States Navy in Vietnam, 1954–1955*, Texas Tech University Press, Lubbock (Texas).

Giáo Xứ Bùi Phát (Bùi Phát Parish). (n.d.), *Lược sử Giáo xứ Bùi Phát* (History of Bùi Phát Parish), available at: http://giaoxubuiphat.com/luoc-su-giao-xu.html (last accessed 1 March 2020).

Giáo Xứ Tân Linh (Tân Linh Parish) (ed.) (2015), *Giáo Xứ Tân Linh: 60 Năm Hình Thành và Phát Triển (1955–2015), Tan Linh Parish: 60-year Formation and Development 1955–2015* (n.p.), Ho Chi Minh City.

Goscha, C. (2016), *Vietnam: A New History*, Basic Books, New York.

Gunn, G. C. (2014), *Rice War in Colonial Vietnam: The Great Famine and the Viet Minh Road to Power*, Rowman & Littlefield, Lanham.

Hansen, P. (2009), *Bắc Đi Cú: Catholic Refugees from the North of Vietnam, and Their Role in the Southern Republic, 1954–1959*, in "Journal of Vietnamese Studies", 4, 3, pp. 173–211. https://doi.org/10.1525/vs.2009.4.3.173

Hsia, R. P. (2018), *A Companion to the Early Modern Catholic Global Missions*, Brill, Boston.

Jacobs, S. (2004), *America's Miracle Man in Vietnam: Ngo Dinh Diem, Religion, Race, and US Intervention in Southeast Asia*, Duke University Press, Durham.

Keane, W. (2007), *Christian Moderns: Freedom and Fetish in the Mission Encounter*, University of California Press, Berkeley.

Keith, C. (2012), *Catholic Vietnam: A Church from Empire to Nation*, University of California Press, Los Angeles.

Luce, D., and Summer, J. (1969), *Vietnam: The Unheard Voices*, Cornell University Press, Ithaca.

McLeod, M. W. (1991), *The Vietnamese Response to French Intervention, 1862–1874*, Praeger, New York.

Ngo, L. A. (2016), *Nguyễn-Catholic History (1770s–1890s) and the Gestation of Vietnamese Catholic National Identity*, PhD thesis, Georgetown University-Graduate School of Arts & Sciences. Thesis, Georgetown University, 2016.

Ngô, T. T. T. (2016), *The New Way: Protestantism and the Hmong in Vietnam*. University of Washington Press, Seattle.

Nguyen, P. V. (2018), *A Secular State for a Religious Nation: The Republic of Vietnam and Religious Nationalism, 1946–1963*, in "The Journal of Asian Studies", 77, 3, pp. 741–771. https://doi.org/10.1017/S0021911818000505

Nguyen, T.-S. (2017), *Inculturation for Mission: The Transformation of the French Notre-Dame des Victoires into Our Lady of La Vang in Vietnam 1998*, in "Missiology", 45, 2, pp. 180–190. https://doi.org/10.1177/0091829616669958

Ramsay, J. (2007), Miracles and Myths: Vietnam Seen through Its Catholic History. In P. Taylor (ed.), *Modernity and Re-Enchantment: Religion in Post-Revolutionary Vietnam*, ISEAS–Yusof Ishak Institute, Singapore, pp. 371–398.

Repstad, P. (2019), *More Dialogue between Approaches: Everyday Religion and Political Religion*, in P. Repstad (ed.), *Political Religion, Everyday Religion: Sociological Trends*, Brill, Boston, pp. 55–66.

Tai, H.-T. H. (2013), *Millenarianism and Peasant Politics in Vietnam, Millenarianism and Peasant Politics in Vietnam*, Harvard University Press, Cambridge.

Taylor, K. W. (2013), *A History of the Vietnamese*, Cambridge University Press, Cambridge.

Taylor, P. (eds.) (2007), *Modernity and Re-enchantment: Religion in Post-revolutionary Vietnam*, Institute of Southeast Asian Studies, Singapore.

Topmiller, R. J. (2002), *The Lotus Unleashed: The Buddhist Peace Movement in South Vietnam, 1964–1966*, University Press of Kentucky, Lexington.

Tran, A. Q. (2017), *Gods, Heroes, and Ancestors: An Interreligious encounter in Eighteenth-century Vietnam*, Oxford University Press, New York.

Trân, T. L. (2005), *The Catholic Question in North Vietnam: From Polish Sources, 1954–56*, in "Cold War History", 5, 4, pp. 427–449. https://doi.org/10.1080/14682740500284747

Trần, T. T. (1978), *Thập Giá Và Lưỡi Gươm (Linh Mục Trần Tam Tinh)* [The Cross and the Blade (Priest *Trần Tam Tinh*)], Nhà Xuất Bản Trẻ (The Publishing House), Ho Chi Minh City.

Vertovec, S. (2007), *Super-diversity and its Implications*, in "Ethnic and Racial Studies", 30, 6, pp. 1024–1054. https://doi.org/10.1080/01419870701599465

Vertovec, S. (2014), *Reading 'Super-diversity'*, in B. Anderson, M. Keith (eds.), *Migration: A COMPAS Anthology*, COMPAS, pp. 86–88.

Vietnam General Statistics Office. (2019), *Completed Results of the 2019 Viet Nam Population and Housing Census*, Government Report, General Statistics Office Publishing House, p. 21, available at: https://www.gso.gov.vn/en/data-and-statistics/2020/11/completed-results-of-the-2019-viet-nam-population-and-housing-census/ (last accessed 20 March 2022).

Werner, J. S. (1976), *The Cao Dai: The Politics of a Vietnamese Syncretic Religious Movement*, PhD Thesis, Cornell University.

Part 2
Asian Diasporas in Italy

Chapter 6
Migration, Religious Super-diversity, and Cohabitation: Notes from Ethnographic Research on the Sinhala Community in Messina (Sicily)

Giovanni Cordova

Abstract

The nexus between religious super-diversity, conflict and peace-building is particularly fitting to the recent history of Sri Lanka. Besides the civil war, which ended in 2009 after 13 years, religion, cohabitation, and conflict are all relevant issues. It could not be otherwise, given the high density of the Sri Lankan religious landscape, which is composed of some of the most widespread religions in the world: Buddhism, Hinduism, Islam, and Christianity. I will propose some reflections starting from ongoing ethnographic research on the Sri Lankan Catholic and Buddhist communities living in the Sicilian city of Messina. Religious super-diversity will be assumed in relation both to the hosting society and to the Sinhala community itself, confronted with dynamics of interaction and cohabitation abroad. I will examine how religious super-diversity is transposed onto the migration phenomenon; how it interacts with and how it is re-shaped within the hosting context. Does the migration experience make differences more marked or, rather, does it reconcile differences promoting cohabitation? How does the relation between migration and super-diversity intervene into religious statuses? Does it make identities more rigid or flexible?

Keywords: Sri Lanka, Catholic Church, Buddhism, inter-rituality, religious coexistence, devotion, civil war

1 Introduction

Long before Vertovec introduced the category of super-diversity[1], Ulf Hannerz, already in the 1990s, claimed that cultural flows within the global "ecumene" could lead to the transformation of social meanings. He argued that this happens through the coordinates of identity and difference, which are usually brought about by the experience of mobility[2]. After all, the extensive literature on transnationalism highlights the numerous ways in which new political communities, affiliations, and feelings of belonging (often subversive and counter-hegemonic) transcend nation states while simultaneously being incorporated within them[3]. This condition can also be referred to as the quality of simultaneity that Peggy Levitt and Nina Glick Schiller define as "living lives that incorporate daily activities, routines, and institutions located both in a destination country and transnationally"[4]. Transnationalism literature emphasizes "how persons simultaneously maintain and shed cultural repertoires and identities"[5], interacting within a location and across its boundaries, sometimes in ways that contradict long-time values. From this assumption derives the opposition between transnational "ways of being" and "ways of belonging". The latter refers to "practices that signal or enact an identity which demonstrates a conscious connection to a particular group", while the first describes the "actual social relations and practices that individuals engage in"[6], independently of their conscious identifications and feelings of belonging.

Regarding the general topic of migration, the value of the notion of super-diversity in enhancing our understanding of religions does not solely reside in the mere description of the plurality of places of worship,

---

1. Vertovec 2007, p. 1025.
2. Hannerz 1992.
3. Glick Schiller et al. 1992; Levitt 2004; Glick Schiller 2004; Riccio 2014.
4. Levitt, Glick Schiller 2004, p. 1013.
5. Ibid.
6. Ibid., p. 1010.

rituals, sacred traditions, dresses, and aesthetic codes[7]. Rather, its potential resides in helping us grasp those relations existing between "religion and other status categories in contexts of migration-driven diversification, such as race, ethnicity, legal status, age, and gender"[8]. This complexification of diversity finds a parallel in the acknowledgment of the "mutual constitution of different kinds of religious difference"[9]: in other words, the notion of super-diversity transposed onto religions calls for the acknowledgment of simultaneous and co-present religious differences (evident in practices, representations, and identities), including those emerging within the same ethnic/social group.

Herein, I will refer to ongoing ethnographic research on South Asian communities rooted in Southern Italy. I will engage with the migration experience of the Sri Lankan Sinhala community in the Italian southern region of Sicily – and more precisely in the city of Messina, one of the Italian cities with the highest concentration of Sri Lankan people. I propose to reflect upon the relationships between Sinhala Catholic and Buddhist communities living in Messina.

Sicily is one of the Italian regions where the Sri Lankan population is more concentrated, together with Lombardy, Campania, Veneto, and Lazio. In Sicily, Sri Lankans are mostly distributed among the three main cities of the region: Palermo, Catania, and Messina. The territory of Messina hosts the highest number of Sri Lankan people (around 4000 according to latest statistical data), who constitute the largest non-EU foreign community in the province.

The research began in the spring of 2021, aiming to explore the connection between migrants and home-making processes in the host contexts through the lens of rituals[10]. I focused principally on Sinhala Catholics, who form the main foreign community in the city of Messina,

---

7. The relation between migrations, mobility, and religion has extensively been studied over the last decades (Bonfanti 2014; Levitt 2003, 2004; Salih 2000; Vertovec 2019).
8. Becci, Burchardt 2016, pp. 1–2.
9. Ibid.
10. The research is part of a Research Project of National Relevance (PRIN_201773AHHL_001 – CUP J44I19001120005), "Migration, blurring boundaries, and homemaking: Anthropological analysis of the rituals/migrations nexus in Southern Italy", which involves the universities of Messina, Catania, Palermo, and Basilicata.

and whose complex and actively structured ritual time-space constitute a useful point of observation for the research objectives. In addition to conducting in-depth interviews to religious personnel (both Sinhalese and Italian) and ordinary believers, my ethnography primarily consisted of the direct participation in the ritual activities performed by the Sinhala Catholic community. This included ordinary and special masses, processions, saints' festivities, catechism, and other celebrations. I also gained access to the organisational structure responsible for the day-to-day running of the Sinhala Chaplaincy of Messina. Furthermore, the research focused on the continuous yet troubled relationship between the Catholic dioceses of Messina (including ecclesiastic figures as well as pastoral and charity associations) and the religious leaders of the Sinhala community. It examined the frictions and attempts at mutual control that are evident in the (futile) efforts played by the dioceses to involve Sinhalese into pastoral activities also for orienting their religiosity toward "correct" patterns of religious behaviour. A shorter part of the research also involved the smaller Sinhala Buddhist community.

In Messina, migrants from Sri Lanka insert themselves in the local economic fabric, mainly as domestic workers and caregivers, though there is also not a lack of businessmen and small entrepreneurs, especially in the field of ethnic catering and commerce. Until the spread of the Covid-19 pandemic, families used to manage a reversible distribution of people between Italy and Sri Lanka. They usually let children attend school in Italy until they obtained long-stay permits or citizenship and then made their way back to Asia, in order to save money and guarantee mastery of the English language. Afterwards, they would again come to Italy. At present, as economic conditions and the political situation in Sri Lanka worsen, things seem to be changing. During the last months I have been tracing unplanned returns to Italy made by mothers or fathers with children in tow, who have to begin attending Italian school in the middle of the school year despite their insufficient linguistic skills.

For the purposes of this study, it is interesting to take into account considerations beyond economic and material well-being, such as the symbolic and immaterial reasons that have been shaping the transnational migration space between Italy and Sri Lanka over the last decades. Religious rituals and practices act not only as home-making tools in the country of arrival, but the symbolic value linked to the role and the presence of Catholicism in Italy's history strongly resonates among Catholics coming from the western coast of Sri Lanka where Catholicism is traditionally rooted[11].

In particular, "the pilgrimage sites and Saints that belong to the host country (St. Anthony of Padua, the Tindari Madonna in the Province of Messina, St. Rosalia in Palermo, and St. Agatha in Catania) serve to increase Italy's symbolic value among Sri Lankan immigrants and to feel the desire for migration among their relatives and friends in the Country of origin"[12]. The religious experience that Sri Lankan people recreate in Italy prompts that "demand for Italy" that seed the cultures of migration here and there (i.e., in the countries of origin and arrival)[13]. Not by chance, many among my Catholic interlocutors are taken aback after they discover that the religiosity lived and shown by Italian people is not as intense as they imagined. "Where I work, my colleagues often blaspheme, and someone is even atheist", once the astonished Amil, one of the catechists within the Messina's Catholic community and member of several charismatic and prayer groups in Italy and Sri Lanka, told me[14].

2 Interaction of Diversities

In this paper, super-diversity will be considered and examined mainly in connection to relations between Sinhala Catholics and Buddhists in Messina. However, to pursue the line of inquiry suggested by numerous studies on super-diversity, which call for an analytical and methodological elaboration of the diverse layers present in the observed context, it will be useful to briefly reflect on another expression of super-diversity. This emerges from the relationship between Catholic Sinhalese and the Catholic Diocese of Messina. We must always keep in mind the role occupied by religion in contemporary European multiculturalism politics.

---

11. Benadusi 2015.
12. Ibid., p. 96.
13. Mara Benadusi (2015) deals with the transnational fluxes of relics, which involves both Catholics and Buddhists, activated through devotion to Saints. The religious and social meaning of relics are particularly evident in the case of St. Agatha in Catania and, as I came to know, the Lady of Sorrows in Syracuse.
14. Encounter held in Messina, 9 September 2021.

As Ester Gallo remarks, "political markers such as 'race' and 'ethnicity' have been replaced by 'faith' as a renewed idiom of recognition by both the state and minorities"[15]. This is particularly true in the case of South Asian communities, who increasingly reject a shared identification as "South Asians" privileging rather religious labels by which to be identified while "structuring connections between different ends of diaspora" and "defining a collective awareness across temporal and spatial distance"[16]. However, these general tendencies must be put in relation to the different ways by which the Church and local expressions of Christianity historically framed the role and the presence of religion (and of religious difference) in each national context.

Furthermore, despite the sharing of a common religious matrix, we need not forget that historical universal religions (such as Christianity) are anything but homogenous, being rather crossed by internal demarcation lines and constant tensions between "unity" and "diversity", as well as between "local" and "universal" declinations of theological, institutional, and devotional repertoires[17]. Moreover, even though in many European countries (like Italy) the Christian and particularly the Catholic religious identity may lead migrants to mitigate their profile of otherness, racialization processes may be paradoxically activated through the main national Church organization's pastoral work. This is the case of the cultural construction of migrants' religiosity, which is often fed by stereotypes, generalizations, and naturalizations encompassing their alleged sincere, authentic, and fervent faith – but heterodox and requiring it to be domesticated in the final analysis[18]. In short, when it comes to ethnic "others", sharing the same Christian confession does not prevent it from turning into cultural difference.

During my fieldwork, I observed how the efforts of the Catholic Church of Messina to involve the Sri Lankan Catholic community in a wide range of pastoral activities and initiatives inevitably intersect with local Sri Lankan religious activism aimed at establishing a "distinctive cultural space" to reinforce and strengthen their unique religious identity[19]. The

15. Gallo 2014, p. 3.
16. Ibid., p. 7.
17. Norget et al. 2017.
18. Gallo 2014.
19. Jacobsen, Raj 2008, p. 4.

Catholic *Migrantes Foundation* of Messina[20], appointed to the pastoral care of migrants, is engaged in the organization of several activities of both religious and charitable nature. In many events dedicated to the issue of migrations and the ecclesial integration of the Sri Lankan community (like the special Masses hosted in the Cathedral of Messina for Sinhala youth's first communions, the Sinhala Masses dedicated to Saints who are objects of particular devotions hosted in churches and shrines of the city where relics or icons of the Saint are kept, as for Saint Anthony of Padua, very popular in Sri Lanka, or still the refugees' and migrants' international days) the archbishop targeted the Sinhalese publically, as have other diocesan priests, thanking them and appreciating their "authentic" faith, and their "strong" and "genuine" devotion that should be looked at by Italians as a pattern of good religiosity[21]. However, these considerations are accompanied by not so subtle, racialized criticisms that the same religious personnel direct at the Sinhala community. This is especially evident when confronting their desire to autonomously manage the religious activities and services hosted in the parish of St. Elia, where they have gathered several days a week for about ten years.

The local ecclesial and pastoral authorities' evaluation of some ritual features of both the ordinary Sinhala faithful (like crawling on the ground toward a sacred icon) and the national chaplain (like drawing a cross with a blessed statue on the day of a particular celebration), seen as archaic acts once detectable also in the West, leads to the Sinhalese being placed on a different temporal scale. During conversations with diocesan religious figures, I was told that Sinhala religiosity requires the pastoral intervention and guidance of the Church. This is because their religious behavior and practices are based on a "miraculous" conception of the relationship between the faithful and God, the Virgin Mary, and other Saints. They are misunderstood and criticized for their exclusive use of the Sinhala language in Masses and for their lack of interest in participation in those ecclesial and pastoral activities not directly focused on their community.

---

20. The *Migrantes Foundation* is a pastoral unity within the Italian Episcopal Conference (CEI). Its aim is to sustain particular Churches in their work of evangelization and pastoral care of migrants, both Italians and foreigners, to promote fraternity, pacific cohabitation and migrants' rights and protection within Christian communities.
21. Cordova 2025a, 2022.

In this sense, we can observe how diversity crosses an institutional, devotional and social body supposed to be unified, adding complexity to the religious matrixes of identity and extraneousness within the "same" Catholic religious field. Another expression of super-diversity that this contribution will focus on in more detailed in the following paragraphs concerns the blurring relations between Sinhala Catholics and Buddhists, which has lead to innovative devotional practices as creative negotiations on the faithful's religious subjectivity.

Religious co-habitation is frequent in Sri Lanka. The wider Indian Ocean region represents an area that challenges our understanding of religious diversity, demanding an approach capable of grasping those (ambiguous) zones of inter-being where traditions and moral worlds are not mutually exclusive, and where someone usually is not called to choose between one pattern of devotion and another[22]. However, these relations expressed through plural worships[23], interrituality[24], visits to shared shrines, prayers addressed to "other" deities, and saints and "hybrid" patterns of daily lived religion, acquire a different light within the experience of migration, as claimed by my fieldwork interlocutors. After all, "religious super-diversity simultaneously develops at global and local scales"[25]. Religious super-diversity presents an "array of options for belonging that reach far beyond their communities and culture and that challenge local religions"[26], impacting both departure and arrival countries[27]. In this sense, "super-diversity" may allow us to conceive of "religion" as a practical category[28], contributing to the ethnographic understanding of the historical and contextual terrains where religions are made and lived, within the "broader social, cultural, political and economic environment in which they are debated [...] and [which] change over time"[29].

22. Michael Carrithers (2000) coined the concept of "polytropy" to refer to convergences and cohabitation in religious life in South Asia.
23. Bastin 2002.
24. Kreinath 2017.
25. Becci, Burchardt 2016, p. 5.
26. Levitt 2003, p. 2.
27. Van Dijk 1997.
28. The concept of "lived religion" helps in directing the observation to people's daily personal experience of faith (Orsi 1985, 1996).
29. Osella, Soares 2020, p. 477.

How does religious super-diversity interact with and how is it re-shaped within the hosting context? Does the migration experience make differences more marked, or does it rather reconcile differences promoting cohabitation? Does it make identities more rigid or flexible?

3   War and Peace: #Gota Go Home!

Sri Lanka has a population of almost 22 million people. The main ethno-linguistic divide is composed of the Sinhala majority (the first language of over 70% of the whole population) and Tamils. However, the Sinhala-Tamil opposition is not as simple and unambiguous as we may think. The taxonomic landscape is much more complex. Muslims, who are mostly Tamil speakers, "constitute an 'ethnic' category, as well as a 'religious' category; Hindus, though, are a 'religious' group but not an 'ethnic' group. Malays are religiously 'Muslim', but 'ethnically' not Muslim. Almost all Buddhists are Sinhala, but not all Sinhala are Buddhist"[30]. As it is easy to understand, this stratified landscape has been targeted by an intensive work of "purification" played by the State – and its ideological and coercive apparatus – since independence, which has attempted to foster the impossible isomorphism of one people-one nation-one place[31].

Nevertheless, it is no coincidence that Sri Lanka has been defined as a complex religious field characterized by the daily intermingling of religious traditions, practices, and rituals[32]. These entanglements have historically shaped inter-religious and inter-ethnic cohabitation as well as social tensions, easily encompassing ethnic and political violence, as Stanley Tambiah has so brilliantly shown in relation to Buddhism[33]. This peculiar condition of pluralism has been interpreted through different key readings.

"Syncretism" is a particularly popular notion thanks to which it is possible to think of the continuous and solid interactions between religions

---

30. Spencer et al. 2015, p. 3.
31. This is particularly evident in relation to neighboring India, the connection to which (especially for what concerns the Hindu heritage in the island) has been strongly denied by the Sri Lankan governments until recent years (Spencer 2003, 2014).
32. Silva et al. 2016; Spencer et al. 2015.
33. Tambiah 1986, 1992.

and devotees, presuming the overlapping of cultural features to such an extent that sooner or later some of each religion's features will creatively blend with those of others. The history of many Sri Lankan multi-religious spaces, such as Adam's Peak[34], Kataragama[35], the Shrine of Our Lady of Madhu, and many other lesser-known sites, along with the ritual practices conducted there, and most importantly the interactions between believers, has led numerous scholars to describe the processes resulting from cultural and religious diversity with the term "syncretism"[36].

However, recent studies – coming, among others, from Sri Lankan scholars – highlight that diversity does not always imply "a permanent overwhelming and alteration of one religion by another". Rather, "people in Sri Lanka's multi-religious landscape use innovations in practice to construct and negotiate religious spaces within their own religions that allow them to interact with other religions – sometimes by momentary amalgamation, sometimes by contestation as need requires – without abandoning themselves"[37]. This approach, even if too reliant upon the post-modernist assumption of the individual agent's capability to negotiate and switch from one register to another (including religion), may help us frame the practices put in place by Sri Lankans placed between the local and the transnational levels.

This history of religious intersections and overlaps, deeply rooted over time, did not prevent the civil war that ravaged the island from 1983 to 2009, due to hostilities between the Sri Lankan government and the northeastern paramilitary separatist group, the Liberation Tigers of Tamil Eelam (LTTE). As suggested by recent analyses[38], the conflict was something more than the mere contrast between Sinhala and Tamils. Rather, it was the culmination of several layers of conflicts that arose since the 1950s mixing the political and economic aspirations of the post-independence youth (including Sinhala youth), the Buddhists' nationalist claims,

---

34. Adam's Peak is a mountain in central Sri Lanka containing a footprint in the rock. For Buddhists, the footprint is that of Buddha; for Christians and Muslims it is that of Adam or St. Thomas; for Hindus, it is that of Hanuman or Shiva.
35. Kataragama is a town in southern Sri Lanka, which is sacred for both Buddhists and Hindus. Here a temple dedicated to God Kataragama, a deity particularly popular in Sri Lanka, is located.
36. Gombrich, Obeyesekere 1988; Goonasekera 2007; Kapferer 1997.
37. Sanmugeswaran 2021, p. 3.
38. Moore 1993; Goodhand et al. 2011; Spencer et al. 2015.

and the spread and re-appropriation of ideologies of liberation fostered by Marxism and echoed at the time of the end of colonialism. Within these frictions, we may find several entanglements between ethnic, religious, and political motifs, in such a way that the civil war cannot be reduced just to the clashes between Sinhala and north-eastern Tamil insurgent groups.

I do not want to retrace the dynamics of the civil war. Rather, I intend to evidence how religion can arise as a "problem" fostering hostilities and war or otherwise act at the margins of the political field (or perform as an intermediate zone crossing political boundaries) to provide people with safety and protection.

In a group work based upon a "collaborative ethnography of war and peace", the authors focus brilliantly on the different ways religions have shaped their responses to the rise of the conflict[39]. In many cases, religion succeeded in finding a place outside the war, doing so "in ways that to some extent ignore the boundaries that divide different religious and ethnic communities"[40]. The authors cite how bigger Tamil Hindu temples (*kovils*) tried to isolate themselves from the hostility generated by the war in the east of the island, providing for spaces of safety and protection that extended beyond Hindus. Oracle rituals held in these temples (and sought in order to address the insecurity and anxieties caused by the war) were the main feature of this "demotic" religiosity[41], based upon a pluralism quite indifferent to inter-religious boundaries. Catholic priests, rather, were active in a more evident way in the realm of public engagement, using their institutional strength (benefiting from the Church international networks and NGOs – like Caritas – that provided for the basic need of Sri Lankans of all faiths and ethnicities) to act as a humanitarian actor thanks to its deep transnational networks and material resources[42].

Turning to Buddhists' role, although Buddhism provided the symbolic reserve for the rise of Sinhala nationalism in post-colonial times[43], is not representable through a single lens. Not all Buddhist monks entered the

39. Spencer et al. 2015.
40. Ibid., p. 31.
41. Lawrence 1997.
42. Johnson 2012.
43. The post-Independence history of Sri Lanka has seen the increasing hegemony of Sinhala Buddhism, that has progressively tended to subsume the identity and

realm of party politics and nationalistic engagement. The development of Buddhist monks' orders (*sangha*) did not follow the same pattern, oscillating between different entanglements between politics, religion, and inter-ethnic relations[44]. In this sense, the interaction between "war" and "religion", and the political mobilization of the latter, cannot be labelled with fixed categories.

Religious cohabitation and conflict do not call into question the civil war exclusively. Muslims and Christians are minorities that throughout the contemporary age have often been targeted with suspicion, if not by concrete discrimination, (even though for different reasons) and are also perceived and classified as ethnic "others".

On 21 April 2019, on the occasion of the Catholic Easter, a series of terrorist attacks hit several churches and hotels. Smaller attacks continued in the following days, causing a total of 267 deaths. According to the Sri Lankan government, the jihadist national *Thowheeth Jama'ath* group executed the attacks. Despite the fact that the main instigators of the attacks are still unknown[45], fear and distrust around Muslims increased, leading to anti-Muslim riots and the rooting of a widespread Islamophobia in the country[46]. In times of political crisis and social tension the presence of Islam and Christianity in Sri Lanka has often been linked to foreign and hidden powers threatening Sri Lankan national integrity and so presented as exogenous and "alien" religions[47]. Consider the extensive transnational connections linking Christians with Europe and North America,

---

      allegiance with the Sinhala nation. To be Sinhala without being Buddhist became more difficult over time (Stirrat 1992).
44. This complex frame epitomized also in the contraposition between different Buddhist training institutions: the cosmopolitan oriented *Vidyodya* and the nationalist anti-Tamil *Vidaylankara* (Seneviratne 1999).
45. https://www.aljazeera.com/news/2022/1/12/sri-lanka-resumes-trials-over-2019-easter-sunday-bombings (last accessed 18 January 2022). Frictions between Catholics and the government became evident when the Colombo archbishop criticized the lack of progress in the investigations. https://www.aljazeera.com/news/2021/4/21/sri-lanka-catholics-slam-govt-over-easter-attacks-probe (last accessed 18 January 2022).
46. Imtiyaz 2020.
47. Pinto 2015. This is particularly evident in the case of Muslims, traditionally identified with the ethnic matrix of Moors, descendants from the ancient Arab traders settling in Colombo around the 9th century.

and Muslims with the Arab Gulf. This is a particularly remarkable point if compared to Buddhism and, even if on a lesser degree, Hinduism, officially presented by competing political powers and institutions as "intrinsic" cultural and religious systems "naturally" rooted in Sri Lankan history and society.

However, despite the continuous "weaponization" of religion pursued by international and regional agencies[48], this island still represents a "single, albeit divided, religious field"[49]. Here, people act a vernacular cosmopolitanism made of practices and feelings of belonging that found a "grammar of plurality" which goes beyond communal and ethnic boundaries[50]. The hard political, social and economic crisis that affected Sri Lanka in 2022 and lead to the resignation of President Gotabaya Rajapaksa has produced a large popular mobilization characterized by striking inter-religious participation[51]. The images of the protests that have circulated globally, accompanied by the viral slogan "#GotaGoHome!", depict believers of all religions (including Buddhist monks, Hindu priests, and Christian pastors and nuns) demonstrating together in public spaces and calling for radical political and institutional change. The presence of religious symbols in the protest has been significant, as evidenced, for example, by the recurring use of icons of the Christ. These were also portrayed by Catholic protesters in symbolic reenactments of the *Via Crucis*, in the presence of followers of other religions, to evoke a parallelism between Christ's sacrifice and the hard life conditions of the impoverished and starving Sri Lankan people. The same can be said for the direct involvement of religious institutional actors (the Sri Lankan Catholic Church and the organizations of Buddhist monks), as witnessed by the active presence of priests and nuns in the streets, being attacked by the army. The social and political mobilization after the current national crisis may have opened up spaces of religious coexistence, though they have not emerged so far. This reveals the conciliatory role played by religious attitudes and beliefs in Sri Lanka. We

48. Rajasingham-Senanayake 2021.
49. Spencer et al. 2015, p. 16.
50. Srinivas 2014.
51. In 2022 Sri Lanka faced the worst economic crisis since its independence in 1948, made of high inflation tax, near-depletion of foreign exchange reserves, and increase in prices of basic necessities.

still have to understand whether the renewed presence of religion in the public space may lead to the overcoming of, rather than the emphasizing of, ethnic and religious boundaries, as recent popular mobilizations seem to indicate.

4 The Buddha and the Christ

Sri Lanka may be considered an interesting non-Western example to apply the notion of "super-diversity" outside the context where it originated. It is not by chance that many of the theorizations about the topic have been developing in relation to South Asia, where the historical co-presence of several religious traditions existed well before the colonial period and the encounter between Christianity and "indigenous" religions. These unique historical, political, and social conditions have inevitably influenced social relations and the ways in which members of different religious groups exist within the same social sphere, spanning a spectrum from close association to antagonistic affiliations[52].

The Sinhala community living today in Messina is mostly made of Catholics[53] which make up more than half of the whole population. Beyond that, a few hundred Buddhists and several dozen Muslims and Hindus comprise the population. However, today in Sri Lanka, Catholics constitute a politically uninfluential community, which is not as relevant as it was in the past. Roderick Stirrat writes about the "political eclipse"[54] of the contemporary Church, due to historical and political reasons I cannot deepen here. However, this is particularly relevant to the topic addressed in this article. Within the context of transnational migrations, what are the social and political implications running through a community that passes from a condition of minority in Sri Lanka to one sharing the main religious tradition of the country of arrival?

---

52. Shah-Kazemi 2006; Mosse 2012; Das 2013.
53. Given the lack of statistical surveys of the religious composition of the Sri Lankan community, I can rely upon the observation conducted at the main rituals, in the Sinhala Chaplaincy, and in shops, markets, and restaurants to sustain that more than half of the whole Sri Lankan population in Messina is made up of Catholics.
54. Stirrat 1992, p. 177.

Consequences are impossible to overlook and directly challenge our understanding of super-diversity. The role of Sinhala nationalism and Sinhala Buddhism in the contemporary Sri Lankan political and cultural scene has opened new avenues for conceptualizing Catholic faith as well as religious practices and rituals. "Growing numbers of Catholics are attending non-Catholic shrines, developing syncretic notions of religious practice, and questioning the basic tenets of the Church's teachings"[55], wrote Stirrat. If, in Sri Lanka, the attendance of Hindu festivals, Buddhist temples, and Catholic Churches and shrines has historically exceeded strict confessional belonging, pointing towards a rather pluralistic dimension, this tendency has increased significantly over the last two decades.

Catholics have always existed within a cultural ecosystem where the political and social significance of other religions was impossible to ignore, even in the "enclaves" of the western coast where the Catholic presence is still well represented today. What has changed is the gradual identification of Catholics with Sinhala nationalist cultural themes after independence, paralleling the increasing significance of ethnic markers over religious ones as the basis for social identity, unlike in the past. By way of example, according to my Sinhala Catholics informants in Messina, the words "tradition" and "rites" (*chāritra*) mark practices conceived as culturally Sinhala/Sri Lankan, but not specifically as Catholic, even when they are performed in the church, during the Mass (like the "traditional" dances performed at the moment of the Offertory). As such, they are understood as different than properly Catholic ritual acts, like prayers (*yākgnā*).

Despite the periodic resurgence of intolerant religious movements making claims for purity and primacy, the history of Sri Lanka is one of diffuse entanglements between the faithful and shared holy places. One of the clearer examples is given by the great Marian Shrine of Our Lady of Madhu, located in the Mannar district, visited by Pope Francis in 2015. The Madhu Shrine is one of the most popular shrines in Sri Lanka, together with the shrine of St. Anne at Talawila in the western coast. The foundational myth of Madhu's Shrine tells of a statue of Our Lady that survived the destruction of the north of the island under Dutch colonial domination and was preserved in the jungle. In 1870, the first annual

---

55. Ibid.

pilgrimage to the Shrine was instituted, though the shrine dates back to the 17th century. During summer, the annual feast for the Assumption of the Blessed Virgin Mary (15 August) is held in the holy site. It is not by chance that in the month of August two of the major Marian feasts of Sri Lankan Catholics in Eastern Sicily, the Our Lady of Tears in Syracuse and the pilgrimage at the shrine of Dinnammare (Messina), also take place.

Sri Lankans in Messina related emotional pilgrimages to the Madhu shrine. To accomplish pilgrimages, they have to plan trips lasting more than two days, given the distance from their home villages and cities mostly located in the southwestern part of the island. Usually, families move to Madhu with relatives and friends, renting minibuses. Upon arrival, they sleep for one or more nights in one of the numerous hostels available for pilgrims. To arrive in Madhu is all but easy. Until a few decades ago, journeys to Madhu were even more difficult and dangerous. To accomplish it safely, the pilgrimage itself was a sign of the grace received from Our Lady, who is still today believed to possess miraculous powers[56].

Moreover, due to its location, it has been one of the regions most affected by the civil war. Madhu is, in fact, in a Tamil speaking area in north-western Sri Lanka, an area claimed by the LTTE as Tamil Eelam. At that time, it was very dangerous to reach. The shrine, which serves as the point of intersection between Sinhala and Tamils, constituted a demilitarized area, hosting camps and thousands of refugees in its internal spaces during the war. However, this did not prevent the occurrence of murders, attacks on means of transportation and shelling, as for example in what has been called the "Madhu Church Massacre" in 1999[57]. During the war, several "penitential pilgrimages" were held, and when the Sri Lankan government re-established its authority over the area at the end of the conflict, the statue of Our Lady was moved into the rebel-held area before being returned.

56. Stirrat (1992) lists some of the beliefs about the healing properties of Our Lady of Madhu and the Shrine itself. Pilgrims took home sand and coconut oil scrubbed on the crosses surrounding the Churches. For the same reason, they used to bring home the rice distributed at the end of Masses, a practice which is still in use today.
57. Responsibility for the attack, which had a reported death toll of forty people, is still widely disputed.

The Shrine in Madhu is of interest for us, however, because it is a holy site shared by several religious confessions and ethnic groups. Catholics, Sinhala, and Tamils, of course, but also Buddhists, Hindus, and Muslims take part in the annual pilgrimage and visit the shrine throughout the whole year. It is noteworthy that the Muslim community contributed to the renovation of one shrine's chapel[58]. Madhu does not represent an exception: even in Messina, Catholic sites are visited by other faithful.

Turning now to the practice of attending Buddhist temples, this was, and still is, fairly common among Catholics in Sri Lanka. Many of the Sinhala Catholics in Messina I have been encountering in my research tell me that they access Buddhist temples during their periodical stays in Sri Lanka. Usually, these visits are made while going out from the native village in order to buy or do something else in bigger cities. Sometimes the visit to the temple happens on the occasion of a Buddhist feast. This is particularly common in mixed families where the patrilineal side is Catholic and the matrilineal one is Buddhist, or the reverse (the first case happens more often, according to the testimonies I collected).

Visits to the temple may be made with the desire to have a look at a different environment, just as a matter of curiosity. Among young Sinhala attending middle schools in Messina, where they have lived since they were no more than six years old, visits to the Sri Lankan Buddhist temples are remembered for their enjoyable character. "It provided me with calm, serenity" Chamila, a 13-year-old girl from Ja'Ela[59] told me, referring to the time she entered a Buddhist temple with her mother during a summer stay in Sri Lanka[60]. Chamila and her family attend the main Sinhala Catholic Chaplaincy in Messina. She and her younger sister, Alisha, have received the sacraments of Confession, First Communion, and Confirmation in Italy. They are assiduous attenders of non-liturgical

58. This information has been given to me by Sinhala Catholics in Messina. It is specifically a plaque on the wall of the Blessed Sacrament Chapel that was affixed in 1979 by a Muslim lawyer in memory of his son (Whitaker 2021).
59. Ja'Ela is a town located in the suburbs of Colombo, from which dozens of Sri Lankans living in Messina come to visit the Buddhist temple located there.
60. Encounter held in Messina, 14 October 2021. To meet the needs of confidentiality expressed by my Sinhala interlocutors, their names have been changed in this paper.

events as well as weekend Masses[61], and both wear the headscarf with the Madonna of Lourdes embroidered on it that Sinhala women wear at Mass and during rosaries. Among their relatives in Sri Lanka there are not Buddhists. Visits to temples are part of the composite landscape of cultural and religious diversity in their country of origin.

I have to specify that neither Chamila nor Alisha know well what Buddhism is. Neither of them would be able to explain it or its cosmological or (a)theological premises to someone not familiar with Buddhism. They know what happens inside temples and they may be able to roughly describe what happens during the *Puja*[62]. They have been familiar with that, but not to the point of being self-conscious of meanings or principles. It is not just a matter of age. Even older Catholics who teach Sinhala to children born in Italy (and to foreign researchers like me), and who master the complex and deep semantic networks of Sinhala language, struggle to explain the meaning of a word whose etymology and usage is rooted in Buddhism. The reason is that they simply do not know the exact definitions of words. "Once I knew, but after decades away from Sri Lanka, living here where Buddhism is a very thin presence, I became unfamiliar with it", my teacher of Sinhala and the catechist and director of the Chaplaincy's Choir, Tharindi, told me. Surely, this relative unawareness does not regard people and families among whose members it is possible to count as Buddhists. However, Chamila was not properly at ease in speaking about her feelings about Buddhist Temples. "My parents don't like that I go to the Buddhist temples here in Messina", she told me. Things may change with migration, and a common practice in the country of origin becomes more problematic in that of arrival.

During my ethnographic research, I often found the presence of Buddhists in Catholic churches and shrines. Sometimes, even for the religious body, it is difficult to trace clear boundaries between the faithful. To provide a brief example, the two Scalabrinian nuns who were

61. In the Sinhala Chaplaincy in Messina, besides Masses, the chaplain and the faithful hold non-liturgical events. Among them, I limit myself to cite the non-liturgical novena for the Madonna of the Perpetual Help, which is very popular in Sri Lanka and happens every Wednesday evening.
62. The *Puja* is one of the main devotional practices of Buddhism, held to express gratitude and respect to Lord Buddha. It is interesting to note that among Sinhala Catholics, *pujaye* is the term for the Mass.

sent to Messina to fulfill the pastoral care requested by the Archbishop of Messina for Catholic ethnic communities, notably Sri Lankans and Filipinos, struggled to accurately identify which parents of the young Sinhala students attending the Chaplaincy's after-school activities were Catholics[63]. Sometimes, after months of attendance in the Sinhala Chaplaincy of Saint Elia, the baroque rectory made available to Sinhalese by the local *Migrantes* office, they discover that the parents of a little girl or boy, having received the Sacrament of the First Communion, are Buddhist even though they regularly attend Masses, take the communion, and go on pilgrimage to Catholic sites. Such ambiguities around religious subjectivities may be interpreted as the effort to please Catholic pastoral institutions and benefit from their services. However, it is also true that in mixed families, in some cases even those children who receive their first Communion and follow the pastoral care provided by the Sri Lankan Chaplain (like the Catechism course), may not define themselves as definitively Christians. Their parents affirm that when their sons are older, they will freely decide if they are Christians or Buddhist. Meanwhile, however, they receive First Communion and the other Sacraments. Such ambivalences, which Coleman would define as "forms of ritual semi-engagement"[64], may be explained by recurring to the argument that "Buddhism is not really a religion; rather, it's a way of life. It teaches you to behave good, not to kill animals, and so on", as many people characterized by multiple religious orientations used to tell me.

Among them was Mayuri, a Buddhist woman who recently returned to Messina, where she had already emigrated when her kids were young. While introducing to me her "100% Catholic" husband, and her two sons[65], Mayuri told me that the latter used to attend Catholic churches, according to the faith of their father's family, already in Sri Lanka, because they studied Buddhist topics at school and it would be preferable to enrich their knowledge on Catholicism. This condition allows for the

---

63. The Congregation of the Missionary Sisters of St. Charles Borromeo Scalabrinians was founded in 1895 by Giovanni Battista Scalabrini. Their mission consists of catechesis, Christian education, social action, and pastoral care of migration. They are often present in centers for arrival and welcoming migrants.
64. Coleman 2014, p. 288.
65. The encounter took place in Messina, 22 April 2022.

permeability of boundaries and practices: the Buddhist monk of Messina comes to their new house to bless it, and a week later the whole family goes on pilgrimage at Lourdes or in other Catholic shrines in Italy. In the house where they recently moved, Mayuri's Buddhist mother placed "in the centre" a big statue of Lord Buddha, brought from Colombo, and Mayuri is planning to make a shelf where she can put images of Christ, in order to let her sons pray at home.

Mixed families originate from mixed marriages, which are sometimes celebrated in the church of Saint Elia in Messina, after the Buddhist wife/husband converts to Christianity and is baptized. In this case, marriage rites are celebrated within the Mass; otherwise, if the Buddhist groom or spouse has not been baptized, the marriage rite held in the church is shorter: the spouses become officially husband and wife only once the Mass is ended and a "private" rite takes place after people have left the church. Except on rare occasions, Buddhist and Catholic families usually allow their young sons to convert for marriage, given the social importance of marriage for the whole family group. Mayuri's mother did not like that her daughter converted to marry a Catholic man but, being a widow, she had no possibility to resist the pressures exerted by her future son-in-law's family, who wanted to celebrate a full mass in the church.

For this reason, in the following years, despite her Buddhist former education, Mayuri would have looked in the direction of the statue of St. Anthony displayed on the related Messina's shrine to seek relief from pains that she felt during her pregnancy.

As we have observed, relatively easy communication and transitions between boundaries do not imply a complete absence of constraints and ties. The Catholic Church requires conversion through baptism, and Mayuri's mother expects her grandchildren to bow in reverential salutation (the same gesture that Sinhala Catholics make in front of their Chaplain) in front of the statue of Lord Buddha as they return home.

Pilgrimages to Catholic Shrines in the provincial territory of Messina are commonly shared by the faithful of other religious confessions. This is the case of the shrine of the Madonna of Tindari, one of the most popular Catholic Shrines in Sicily. Sri Lankans[66] come from all over Italy to

---

66. Mollica 2000; Faranda 2009.

visit the shrine on the occasion of their annual Feast organized in May, whereas the traditional Feast of Tindari is held in September[67].

The dark-skinned Madonna of Tindari is the object of a very deep devotion, especially in Sicily and by both Sinhalese and Tamils. Just as Sicilians do, Sri Lankan parents also name their sons Tindaro and their daughters Tindara – or sometimes just Tindari for both genders. During my research I acknowledged that the Madonna of Tindari became an object of devotion about fifteen years ago. At that time, one of the first Sinhala chaplains in Sicily, who was at that time residing in Catania, fostered the faithful to discover the cult for the Tindari's Madonna and encouraged the organization of visits and pilgrimages to the shrine. Among the reasons for why this cult has become as popular as it is today is the historical configuration of Sri Lankan Catholicism. As the first Oratorian missionaries came from Goa (southern India) in the twentieth century, they made massive use of devotion for Saints and Madonnas to let Catholicism take root[68]. Equally, the dark color of this Madonna fosters Sinhalese identification with this Marian figure along the axes of "racial" and ethnic difference. "It's our Mother. She's brown, like us", Amil, a catechist in the parochial group, once told me[69].

Visits and pilgrimages to Tindari can be made by single families or larger groups. In the latter, they rent a minibus. It is especially before the periodic return to Sri Lanka that they go to the shrine, seeking the Madonna's grace and benediction before accomplishing a long journey to South Asia. Another common occasion for going to Tindari is for the beginning of the new year. On 1 or 2 January it is possible to note hundreds of Sri Lankan pilgrims attending the shrine, taking part in the Mass and laying down flowers for the Madonna while addressing personal prayers to Her. In many cases, people bring particular objects and documents to the shrine, including the keys of a car just bought, or the permit papers for a being examined by local authorities.

---

67. It should be noted that many Catholic Communities (not only Sri Lankans) in Sicily celebrate feasts for Mary and the Saints (Madonna of Tindari and Dinnammare, St. Nicola in Messina, St. Agata in Catania) in different dates than the traditional ones of the Italian Catholics' calendar.
68. Stirrat 1992.
69. Encounter held in Messina, 9 August 2021. On this issue, see Cordova 2025b.

The Madonna of Tindari is deeply beloved by Buddhists, who respect her powerful and graceful virtues. They do not just visit the shrine, mingling with Catholics. They also perform ritual practices, especially during critical moments in life. Women passing through difficult pregnancies, for example, walk crawling from the entrance to the main altar to make a vow to the Madonna – an act of piousness once very common among Italian women. I personally know Buddhist women who engaged in this practice when pregnant, asking their husbands or relatives to record a video of the ritual to send to the family residing in Sri Lanka. This is how a transnational ritual space comes to be constituted, introducing practices and ideas in contexts where they were relatively unknown or not practised.

Religious entanglements are easily observable in the Sinhala ritual space in Messina and beyond, in "ethnic" restaurants and markets where Catholic and Buddhist iconographies are equally present in the same shop. The co-presence of statues and paintings depicting the Buddha, as well as Catholic figures particularly revered among Sri Lankans – Jesus Christ, the Madonnas of Lourdes, Fatima, and Tindari, St. Francis, St. Anthony of Padua, and St. Sebastian – might cause disorientation for observers unaccustomed to the flexibility of ritual scenes and pantheons. Even in Buddhist *Vihāras* in Messina[70], Catholic votive candles with the face of the popular St. Pio find their place among flowers and other objects of the Buddhist cult. In this regard, and answering my questions, a monk at one of the two temples in Messina confirmed to me that for Buddhists it is not a problem to attend Catholic churches and shrines. Sacred figures, like the Madonna of Tindari, are considered with deep respect if not devotion. Buddhists can pay tribute to saints and Madonnas whose grace, miracles, and powers are not called into question, revealing what has been described as that "accommodation of 'other' deities, powers, indigenous spirits, and ritual practices"[71] that is easy to see in Sri Lankan sacred sites and places of worship. "Remember", the young monk who had arrived in Italy five years ago from Anuradhapura, told me, "Buddhism is a research, a pathway". His comment aimed at distinguishing Buddhism from the stricter

---

70. *Vihāra* is the main room of the temple, where prayers take place in the presence of a large statue of the Buddha.
71. Rajasingham-Senanayake 2021, p. 14.

ritual and the formal codifications and rules followed by practitioners of other religions[72].

5 Plural Conclusions

In Tindari and other Catholic shrines, including those in Buddhist temples which are sometimes attended by Catholics, we see the formation of interfaces crossing religious boundaries and extending ritual space[73]. Nothing here is of exception in the Indian Ocean Region, where there is "accommodation and localization of diverse cultural forms, flows, and forces, including doctrinally monotheistic religions (Christianity and Islam), despite the latter's apparently 'jealous' god/s"[74]. Even in migration contexts, the everyday ritual religious practice reveals shared traditions and cultural motifs of devotion, reshaping civic negotiations of interaction between social groups.

Moreover, migration brings an extension of the singular religious field towards zones of interconnection. Interested in Buddhists' devotion to the Tindari's Madonna, I asked many Buddhists (including one of the monks residing in Messina) for some explanation about that. I was intrigued by the eventual overlapping of the image of the black Madonna and that of Pattini, a female deity incorporated from Hinduism in the Theravada Buddhist pantheon, which throughout Sri Lankan's history had already included Hindu gods and assimilated *Veddha* cultural practices[75]. Pattini (Kannaki for Tamil Hindus) in Sri Lanka is considered the goddess of fertility and health and the protector of the island and is worshipped by both Tamils and Sinhala and, in turn, transmitted to Sri Lanka from

---

72. Encounter held in Messina, 27 January 2022. By saying that, the monk reproduced a common polemic *topos*, often employed by Protestants when targeting the empty ritualism of Catholicism (Norget et al. 2017). Concerning the definition of Buddhism as a religion, see Southwold 1978.
73. Samnugeswaran 2021.
74. Rajasingham-Senanayake 2021, p. 14.
75. Gombrich, Obeyesekere 1988; Obeyesekere 1966, 2004. However, this possible connection could be extended to other Madonnas (Our Lady of Lourdes, Our Lady of Fatima, etc.), to whom Sri Lankan Catholics are strongly devoted. Here I consider the Tindari's Madonna because she is a "new" sacred figure that Sri Lankans discover through migration.

Southern India[76]. Pattini, "meaning 'faithful and chaste wife' in Sanskrit [...] is a guardian of Buddhism, and a *bodhisattva* aspiring to attain Enlightenment"[77]. Furthermore, devotion to Pattini has increased during and after the civil war, especially in the areas involved in the conflict.

Without having the possibility to deepen this topic, I limit myself to considering how myths and rites concerning Pattini focus on the mother-child relation. Not coincidentally, Pattini is called *Pattini Amma* by Buddhists, where *amma* means "mother" in Sinhala. Moreover, according to Obeyesekere[78], South Indian merchants devoted to Pattini borrowed from West Asia the religious and cultural motif of the *mater dolorosa*, within which the worship of Pattini has been built in Sri Lanka, following the myth, where Pattini was a chaste wife and a hungry widow. The *Maniyo* (mother) motif is strongly related to the Catholic figure of the Virgin Mary and is explicitly evoked by Sinhala Catholics and Buddhists in rituals, songs, and discourses about religion.

Do Sinhala Buddhists in Messina overlap the Madonna of Tindari with the goddess Pattini? Not at all. People I talked to have grasped commonalities between the two figures and devotional motifs, but only after I introduced the suggestion. According to them, the Madonna of Tindari has successfully fit the cosmological and ritual horizon that fosters Buddhists' religious practice. She is a figure whose worship does not present a contradiction or an offence to the Buddhist sacred and ritual space (as the Buddhist monk told me), grafting on cultural motifs, moral registers, and religious themes already known and possessed in Buddhism. In other words, this Madonna (just as, to a minor degree, other Saints beloved by Buddhists) has become another piece of the extended Buddhist choreography[79]. Rather than thinking in terms of uniqueness and monolithic overlaps, it is surely more fruitful to think through the registers of complexity and plurality.

The frames depicted across these pages testify to how diversity in Sri Lanka can seamlessly evolve into everyday cohabitation, built on a foundation of encounters, overlaps, entanglements, interstices, and interfaces.

76. Obeyesekere 1984.
77. de Alwis 2021, p. 73. For Buddhism, *Bodhisattva* is one who joints the Enlightenment and so is on the path towards the *Buddhahood* state.
78. Obeyesekere 1984.
79. Barkan, Barkley 2014.

Without overstating these premises, the Indian Ocean region emerges as an area that challenges our comprehension of religious super-diversity. It calls for a fresh – and possibly ethnographic – approach, one that is capable of understanding the zones of inter-being where traditions and moral worlds coexist without being mutually exclusive, and where individuals are not typically forced to choose between one pattern of devotion and another.

However, I would like to end this contribution by evoking some questions arising from my fieldwork in Messina. With respect to Sri Lanka, religions and rituals "on the move" enlarge on a trans-national scale the existing options for identity and belonging, reaching frequently to alter local religious structures, forms, and practices. In other words, the interaction and the inter-relation between "diversities" may lead to original scenarios, that respond to the religious landscape of migration, where Catholicism is the majority religion and Buddhism a minority one, at the contrary than in Sri Lanka. This condition engenders greater possibilities to act on the part of religious personnel and ordinary believers.

On many occasions, like Sunday Masses, the Sinhala chaplain exhorts the faithful not to attend Buddhist temples and, most of all, to not bow in front of the monk, while recognizing at the same time the historical multi-vocal influence that Buddhism exerted over Catholicism.

Shops, markets, and restaurants have plenty of the two religions' symbols, and Catholic shrines are attended by Buddhist faithful. However, political, economic, and religious infrastructures overlap even more evidently in the narrower communities of the diaspora. In many cases, the Sinhalese already knew each other well before migration, transplanting abroad village or town relations – with their load of sympathy as well as rivalry and competition. In Messina, religious practices and (inter)confessional belonging are charged by such preconditions. Some of the more influential Catholic members of the Sinhala community attend reluctantly those restaurants and shops owned by Buddhist people who are subjects of rumor for their formidable entrepreneurial rise in Messina. If Chamila and Alisha can freely visit Buddhist Temples on the occasion of their trips to Sri Lankan cities, as reported in the previous pages, in Messina their parents do not appreciate that they can be seen and identified by the networks of Buddhist people involved in the care of the Temple. Religious belonging strictly intersects new or already existing social relations and personal acquaintances, and from such entanglements results in the overall social and cultural reproduction of the Sinhala community "far from home".

Migration and super-diversity is a dynamic nexus, and its outcome is unpredictable, as it relies on several variables such as the economic and political situation in both countries of origin and arrival, the pattern of migration chains, and age and gender coordinates, just to name a few. Furthermore, the concept of super-diversity compels us to reflect not only on the interactions between diversities that I have discussed throughout this contribution but also on the very nature of diversity itself. What does "diversity" mean for young people growing up in an environment where Buddha and Christ coexist within the same household spaces? And how does super-diversity manifest for those same young individuals who partake in their First Communion amidst visits to a Buddhist temple and subsequent pilgrimages to a Catholic church? At the same time, super-diversity reveals its usefulness to look at the ways by which sharing the same religion does not prevent the attribution of alterity, following ethnic and racialized divides not difficult to observe, as I evoked in relation to the experience of Sinhala Catholics in Messina. This is why the notion of super-diversity represents less a prescriptive analytical concept rather than a useful way of looking at how identity, belonging, and diversities reshape between the Indian Ocean and the Mediterranean, calling for further research and reflection.

Author Biography

Giovanni Cordova is a social anthropologist whose main research interests span from religions and rituals (with special reference to Islam and Christianity) to migrations, with an areal expertise on North Africa and, more recently, South Asia. He has conducted fieldwork in Tunisia and Italy. He is currently Research Fellow in Ethno-Anthropological Disciplines at the Department of Humanities of the University of Naples "Federico II". His most recent research project concerned the study of the devotional and ritual realms among the Sri Lankan communities living in Sicily, exploring the co-existence between universal religious values, local forms of religiosity, and migrants' religious experiences.

References

Barkan, E., Barkley, K. (eds.) (2014), *Choreographies of Shared Sacred Sites: Religion, Politics, and Conflict Resolution*, Columbia University Press, New York.

Bastin, R. (2002), *The Domain of Constant Excess: Plural Worship at the Munnesvaram Temple in Sri Lanka*, Berhahn, New York.

Becci, I., Burchardt, M. (2016), *Religion and Superdiversity: An Introduction*, in "New Diversity", 18, 1, pp. 1–7.

Benadusi, M. (2015), *Sacred Spaces and Border Crossing: Sinhalese Dreams of a Sri Lanka-Sicily Round Trip*, in "Sri Lanka Journal of Social Sciences", 38, 2, pp. 95–105. https://doi.org/10.4038/sljss.v38i2.7394

Bonfanti, S. (2014), *Religioni*, in B. Riccio (ed.), *Antropologia e migrazioni*, CISU, Roma, pp. 117–127.

Carrithers, M. (2000), *On Polytropy: Or the Natural Condition of Spiritual Cosmopolitanism in India: The Digambar Jain Case*, in "Modern Asian Studies", 34, 4, pp. 831–861. https://doi.org/10.1017/S0026749X00003991

Coleman, S. (2014), *Pilgrimage as Trope for an Anthropology of Christianity*, in "Current Anthropology", 55, S10, pp. S281–S291. https://doi.org/10.1086/677766

Cordova, G. (2022), *Il Dio dei miracoli. Chiesa "universale" e singalesi cattolici a Messina*, in "L'Uomo. Società, tradizione, sviluppo", 12, 2, pp. 7–37.

Cordova, G. (2025a), *In His Image: 'Good' Migrants and the Catholic Church in Southern Italy*, in *"Journal of Ethnic and Migrations Studies"*, pp. 1–17. https://doi.org/10.1080/1369183X.2025.2454008

Cordova, G. (2025b), *Madri in prestito. Rituale, appartenenza e devozione mariana tra i singalesi cattolici a Messina*, in M. Benadusi, G. Cordova (eds.), *Tra Oceano Indiano e Mediterraneo. Rituali, ostilità e convivenza nelle migrazioni dallo Sri Lanka*, Argo, Lecce, pp. 49–84.

Das, V. (2013), *Cohabiting an Interreligious Milieu: Reflections on Religious Diversity*, in J. Boddy, M. Lambek (eds.), *A Companion to the Anthropology of Religion*, Wiley Blackwell, New Jersey, pp. 69–84.

de Alwis, M. (2021), *Divine Eyes on the Sorrows of Lanka. Post-war Devotion to Pattini-Kannaki*, in M. P. Whitaker et al., *Multi-religiosity in Contemporary Sri Lanka*, Routledge, London, pp. 73–85.

Faranda, L. (2009), *Viaggi di ritorno. Itinerari antropologici nella Grecia antica*, Armando Editore, Roma.

Gallo, E. (2014), *Introduction*, in E. Gallo (ed.), *Migration and Religion in Europe. Comparative Perspectives on South Asian Experiences*, Ashgate, Farnham, pp. 1–27.

Glick Schiller, N. (2004), *Transnational Theory and Beyond*, in D. Nugent, J. Vincent (eds.), *A Companion to the Anthropology of Politics*, Blackwell, Malden, pp. 448–467.

Glick Schiller, N. Basch, L., Blanc-Szanton, C. (1992), *Towards a Transnational Perspective on Migration*, New York Academy of Sciences, New York.

Gombrich, R. F., Obeyesekere, G. (1988), *Buddhism Transformed: Religious Change in Sri Lanka*, Princeton University Press, Princeton.

Goodhand, J., Sørbø, G. M., Goodhand, J., Klem, B., Nissen, A. E., Selbervik, H. (2011), *Pawns of Peace: Evaluation of Norway's Peace Efforts in Sri Lanka, 1997–2009*, NORAD, Oslo.

Goonasekera, S. (2007), *Walking to Kataragama*, International Centre for Ethnic Studies, Colombo.

Hannerz, U. (1992), *Cultural Complexity. Studies in the Social Organization of Meaning*, Columbia University Press, New York.

Imtyiaz, A. (2020), *The Easter Sunday Bombings and the Crisis Facing Sri Lanka's Muslims*, in "Journal of Asian and African Studies", 55, 1, pp. 3–16. https://doi.org/10.1177/0021909619868244

Jacobsen, K. A., Raj, S. J. (2008), *Introduction: Making an Invisible Diaspora Visible*, in K. A. Jacobsen, S. J. Raj (eds.), *South Asian Christian Diaspora: Invisible Diaspora in Europe and North America*, Ashgate, Farnham, pp. 1–16.

Johnson, D. (2012), *Sri Lanka – a Divided Church in a Divided Polity: The Brokerage of a Struggling Institution*, in "Contemporary South Asia", 20, 1, pp. 77–90. https://doi.org/10.1080/09584935.2011.646076

Kapferer, B. (1997), *The Feast of Sorcerer: Practices of Consciousness and Power*, University of Chicago Press, Chicago.

Kreinath, J. (2017), *Interrituality as a New Approach for Studying Interreligious Relations and Ritual Dynamics at Shared Pilgrimage Sites in Hatay, Turkey*, in "Interreligious Studies and Intercultural Theology", 1, 2, pp. 257–284. https://doi.org/10.1558/isit.33618

Lawrence, P. (1997), *Work of Oracles, Silence of Terror: Notes on the Injury of War in Eastern Sri Lanka*, PhD Thesis, University of Colorado.

Levitt, P. (2003), *"You Know, Abraham Was Really the First Immigrant": Religion and Transnational Migration*, in "Transnational Migration: International Perspectives", 37, 3, pp. 847–873. https://doi.org/10.1111/j.1747-7379.2003.tb00160.x

Levitt, P. (2004), *Redefining the Boundaries of Belonging: The Institutional Character of Transnational Religious Life*, in "Sociology of Religion", 35, 1, pp. 174–196. https://doi.org/10.2307/3712504

Levitt, P., Glick Schiller, N. (2004), *Conceptualizing Simultaneity: A Transnational Social Field Perspective on Society*, in "The International Migration Review", 38, 3, pp. 1002–1039. https://doi.org/10.1111/j.1747-7379.2004.tb00227.x

Mollica, M. (2000), *Tindari: Dalla città greca al culto della Madonna Nera*, Armando Siciliano editore, Messina.

Moore, M. (1993), *Thoroughly Modern Revolutionaries: The JVP in Sri Lanka*, in "Modern Asian Studies", 27, 3, pp. 593–642. https://doi.org/10.1017/S0026749X00010908

Mosse, D. (2012), *The Saint in the Banyan Tree: Christianity and Caste Society in India*, University of California Press, Berkeley.

Norget, K. et al. (eds.) (2017), *The Anthropology of Catholicism: A Reader*, University of California Press, Berkeley.

Obeyesekere, G. (1966), *The Buddhist Pantheon in Ceylon and its Extensions*, in M. Nash (ed.), *Anthropological Studies in Theravada Buddhism*, Yale University Press, New Haven, pp. 1–26.

Obeyesekere, G. (1984), *The Cult of the Goddess Pattini*, University of Chicago Press, Chicago.

Obeyesekere, G. (2004), *Where Have all the Veddas Gone? Buddhism and Aboriginality in Sri Lanka*, in N. Silva (ed.), *Hybrid Island*, Social Scientists' Association, Colombo, pp. 1–19.

Orsi, R. (1985), *The Madonna of 115th Street: Faith and Community in Italian Harlem, 1880–1950*, Yale University Press, New Haven.

Orsi, R. (1996), *Thank You, St. Jude: Women's Devotion to the Patron Saint of Hopeless Causes*, Yale University Press, New Haven.

Osella, F., Soares, B. (2020), *Religiosity and its Others: Lived Islam in West Africa and South India*, in "Social Anthropology", 28, 2, pp. 466–481. https://doi.org/10.1111/1469-8676.12767

Pinto, L. (2015), *Being a Christian in Sri Lanka. Historical, Political, Social, and Religious Considerations*, Balboa Press, Bloomington.

Rajasingham-Senanayake, D. (2021), *Spaces of Protection, Healing, and Liberation: Religious Polyphony, Geopolitics and Colonial Construction of the Violence of "Others"*, in M. P. Whitaker, D. Rajasingham-Senanayake, P. Sanmugeswaran, *Multi-religiosity in Contemporary Sri Lanka*, Routledge, London, pp. 13–31.

Riccio, B. (ed.) (2014), *Antropologia e migrazioni*, CISU, Roma.

Salih, R. (2000), *Moroccan Migrant Women*, in R. Grillo et al. (eds.), *Here or There? Contrasting Experiences of Transnationalism: Moroccans and Senegalese in Italy*, CDE, University of Sussex.

Samnugeswaran, P. (2021), *Negotiating with Innovative Multi-Religious Spaces, New Religious Pluralism, and Geo-Religious Powers in Post-War Sri Lanka*, in M. P. Whitaker, D. Rajasingham-Senanayake, P. Sanmugeswaran, *Multi-religiosity in Contemporary Sri Lanka*, Routledge, London, pp. 3–12.

Seneviratne, H. L. (1999), *The Work of Kings*, University of Chicago Press, Chicago.

Shah-Kazemi, S. (2006), *Islam and Religious Pluralism*, Islamic Publishing House, Toronto.

Silva, K. T., Niwas, A., Wickramasinghe, W. M. K. B. (2016), *Religious Interface and Contestations between Buddhists and Muslims in Sri Lanka: A Study of Recent Developments in Selected Multi-Religious and Cross-Cultural Sites*, International Centre for Ethnic Studies, Colombo.

Southwold, M. (1978), *Buddhism and the Definition of Religion*, in "Man", 13, 3, pp. 362–379. https://doi.org/10.2307/2801935

Spencer, J. (2003), *A Nation 'Living in Different Places': Notes on the Impossible Work of Purification in Post-Colonial Sri Lanka*, in "Contributions to Indian Sociology", 37, 1–2, pp.1–23. https://doi.org/10.1177/006996670303700102

Spencer, J. (2014), *Anthropology, Politics, and Place in Sri Lanka: South Asian Reflections from an Island Adrift*, in "South Asia Multidisciplinary Academic Journal", 10, pp. 1–16. https://doi.org/10.4000/samaj.3812

Spencer, J., Goodhand, J., Hasbullah, S., Klem, B., Silva, K. T., Korf, B. (2015), *Checkpoint, Temple, Church, and the Mosque: A Collaborative Ethnography of War and Peace*, Pluto Press, London.

Srinivas, T. (2014), *Engaged Cosmopolitanism and Religious Pluralism in an Era of Globalization*, in M. Rovisco, S. Kim (eds.), *Cosmopolitanism, Religion and the Public Sphere*, Routledge, London, pp. 101–120.

Stirrat, R. (1992), *Power and Religiosity in a Post-Colonial Setting: Sinhala Catholics in Contemporary Sri Lanka*, Cambridge University Press, Cambridge.

Tambiah, S. J. (1986), *Sri Lanka: Ethnic Fratricide and the Dismantling of Democracy*, University of Chicago Press, Chicago.

Tambiah, S. J. (1992), *Buddhism Betrayed? Religion, Politics, and Violence in Sri Lanka*, University of Chicago Press, Chicago.

Van Dijk, R. (1997), *From Camp to Encompassment: Discourses of Trans-subjectivity in the Ghanaian Pentecostal Diaspora*, in "Journal of Religion in Africa", 27, 2, pp. 135–159. https://doi.org/10.2307/1581683

Vertovec, S. (2007), *Super-diversity and its Implications*, in "Ethnic and Racial Studies", 30, 6, pp. 1024–1054. https://doi.org/10.1080/01419870701599465

Vertovec, S. (2019), *Talking Around Super-diversity*, in "Ethnic and Racial Studies", 42, 1, pp. 125–139. https://doi.org/10.1080/01419870.2017.1406128

Whitaker, M. P. (2021), *Innovation and Multi-religiosity at Sri Lankan Interfaces*, in M. P. Whitaker et al., *Multi-religiosity in Contemporary Sri Lanka*, Routledge, London, pp. 32–42.

Chapter 7
"Out-of-place" Muslims: Public Islam and Youth Activism in Sites of Modernity

Andrea Priori

Abstract

This chapter, based on ethnographic research among young people with Bangladeshi origins in the city of Rome, examines different expressions of religious activism in order to shed light on the relationship between the public sphere, Islam, and sites of modernity in migratory contexts. The analysis highlights two differing approaches to public expressions of religion: one that emphasises intertextuality between different ir-religious repertoires and follows a paradigm of interculturality; the other based on an idea of mutual untranslatability and reliant on values typically associated with multiculturalism. Both approaches mobilise the grammar of Islam within civic and political pathways with meanings drawn from the different positionalities of the people and organisations involved, and which stage a discourse on public Islam in theatrical and topological forms that highlight deep interconnections between Islam and "modernity". They therefore challenge the monotheism of reason that tends to exclude Muslim actors from a normative, and ultimately biased, concept of the public sphere.

Keywords: Islamic associations, madrasahs, migration, public Islam, space

As for the righteous, they will be in a secure place. Amidst gardens and springs. Dressed in silk and brocade, facing one another[1].

1. Qur. XLIV:51–53.

1 Introduction

This chapter deals with the different expressions of public Islam within the so-called Bangladeshi community of Rome, paying particular regard to younger generations[2]. Despite being based on a localised scenario, many of the observations made here could be applied to the situation of public Islam in Italy in general, and in some cases even in Europe, because many of the dynamics and attitudes can also be found in other local contexts among young Muslims with different national backgrounds[3]. This is perhaps not so surprising, at least when considering that those who have to cope with being "Muslims in a non-Muslim country" experience many similar negative aspects and forms of otherisation.

The internal diversity of the public Islam that I analyse can be considered a form of religious super-diversity, constructed at the intersection of generation, education, and other socio-cultural determinants, and being essentially located between two poles. On the one hand, this is an approach to activism that emphasises sameness and interculturality, leveraging the image of a self-disciplined Islam which embraces the supposed value of an "integration in Italian culture". On the other hand, it is an approach which stresses differences between a Muslim minority and "Italians", whose relationships with the mainstream can be likened to multiculturalism, and which reacts more explicitly to the treatments experienced by Muslim people in Italy. Although individuals within both paradigms are compelled to reach out to a hegemonic culture which often conveys ideas

2. My work draws from the ethnographic research project *(Un-)typical utopias – Visions of the future from adolescents at Islamic schools in Bangladesh and Italy*, funded by the Gerda Henkel Foundation. Fieldwork took place in Rome between 2018 and 2020 and mainly involved three Bangladeshi mosques-madrasahs; a group of young activists engaged with the Giovani Musulmani d'Italia association (GMI), a group of young people attending a socialisation centre managed by a local council, and young people associated with other mosques. The methodology included participant observation, recorded interviews (21) and focus-group discussions (8), together with a large number of informal interviews, and the collection of materials such as pamphlets, videos, and even poems. The research group is made up of young people of Bangladeshi descent from 12 to 27 years old, mainly boys and young men. The names of my interlocutors and the madrasahs have been changed, and some biographical details were also altered in order to protect the identity of the research participants.
3. Schmidt 2004; Jonker, Amiraux 2006; Hamid 2011.

that are Islamophobic[4], "integrated" activists tend to downplay such problems, often shifting the attention to the "shortcomings of the Muslims", or to the incapacity of the first generation (i.e., those who migrated to Italy) and their young emulators to "understand the Italian context", to use the words of my interlocutors. By contrast, those who have a more separatist approach tend to emphasise the injustices suffered by Muslims, including the ongoing closures of migrant mosques, incidents which unevenly affect the two groups of activists featured in this article[5].

The polarisation between integrated and separatist activisms is to a large extent generational. We can say that integrated activism is typical of young people, a category that in the case of Italian Muslims largely overlaps with that of the "second generation", or the children of migrants, while separatist activism pertains to "the adults" or the first generation, persons with a direct experience of migration. However, this does not simply mean that young Muslims invariably emphasise "integration". In fact, those young people whose civic engagement is based around mosques and madrasahs, and which is therefore subordinated to strategies developed by adults, tend to reproduce those adults' models of activism. This notwithstanding, many of them did express the desire to embrace a more independent approach, and the idea of an activism which relates more to larger society. In contrast, integrated activism is more typical of individuals and organisations whose social networks are not completely dependent on mosques and madrasahs. In the case of youth activism, this essentially encompasses members of the Giovani Musulmani d'Italia (Young Italian Muslims) association (GMI), the only Islamic youth association in Italy, who are the descendants of migrants of diverse origins[6]. This is not to say that the characteristics that I ascribe to an integrated activism are peculiar only to members of this organisation, rather that they represent a generational ethos drawing from sedentarization processes typical of youth whose relationship with mainstream society, and with the public sphere, is inevitably different from that of their parents, who arrived in Italy as adults[7].

4. Sciortino 2002; Rivera 2003; Alietti, Padovan 2020.
5. See footnote 31.
6. Frisina 2006; Della Porta, Bosi 2010.
7. Priori 2021.

The fact that these tendencies take root in different organisations also has important implications with regards to other aspects of these distinct ways of going public. Separated activism in the context of mosques is essentially based on male homosociality and seems to directly rely on an effective exclusion of women from the public sphere, or at least on their confinement to an ancillary role. In contrast, in a civil society organisation like the GMI, young men and women share the same forms of involvement, although all members of Bangladeshi origin were males at the time of my research. In addition, the incorporation of an Islamic aesthetic varies in the different contexts, as in the case of mosques and madrasahs, where young people wear clothes that are considered appropriate in the Islamic tradition, resulting in an augmented exposure to Islamophobia in public spaces. In contrast, among the integrated activists, only women dress with an Islamic aesthetic, at least insofar as they wear a veil, while men dress themselves mostly in casual clothes, wearing "Islamic clothes" only on special occasions.

For the remainder of this chapter, after an excursus about the public role of Islam in Europe, and on the characteristics of the two groups of Italian-Bangladeshi youth on which this contribution is based, I will analyse their rhetoric and practices in order to outline how their different approaches to activism are formulated and professed, particularly with regards to the use of public spaces.

2   Public Islam and Public Spaces

At first glance, the relation between the "public sphere" and religion in Europe seems to be a controversial one. Due to the counterproductive role played by the temporal power of the Catholic Church in processes of modernity, religion is often excluded from (or inadequately included in) enlightened or normative definitions of the public sphere[8]. Nevertheless, although religious actors *de facto* do still play a quite prominent role in the public spheres of many countries, any talk of "problems" seems to concern Islam in particular rather than religion in general, as Muslim

---

8.   Habermas 1990, 2006; Rawls 1993; Dreyer, Pieterse 2010.

subjectivities tend to be otherised, silenced, or excluded from the ideas of civility and civilisation[9].

The examples provided by my young interlocutors highlight that despite attempts to silence Muslim voices, a "public Islam" is indeed active at various levels of civic debate. Muslims' religiously inspired engagement is based on "highly diverse invocations of Islam", with the aims of positively influencing the situation of Muslims in the country and pursuing the common good for society as a whole[10]. This engagement is exemplary of the multivocality which characterises the public sphere as a domain where not only secular and religious views are confronted, but also perspectives inspired by different religions, or different interpretations of the public role of the same religion, coexist. In Italy, like in other European countries[11], or in countries like Egypt[12], this has meant that participation in democratic processes or civil society rituals has taken the place of establishing alternative policies which are supposedly "Islamic" in nature. The idea that there exists an unbridgeable gap between Islam and the "democratic" forms of government promoted by the Western secular bourgeoisie has become, to a large extent, obsolete[13], as has the "secularisation thesis"[14], which depicts the secularisation of society as an inevitable outcome of the processes of modernisation, a theory which in recent decades has been disproved by the evident revival of the public role of religion[15]. Specifically in Bangladesh the Liberation War, in which Islamic groups colluded with the Pakistani army to enact harsh repressions upon the independence movement, instilled in many a conviction that a secularist (and "modern") state and Islam are reciprocally and irremediably incompatible. This conviction has been giving way to more nuanced positions, which strategically incorporate elements from both ideological fields and recombine them into a middle-class way of life, in which a deep identification with so-called modernisation processes does not automatically exclude Islam as an idiom capable of expressing values

9. Said 1978; van der Veer 2016.
10. Eickelman, Salvatore 2006, p. 98; Hasan 2009.
11. Song 2012; Mapril, Blanes 2013.
12. Schielke 2011; Sparre 2017.
13. Bayat 2007.
14. Taylor 2007; Geertz 1968.
15. Casanova 1994; Joas 2009.

with broad social recognition, and providing social movements with a lexicon that can be easily appropriated by the crowds[16].

The Italian Bangladeshi youths with whom this chapter is concerned are definitely a case in point, stemming as they do from families which do not have strong allegiances with Islamic actors, but on the contrary, from parents who opted for secular and Westernised lifestyles by emigrating to a European country. This "disruption of a traditional order", as Sayad put it[17], is often counterbalanced by a focus on the "preservation" of religious beliefs, typical of the processes of ethnicisation that often accompany emigration. Parents often hold traditional and even essentialist views of Bangladeshi identity, understanding it as something static or as some sort of "essence", rather than as something that changes over time due to transculturation processes. This means that younger generations often receive a religious education that is more exhaustive than their parents did in Bangladesh, in an effort to prevent them from losing what their parents have conceived of as an essential Bangladeshi identity. This (re)discovering of religion, besides being part of developments in migratory processes and global trends nurtured by the growing popularity of Islamic content in both traditional and digital media, in many cases is also fuelled by petty-bourgeois conformism. In fact, if in the 1970s and early 1980s ignoring religious education in the name of a secularism inspired by the Nehruvian socialism of the Awami League was eminently fashionable[18], nowadays a respectability which is instrumental to the preservation of the *izzat* (prestige) of a middle-class family includes the duty of Islamic education.

The distinct approaches to activism discussed in this article are rooted in the different ways in which members of the so-called second generation react to the models presented to them in the madrasahs run by

16. Huq, Rashid 2008; White 2012; Hasan 2017.
17. Sayad 1999.
18. The ruling Awami League party in Bangladesh was at the heart of the Bangladeshi independence movement and initially pursued a moderately socialist and highly secular policy, inspired by the non-alignment positions of former Indian Prime minister Jawaharlal Nehru. The socialism of the Awami League, however, soon gave way to a markedly liberal approach in economics, and in recent years its secularism, which since the 1990s has adopted a hard line against Islamic organisations because of the spread of fundamentalism in the country, seems to have found softer interpretations, and is more inclined to open a dialogue with "moderate" religious organisations.

Bangladeshi migrants in Rome, where they receive a religious education. On the one hand, some youths identify with a model of activism typical of the generation of mature adults who grew up in Bangladesh, that is, a model based on proselytism, the fulfilment of the ritual calendar, and the transmission of knowledge from the Qur'an on the basis of a mnemonic methodology. On the other hand, there are youths, making up the majority in this study, who dislike the cultural model proposed by mosques and madrasahs, and who, in some cases, have developed other forms of religious participation. The groups also differ in the way in which they present themselves in public, the latter group choosing not to follow the example of their elders, which until a few years ago was the only way in which Islamic actors made themselves visible in Rome. The approach to activism I have described as "separatist", and as typical of the elder generation, engages with the public arena mainly by means of protests against the closure of mosques and madrasahs by the authorities following breaches of safety and building regulations[19]. In 2016, one of these protests received an impressive amount of media coverage as it took place in front of the iconic Colosseum, marking a temporary appropriation of a global centrality by actors, the migrants' mosques, which are relegated in the extreme to spaces that are peripheral, informal, and in every sense of the word, underground. It is no coincidence that many of these mosques are located in basements, and it is precisely against this situation of perceived self-ghettoisation that some segments of the Bangladeshi second generation, along with other young Muslims from diverse national backgrounds, and a growing number of Muslims of Italian origin, are coming together under such slogans as: "Let's get out of the basements". In fact, the typical first generation activist is busy with administrating the mosque, its organised rituals, its madrasah, and its flows of donations, motivated by a fundamental desire to be able to continue to remain confined in spaces of worship, in the belief that this is the only way to be left relatively free to practise Islam in a country where it is barely tolerated. In addition, the first generation, together with younger people who cooperate with mosques and madrasahs, has been seemingly forced to go public in order to have their voices heard. By contrast, for the segment of the younger generation that attempts to put into practice a different way

---

19. Russo 2018.

of relating to the surrounding society, being visibly present as Muslims in public spaces is something which is aspired to and actively practiced.

This differing relationship with the urban space, and with other sites of modernity such as schools, universities, conference halls, and parliaments, is connected to another important aspect of the public sphere: practices, namely spatial practices. The public sphere is not only a discursive space, and both verbal and non-verbal performances are capable of influencing its constitution, as demonstrated by the strong impression that the mere image of a large group of Muslims kneeling in prayer in front of the Colosseum created, a much more lasting impression than that produced by their protest statements. Some years later, few remember what those "out-of-place" Muslims wanted, but many vividly recall the visual impact of the scene.

The public can be defined phenomenologically as a world of appearances where things can be both "seen" and "heard"[20], and consequently going public is not only a matter of what is said, but it is also about where it is said, and the theatrical effect elicited by the presence of a given category of people in a given kind of place. In this sense, another specific aspect of the current manifestations of public Islam, not only in Rome and in Western contexts but at a global level, is that we are more often seeing people with Islamic attire in sites of modernity. In these locations, the very presence of a *hijab*, for example, is in itself an act of disruption to a consolidated symbolic order[21]. In this way, Islam gains visibility through the eyes of mainstream society, as it is mobilised in the creation of public selves that reconcile religion with an idea of modernity[22]. In this sense, the "Islamic city", intended as an imagined social space epitomising a model of society as envisioned by my interlocutors, is not just another city structured around a theocratic order[23]; it is the city in which they already live, in which the vestiges of inherently secular manifestations of modernisation serve as a stage for verbal and non-verbal performances that re-politicise religion in accordance with the grammar of "secularised" politics. The Tahrir Square movement in Egypt[24], like the Hefazat-e-Islam

20. Arendt 1957; Villa 1992.
21. Göle 2002; Mapril, Blanes 2013; Sounaye 2018.
22. Esposito, Burgat, 2003; Malik 2003; Masud et al. 2008.
23. Mongin 1987.
24. Telmissany 2014.

in Bangladesh[25], gained strength because of their visibility in the urban space, and through their capacity to appropriate the repertoire of social movements. And it is in this sense that all the actors involved with my research recognise the validity of participative processes in the bourgeois state, even though the ideas of how that participation might take place differ. The separatists base their participatory ideas on public protests, while integrated activists conceive of participation more as an involvement in the rituals of civil society[26]. In this respect, an important element of differentiation within Bangladeshi public Islam in Rome lies in the conception of urban spaces. The first generation, together with younger people who cooperate with mosques and madrasahs, look at such spaces as places to be reluctantly occupied, that is, only for protests. This represents a logic that reciprocates (and reacts to) the encroachment of authorities into the separate spaces of the sacred, represented by mosques. In contrast, younger people who follow a strategy based on "integration" believe that public spaces should also be purposed for everyday practices such as prayers, until the presence of Muslims praying in a public square "becomes normal", to use the words of a young activist from the GMI association. In this way, the production of a religious citizenship in migratory contexts can be articulated in terms of a "right to the city"[27].

3 The Two Paths of Muslim Activism in Rome

Two of the groups I examined in my research exemplify the two approaches to activism that I have previously introduced, the "integrated" and the "separatist", the former referencing members of the GMI association, or more specifically members of its Roman branch with Bangladeshi origins, and the latter young people from the Quranic School of Rome

---

25. Zaman 2016.
26. The increasing participation in electoral processes via local parties, often linked to the political centre-left, is also emerging as an important trend. The 2021 municipal elections in Rome saw the participation of a number of young Muslim candidates of Bangladeshi origin, although none of them were part of the GMI. In the same elections, two of the Bangladeshi mosques involved in my research supported a Muslim candidate of Italian origin who was strongly committed to the cause of the right to worship.
27. Hudson 2003; Salguero, Hejazi 2021.

(QSR), a madrasah which, during my fieldwork, held activities in two Bangladeshi mosques. The two organisations have differing histories and missions. The GMI was formed in the aftermath of 9/11 in order to convey a reassuring image of Islam, to promote the idea that being an "Italian Muslim" is not a contradiction in terms, and to provide a space where young activists can organise their agenda independently of elders[28]. The QSR, being a madrasah, is not as such an organisation made by or of youths, rather it was made for youths, and its mission is to provide religious tuition to the children of Bangladeshi migrants. If the GMI is governed by young people, in the QSR young people are not represented on the governing board. Rather, most youth participants are simply students, while a few young teachers and advanced students participate in non-educational activities organised by both the madrasah and the mosques, without being involved in related decisions. While the GMI emphasises relations with larger society, the QSR has fewer relationships with non-Muslim actors. Moreover, the majority of its interactions with local authorities involve law enforcement bodies and disciplinary processes, such as "anti-terrorist" searches or building safety inspections. In 2016, the closure of a number of mosques due to safety and building regulation violations prompted a mosque which was hosting QSR activities to join the political mobilisation which culminated in the prayer action at the Colosseum. A few years later, the problems also began to impact the QSR itself. The mosque hosting its activities was partially closed to the public in the summer of 2018, and nine months later during celebrations for the end of the school year another police raid led to the closure of the entire space. If the partial closure was accepted with some understanding, the complete closure sparked a new cycle of protests. In response, a further police raid in June 2020 led to the closure of yet another mosque, to which the activities of the QSR had been moved in the meantime.

The experiences of the GMI are totally different. Its relationships with larger society do not centre around the disciplinary powers of police but instead entail mostly positive moments such as participation in encounters with members of political institutions, or events of interfaith dialogue in sites of modernity like universities and conference halls. Members of the association are representatives of an Islam that aims at not only being

---

28. Frisina 2006.

more extroverted and "Italian", but also more cultured. In fact, unlike the board members of the mosques and madrasahs and the young people who participate in their initiatives, the GMI are invariably university students or young professionals who have recently graduated, who are more accustomed to the language of civil society and aware of the ways in which a public Islam that aspires to be European is currently expressing itself in other countries, especially the UK. Thus, while GMI members enjoy access to a cosmopolitan milieu where it is possible to reach out to non-Muslim subjectivities, young people associated with the QSR do not.

One factor in these different positionalities is surely age, influencing as it does education and the capabilities to reach out to larger society. In fact, at the time of research the GMI members were all young men aged between 21 and 27 years, while in the QSR my interlocutors ranged in age from 12 to 21. More specifically, in the QSR, my interactions mainly were with those participating in the *hifzo*, the section of memorization of the Qur'an, whose students were all males between 12 and 16, and whose teachers were two young men aged 21 and 18 respectively. During public events and internal ceremonies a few ex-QSR students (invariably males) around 18 years of age also showed up[29]. This means that although most of the QSR students may have the opportunity to attend university in the future, at the moment they are not old enough to do so, while for the older members not enrolling in university is a personal choice. The two young teachers, for example, preferred to invest in a madrasah education, and undertook an important part of their Islamic studies in Bangladesh.

These positionalities, together with the relational assets and internal compositions of the two organisations, inevitably affect models of participation and the agency of the individual youths. In this sense, the GMI represents a quasi-ideal site for the expression of youth agency, as explained by Nazmul, a 24-year-old university student:

> Hence, it is important to try to create a community of young people, who can understand things and who represent the future, and this is what we are trying to do. Hence, [we look at whether] we can

---

29. An important common element between the two groups is gender, as both young people from the *hifzo* of the QSR and the Bangladeshi activists of the GMI are cis men who enjoy a patriarchal dividend in terms of access to the public sphere (Fraser 1990).

help the first generation in some way, we talk about our fathers, their faults, and this makes you understand how to go forward.

By contrast, the situation in the QSR is very different. Here, young people simply follow the path that the adults have marked out, as outlined by Abdul, a 21-year-old teacher:

Anything we do, we do it with the adults, always. We do the same thing, both adults and youths.

[Researcher] *Why is there this difference between the two groups [QSR and GMI]?*

I don't know. What comes to my mind [...] off the top of my head [...] in cultural terms, is that it's because we entered the mosque when we were children, and for this reason we didn't find another path [...]. [This] creates a mentality, you stay with the mosque, you don't leave the mosque, this is what the imams teach you [...].

Continuities between the approaches of the first generation and that of younger people like Abdul do not go unnoticed by the GMI members. For this reason, their critiques of the elders are sometimes also applied to the madrasah students[30]. Asad, a 24-year-old university student, explains:

What's their problem? I tried to highlight this thing also with the adults, but I learnt from experience that this doesn't work [...]. [These boys] Are not interested in what surrounds them. Their acts are based merely on a simple routine [...]. They say their prayers, good! They read the Qur'an? They respect Ramadan? Good! [When you ask them:] "What do you think about what you're doing?", a question which attempts to elicit an opinion, they will hesitate to answer. That's a problem!

Despite the nuances of their respective accounts, both Asad and Abdul imply that differences in the two environments in terms of youth agency and attitudes originate in the peculiarities of the mosque as a learning

---

30. In this regard, it should be noted that although all GMI members also completed the first three levels of the madrasah curriculum, they did not identify with the model of religious knowledge and activism proposed by the adult generation.

environment characterised by a specific "culture". In the mosque/madrasah Islamic knowledge is *reproduced* through memorization and young people are subordinated to the adults while, in the GMI, the capacity to *produce* a rational argument about religion is highly valued and, despite evident hierarchies between newcomers and older members, there is no generation of "parents" to whom one must subordinate oneself.

Despite this, there also appear to be limits connected to the number and the age of young people who can be involved in moments of activism. In the QSR, underage youths do not participate in the organisation of public activities, and most of the older students drift away from the madrasah. As a result, at the time of my fieldwork, apart from occasional support provided by some young men, only two young adults were involved on a regular basis with the activities of the QSR, something which inhibits the possibility of a generational path to a public Islam. This is not to say that these youths are unwilling to propose their own ideas for conveying the meanings of Islam to non-Muslim people. In fact, even those who follow the separatist example of the adults are interested in relating to the broader society but lament a lack of cooperation on the part of other young people, as explained by Abdul:

> For the time being, there is nobody of my age. Nobody in his twenties. The kids are there but they mostly go to school. If you go to school, you are also busy with homework, and in addition you go to the madrasah, thus there is no time left to invite people and make them understand what Islam is.

Abdul expresses a sense of loneliness which is absent from the discourses of the GMI's members, and points to the lack of appeal for young people exerted by traditional forms of religious engagement. The situation in the two mosques in which the QSR is based is similar to that of other Roman mosques. For most young people, their continuative presence at a mosque is a duty which ends with the completion of the first three levels of the madrasah syllabus, provided that their parents are satisfied and choose not to enrol their child at the *hifzo*. Membership in the GMI, however, is presented as an act of free will, a choice that enables connections to young people from different national backgrounds, and not only Italian Bangladeshis. This fosters a feeling of being part of a large and internally diverse group of Muslim youth, who feel able to "understand things", as

Nazmul stated. A camping trip organised by the GMI during the summer of 2019 welcomed dozens of people in their twenties from around Italy. Conversely, when, in the same period, I took part in a beach trip organised by the QSR, three coaches were needed to transport all the students and parents, yet there were only a handful of young people between the ages of 18 and 30.

Thus, despite wanting to move towards an idea of activism more akin to that promoted by GMI members, young people like Abdul end up renouncing a comparable generational pathway to a public Islam and reproducing many of the attitudes of the adults. This is reinforced by the tendency of the madrasah group to conceive of themselves as a separate body that asks only to be "left alone". This is how Abdul responds when I ask him what Italians should do to help his mosque:

> Ok, in my opinion, the Italians don't have to do anything, as long as they leave us alone. That's the main thing. And then, if they want, they can come to us sometime and see what we do, so as to understand better [who we are]: "What are you doing? We want to see how you produce guns, bombs". We want them to come sometimes to see that we don't do anything bad. [...] [I]f an Italian enters the mosque and sees that everything is peaceful, he will tell his relatives: "They don't do anything bad, why should we disturb them"?

The sarcasm expressed by Abdul with regard to Italians who would only enter a mosque to observe how bombs are produced is typical in the QSR. Here, an experience such as the closure of the mosque adds up to a series of episodes in which people feel that they are under attack as Muslims. Unlike the GMI, in the QSR young people are more willing to recount these events. During the early stages of my fieldwork, they tended to downplay the effect of such actions. Once police repression on their mosque intensified, however, they showed a greater willingness to share episodes of Islamophobia, which significantly take place in sites of modernity, such as city streets or classrooms. Imran, a 13-year-old *hifzo* student, explains:

> They think they are superior and say: "No, Islam is not what you say", or "Catholicism is better". [...] [M]y teacher of religious education at school keeps saying: "You had no choice, you were born

Muslim, and you had to embrace Islam". He even gave some examples: "If I gave you only bananas you would eat only bananas, but if I gave you also apples, pears, oranges…".

Similarly, Nurul, an 18-year-old teacher in the QSR, recalls one of the many episodes of Islamophobia that he has suffered as he was walking down the street in Torpignattara, a neighbourhood that, ironically, is identified as the Roman Banglatown: "Two days ago, I was walking in the street, there were four of us, a man said, 'we need Mussolini here! Mussolini would take care of you!' […]. They do not think of us as men, as persons".

If "Italians" are sometimes described in the QSR as threatening, among the GMI members there is a clear desire to avoid self-victimising. The Bangladeshi members of the association prefer not to talk about Islamophobia, and when they do so, they tend to use moderate tones and to underline faults in the "Muslims". The closure of the mosques is a case in point, as it is generally blamed on the "Bangladeshi community"[31]. When I ask Asad whether the city council is responsible for the situation, due to it not offering a clear path to comply with regulations, he explains:

> To tell the truth, it is not completely on the Council […] the first responsibility is on them [*the Council*], but the point is that the community too does not have a clear vision on this issue. In mosques, more than a hundred people gather together, and it is not acceptable that some do not have emergency exits […]. […] [I]f the community wanted to change the situation, change its approach, if they started to care more about people's safety, their own safety, we probably would already have a regulation [on prayer rooms].

Based on this view, even the responsibility for practices such as racial profiling is shared by Muslim people, as illustrated by Tareque, a 24-year-old artist, when talking about controls at airports and railway stations which primarily target people in Islamic attire:

> More importantly, it is up to you to change your attitude, because if your mindset is similar to theirs… [if you think:] "No! They are

---

31. This could also be related to the fact that the mosques usually attended by members of the GMI were closed only for short periods of time, while the two mosques connected to the QSR endured harsher penalties.

searching me because I look like a terrorist" […] if you think in the same way, things do not change, there will always be hostility. On the contrary, being sympathetic can change attitudes […] I mean, in order to change the other, you need to change yourself first.

The strategic orientation of the GMI seems to be about how to communicate one's Muslimness while avoiding the binary "victim of Islamophobia" or "potential terrorist". In fact, in their words episodes of intolerance generally happen to other people. Phrases such as "it is up to you" or "I have been lucky" are recurring elements in their discourses. Nevertheless, episodes of Islamophobia involving GMI members did indeed emerge in many interviews, as in the case of Saeed, a 22-year-old university student:

> I've been very lucky! But, for example, verses on war [from the Qur'an] are the most misinterpreted […]. This influences young people at school, even Bangladeshis. When a terrorist attack happens, people ask you: "So, are you going to blow yourself up too?" I mean, this happened also to me. At a certain point, people made these jokes also with me.

In this sense, "being lucky" essentially seems to mean that the members of the GMI feel more empowered in coping with episodes of Islamophobia, while in the QSR the closures of the two mosques exacerbated disillusionment along with a sense of powerlessness. Among the GMI members optimism is very much the norm, and their experiences of being treated as subordinated subjects is counterbalanced by a stronger set of social assets, particularly when compared to the young people in the QSR.

These differences in social assets, the differing practices of the two groups, together with their contingent experiences, cause the same basic ideas to be articulated and expressed differently. For example, both groups share a discursiveness which values relations with non-Muslim people and a peaceful and inclusive concept of Islam, yet differences in the relationship with mainstream society fuel important divergences in visions of activism. For the young people in the QSR the idea of connecting with non-Muslim people remains an abstract one and is accompanied by statements of a decidedly more separatist nature. On the contrary, GMI members have deeper interactions with the mainstream, and consequently exhibit an ethos of connectivity with hopes that a resulting exposure to diversity will increase their self-awareness as Muslims, while at the same time offering an opportunity to "learn from the other", as explained by Saeed[32]: "So, for example, in an ideal society I see not only Muslims but also non-Muslims, so I can learn from that person and that person can learn from me. This is the thing we have to encourage".

In the perception of the "integrated" activists, relations with mainstream society inevitably entail the act of coming out from only "places of worship" in order to affirm the presence of a visible Islam at a series of strategic sites, among which the urban space and universities seem to play important roles. Tareque explains:

> [W]e should really start putting things into practice, everywhere, in public parks, in the street, not only in places of worship. I mean, for me, people are starting to get used to seeing that, in any case, Islam is there [...] it will become a normal thing. I mean, based on this you can prompt curiosity among people. This happened to me when I was doing my prayers at the university, in the end there was much more curiosity, mental openness. [...] Actually, some [...] many students [...] I don't know [...] from Sapienza, from Tor Vergata [*universities*], from different places don't [...] they don't pray, as if ashamed.

Feeling free to pray wherever one wants is a tangible sign of an establishment of positive relations with those sites of modernity whose physical access also denotes a more metaphoric access to the public sphere, and in this respect all members of the GMI say that they have found at the university they attend a sort of small utopia, where their religiosity is not feared. The young people from the QSR also cherish a quite similar idea about the emergence of Muslim people at strategic sites, but for the students and teachers of the madrasah things are more difficult. For the QSR's youths, relations with sites such as universities and conference halls do not exist – at least not yet, experiences of school sociality are

---

32. In this regard, it is worth noting that while the young people of the QSR are not inherently introverted but, on the contrary, do wish to have more contact with "non-Muslims", some members of the GMI, in spite of a rhetoric strongly oriented towards a relationship with "the others" and practices that realise this ideal within constrained space-times, still admit to having a propensity of hanging out with observant Muslims.

sometimes connected to Islamophobia, and those of the urban space also tend to be negative. Abdul explains:

> In Rome we could organise, every week or every month, in a park or some other open-air place, an event where we offer food to everyone, where we distribute our publications, or where someone talks about Islam and people can listen and give their opinions [...]. But to organise something like that you need more young people, not just one or two.

The possibility of organising such events is not only hindered by a lack of young people, but there is also the feeling that the larger society has a fear of the presence of Muslims in public spaces. Abdul even thinks that it was an encroachment in a public space by his mosque, which had organised a religious festival in a fairly central public square on the very day of the second police raid, that caused its closure.

> This is what happens to Islam and Muslim people, people only get negative information [from the media] about Islam and so they think that Muslims are wicked, they bring negative things, they are people who put bombs in public spaces. This is the problem!

> All of a sudden, an inspection arrived on Sunday, they stepped inside and after a while the mosque was gone [...]. Why that inspection? Are we terrorists? Did we put a bomb somewhere? [...] Since we organised an Islamic festival in [...] [*name of a city square*], they must have thought: "How did they do it? How is that possible? Which mosque do they come from?" So, someone gave the order: "To find the organisers and close their mosque!"

As we have seen, the relationship of the young people from the QSR with spaces of modernity is constantly overshadowed by threats of violence: the alleged violence acted out by "Muslims" against the rest of society, and the violence actually experienced in the form of Islamophobic attitudes, which for many people means that the presence of a person dressed "as a Muslim" in a street, square, or classroom is somehow "inappropriate" and "dangerous". These experiences of violence are also partly shared with young people in the GMI, although the latter have opportunities to counterbalance these negative episodes with experiences of situations in which the latent civil war between Christians and Muslims, expressed through acts of Islamophobia, is suspended and supplanted by a different set of relationships, as we will see in the next section.

4 Staging a Public Islam

Insofar as sites of modernity such as schools and urban spaces seem to represent preferential places for Islamophobic episodes, in order to establish a public Islam young people from both groups see these locations as strategic sites, yet their perceptions differ in three important ways. Firstly, the QSR has developed a prevailing, if not exclusive, relationship with public urban spaces such as squares, while GMI members focused more on institutional sites such as lecture halls and conference centres, although they do indeed desire to establish their presence in urban spaces as well. Secondly, while for the QSR and the two studied mosques relations with sites of modernity mainly take the form of protests, affirming a separation between "Muslims" and "others", for the GMI a presence in places where ideas are peacefully discussed and respectfully confronted implies a participation in exchanges with "the other" where a climate of interconnectedness is created. Thirdly, both the young people and the adults from the QSR are generally reluctant to occupy public spaces, as they do not feel comfortable or secure in doing so, while the young people from the GMI are much more at ease when going public. In order to outline how these differences are expressed in non-verbal terms, I will look at a few events participated in or organised by the GMI and the QSR.

The GMI members, during the almost two years of my fieldwork, in addition to attending a number of internal training events or those with the exclusive involvement of other Islamic organisations, also took part in public meetings devoted to interfaith dialogue. In these meetings, organised by university departments, cultural institutions, or local associations, people from different religious backgrounds are brought together with secular people (often scholars), in a sort of ideal environment in which everyone is equal. In these liminal settings, a conditional form of society is represented where the power relations between Christianity and Islam, or between secular and religious knowledge, are temporarily abolished. In this way, the participants create a situation characterised by an equality of different religions and cultural repertoires, albeit in a limited space-time, and celebrate the production of a dense network of interconnections and reciprocal translations between the different epistemes that inhabit the public sphere.

A meeting on interfaith dialogue that took place in April 2019, attended not only by the GMI but also by representatives of youth associations of other religions, such as Adventists, Jews, Sikhs, and Catholics, as well as by scholars who deal with the religious, provides an excellent example of the dynamics which take place in these scenarios. Everyone sits at the same table, so that no obvious hierarchy is present. Young representatives of minority religions who – especially in the case of the representatives of Islam, usually have a minor voice in the public sphere, play a leading role. Although some of the scholars present also pose questions from time to time, it is the young people from the religious associations (including the GMI) who have most control over the topics that are discussed. This is a situation completely reversed from that of everyday life, where the members of the GMI (and in general all the young people involved in my research) are forced to answer a barrage of questions about Islam that they perceive as inappropriate, and biased.

It is precisely the experiences of being approached in the wrong way by "others" that forms one of the common pillars at interfaith dialogue events among young people from different religious affiliations. During the meeting of April 2019, for example, a scholar asks the representatives of the various associations whether they experienced "negative episodes" and forms of discrimination. Asad, from the GMI, speaks of the problems with his former schoolmates, a Jewish boy tells of "clashes" and "unpleasant episodes" at school and in the street, and a Sikh girl politely complains of suspicious attitudes not so much because of her religion, which only a few seem to know about, but because, due to her attire, she is often mistaken for a Muslim. At the same time, a young Catholic woman expresses solidarity with the young people, while someone from the audience highlights that "even Catholics are targeted sometimes".

The commonality between the situations experienced by participants is not restricted only to negative episodes but is also based on a shared principle, namely the mutual translatability of the various religious idioms. In fact, during such encounters the ideas that, despite its different articulations in the various religions, "God is one" and "spirituality remains the same", are fundamental tropes. In order not to exclude anyone, least of all the scholars moderating the event, this principle of translatability is also extended to secular and scientific knowledge. Nurul from the GMI explains that although not a "scientific book", the Qur'an contains a lot of scientifically relevant information and points out that although he is very religious, as a physicist he recognises himself fully in the scientific discourse, in accordance with recent developments in Islamic thought[33]. He posits that science and religion reveal various forms of intertextuality and emphasises the need to translate religious content into "everyday language" so that it might be "modern" and "attractive to young people". After Nurul's speech, everyone expresses their approval for the idea of a commonality in diversity, supporting in this way a model of an intercultural society that does not keep differences separate but, on the contrary, promotes the search for common elements. At the same time, a line of continuity is drawn between "religious tradition" and "modernity".

At the end of the encounter the participants take photos together to post on various social media platforms as tangible evidence of a common identification, one that does not rest simply on the possibility of creating connections between "Italians" and "Muslims", but implies that one can be both, just as it is possible to be "Italian Sikhs" or "Italian Hindus".

The situation with regards to the QSR is different. Here, although most young people do not refer to Italians as others, members of the first generation, together with some younger men, regularly make a distinction between "Bangladeshi Muslims" and "Italians". This attitude is fostered not only by the experiences of arriving in Italy as adults, one which is typical of first generations, but also, in this case, by a relationship with authorities and mainstream society that confirms and deepens this separation, as demonstrated by one of the many protests against the closure of the mosque in which the madrasah's activities usually took place.

At the beginning of May 2019, the mosque, with the help of a secular association of Bangladeshi migrants experienced in political conflicts, organised a public prayer in a square on the eastern outskirts of Rome, the first of a series of protests against the mosque's closure. The tone of this event was blatantly different from that of the interfaith dialogue event described above, but first of all it was the visual and topological

---

33. Gardner, Hameed 2018; Unsworth 2019.

organisation that was different. While at the event attended by the GMI all the participants were seated next to each other, intermingling and thereby expressing a presumed absence of hierarchy and relevant differences, at the protest prayer there were strict separations and a very clear division of the roles of "Italians" and "Bangladeshis". All of the people in the centre of the square, where the prayer space is organised, were not only Muslims, but Muslims with Bangladeshi origins. I was the only person present who did not fit into this category. Other Muslims, meaning not only non-Bangladeshis but also those Bangladeshis belonging to other mosques, do not participate in the protest. Indeed, developments resulting from the 2016 protests have shown that, cynically speaking, if you are not directly affected by the closures, it is more convenient not to get involved. The "Italians" keep to the fringes of the square and significantly belong to two categories: plain-clothed policemen and journalists from local newspapers. As often happens in these settings, the way police and journalists approach the situation creates an effect similar to that of colonial expositions, where potentially ferocious creatures are kept within a delimited area and observed from a safe distance by supposedly civilised counterparts. Not only is there no sense of commonality between the two realities, but there is also no verbal communication at all, only a mutual scrutiny or monitoring. The setting also seems to do little to disrupt perceived hierarchies, as the authority of police and journalists is juxtaposed against a lack of it for those who are otherised, both as Muslims and as migrants, even though many of the youngest were born in Rome.

Important differences between the two contexts also exist in the roles of women and young people. There were no women of Bangladeshi origin at the interfaith dialogue attended by the GMI, but despite this, women still played a prominent role in it. In contrast, women were completely absent from the protest prayer. Similarly, at the interfaith dialogue young people play a pivotal role, while at the public prayer they are essentially employed to increase the number of protesters. There were about 20 teenagers and a few young men present, but it is not up to them to decide what to do or to explain the reasons for the protest to the few onlookers. They limit themselves to participating in the prayer. There was an introduction before the prayer where the reasons for the protest were explained, but the role of the spokesman was assigned to the president of the secular association which supported the protest. His speech focused on an aspect of the closure that had profoundly outraged the community of believers from the mosque: The *minbar*, that is, the small pulpit used for the sermon, was equated with a stage and the police had accused the imam of performing a show without the necessary permission. "It's like they spat in my face", he announced. "With all due respect to Italian laws, this is an abuse of power, in my country these things don't happen". The substance and tone of his speech are in stark contrast with any ethos of connectivity such as that expressed by the GMI. If the GMI could be said to promote the idea of an Italian Muslimness, and a confidence that such a concept might be easily accepted by the public, the protesters from the mosque have internalised the idea of an irreconcilable distance between them and "the Italians", even though some of them are Italian citizens themselves. "My country" in the discourse of the mosque/madrasah is not Italy, rather it is Bangladesh[34].

If the attitude of the GMI might be described as intercultural, although it does not exclude certain degrees of both assimilationism and multiculturalism, that of the madrasah group is decidedly multiculturalist. For them, Italians and Bangladeshis, or Christians and Muslims, are irreconcilable realities which can coexist and cohabit with each other but cannot be reciprocally translated. For this reason, the only demands from this sector of the Muslim-Bangladeshi community is that they be left free to practise their religion in spaces separated from the rest of society.

Similar dynamics to those at the protest prayer can also be seen during another of the protests organised by the mosque, an *iftar* (the breaking of the fast at day's end during Ramadan) which took place in another public square a few days later. In this case, the contrast to the GMI is perhaps even more evident, as they also organised an *iftar* during the same period, yet the GMI's *iftar* was not an act of protest but an event characterised by a festive atmosphere and the participation of a large number of non-Muslims. At the *iftar* protest organised by the mosque connected to the QSR, as in the public prayer, there was a sharp separation between "Bangladeshi Muslims" and "Italians". The "Italians" do not take part in the breaking of the fast, with the exceptions of myself, a university

---

34. Tellingly, in some demonstrations the protestors campaigned both for the right to worship and for the rights of migrants, for example in June 2020 in front of the Rome City Hall.

student, and a Muslim of Italian origin who, two years later, would run as a candidate in local elections with the support of the mosque[35]. On this occasion the event is watched by a police riot squad, and the journalistic presence is also greater. A substantial group of women also take part this time, separated from the male protesters by a fenced-off area. Once again, the same elements that were present in the prayer protest can be observed: a clear separation between Muslims and non-Muslims as well as between men and women, a relationship between "Italians" and "Muslims" which ranges from disciplining to spectacularisation, and a certain degree of marginalisation of young people. Once again, use of the microphone is the privilege of the elders, who repeat the same arguments they made during the protest prayer. As the speeches continue, most of the young people are becoming bored; many had been helping to set up the event since early afternoon and would simply like to go home. I ask Nurul, one of the teachers, about what the next steps in the protest might be, and he replies that he has no idea: "They [*the adults*] decide and then let us know. I don't know anything". In addition, some participants appear to be more worried than happy about the large attendance, as they fear that the situation might provoke and attract attacks from Islamophobic organisations: "If someone shoots then they will blame us", comments Abdul, the other teacher. While we are cleaning up the rubbish after the *iftar*, in the act of removing beer bottles which were clearly not left by those who took part in the meal, Nurul comments caustically: "We'd better remove these too, otherwise they could say that we left them here".

In contrast, the *iftar* organised by the Roman branch of the GMI in May 2019 depicts completely different relationships between the diversities. The event takes place at the University of Sapienza, where many members of the association study, and involves several categories of people: Muslim students, students from other religious backgrounds, members of other associations, professors, and university staff. The assortment of people who speak at the microphone is not limited to Muslims; there are also representatives from the university's diversity office, academics, and student representatives. All speakers criticise Italian society for not being inclusive enough towards Islam, albeit in restrained tones. In this way, a discourse that in events organised by the

---

35. See footnote 26.

mosques is the exclusive prerogative of Muslims, is also taken on by the "others". Nonetheless, young Muslim activists have a leading role, one which, judging by their radiant faces, they have long coveted. Not only do they get the opportunity to provide guidance on the place and times for activities such as prayers to an audience of Muslims, but also the opportunity to lecture others on how to behave in such situations as well as on ethical issues such as food waste and respect for the environment. During the event, features of an ideal society are acted out, in which, to use the words of two GMI members, "people reach[ing] out to each other", and a "curiosity towards the others" are the norm. After the speeches, different categories of people sit and eat together, chatting amicably. Two young Muslims illustrate different traditions in the preparation of food for the *iftar* to non-Muslim people, a young man of Italian origin and a member of the Buddhist sect Soga Gakkai talk to a GMI member about differences between Islam and Buddhism, and a group of people chat about continuities between Islam and Christianity. This situation contrasts starkly with the absence of communication between diversities at the *iftar* event organised by the mosque and mirrors the different relational assets of the two groups. While relationships between the mosques hosting the QSR and institutions pass mainly through the interface of the police or judiciary and take on disciplinary forms, the GMI forms contacts with academics and representatives of civil society, interlocutors who are in a position to provide an additional legitimacy to the association, fostering feelings of being accepted within the public sphere in its members. The GMI activists, therefore, are able to frequent with relative ease those sites of modernity in which many other Muslims, such as students who are "ashamed to pray at university" according to one respondent, feel out-of-place.

5 Conclusion: A Monotheism of Reason vs. A Polytheism of Values

As we have seen in this chapter, biased representations of Islam as a threatening presence that are conveyed in Italy by mainstream media and politicians[36], and with which the interlocutors in my research deal with

36. See footnote 4.

during their daily lives, are contradicted by the ethnographic research evidence. Analysis of the discourses and practices of young people of Bangladeshi origin shows that, far from having intentions to build a theocratic order, on the contrary, they want to take part in the public sphere using languages and modalities that are acceptable to the society in which they live. In this sense, the findings of my fieldwork concur with those of numerous scholars concerned with Muslim activism in various countries[37]. Not only does Islam prove to be less threatening than is represented by the rhetoric of politicians and media platforms, but it is also much more complex and internally super-diverse. As we have seen, there are various ways of conceiving a public role for Islam and, in the cases presented here, both of these two distinct approaches distance themselves from stereotypes of jihadism by connecting with ideas of modernity and models of participation that, until recently, were believed to be the exclusive prerogative of "secular culture". This secular culture proclaims a total separation from the influence of religion on the one hand, while on the other it actually offers a preferred path for the public towards more familiar, and more powerful, realities, which in Italy are represented by Christian actors, or others considered less "dangerous" (i.e., politically assertive) than Muslims, such as Buddhists.

We have also seen how this internal diversity of Islam is constructed at the intersection of varying features or dynamics. Generational background, specifically with respect to migration, surely plays an important role, insofar as the specific life-experiences and hysteresis of the habitus of the first generation of Bangladeshis in Rome prevent them from adhering to a more extroverted model of activism. The ways in which a section of the second generation are indeed "going public" are inextricable from the generational assets which they draw from sedentarization processes in terms of language or education. However, it is the intersection of generation with other determinants that seems to make the telling differences. Differences in educational paths, personal trajectories that in some cases involve sites in Italy and Bangladesh and entail different relational assets, or alignments with organisations that have divergent relationships with the authorities and mainstream society in general, play a pivotal role in directing the rhetoric and practices of young Muslim activists. Those

---

37. For bibliographical references see footnotes 3, 10, 11, 12, 13, and 16.

who, by virtue of their personal assets or membership in a group, have greater capacities to relate to the public sphere and wider society seem to be more inclined towards interculturality, "integration", and connectivity, while those who are less able to do so are more prone to a separatism typical of multiculturalism.

As we have seen, in spite of these differences, both of the realities under scrutiny promote a peaceful image of Islam and express their claims based on a grammar of participation in the processes of "democratic" society, as they are understood based on the knowledge and culture of diversity with which they are imbued. In this way, "separatist" or "integrated" activists express two distinct concepts of pluralism, the former based on an idea of the public as terrain where irresolvable diversities between epistemes are staged, while the latter implies rather that the same episteme is articulated differently, producing different language games that ultimately express similar concepts. To put it another way, the different approaches to activism entail a juxtaposition between an irreducible heteroglossia and an ethos of translatability. Despite this disparity, they share the common trait of looking at the public as an internally diverse domain where a "polytheism of values" does admit the possibility of different discourses and practices[38].

Normative notions, such as Habermas' concept of "communicative rationality", seem to have a limited scope in describing the phenomenological reality of the public because, as we have seen, there is also a non-verbal and performative dimension of the public, in which it is extremely difficult to assess the "rationality" of arguments that are put forth in embodied and topological forms. In this "theatrical dimension" of the public space[39], what is staged is not a text in the common meaning of the term, it is rather a "didactic performance" which often prefigures a model of society towards which one aspires[40]. A stance that sees the public as the monocratic domain of an Apollonian "monotheism of reason"[41] is

38. Villa 1992, p. 716.
39. Amiraux, Jonker 2006, p. 14.
40. Göle 2002, p. 177.
41. The expression "monotheism of reason" appears in the Hegelian manuscript *Oldest System Program of German Idealism*, where it is contrasted with a "polytheism of the imagination", a dialectic that Manoussakis (2012) traces back to that between Apollonian and Dionysian. In my case, a monotheism of reason is understood as

inadequate in its accounting for the complexity of super-diverse societies because these societies are cohabited by not only differing ir-religious affiliations but also by different interpretations of the same ir-religious repertoire. In addition, the emphasis placed on the discursive dimension by this monotheism of reason fails to account for the phenomenological reality of the public sphere, as a domain which is formed not only through discourses but also through practices, including spatial practices.

In this sense, we have also seen how the sites of modernity presented here offer different levels of accessibility to visible Muslims, with quasi-utopian settings such as conference halls and university departments associated with the virtues of dialogue and mutual understanding, juxtaposed against places such as urban spaces and schools which represent minefields to most Muslim people. Muslim youths are currently attempting to repurpose these problematic sites as stages, in order to convey "social gestures of transparency" aimed at destigmatising Islam[42]. Through these actions they ultimately aim for the inclusion of Islam in a society which lacks realistic representations of what a Muslim organisation (and a Muslim person) actually are, and as a result does not fully recognise them as actors in the public sphere, although in fact they have already been present in it for years.

Author Biography

Andrea Priori, an anthropologist concerned with migrations and im-mobilities with a focus on Bangladesh, currently holds an MSCA Global Postdoctoral Fellowship at Roma Tre University/Université de Lausanne. Their main research interests include the construction of masculinities, migrants' political self-organization, and the intersection of im-mobility, politics, and ir-religiosity. Priori has published a monograph on Bangladeshi migrations entitled *Romer probashira* (2012, Meti Edizioni), various book chapters and peer-reviewed articles, and

---

the attempt to exclude *a priori* some actors from the public sphere because they are "irrational" and can be contrasted with a "polytheism of values" (Villa 1992), which accounts for the irreducible diversity of the value systems which inhabit the public sphere.

42. Salguero, Hejazi 2021, p. 94.

has co-edited special issues for the journals *New Diversities, Migration Letters*, and *Religion and Society*.

References

Alietti, A., Padovan, D. (2020), *Islamophobia in Italia – Rapporto nazionale 2018*, Istanbul, SETA Publications, available at https://setav.org/en/assets/uploads/2020/04/R156It.pdf (last accessed 13 January 2022).

Amiraux, V., Jonker, G. (2006), *Introduction: Talking about Visibility – Actors, Politics, forms of Engagement*, in G. Jonker, V. Amiraux (eds.), *Politics of Visibility: Young Muslims in European Public Spaces*, Transcript, Bielefeld, pp. 9–20.

Arendt, H. (1957), *The Human Condition*, University of Chicago Press, Chicago.

Bayat, A. (2007), *Making Islam Democratic: Social Movements and the Post-Islamist Turn*, Stanford University Press, Stanford.

Casanova, J. (1994), *Public Religions in the Modern World*, University of Chicago Press, Chicago.

Della Porta, D., Bosi, L. (2010), *Young Muslims in Italy: Parma and Verona*, Aarhus, CIR-Aarhus University, available at https://pure.au.dk/portal/files/32769822/Rapport3.pdf (last accessed 13 January 2022).

Dreyer, J. S., Pieterse, H. J. C. (2010), *Religion in the Public Sphere: What Can Public Theology Learn from Habermas's Latest Work?*, in "HTS Teologiese Studies/Theological Studies", 66, 1, pp. 1–7. https://doi.org/10.4102/hts.v66i1.798

Eickelman, D. F., Salvatore, A. (2006), *Public Islam and the Common Good*, in "Etnográfica", 10, 1, pp. 97–105. https://doi.org/10.4000/etnografica.3004

Esposito, J., Burgat, F. (2003), *Modernizing Islam: Religion and the Public Sphere in Europe and the Middle East*, Hurst & Co., London,

Fraser, N. (1990), *Rethinking the Public Sphere: A Contribution to the Critique of Actually Existing Democracy*, in "Social Text", 25–26, pp. 56–80. https://doi.org/10.2307/466240

Frisina, A. (2006), *The Invention of Citizenship Among Young Muslims in Italy*, in G. Jonker, V. Amiraux (eds.), *Politics of Visibility: Young Muslims in European Public Spaces*, Transcript, Bielefeld, pp. 79–101.

Gardner, V., Hameed, S. (2018), *Creating Meaning through Science: "The Meaning of Life" Video and Muslim Youth Culture in Australia*, in "Journal of Media and Religion", 17, 2, pp. 61–73. https://doi.org/10.1080/15348423.2018.1531622

Geertz, C. (1968), *Islam Observed: Religious Development in Morocco and Indonesia*, Yale University Press, New Haven.

Göle, N. (2002), *Islam in Public: New Visibilities and New Imaginaries*, in "Public Culture", 14, 1, pp. 173–190. https://doi.org/10.1215/08992363-14-1-173

Habermas, J. (1990), *Moral Consciousness and Communicative Action*, MIT Press, Cambridge.

Habermas, J. (2006), *Religion in the Public Sphere*, in "European Journal of Philosophy", 14, 1, pp. 1–25. https://doi.org/10.1111/j.1468-0378.2006.00241.x

Hamid, S. (2011), *British Muslim Young People: Facts, Features and Religious Trends*, in "Religion, State and Society", 39, 2–3, pp. 247–261. https://doi.org/10.1080/09637494.2011.600582

Hasan, M. (2017), *The Language of Youth Politics in Bangladesh: Beyond the Secular-Religious Binary*, in "RESOLVE Network Research Brief", 1, pp. 1–18. https://doi.org/10.37805/bgd2017.5

Hasan, N. (2009), *The Making of Public Islam: Piety, Agency, and Commodification on the Landscape of the Indonesian Public Sphere*, in "Contemporary Islam", 3, pp. 229–250. https://doi.org/10.1007/s11562-009-0096-9

Hudson, W. (2003), *Religious Citizenship*, in "Australian Journal of Politics and History", 49, 3, pp. 425–429. https://doi.org/10.1111/1467-8497.00296

Huq, S., Rashid, S. F. (2008), *Refashioning Islam: Elite Women and Piety in Bangladesh*, in "Contemporary Islam", 2, 1, pp. 7–22. https://doi.org/10.1007/s11562-007-0029-4

Joas, H. (2009), *Does Modernisation Lead to Secularisation?*, in W. Gräb, L. Charbonnier (eds.), *Secularization Theories, Religious Identity and Practical Theology*, Lit Verlag, Münster, pp. 25–34.

Jonker, G., Amiraux, V. (eds.) (2006), *Politics of Visibility: Young Muslims in European Public Spaces*, Transcript, Bielefeld.

Malik, I. H. (2003), *Islam and Modernity: Muslims in Europe and the United States*, Pluto Press, London.

Manoussakis, J. P. (2012), *The Philosopher-Priest and the Mythology of Reason*, in "Analecta Hermeneutica", 4, pp. 1–18.

Mapril, J., Blanes, R. L. (eds.) (2013), *Sites and Politics of Religious Diversity in Southern Europe*, Brill, Leiden-Boston.

Masud, M. K., Salvatore, A., van Bruinessen, M. (eds.) (2008), *Islam and Modernity: Key Issues and Debates*, Edinburgh University Press, Edinburgh.

Mongin, O. (1987), *La cité islamique*, in "Esprit", 129–130, 8–9, pp. 63–65.

Priori, A. (2021), *Young People First! The Multiple Inscriptions of a Generational Discourse of Muslimness Among Italian-Bangladeshi Youths*, in "Migration Letters", 18, 1, pp. 97–108. https://doi.org/10.33182/ml.v18i1.1058

Rawls, J. (1993), *Political Liberalism*, Columbia University Press, New York.

Rivera A. (2003), *Estranei e nemici*, DeriveApprodi, Rome.

Russo, C. (2018), *Musulmani di Roma. Spunti di riflessione da una etnografia*, in A. Saggioro, C. Russo (eds.), *Roma città plurale. Le religioni, il territorio, le ricerche*, Bulzoni Editore, Rome, pp. 285–371.

Said, E. W. (1978), *Orientalism*, Pantheon Books, New York.
Salguero, Ó., Hejazi, H. (2021), *Multiculturalism, Gentrification, and Islam in the Public Space: The Case of Baitul Mukarram in Lavapiés*, in "Migration Letters", 18, 1, pp. 85–96. https://doi.org/10.33182/ml.v18i1.1057
Sayad, A. (1999), *La double absence Des illusions de l'émigré aux souffrances de l'immigré*, Editions du Seuil, Paris.
Schielke, S. (2011), *The Arab Autumn? On the Continuity of Uprising in Egypt*, in "Suomen Antropologi: Journal of Finnish Anthropological Society", 4, pp. 76–79.
Schmidt, G. (2004), *Islamic Identity Formation Among Young Muslims: The Case of Denmark, Sweden and the United States*, in "Journal of Muslim Affairs", 24, 1, pp. 31–45. https://doi.org/10.1080/1360200042000212223
Sciortino G. (2002), *Islamofobia all'italiana*, in "Polis. Ricerche e studi su società e politica in Italia", 1, pp. 103–123.
Song, M. (2012), *Part of the British Mainstream? British Muslim Students and Islamic Student Associations*, in "Journal of Youth Studies", 15, 2, pp. 143–160. https://doi.org/10.1080/13676261.2011.630995
Sounaye, A. (2018), *Salafi Youth on Campus in Niamey, Niger: Moral Motives, Political Ends*, in E. Oinas, H. Onodera, L. Suurpää (eds.), *What Politics? Youth and Political Engagement in Africa*, Leiden, Brill.
Sparre, S. L. (2017), *Experimenting with Alternative Futures in Cairo: Young Muslim Volunteers between God and the Nation*, in "Identities", 25, 2, pp. 158–175. https://doi.org/10.1080/1070289X.2017.1400276
Taylor, C. (2007), *A Secular Age*, The Belknap Press of Harvard University Press, Cambridge.
Telmissany, M. (2014), *The Utopian and Dystopian Functions of Tahrir Square*, in "Postcolonial Studies", 17, 1, pp. 36–46. https://doi.org/10.1080/13688790.2014.912194
Unsworth, A. (2019), *Discourses on Science and Islam: A View from Britain*, in S. H. Jones, R. Catto, T. Kaden (eds.), *Science, Belief and Society: International Perspectives on Religion, Non-Religion and the Public Understanding of Science*, Policy Press, Bristol, pp. 263–288.
van der Veer, P. (2016), *The Value of Comparison*, Duke University Press, Durham and London.
Villa, D. R. (1992), *Postmodernism and the Public Sphere*, in "The American Political Science Review", 86, 3, pp. 712–721. https://doi.org/10.2307/1964133
White, S. C. (2012), *Beyond the Paradox: Religion, Family and Modernity in Contemporary Bangladesh*, in "Modern Asian Studies", 46, 5, pp. 1429–1458. https://doi.org/10.1017/S0026749X12000133
Zaman, F. (2016), *Agencies of Social Movements – Experiences of Bangladesh's Shahbag Movement and Hefazat-e-Islam*, in "Journal of Asian and African Studies", 53, 3, pp. 339–349. https://doi.org/10.1177/0021909616666870

Chapter 8

The Digital Darśana: Celebrating Durgā Pūjā 2020 During the Pandemic

Valeria Giampietri, Randa Khalil, and Ludovica Tozzi[1]

Abstract

    The chapter analyses the way one of the main Hindu religious festivals, the Durgā Pūjā, has been celebrated by the Hindu Bangladeshi and Indian diasporic community in Rome, specifically in the neighbourhood of Tor Pignattara, during the pandemic in October 2020. The focus of the present research is the process of adaptation of Durgā Pūjā during the pandemic along with the essential role of the internet and technologies that allowed worshippers to overcome Covid-19 restrictions and geographical borders for the people of Tor Pignattara district.

Keywords: religions, Hinduism, heritage, Bengali culture, diaspora, media, Covid-19

---

1. The chapter is the result of collective ethnographic research conducted by Valeria Giampietri, Randa Khalil, and Ludovica Tozzi. Specifically, while the Introduction (section 1) and the Conclusion (section 5) have been collectively written, the author of section 2 is Ludovica Tozzi, the author of section 3 is Randa Khalil, and the author of section 4 is Valeria Giampietri. This chapter summarises the volume written by the chapter's authors and edited by Carmelo Russo, published in 2023.

1 Introduction

Durgā Pūjā, also known as *Navarātrī*, is one of the most important and eminent Hindu festivals, celebrated all over the world and the Indian subcontinent, especially in the northeastern regions, such as West Bengal, Orissa, and Assam, but also in other countries like Bangladesh, Nepal[2], etc. Navarātrī is the regional festival of West Bengal, where it is celebrated in a very pompous way and it is majorly recognised as the most important national holy day in the Bengali Hindu calendar[3]. This worship has gradually evolved to celebrate Durgā's folk identification as the mother and daughter of Hindu Bengali peoples who reside in India, Bangladesh, and worldwide as part of several diasporic communities[4]. Besides South Asian states, such as the above-mentioned ones, increasingly more countries throughout the European continent, such as Great Britain, Germany, Sweden, Netherlands, and Italy[5] have recently hosted Durgā Pūjā annual celebrations. The more the Bengali community – whether its members come from India or Bangladesh – increases, the more Durgā Pūjā festivals become a public and social event involving a progressively wider audience in the host countries[6]. Durgā Pūjā is a festival that lasts ten days and ends with *Vijayā Daśamī*, or the Victory Tenth day, when the slaying of the demon Mahiṣa by the hand of Goddess Durgā is celebrated.

Alongside *Daśamī*, the last five days of Navarātrī are particularly significant too, when some of the most eminent manifestations of the Goddess – like the child Durgā form, also known as Kumārī, the Goddess Kālī, the fierce manifestation Cāmuṇḍā, and others – are worshipped. During

2. Sarkar 2012, p. 325.
3. McDermott 2011, p. 247.
4. Ibid., pp. 126–129.
5. Despite the lack of scientific material, which proves the scarcity of academic research on contemporary Durgā Pūjā, celebrations internationally, it is possible to find a plethora of online blogs and social media accounts, held by Bengali diasporic community managers or referents that take care of explaining and inviting people to religious and cultural events, such as Durgā Pūjā celebrations. There are some examples listed in the Webography section in the references.
6. An example of this phenomenon is visible in North America, where Durgā Pūjā celebrations have grown steadily in number since the mid-1960s, when the first groups of Bengalis who had come under the new immigration laws moved, settled down, and started to commemorate their religious heritage (McDermott 2011, p. 225).

the whole festival, many different artistic events take place and animate the public space: numerous dancing, singing, and theatrical plays are performed to create an enjoyable atmosphere that makes people live a unique experience. Therefore, Durgā Pūjā is not only a religious event but also a socio-cultural festival that exceptionally has the power to bind people together and reaffirm religious values. In October 2020, the Covid-19 pandemic, which had broken out in March of that year, spread across Italy and worldwide in a second wave of contagion. The pandemic emergency completely disarranged and shocked economic and socio-political life in Italy. Consequently, several precautionary measures were taken to keep social distance and contain the spread of the virus. Also, religious life and meetings underwent a radical change: all religious places were closed, and ceremonies got suspended too. The ministerial decree of 13 October 2020, the last before the celebration of Durgā Pūjā, banned gatherings and allowed only a certain number of people at a time to have access to religious places, considering their size and specific characteristics, in order to guarantee at least one metre of social distance.

The following sections aim to analyse, after a theoretical overview of the Durgā Pūjā festival's historical framework, how the two Hindu temples in Tor Pignattara celebrated Navarātrī while dealing with the pandemic restrictions, and what kind of solutions were proposed to lead religious ceremonies with the help of technology, broadcasting tools, and social media. Finally, the last section examines the role played by technologies among diasporic groups and how online religious activities have gained a central role within worshippers' communities in a displacement context.

2 Durgā Pūjā: A Journey Through the History and Cultural Impact of Bengal's Major Festival

2.1 Tracing the Devī

The ritual and the festival of Durgā Pūjā, as we know them today, have been changing and keep changing with the passing of time. Both mythology and the popular recognition that the Goddess gained among Hindu worshippers' communities have a long history of transformation and renovation, through a process of transversal interaction between top-down cultural forces and local traditions. As Sarkar states, it is impossible to trace back in time the origins of both the myth and the ritual dedicated to Goddess Durgā, especially before the colonial presence. Still, we will try to investigate some of the turning points of this undefined process[7]. The first rituals in honour of the Devī can be traced back to prehistoric times (2nd millennium BCE) when the Devī reflected an unclear divine and generative power that declined in different forms and expressions according to regional heterogeneous traditions. The Goddess's personality and hagiography got shaped by popular narratives, through the oral vehicle of songs and poems, and by the elitist Brahmanical culture based on a corpus of Sanskrit texts. In fact, codified references to the Devī can be found in some puranic texts, such as the 6th century *Devī-Māhātmya* section of the *Mārkaṇḍeya Purāṇa* and in several Śākta Purāṇas, such as *Bhaviṣya Purāṇa*, *Brahmavaivarta Purāṇa*, *Devī Purāṇa*, and many others[8]. Devī's mythology is also included in the two main Indian epics: the *Mahābhārata* and Kṛttibās's Bengali *Rāmāyaṇa*[9]. Furthermore, references to the celebration of *pūjā* performances to the Devī in Bengal can be found in several late mediaeval texts, like *Maṅgalkāvya*, the *Viṣṇuyamalā* of the 15th century, and the *Caitanyamaṅgal* from 1538–1550[10]. Therein, the *pūjā* is described as an event, a festival to come together and play musical instruments in the month of Āśvin[11].

Through the dialogue between the prehistoric cult of a divine feminine power, identified as the Cosmic creatrix and Mother, the Brahmanical-Puranic narratives, the *Śākta* cultural movements[12], and other transversal local traditions, the Devī started to be recognised as an ambivalent figure: a symbol of fertility, a source of creative energy, and a furious and fierce erotic being with a feminine aspect. Moreover, through the involvement of the Devī into the sexualised philosophical and ritual Tantric context[13], the

7. Sarkar 2012, p. 325.
8. McDermott 2011, p. 12.
9. Ibid.
10. Ibid., p. 13.
11. The seventh month of the lunisolar Hindu calendar. The month of Āśvin corresponds to the Gregorian calendar months of September and October.
12. Śākta traditions enhance the figure of the Goddess and recognise the centrality of the Goddess's creative energy (śakti). Through śākta texts, this religious tradition became explicit both in its puranic and tantric manifestations. Flood 1996, p. 238.
13. McDermott 2011, p. 165.

Goddess got to be recognised also as both a life keeper and a death bringer. Such ambiguous features are typical of a great number of other different Goddesses, from both local and pan-Indian traditions, who started to be identified as manifestations of a sole Devī, also known as Mahā Devī[14], as a result of the intersection of the so-called "Deshification"[15] – that is, the influence of local and indigenous cultures on Brahmanical religion – and Sanskritization processes.

There is no evidence of a "Great Goddess" in the *Vedas*, as Flood writes, there is textual evidence only from the mediaeval period and it suggests non-Vedic, and probably non-Aryan, origins[16]. Furthermore, local traditions centred on the Devī's worshipping revealed a strong ritual connection with polluting organic material, in contradiction with the mainstream Brahmanical system, therefore such practices denote a possible counterhegemonic origin. The main and most famous form of the Devī is Goddess Durgā, described in many puranic texts (*Devībhāgavata Purāṇa, Devī Māhātmya, Mārkaṇḍeya Purāṇa*) as *Mahiṣāsuramardinī*, the slayer of Mahiṣāsura[17] which represents a threat for cosmic and worldly order[18]. Another one of the most popular Goddess's forms, which is strongly influenced by Tantrism, is the Kumārī: the non-menstruating child form of the Goddess that incarnates and symbolises the powerful, but also contained, creative potential of a woman-to-be, although the martial element is not directly manifested[19]. As a matter of fact, the Kumārī

14. Translatable as "Great Goddess", a deity fully recognized by Brahmanical orthodoxy. Flood 1996, pp. 237, 246.
15. *Deshification* is the opposite of *Sanskritization*, the process by which the Sanskritic tradition simultaneously absorbs and transforms those same popular traditions and shapes them according to the Brahmanical value system. The two processes of Sanskritisation and Deshification beget each other and interact mutually in time. Doniger 2010, p. 6.
16. Flood 1996, p. 244.
17. Mahiṣāsura is a Sanskrit name composed of two terms: *Mahiṣa* "buffalo" and *asura*, usually translated as "demon". In Vedic literature, the term *asura* is used to refer to a class of supernatural beings considered as the counterpart of *devas*, the Gods (literally "shining ones"). In modern Hinduism, *asura* can be considered as "anti-god" related to chaos and disorder, more specifically to adharmic situations and evil actions which have negative consequences on the existing. Flood 1996, pp. 58–59.
18. Ibid., p. 239.
19. The worship of a supreme feminine deity has been the focus of many twentieth-century, controversial reinterpretations of the cult of the Great Goddess also in

can be considered conceptually close to the early recognition of the Devī as Durgā. The myth of Durgā as *Mahiṣāsuramardinī* has given birth to a codified iconography of the Goddess represented while beheading the demon Mahiṣa, laying on her vehicle, the lion, holding different kinds of arms in her multiple hands. The first representations of Durgā as the demons-slayer are traced back to the period between the 7th and 8th centuries[20] and it is still the most famous representation of the Goddess.

Such a powerful feminine model stands openly in contrast with the Brahmanical prescription of gender roles and behaviour in society as presented in normative texts, like the *Dharmaśāstra*[21], whose depiction of women is passive as their role is to be submitted to male authority[22]. Starting from the interaction of shastric texts and socio-economic shifts, the narrative about the powerful Durgā *Mahiṣāsuramardinī* started changing, causing a re-arrangement of Durgā's identity as a less violent and furious divine being. McDermott states that by the 14th and 15th centuries, with the mediaeval texts of *Caṇḍīmaṅgalakāvya* and the 16th century-*Durgāpūjātattva*, we have the first references to the maternal nature of the Goddess[23]. By the late 18th century, the explicit link between Durgā and Pārvatī/Umā, the archetypical loving wife and daughter, was

---

    Pagan and Judeo-Christian traditions, Tantrism, and Germanic mythology in order to enhance the existence of a common primaeval nurturing Mother worshipped in her triple form of Maiden-Virgin, Lover-Mother, and Dark-Mother. Revivalist theories put profound emphasis on women's bodies and sexuality, menstruation, birth, and deadly potential, trying to demonstrate how Goddess-centred pantheons also mirrored a supposed matriarchal ancient society. Cusack 2017, pp. 346, 357.

20. Flood 1996, p. 248.
21. *Dharmaśāstra* is the ancient Indian body of jurisprudence that is the basis, subject to legislative modification, of the family law of Hindus living in territories both within and outside India (Stefon 2021).
22. Imposing a patriarchal system and the subsequent submission of women through religious narrative and legislature has been recognised as a common pattern of other ancient and modern religious systems like Pagan, Judeo-Christian, and Neopagan traditions. On the other hand, ancient and modern witchcraft practices, and Tantrism, for example, were controversially interpreted as counter hegemonic traditions whose female-body-sex-centred rituals have the power to repristinate ancient matriarchal values and criticise masculine norms imposed by monotheistic unity (Cusack 2017, pp. 336–343, 347).
23. McDermott 2011, p. 91.

made and it is traceable in Bāṇa's *Caṇḍīśataka*[24]. The dual nature of the Goddess – one as a fearless virgin and warrior with tribal origins and one as the benevolent and submissive mother/daughter – kept evolving over time and it was constantly used to create a cultural connection between Hindu women and the Goddess. Such a narrative about Durgā has historically been involved in nationalist policies of gender control, making the divine figure a model for all female members of the worshippers' community, a phenomenon which got intensified especially between the 18th and the 20th centuries, during the independentist and the Hindu nationalist movements (1905–1917). By that time, in order to fulfil the independentist policy, reformists needed a culturally Indian symbolism, which is why they tried to move emphasis towards the Goddess's maternal rather than her martial self. By the late 17th century, the iconography linked to Goddess Durgā also started changing: the representation of the Goddess as a demon slayer was kept more or less the same, but the main idol was sided by four Gods, Durgā's sons and daughters Kārtikeya, Gaṇeśa, Lakṣmī, and Sarasvatī, in a one-piece traditional idol. Durgā's *mūrti*[25] is essential for hosting the Goddess' *prāṇa*[26], which is believed to descend on Earth and inhabit the *mūrti* from the sixth to the last day of Navarātrī. The *mūrti*, whether it is a *ghaṭ*[27], a picture, or an anthropomorphic statue, is essential to receive the *Darśana* of the Goddess, the most intimate form of contact with the divine that Hindu worshippers can have, plus an act of blessing[28]. Today, even if Goddess Durgā is still recognised as a warrior and a demon slayer, she is praised like a mother, a mother for humankind, a mother to call and praise when in need. Nonetheless, she is also treated like a married-off daughter who has the chance to go back to her paternal home – every Hindu family's house – once a year during holidays, leaving it and the worldly dimension again by the end of the festival through the sacred immersion ritual, the *Visarjana*.

---

24. Sarkar 2012, p. 338.
25. Anything which has a definite shape and physical limits consecrated for worship, which during ritual becomes an embodiment or incarnation of the deity.
26. The vital Breath, essence, life.
27. Earthen pot of water.
28. McDermott 2011, p. 109.

2.2 A Celebration for Kings and Peasants

Durgā Pūjā is a festivity originally linked to the harvest season, which is why the ritual praxis is built upon agricultural symbolism, fertility developed within the rural agricultural classes, and martial and metaphysical elements[29]. It is possible to affirm that the rituals to the Goddess originated from the lower social strata, spread, and were adopted by the upper classes as a result of the Deshification process. As Rodrigues states, side by side with fecundity, a key feature of the Devī is her role as a granter and legitimiser of royal power. The puranic myth that describes the Goddess as a demon slayer, identifying her victory as the triumph of Good over Evil[30], gave a compelling narrative to associate with royal and influential dynasties, enhancing their ability in warfare and their fierce attitude towards enemies as an apotropaic tool for their wealth and properties. The special status of Durgā Pūjā stems from its historical origins as a celebration built up and performed by royal and high-middle-class families to gain social prestige and economic wealth, a process that remains active today.

The autumnal Durgā Pūjā takes place during the lunar month of *Āśvin*, which occurs on the first nine nights of the waxing new moon (Navarātrī). The last four to five days of Navarātrī are the most important ones: on the sixth day the Devī is awoken in the bilva tree, with mantra recitations in a rite called *Bodhana*; on the seventh day, the deities are invited to reside for the duration of the festival in the plants and the *ghāṭ*, and the worship of the Kumārī takes place; on the eighth day, the fiercest form of the Goddess, *Cāmuṇḍā*, is worshipped; the ninth day is the most important one because by that day the greatest animal sacrifices occur; and finally the tenth day, *Daśamī*, is when the triumph of Durgā over the demon Mahiṣa is celebrated. According to mythology, on the tenth day, Goddess Durgā is believed to return to her husband, to God Śiva's home on mount Kailāsa. Hence, the last rituals celebrate the moment of farewell, when the Goddess takes her leave of the family that hosted her and goes away through the *Visarjana*, "the immersion of the idol into a watercourse". By the mid-19th century, Durgā Pūjā started being held as a collective enterprise by many groups of enthused citizens and it started following

---

29. Rodrigues 2003, p. 15.
30. See footnote 19.

marketing and economic logic. By the turn of the twentieth century, Durgā Pūjā became a *Sārvajanīna Pūjā* or "*pūjā* for all", a public celebration for everyone, regardless of religious or socio-cultural differences[31].

Today, Durgā Pūjā is a festival that completely transforms both private and public spaces, a transversal event that turns familiar neighbourhoods into extraordinary, liminal spaces, where "internal community boundaries are tactfully retained so that people across classes and religion can participate, even if to a limited extent, in the revelries, feasting, and entertainments that take place"[32]. The cities and villages get totally rearranged for the occasion: *paṇḍāls*, which stand as temporary temples to host the *mūrti*, are built all over; the streets get decorated, colourful, and clean; theatrical, singing, and dancing spectacles are performed during the ten days to entertain the vast and heterogeneous audience. Increasingly spectacular ornaments and performances are prepared and financed by middle-class individuals and private companies at each festival, in order to gain prestige and money, giving rise to competitive but also amusing contests for prices, adapting a socio-cultural event to marketing strategies.

2.3 Mother Durgā's Displaced Children: Diaspora and Ritual

Durgā Pūjā is mainly an urban festival that "becomes a liminal site for imaginary journeys in time and space across India and the globe, inculcating new tastes in archaeological tours, heritage viewing, art, and craft consumption", as Ray claims[33]. The increasingly larger Hindu Indian and Bangladeshi communities residing abroad – in Hong Kong, the United States, and London among others[34] – started to celebrate Durgā Pūjā publicly by the end of the last century, with the attempt to recreate the traditional local celebration and at the same time giving rise to new peculiar and intercultural traditions.

Goddess Durgā is praised in her role of married daughter and Mother of humankind who visits her paternal family once a year to subsequently go back to her husband's home, as McDermott asserts. The filial symbolism accentuates the love-in-separation feeling at the heart of the event,

---

31. Ray 2017, p. 12.
32. Ibid., p. 3.
33. Ibid., p. 37.
34. McDermott 2011, pp. 224–240.

as well as the sense of loss and longing[35]. Such a narrative encourages a feeling of identity and belonging in a diasporic community abroad. It further intensifies the emotion of *viraha*[36] shared by both the displaced worshippers and the Goddess herself, who is also perceived as the icon of the Motherland or 'Bhārat Mātā'[37]. Regarding this topic, Chatterjee maintains that the peculiar fluidity of Goddess Durgā's personality is very relatable for those displaced groups who constantly negotiate and reshape their identity after leaving their homeland[38]. Immigrants' resettlement in a host country requires tremendous changes that provoke nostalgia, confusion, and a sense of loss. As Vásquez states, diasporic livelihood enhances a feeling of unity and cohesion in a hostile host country, allowing its members to imagine themselves as a unified ethnos[39].

Nevertheless, according to Vertovec[40], it is necessary to apply a multi-dimensional perspective on diversity for a better understanding of immigration and multicultural hosting milieu, moving beyond "the ethnic group as either the unit of analysis or sole object of study"[41]. While presenting his dissertation on super-diversity[42], Vertovec points out that any human group from a given country presents extreme internal variety[43]. In fact, the Bengali regional flavour of events like Durgā Pūjā, for example, leads to a certain exclusivity also in a diasporic community, to the extent that ethnicity and shared culture can override religion: non-Bengalis are certainly not unwelcome, but they tend to be absent, while Muslim Bengalis or Bangladeshis often join and are welcomed in[44]. Nevertheless, considering again multiple variables other than ethnicity, remarkable linguistic, economic, political, and cultural differences among Bangladeshi,

---

35. Ibid., p. 99.
36. Separation, the anguish of separation or absence.
37. Rodrigues 2003, p. 347.
38. Even though Chatterjee's (2020) study is an analysis of the symbolic and actual link between Durgā Pūjā and post-Partition displaced women, the results of his research can be applied to this work too.
39. Vásquez 2010, p. 128.
40. Vertovec 2007, p. 1026.
41. Glick Schiller 2006, p. 613.
42. Vertovec 2007, p. 1025.
43. Ibid., pp. 1031–1032.
44. McDermott 2011, p. 237.

West Bengali, and Indian Bengali people[45] become evident in everyday life and during cultural events. West Bengali diasporic communities, for instance, tend to be older, more well-established, and wealthier, and their members belong to educated and economic elites, while Bangladeshi community members tend to be part of the economic migration, they have a recent history of displacement, and often are employed in less well-paying jobs, tending to feel more connected to Bangladesh.

Public and religious life gets affected by such discrepancies among West Bengali and Bangladeshi diasporic communities. The way they celebrate Durgā Pūjā reflects political tension: Hindus in West Bengal constitute the majority of the population, so their religious identity is not under threat in their country. At the same time, Hindu Bangladeshis got deeply traumatised by the political backlashes against them that have occurred since the early 1990s. Diasporic communities tend to get affected by the current political situation in their home countries, which is why Bangladeshi Hindus, for example, celebrate Durgā Pūjā "with a wary eye to communal tension"[46] and their festival can have a strong political connotation also abroad. Not only do political and economic issues affect the way diasporic community celebrate Durgā Pūjā, but such a great event also undergoes a series of necessary practical changes in a displacement context: ritual time gets generally shortened in order to adapt it to laboral and educational schedule of students and workers; public *paṇḍāl* and structures built for the occasion are exchanged with close and circumscribed spaces since the event does not affect the totality of residents but just a small part of them; some procedures of the ritual praxis need to be changed, like the *Visarjana* or the immersion of the *mūrti* performed on *Daśamī*, since in American and European countries, for example, people have to follow anti-pollution rules. The community cannot afford to buy a different *mūrti* every year as it should be, that is why the idol is kept intact for at least five years and the farewell rituals[47] before the *Visarjana* get changed too, and so on. Lastly, diaspora consequences on gender relationships need special attention too. Al-Ali affirms

45. Bengali people residing in Indian States other than West Bengal have experienced direct and/or indirect migration from West Bengal or Bangladesh.
46. McDermott 2011, pp. 230–231.
47. During the traditional farewell rituals, married women symbolically feed the Goddess with sweets (McDermott 2011, p. 230).

that the diaspora provides enabling contexts in which existing gender ideologies and relations are both reiterated and challenged. South Asian women have the chance to appeal to more liberal legislatures and have access to economic resources and rights, but they are also subjected to the possible consequences of hardening the notions of "cultural authenticity" and "traditions"[48]. In the host countries, women are expected to fulfil the same social and domestic duties as they did in their own country. They are expected to follow the shastric ethics and carry out their reproductive, domestic, and religious roles looking at virtuous Goddesses, like Durgā, as their behavioural models.

In the following sections, special attention will be drawn to an actual example of Durgā Pūjā celebrated by the Hindu Bengali community in Rome, more specifically in the neighbourhood of Tor Pignattara, in 2020, during the Covid-19 pandemic. Subsequently, it will become clear how and why displaced communities reinvent themselves, their rituals, and their habits to survive in the host country.

3   Pandemic Durgā Pūjā

3.1 *Pandemic Durgā Pūjā: The Case Study of Tor Pignattara's Temples*

The Covid-19 pandemic challenged people's lives from many points of view, including a religious one. Religious places in Italy have been forced to follow all the restrictions that the Italian government imposed: the obligation to wear masks, the social distancing, and the reductions in the number of people allowed in a closed space are just a few examples of the changes that worship places had to deal with. And, inevitably, these issues had an important impact on the way religious communities celebrated rituals.[49]

---

48. Feminist scholars have fought to deconstruct the image of South Asian women as passive and agency-less. Indeed, it is important to remember that agency and involvement in decision-making processes within the household, but also within larger communities, are always maintained and even empowered in a certain way through participation in religious and cultural events (Al-Ali 2010, p. 20).
49. Consiglio dei ministri della Repubblica Italiana 2020.

As previously mentioned, this paragraph will analyse the celebrations of Durgā Pūjā in 2020, held from the 22–26 October, in Tor Pignattara, Rome, taking into account the restrictions put in place because of the pandemic. The analysis will look at two specific case studies: the first one is the Om Hindu Mandir at Via Amedeo Cencelli 23/A[50] and the second one is the Puja Udjapon Parisad at Via Guido Cora 21, which are the two Hindu temples in this district. Before presenting the main argument, it is important to understand the reason why the research is based on this area of Rome.

Tor Pignattara is a district that counts a large number of foreign people living there: it is a "multiethnic" place, as well as a multireligious one. It is a historic Roman outskirt of the eastern area[51], and in the last twenty years it has been hit by strong migratory flows, especially from the Asian continent. Indeed, as Carmelo Russo claims[52], Tor Pignattara is a peculiar district, that we can define as "super-diverse", and that hosts several worship places belonging to different religions: four Catholic parishes, four mosques, four Pentecostal churches, two Hindu temples, and one Buddhist temple[53].

Another important feature worth noting is that both the places of worship analysed for this research are peculiar. From the architectural point of view, what we see when we go to the temples are former shops being used as spaces of worship, and this is a feature that the Hindu temples share with the mosques of the area (and they are not the only ones)[54].

50. In this chapter and the following one, we decided to leave "Via" in the Italian language, avoiding translating with the corresponding English "Street".
51. Ficacci 2007, p. 9.
52. Russo 2017, p. 152.
53. Ibid.
54. Article 8 of the Italian Constitution states that all religious confessions are equally free before the law and that they have the right to organise themselves according to their statutes, so long as they do not conflict with the Italian legal system. It establishes that their relations with the State are regulated by the law based on agreements with the relevant representatives. Unlike other religious denominations, Islam does not have an agreement (Intesa) with the Italian State. A big problem in this sense is the lack of an association that is clearly representative of the majority of Muslims in Italy. This depends on various factors, including the complexity of the Islamic religious reality, which is varied within it and does not have a single legal representation.

This is a relevant aspect that shows all the difficulties that religious communities might face in finding or creating a new space for themselves and their religious activities. This depends on many issues. One of these is related to the fact that religions settle themselves in urban spaces and need to interact and negotiate with the territory in which they are located (as well as with other religious communities). The allocation of religions in urban space occurs in a complex way, through stratifications. Through the sociological analysis of Becci, Burchardt, and Giorda it is possible to identify different ways of settling religions. What the three authors define as "Place-Making" is the process that concerns the religions that we can define as migrant or diasporic ones, among which it is possible to consider Hinduism[55].

When we talk about Hinduism in Italy, it is important to note that it was officially recognised in 2012, by the government of Mario Monti, through an agreement with the Italian Hindu Union (UII), which is an association managed mainly by Italians. It is indeed important to emphasise that Hinduism in Italy is presented as a young reality, which is constituted mainly in two "branches": the first is characterised by Italian citizens who have approached the Hindu religion, and the second is determined by migratory flows. Unlike Puja Udjapon Parisad, the Om Hindu Mandir belongs to UII and is the only temple in Rome to be part of it. The *mandir*'s entry into the UII was recorded in 2016 after the organisation included the Bangladeshi temple community in some public religious activities[56]. Both the Om Hindu Mandir and the Puja Udjapon Parisad are managed by Bangladeshi communities. As a matter of fact, the Bangladeshi community is the biggest foreign group present in the 5th Municipality[57], in

---

The agreement offers various religious confessions, different from the Catholic one, the opportunity to have advantages within the civil life of the State. In general, these advantages materialise in many ways. One of these is having rules for the construction and protection of religious buildings and the enhancement of assets regarding each confession's historical and cultural heritage, as a guarantee of their respective cultural identities. Russo, Tamburrino 2015, pp. 15–22.

55. Becci et al. 2017, pp. 82–85.
56. Scialdone 2018, pp. 246–250.
57. The term "Municipality" means what in English is defined as Local Council. See Chapter 9.

which Tor Pignattara is located[58]. For this reason, the area is also called "Banglatown"[59].

Moreover, Broccolini underlines that the local Bangladeshi community is embedded within transnational networks; however, it is re-establishing a "locality" within the lines of a politics of diaspora that employs dominant Western values – such as that of urban requalification – in the name of safeguarding national moral values. The diaspora thus becomes an engine that "refunds" the space of landing within a national belonging. Furthermore, the Bangladeshi communities have activated forms of social, economic, and associative life in the territory, which they perceive and represent as positive and requalifying for the territory[60].

As also Andrea Priori notices, the recovery and changes that have taken place in the area since the second half of the 1990s have their main agent in migrants, including especially those from Bangladesh who have been playing a leading role[61]. Indeed, the presence of the Bangladeshi community in Tor Pignattara is usually very evident in the streets during the celebrations of Durgā Pūjā, but during 2020 this kind of tradition had to change because of the "extraordinary", in the sense of non-ordinary, time that the world faced and is still facing.

3.2 Durgā Pūjā Celebrations

On the one hand, conducting the research and being part of the celebrations, in both temples, was not easy at the beginning since it was difficult to get in touch with them, and the attendees were often families of those who ran or attended the temple assiduously. However, on the other hand, once permission was obtained from the temple managers, there was a great reception from the participants. As researchers, we actively took part in the rites, invited by devotees, who answered our questions with pleasure and with the desire to share their traditions as they happened in the past when the celebrations were open to the public.

What emerged is that the restrictions that the temples faced and the rules that they had to follow, of course, put limits on the performances

---

58. Roma Capitale 2021.
59. Broccolini 2017, p. 164.
60. Ibid., p. 165.
61. Priori 2014, p. 64.

held during Durgā Pūjā. First, there were concerns about non-compliance with the rules, possible controls, and the consequences of bad organisation. We first noticed that some men were at the entrance of both temples, inviting people to register themselves on a book register for tracking.

Moreover, consuming ritual offerings, since food is undoubtedly a central aspect of Hindu liturgy, has undergone a series of practical changes. Already in 2019, the celebration of Durgā Pūjā was stopped because of issues concerning food. The administration of the Puja Udjapon Parisad had obtained from the 5th Municipality the authorization for the use of a former councilor chamber located at Via Acqua Bullicante. It is a space that the associations of the district use for meetings and debate activities. On 7 October, however, the police dispersed the worshippers who were already in the hall, closing the venue to the public. A delegation of citizens went to the Town Hall to understand the reasons for the closure because the traffic police, while carrying out the ordinance, had not found any infringement of the safety regulations. Eventually, it turned out that the reasons behind the police intervention were the presence of a gas cylinder, food delivery, and a tray for free offerings[62].

Of course, during the 2020 celebration, due to the recommendations regarding the spread of the virus and the restrictions, the way of offering the *prasāda*[63] changed, too. For example, the Udjapon Parisad temple forbade eating the *prasāda* inside the temple and distributed it in disposable containers to each devotee. In the case of the Om Hindu Mandir, this change did not happen. The food was served as usual in the *thālī* and consumed inside the temple.

In both temples the number of people was reduced, and no more than 30 people were present in religious halls. Considering the small number of people and the fear of being controlled by public security, nothing could be heard or seen from the outside. Normally, during Durgā Pūjā there are huge processions and public singing and dancing performances that involve many devotees and inevitably change the ordinary appearance of the area. But what changed in 2020 was the standard mode of

---

62. See Chapter 9.
63. The *prasāda* is the sanctified food offered to the Gods and Goddesses that is then shared with the devotees. It is an essential part of every *pūjā* and, normally, it is served on metal dishes called *thālī* and is eaten with the hands.

carrying out the celebration. While, in the past, the two temples had put a lot of effort into trying to involve as many devotees as possible, in gathering a large number of people, and in putting up a celebration as true to the original festival in India as possible, this time they did quite the opposite: they tried their best to avoid a large gathering and, instead, strived to find new ways to celebrate. Moreover, previously, there used to be a multicultural and multi-religious audience. Anup Kumar, president of the Om Hindu Mandir, during an interview conducted by us[64] on 21 October 2020, explained that people who usually attend Durgā Pūjā are Sikhs, Muslims, and Christians, but because of the Covid-19 restrictions only the close Hindu members of the community temple were allowed to take part in the festival and the rituals. Moreover, Kumar declared that also people from Indian states such as Bhutan, Nepal, and Italy attend religious rituals and events at the *mandir*. In 2020, the recorded attendants in both temples were mostly Hindus from Bangladesh, but with slightly different generational presences. In fact, the Udjapon Parisad temple counted not only families, as in the Om Hindu Mandir, but also university students, two of them from West Bengal.

Usually, both women and men belonging to the diasporic communities get involved in Durgā Pūjā celebrations. In fact, in the last four or five days of Navarātrī, when one-day-long celebrations take place, women attend rituals and celebrations more assiduously. Since most of them do not have any jobs, they have more time than their male counterparts to participate in the long Durgā Pūjā celebrations and Hindu rituals in general. Religious life has a crucial role in the lives of Hindu Bengali women who migrated to Rome. During Navarātrī, women were the ones who took care of preparing food and garlands. Some of them were even helping the Brahmins who were conducting the rituals, handing over to them all the necessities for the ritual performances. In both temples, on the last ritual day dedicated to the women, men also took an active part in the celebration. Since dances and spectacles were not allowed, however, they played drums and performed small instrumental interludes between one ritual phase and the other. Even if women are not allowed to play any instrument during rituals, they are the ones who have a more active part

---

64. Anup Kumar, interviewed by Ludovica Tozzi and Randa Khalil, Rome, 21 October 2020.

in the ceremonials. They are also dressed in a pompous way, as the tradition wants. The 2020 celebration made no exception: women wore *sāṛī*[65], decorated their hair tails, wore showy make-up, and they dressed up their female children with the same care. Also, they took part in the rituals, passing the food and all the necessities to the Brahmins.

Some of them came to the temple bringing their small children, who did not go to school for the occasion. Even this small act alone is a clear example of the ongoing attempt to pass religious values and traditions to the younger generations who are growing up as members of the Italian Bangladeshi community, in a different cultural environment than the one their parents grew up in. Some of the children we met at the temple during celebrations were talking to each other in Italian, while all the adults were speaking to each other in Bengali. This is something that demonstrates the identity issues and challenges that second generations currently face. This can also be analysed through Vertovec's concept of "super-diversity" and the identification of the city as a basin of plurality in which social, religious, and cultural affiliations are added to the individual biographies of each citizen. This results in the multiplication of diversities among individuals and groups, such as generational and gender differences, in a society continuously in transformation[66].

Moreover, due to cultural and social changes tied to migration, Brahmins in Rome are not as many as they can be in India or Bangladesh or in other European cities where diasporic Bengali-speaking communities are bigger. In Rome, Brahmins do not live in the temples, so they normally have to move to celebrate the many Hindu rituals. That is why Brahmins conduct a sort of "itinerant" activity since they serve several temples in town. Brahmin Sumon Chakrabartee, for example, lives in Centocelle and he must move around the city and come to Tor Pignattara every time he is required to attend a celebration. For instance, he arrived late on the last day of the 2020 celebrations in the Udjapon Parisad temple. This apparently trivial occurrence contributes to showing the difficulties and the peculiarities of being part of a diasporic community, as well as the necessity of celebrating holy days, traditions, and festivals. Liturgy of Hindu rituals requires the essential presence of Brahmins who play

---

65. The *sāṛī* is an Indian traditional female indument.
66. Vertovec 2007, pp. 1049–1050.

a fundamental role in the diasporic community. They are the ones who enable religious life to continue abroad, and who strive to keep a displaced tradition that is rewritten day by day by the diasporic community alive.

Furthermore, according to the diasporic communities' traditions, even in Rome the *mūrti* is preserved and changed every five years. In the past years, the Om Hindu Mandir's statue was made by a Muslim craftsman, while in 2020 it was made on a smaller scale and brought to Ostia, where it was released into the sea. Since it is illegal to throw any kind of material into the Tevere river, right after the farewell rituals of *Daśamī* took place, the men worshippers who were attending the rituals in both the temples brought the little *mūrti* to the sea, to Ostia. The Udjapon Parisad worshippers struggled to find a statue, so they ended up having the image of the Durgā and the *ghaṭ* only, that they eventually took to the beach.

What emerged during this research is that the managers of the two Hindu temples in Tor Pignattara really wanted, and worked hard to perform, Durgā Pūjā rituals according to the tradition, keeping it authentic to the extent possible. Even though a smaller number of people had the chance to participate in person in the celebrations because of the fear of Covid-19, the atmosphere was joyous, and the temples' administrators were still able to stay active during Navarātrī.

Despite not sharing the urban space outside the temples, as happened during the previous celebrations, people attempted to attend and celebrate religious rituals normally. Some of them were heard talking about the pandemic and the shock it caused. Brahmins and devotees also prayed to have a normal life soon and tried to give some religious explanation for the new reality. The pandemic had a strong impact on the ritual performances, not only from the organisational point of view but also from the devotional one. Worshippers tried very hard to find a new balance between the restrictions and the will to attend rituals at the temple. The struggle to find a balanced way to celebrate Durgā Pūjā has emerged also through the study of the online modalities made available for the occasion, as we analyse in the next paragraph.

4 Digitizing Devotion: Observing Durgā Pūjā in a Virtual Environment

4.1 The Celebration of Durgā Pūjā on Social Networks

The two Hindu temples of the Tor Pignattara district in Rome, the Puja Udjapon Parisad and the Om Hindu Mandir, have responded to the Covid-19 pandemic emergency and the subsequent restrictions, by proposing alternative ways to follow the *pūjā*. In particular, the temples provide the devotees with the possibility to follow the ritual online.

In this section, we will first present the different prayer alternatives available to devotees and then introduce the idea of "digital religion" as a further tool of analysis. This concept will be deployed to explore whether obtaining the *Darśana* online is considered valid. The Puja Udjapon Parisad managers have transmitted occasional live broadcasts via the private Facebook profile of a *pūjā* participant in the temple, but they shared live broadcasts also in a private Facebook group specifically created for the temple. Both the profile and the Facebook group were in Bengali language. Managers of the temple also shared information on their private Facebook profiles about the celebration of Durgā Pūjā in the temple due to the Covid-19 situation, and invited people not to go to the temple, but to follow the live shows on Facebook instead. Similarly, the Om Hindu Mandir administrators transmitted live broadcasts on a private Facebook profile of the temple called "Om Hindu Monder". Here, the broadcasts were much more frequent than those at the Puja Udjapon Parisad temple. It is evident that the online broadcast of Durgā Pūjā was intended for a limited audience (i.e., temple-goers who personally knew the people who would transmit the broadcasts and who did not have the opportunity, or perhaps those who were afraid, to go to the temple). Both profiles and groups were all in Bengali which shows that the Facebook broadcast of the celebration was not done with the aim of reaching a wider audience.

When talking about the online broadcast of the 2020 celebration of Durgā Pūjā, it is also important to mention the Italian Hindu Union which announced, both on social networks (Facebook and Instagram) and its website, the screening of live streams from some temples in Italy on the occasion of Durgā Pūjā. It also scheduled an online meeting for Sunday, 25 October 2020, with a Hindu family from Calcutta. The spread of the

Covid-19 pandemic also caused restrictions in India, and it limited the celebrations in the temples. The family, therefore, during a meeting on Zoom has shown how they were traditionally celebrating Durgā Pūjā at home. During the broadcast, live images of the celebration from various temples in Italy were also shown, and members of the Union also shared some slides, providing the public with information about the holiday and its significance.

When comparing the live streams from Om Hindu Mandir and Puja Udjapon Parisad temples with those of the Italian Hindu Union, their different intent appears obvious. The purpose of the two temples in Rome was to involve people from a small community (Bengali-speaking Hindus) in a Hindu celebration, particularly given the impossibility of going to the temple due to the pandemic. On the contrary, the purpose of the Italian Hindu Union was to share information and reach a wider audience: most of the people who followed the live shows were, indeed, Italian, and the explanatory presentations about Durgā Pūjā were clearly intended for a non-expert public audience. This difference can be explained by the fact that the Italian Hindu Union is officially recognised by the Italian State as a religious confession. Therefore, it is one of the religious or cultural associations that Italian citizens can decide to devolve their 8x1000 to[67]. Italian Hindu Union's purposes are, in fact, to represent all the Hindus living in Italy and the protection, coordination, practice, and study of Hindu culture and religion[68]. Furthermore, despite the differences between Om Hindu Mandir, which is part of the Italian Hindu Union, and the Puja Udjapon Parisad, which is not, how the two temples reacted to the restrictions imposed by the Covid-19 pandemic are similar.

4.2 Digital Religion: Is It Possible to Pray Online?

It is evident that social media has played a primary role in this particular period. New technologies have changed our lives and, no doubt, many things have been simplified, such as being in contact with people who are

---

67. The 8x1000 is the share equaling 0.8% of the annual income tax return taxpayers can choose to devolve to a religious denomination, recognised by the Italian State, as provided by Italian law.
68. UII 2021.

very far from us. Moreover, they offer migrants the possibility of preserving a continuous and in real-time relationship with the contexts, speeches, and images of their native country and allow richer and stronger connections with the local community or with other diasporic communities with which they can share an experience, a narration, a story[69]. According to Appadurai, "these new forms of electronically mediated communication are beginning to create virtual neighborhoods, no longer bounded by territory, passports, taxes, elections, and other conventional political diacritics, but by access to both the software and hardware that are required to connect to these large international computer networks"[70]. He thus argues that diasporic groups are changing as a consequence of the spread of new technologies. In particular, Appadurai claims that "the global flow of images, news, and opinion now provides part of the engaged cultural and political literacy that diasporic persons bring to their spatial neighborhoods"[71]. However, as a consequence of this new pervasiveness of communication technologies, activities such as checking emails, searching for information on the internet, and having virtual friendships on social networks have now become a significant part of many people's everyday lives.

Indeed, the offline and online spheres are no longer autonomous and discrete dimensions. Rather, they exist in contiguity with one another, constantly mixing and feeding on each other. This has inevitably changed how people practise religion, too. The impact of new technologies on religious practices has been so powerful that scholars coined the term "digital religion" to describe this scenario. According to Campbell, "digital religion" is the term used to define the significant changes in the ways that people practise religion that occurred in the last few decades as a consequence of the spread of communication technology. "Digital religion", she states, "does not simply refer to religion as it is performed and articulated online, but points to how digital media and spaces are shaping and being shaped by religious practice"[72]. In this regard, it is important to mention the website "Saranam"[73]. The blog was created to

69. Matteucci 2020, p. 61.
70. Appadurai 1996, p. 195.
71. Ibid., p. 197.
72. Campbell 2012, p. 1.
73. http://saranam.com.

"do whatever it takes to help Hindus around the world meet their own needs in the realm of religion, spirituality, morality, and the Hindu value system"[74], but it also offers a lot of suggestions to Hindus all over the world, such as films to watch and songs to listen to. There are also a lot of websites that offer the opportunity to celebrate an online *pūjā* as, for example, the Vishwanath temple in Varanasi[75] that allows the devotees to follow the puja celebration broadcast live from the temple every day. As Cristopher Helland states when talking about the use of technology by diasporic communities, "[t]hese are people on the global frontier looking for a connection with their places of origin rather than with the community in which they now live"[76].

But does the online ritual have the same validity as a religious ritual performed in a sacred place? Émile Durkheim defined ritual as a tool to maintain social cohesion; performing rituals creates a sense of community. Helland claims that "Durkheim believed that the real role and function of ritual was to maintain the society. Through ritual practice, people felt a real sense of belonging and social cohesion [...] and felt that they were part of something larger and greater than themselves"[77]. It is possible to analyse the online ritual taking into consideration Dukheim's definition of "ritual". On the one hand, it might be thought that watching a Brahmin perform the ritual in a temple, through a computer's screen alone at home leads to the lack of that sense of community Durkheim talks about. This lack is also accentuated by the absence of the whole set of sensorial experiences that characterise the ritual, such as the colours and smells normally present in the temple during a *pūjā*. Moreover, in the case of religious communities in the diaspora, the temple is not only a religious place in which to perform a ritual, but it is also a space where members of the community can meet, talk in their own language, and share common memories and traditions. On the other hand, however, the new social media offer the devotees the opportunity to create "online communities", such as, for example, groups on Facebook, or even the possibility to participate in rituals performed in their native country, without having to go back there.

74. Helland 2007, p. 970.
75. https://shrikashivishwanath.org/online/live_darshan.
76. Ibid.
77. Helland 2012, p. 26.

These online communities that technological innovations contributed to creating can be described through the concept of "imagined communities", which Benedict Anderson coined to define "the nation":

> A nation, it is an imagined political community and imagined as both inherently limited and sovereign. It is *imagined* because the members of even the smallest nation will never know most of their fellow members, meet them, or even hear of them. [...] The nation is imagined as limited because [...] it has finite, if elastic, boundaries, beyond which lie other nations[78].

Online communities reflect these characteristics. O'Leary, as cited by Helland, argues that "ritual needs to be geographically located in a communal space and landscape, and it was in the ritual activity itself that the group turned cyberspace into a place where this could occur"[79]. Heinz Scheifinger claims that "if a ritual appears to be transformed online but it is still deemed to be acceptable, then it suggests that the ritual itself has not changed significantly and that there are unlikely to be fundamental changes in the religious experience that it gives rise to"[80]. The validity of the Hindu ritual online is also confirmed by the possibility to practise the *Darśana*. The *Darśana* is one of the key elements of the ritual and it involves a devotee gazing into the eyes of the deity to receive blessings. Heinz Scheifinger claims that it is possible to practise the *Darśana* through a computer screen thanks to the opportunity in Hinduism to replicate the deities[81].

As shown above, social media played a fundamental role during the celebration of Durgā Pūjā in 2020, when the restrictions imposed by the Covid-19 pandemic limited regular festival celebrations. However, the fieldwork conducted in Tor Pignattara has shown a much more complex picture. The interviewees proved to be able to appreciate the possibilities offered by new technologies but, at the same time, they highlighted some of the shortcomings of following the ritual online. The words of Binita Nath, a Hindu Bengali woman from Assam who was at the moment of

---

78. Anderson 1991, pp. 6–7.
79. Helland 2012, p. 26.
80. Scheifinger 2012, p. 121.
81. Ibid., pp. 125–126.

the interview residing in Rome, perfectly sum up the ambiguous attitude many of the devotees have towards the online *pūjā*:

> The internet and social media have now become very important in our life. We can't even imagine our lives without these kinds of technologies. So, during the Durgā Pūjā festival, since we couldn't go and celebrate in the temple, we had the chance to sit at home, in front of a telephone or a computer in Italy and see how *Durgā Mātā* is in any Hindu temple around the world. It's obvious that you cannot do anything with your own hands, you can't offer food or a flower. That is indeed the main difference: normally worshippers can actually see what it's happening inside the temple. The most important thing about online religious rituals is that you can not only see what happens in Italian Hindu temples, but you can also see what is happening in India or Bangladesh simultaneously. You have the opportunity to go "back home" virtually and celebrate the *pūjā* with the family in your native country. I think that the internet plays a great role also in sharing information. I could ask if I had permission to go to the temple or not through the internet and social networks. These kinds of things, like information processing, are much faster on the internet, because of social media, Facebook pages, and all. For me, this is a blessing, I can't imagine how we would handle the Corona situation without the internet and media because awareness and information are now so easy to propagate thanks to the internet and social media. Of course, that's very important[82].

It is evident that Binita Nath recognises the benefits that new technologies offer to diasporic communities but, in the case of Durgā Pūjā, she has not been able to replace the ritual celebrated at the temple with the online one. She insisted with the managers of the temples that they allow her to go there even just ten minutes during the *pūjā* to have the *Darśana*: "we could see it from social media but that doesn't give you that feeling unless you have the chance to go around and get the vibes of Durgā Pūjā"[83]. Restricting access to the temple did not just mean not performing a ritual – the main ritual in the case of the Durgā Pūjā festival – but also keeping people away from their origins. It is possible to affirm, therefore, that restrictions caused by the Covid-19 pandemic have limited the religious

---

82. Binita Nath, Zoom interview by Ludovica Tozzi, Rome, Italy, 27 December 2020.
83. Ibid.

life of many devotees, but, at the same time, that the internet and technology have been – and still are – a successful tool for overcoming pandemic and geographical limitations.

5 Conclusion

During the 18th and 19th centuries, Durgā Pūjā became a popular festival for Hindu worshippers all over the Indian Subcontinent and around the world. Thousands of people who migrated from India and Bangladesh to Western countries in the last decades had to start a new life, reconstruct their identities, and get used to new habits. According to the ISTAT[84] 2020 census, the number of Bangladeshi immigrants who have come to Italy has grown to 158,020 while immigrants from Indian countries total 165,512. Of those, some 32,810 Bangladeshi and 11,477 Indian immigrants currently reside in Rome[85]. The growing Indian and Bangladeshi communities are changing demographic and cultural statistics, drawing attention to neglected social and cultural issues.

As for the rest of the American, Middle Eastern, and European cities where Bangladeshi and Indian diasporic communities are constantly growing, it has become impossible to ignore the enormous impact that a regional festival like Durgā Pūjā has in Rome. Celebrated by Hindus and Muslims as well as Sikhs, Christians, and others in Bangladesh, India, and all over the world, Durgā Pūjā is increasingly gaining traction, especially in the multicultural and interracial suburb of Tor Pignattara. The spiritual, cultural, and folkloric baggage that is carried by the Bengali community is displayed and reiterated during such events, "through the use of the vernacular, the regional style of celebrating Navarātrī, and the showcasing of regional dress, cuisine, and arts"[86]. Even though Bengali diasporic group is internally divided by socio-political, economic differences, local and familiar traditions, Goddess Durgā is still identified as a national symbol that nourishes their perception of a shared religious background[87]. While,

---

84. ISTAT is the acronym for National Institute of Statistics.
85. ISTAT (2021); Roma Capitale (2021). For many details inherent in the 5th Municipality, see Chapter 9, par. 1.
86. McDermott 2011, p. 237.
87. Ibid., p. 240.

on the one hand, the whole community struggles for recreating even a small part of what they have lived and remembered about the great Durgā Pūjā that took place in the streets of Kolkata, Dhaka, or Banaras, on the other hand, it is also generating unprecedented and *ad hoc* examples of Navarātrī festival, according to the external environmental influences that change in every place of the world.

If recreating a cultural and religious event abroad is tough work for the Hindu Bengali community in Rome, dealing with the Covid-19 pandemic created a series of incommensurable challenges. The prohibition of gatherings, limited access to any religious spaces, social distancing, and mandatory obligation of wearing masks transformed a public ceremony into a cause of anxiety and fear of both contagion and normative infractions. During Durgā Pūjā 2020, celebrating and entering a temple through a display brought Bengali people from different places in Italy together, making them perform the same unusual rite and celebrating the festival values of "transformation", "blessing", "loss", "hosting", and "gratitude" through an intangible space. Technologies have indeed created new methods to live religious experiences thus religion itself permeated these new virtual spaces. Faith has become the impulse for worshippers to create online communities and blogs and to reiterate traditional values through new platforms in order to reach everyone, everywhere.

Nevertheless, even if technology is gradually allowing people to live religious experiences online, especially during the Covid-19 pandemic, many worshippers still find it difficult to celebrate rituals online instead of attending them physically. Durgā Pūjā, especially for diasporic communities, has always been a unique occasion to create friendships and live a cathartic experience that could make them feel closer to their home country. Resilience was the force that motivated the young Hindu Bengali community in Rome to lead its cultural events as an expression of collective and individual religious enthusiasm, and technology was the instrument to connect them with other worshippers in Rome and with their families thousands of kilometers away.

Author Biographies

Valeria Giampietri is a PhD candidate in Civilizations of Asia and Africa at Sapienza University of Rome, with a focus on language, literature and cultures of the Indian subcontinent. She has published essays and scientific articles in journals and collective volumes, reviews, and she has participated in conferences. Her research interests are ritual practices, gender, migration, and transcultural studies.

Randa Khalil is a PhD candidate in History and Cultures of Europe at Sapienza University of Rome. She is conducting a research project that investigates contemporary Indian feminist theatre between India and Europe. Her research interests focus on theatre, gender, religions, and migrations.

Ludovica Tozzi is a PhD candidate in Civilizations of Asia and Africa at Sapienza University of Rome. Her academic career is focused on Hindi and Bengali languages and literatures, societies, and cultures of the Indian Subcontinent. Her research interests are centred on literature, gender studies and narratives, history of religions, and performance studies.

References

Al-Ali, N. (2010), *Diaspora and Gender*, in K. Knott, S. McLoughlin (eds.), *Diasporas: Concepts, Intersections, Identities*, Zed Books Ltd, London, pp. 118–122.

Anderson, B. (1991), *Imagined Communities: Reflections on the Origin and Spread of Nationalism*, Verso, New York.

Appadurai, A. (1996), *Modernity at Large: Cultural Dimensions of Globalization*, University of Minnesota Press, London.

Becci, I., Burchardt, M., Giorda, M. (2017), *Religious Super-diversity and Spatial Strategies in Two European Cities*, in "Current Sociology", 65, 1, pp. 73–91. https://doi.org/10.1177/0011392116632030

Broccolini, A. (2017), *Patrimonio e mutamento a Torpignattara/Banglatown*, in A. Broccolini, V. Padiglione (ed.), *Ripensare i margini. L'Ecomuseo Casilino per la periferia di Roma*, Aracne, Roma, pp. 148–163.

Campbell, H. A. (ed.) (2012), *Digital Religion: Understanding Religious Practice in New Media Worlds*, Routledge, London.

Chatterjee, M. (2020), *The Oral Tradition of Agomoni Songs as Intangible Heritage: ReReading the Marital Migration of the Bengali Bridal Diaspora*, in "postScriptum: An Interdisciplinary Journal of Literary Studies", 5, 2, pp. 202–214.

Consiglio dei ministri della Repubblica Italiana. (2020), *Decreto del presidente del Consiglio dei ministri 13 ottobre 2020*, in "Gazzetta ufficiale della Repubblica italiana" (https://www.gazzettaufficiale.it/eli/gu/2020/10/13/253/sg/pdf; consultato il 5 agosto 2022).

Cusack, C. M. (2017), *The Return of the Goddess: Mythology, Witchcraft and Feminist Spirituality*, in "Handbook of Contemporary Paganism", pp. 335–362.

Doniger, W. (2010), *The Hindus: An Alternative History*, Penguin, New York.

Ficacci, S. (2007), *Tor Pignattara: Fascismo e Resistenza di un quartiere romano*, Milano: FrancoAngeli.

Flood, G. (1996), *An Introduction to Hinduism*, Cambridge University Press, Cambridge.

Giampietri, V., Khalil, R., Tozzi, L. (ed. C. Russo) (2023), *Una festa hindu in un quartiere di Roma. La Durgā Pūjā a Tor Pignattara durante il covid-19*, Carocci, Rome.

Glick Schiller, N., Çağlar, A., Guldbrandsen, T. C. (2006), *Beyond the Ethnic Lens: Locality, Globality, and Born-again Incorporation*, in "American Ethnologist", 33, 4, pp. 612–633. https://doi.org/10.1525/ae.2006.33.4.612

Helland, C. (2007), *Diaspora on the Electronic Frontier: Developing Virtual Connections with Sacred Homelands*, in "Journal of Computer-Mediated Communication", 12, 3, pp. 956–976. https://doi.org/10.1111/j.1083-6101.2007.00358.x

Helland, C. (2012), *Ritual*, in H. A. Campbell (ed.), *Digital Religion: Understanding Religious Practice in New Media Worlds*, Routledge, London, pp. 25–40.

Istat – Istituto Nazionale di Statistica (2021), *Census of Population and Housing Years 2019–2020. Demographic Characteristics and Citizenship: Geographical Area and Countries of Citizenship Municipalities*, in "Censimenti Permanenti: Data Warehouse", available at: http://dati-censimentipermanenti.istat.it/?lang=it&SubSessionId=418fd3f0-db3c-42fc-bded-7d78334adc0f (last accessed 7 January 2022).

Matteucci, I. (2020), *Le comunità di migranti online e le reti comunicative digitali transnazionali*, in "Agathos: An International Review of the Humanities & Social Sciences", 11, 1, 20, pp. 57–72.

McDermott, F. R. (2011), *Revelry, Rivalry, and Longing for the Goddess of Bengal: The Fortunes of Hindu Festivals*, Columbia University Press, New York.

Priori, A. (2014), *Il genius loci migratorio di Torpignattara*, in C. Cellamare (ed.), *Roma città autoprodotta. Ricerca urbana e linguaggi artistici*, ManifestoLibri, Roma, pp. 63–73.

Ray, M. (2017), *Review Article: Goddess in the City: Durgā Pūjās of Contemporary Kolkata*, in "Modern Asian Studies", pp. 1–39.

Rodrigues, P. H. (2003), *Ritual Worship of the Great Goddess: The Liturgy of the Durgā Pūjā with Interpretations*, in K. K. Young (ed.), *McGill Studies in the History of Religions, A Series Devoted to International Scholarship*, State University of New York Press, Albany.

Roma Capitale (2021), *Popolazione iscritta in anagrafe – Stranieri al 31 dicembre 2020 per municipio, genere e cittadinanza*, Tab. 12, available at: https://www.comune.roma.it/web/it/roma-statistica-popolazione1.page (last accessed 7 January 2022).

Russo, C. (2017), *Patrimonializzare il sacro. Tor Pignattara e i luoghi di culto dell'altro*, in A. Broccolini, V. Padiglione (ed.), *Ripensare i margini. L'Ecomuseo Casilino per la periferia di Roma*, Aracne, Roma, pp. 148–163.

Russo, C., Tamburrino, F. (2015), *Luoghi comuni, luoghi in comune. Percorsi di dialogo e conoscenza a partire dai luoghi di culto della provincia di Roma*, Centro Astalli, Roma.

Sarkar, B. (2012), *The Rite of Durgā in Medieval Bengal: An Introductory Study of Raghunandana's Durgāpūjātattva with Text and Translation of the Principal Rites*, in "Journal of the Royal Asiatic Society", 22, 2, pp. 325–390. https://doi.org/10.1017/S1356186312000181

Scheifinger, H. (2012), *Hindu Worship Online and Offline*, in H. A. Campbell (ed.), *Digital Religion: Understanding Religious Practice in New Media Worlds*, Routledge, London, pp. 121–127.

Scialdone, M. (2018), *Buddisti e induisti nelle migrazioni. Rapporti centro-periferia tra orientalismi e reti istituzionali*, in A. Saggioro, C. Russo (eds.), *Roma città plurale. Le religioni, il territorio, le ricerche*, Bulzoni, Roma, pp. 239–253.

Stefon, M. (2021), *Dharmaśāstra*, in "Encyclopedia Britannica online", available at: https://www.britannica.com/topic/dharma-religious-concept (last accessed 16 October 2021).

UII. (2021), Unione Induista Italiana Sanātana Dharma Saṃgha, *Chi siamo – Online blog*, available at: https://www.induismo.it/en/unione-induista/ (last accessed 28 December 2021).

Vásquez, A. N. (2010), *Diasporas and Religion*, in K. Knott, S. McLoughlin (eds.), *Diasporas: Concepts, Intersections, Identities*, Zed Books Ltd, London, pp. 128–133.

Vertovec, S. (2007), *Super-diversity and its Implications*, in "Ethnic and Racial Studies", 30, 6, pp. 1024–1054. https://doi.org/10.1080/01419870701599465

Webography

Bengali Association of Gothenburg. (2019), *Bengali Association of Gothenburg*, in "Facebook", https://www.facebook.com/BengaliAssociationofGothenburg/

Dev, A. (2021), Keeping Faith, in "The British Bengalis", https://www.thebritishbengalis.co.uk/theblog/special-reports/durga-puja-2020-kit/keeping-faith

Hindu Forum Sweden. (n.d.), *Hindu Forum Sweden Organisation*, in "Facebook", https://www.facebook.com/hinduforumsweden

Hoichoi Bengali Community of the Netherlands. (2017), in "Hoichoi Website", https://www.hoichoi.nl/

Indischer Kulturverein Bharat Samiti e.V. (2020), *_indischerkulturverein*, in "Instagram", https://www.instagram.com/_indischerkulturverein/

Unione Induista Italiana. (2021), *Unione Induista Italiana Sanatana Dharma Samgha*, https://www.induismo.it/

The Hong Kong Bengali Association. (1998), হংকং বেঙ্গলি অ্যাসোসিয়েশন, https://hkbaonline.com/hkba/about_hkba

Interviews

Kumar, Anup. Interviewed by Ludovica Tozzi and Randa Khalil, Rome, Italy, 21 October 2020.

Nath, Binita. Zoom interview by Ludovica Tozzi, Rome, Italy, 27 December 2020.

Chapter 9
Religious "Superconflict": Durgā Pūjā and a Muslim Funeral in a Plural District of Rome, Italy

Carmelo Russo

Abstract

This contribution investigates ambiguity and conflicts that latently lurk among relational and political practices with which several people and groups operate and interact in Tor Pignattara, a semi-peripheral super-diverse district of Rome, Italy. Two events, the Hindu festival of Durga Puja (4–8 October 2019) and a Muslim funeral (30 October 2017), are considered as lenses to investigate responsibilities, competition, rivalry, and incomprehension that gave rise to an "impossible mediation" perception, caused by district "incompatible attitudes". The aim is to emphasize, through two concrete cases, that questions focused on foreign religious minorities involve complex ethical and ideological standings, which imply conflict, opposition, and manipulation caused by different visions – banal cosmopolitanism and banal nationalism – Italian residents, political factions, and institutions have about migration, coexistence, and social inclusion.

Keywords: religious conflict, Muslim Funeral, Durgā Pūjā, banal cosmopolitanism, banal nationalism

1 Introduction: Tor Pignattara as a Super-diverse Place

This contribution[1] investigates ambiguity and conflicts that latently lurk among relational and political practices with which several people and groups operate and interact in Tor Pignattara, a semi-peripheral district of Rome, Italy. These attitudes contrast the process to take advantage of the value of the cultural heritage inherent in intangible religious elements, such as festivals, ceremonies, and rituals, which could constitute a "bridge" between Italian citizens and those who have migrant origins[2]. Foreign people generate a variety of rites, religious practices, and actions that enrich the intangible religious landscape of Tor Pignattara. Nevertheless, some friction among different parts of the inhabitants slowed the peaceful coexistence in the district. This issue is most striking in rapidly globalizing European cities where the interweaving of ethnic and racial differences has become increasingly complex under the impact of global migration[3].

Rome's territory is divided into fifteen municipalities. Tor Pignattara is part of the 5th Municipality and coincides to a good degree with the urban area 6A. Official statistics inherent in Roma Capitale, updated on 31 December 2020, indicate that the 5th Municipality presents an immigrant resident percentage of 17.3%. In absolute figures, out of fifteen in total, the Municipality ranks second for foreign presence, with 42,184 units, after the 6th Municipality with 44,623. The 5th Municipality is divided into twelve urban areas of which 6A-Tor Pignattara contains the greatest number of non-Italians, registered at 10,730 as of 31 December 2020. Almost one-third (32.6%) of 5th Municipality migrants reside there, thus the foreign incidence rises to 22.5%. Among the 155 Roma Capitale urban areas, 6A-Tor Pignattara is the fourth area for the concentration of migrant

1. This research is part of the project "*RELCAPETOWN – Religious Super-Diversity in Cape Town. Dynamics of Leadership and Territorialization Through Religious Spaces in the Migration Process*", which has received funding from the European Union's Horizon 2020 research and innovation programme under the Marie Sklodowska-Curie grant agreement No. 886578. It is hosted by Sapienza University of Rome and managed by the author of this article.
2. Arizpe, Amescua 2013. Particularly relevant are Chapters 5 and 9, respectively written by Jesús Antonio Machuca (2013) and Cristina Amescua (2013). See also, among others, Charrad, Adamas 2011.
3. Eade 2012; Ukah 2012.

residents, after 8F-Torre Angela, 8G-Borghesiana, and 1E-Esquilino[4]. Tor Pignattara is also characterized by extreme national variability: people from 131 nations reside there. Among them, Bangladeshi people are the majority, consisting of 3,273, corresponding to 30.5% of all foreigners in the district, and 33.9% of Bangladeshi people in the 5th Municipality (9,645). It is useful to underline that this citizenship is the third national migrant community in Rome (32,810), while only the eighth in Italy[5].

This statistical data defines Tor Pignattara as a super-diverse area[6]. As Vertovec noted, the "new immigration" has brought with it emergent forms of prejudice, inequalities, segregation, and racism[7]. In Tor Pignattara, conflicts sometimes emerge with uproar and exposure. This essay is focused on two events: the Hindu festival of Durgā Pūjā (4–8 October 2019) and a Muslim funeral (30 October 2017). I have considered them as lenses to investigate the responsibilities, competition, rivalry, and incomprehension that gave rise to an "impossible mediation" perception, caused by district "incompatible attitudes". The aim is to emphasize, through two concrete cases, that questions focused on foreign religious minorities involve complex ethical and ideological standings, which imply conflict, opposition, and for some Italian residents, political factions and institutions' manipulation.

In particular, the 2019 Durgā Pūjā and the 2017 Islamic funeral, as will be seen, shed light on the Municipal Council and right-wing political movements' responsibilities. The first is chaired by Giovanni Boccuzzi and affiliated with the Movimento 5 Stelle (Five Star Movement). In June 2016 the Movement won the municipal elections for the mayor of Rome and attained thirteen of the fifteen municipalities. In the 5th one, Giovanni Boccuzzi replaced Gianmarco Palmieri, a staunch Democratic Party leader, as president. The Movimento 5 Stelle was founded by the Italian comedian Beppe Grillo in 2009 in order to offer an alternative to the voters against the two-party system and the "political caste". Its rapid success depended in large part on the profound distrust many Romans (and Italians in general) had towards their local institutions. The main

---

4. Roma Capitale 2021.
5. Ibid.
6. Vertovec 2007, 2019; Vertovec, Meissner 2015.
7. Vertovec 2007, p. 1045.

Movement's revolutionary practice – emphasized by rhetorical claims – lies in the web-based participatory democracy, in the struggle against the "corrupted establishment", and in the notion of citizenship that motivates the supporters and activists who seek to reconnect Italians with their public institutions[8]. On the other side, relevant agents of the questions, as shown below, are right-wing parties' politicians and sympathizers and conservative people.

The theoretical framework that enabled us to analyse this process is, on one hand, the category of super-diversity[9], especially its religious acceptation[10]. On the other hand, it is inscribed into socio-political and identitarian dynamics which have trivialized and simplified variation[11] of cosmopolitanism[12] and nationalism[13].

As concerns methodology and sources, this essay is based on reflections and analyses following the two events already mentioned. The ethnographic familiarity with the context of Tor Pignattara[14] favoured the access to information and the realization of interviews carried out after the two events with participants of different backgrounds. Together with these interviews, informal dialogues with some interlocutors[15], direct observation, and some articles found on the web, represent the sources I have drawn on. Some contributions from the local online newspaper

8. Bock 2021.
9. Vertovec 2007, 2019; Vertovec, Meissner 2015.
10. Becci, Burchardt 2016; Becci et al. 2017.
11. Squarcini 2019; Vereni 2017, pp. 139–141.
12. Beck 2002, 2011.
13. Billig 1995. Vereni (2017) notes that Ulrich Beck coined the category of "banal nationalism" by having as a reference that of "banal nationalism" proposed by Michael Billig.
14. I started attending Tor Pignattara for research in 2014 when I carried out preliminary fieldwork together with Francesco Tamburrino for Centro Astalli (Russo, Tamburrino 2015). Since the following year, I collaborated with the Ecomuseo Casilino ad Duas Lauros – a territorial museum organisation, managed by an association of the same name, recognised by the Italian State – focusing on the theme of the sacred and also-concerning migration.
15. In order to protect the identities of the interviewees and interlocutors and also considering the sensitivity of the topics dealt with, I have chosen to limit myself to quoting their words, avoiding indicating generalities and information that could allow their recognition. I translated their speeches from Italian to English and did the same for newspaper articles and other written sources.

"RomaToday" – those of G. N. (2 November 2017)[16], Ginevra Nozzoli (1 September 2017), and Ylenia Sina (7 and 10 October 2019) – constitute the starting point with which I developed sections 2 and 3, in which the chronicle is intertwined with oral sources and initial reflections. These articles provide feedback about the Hindu festival and the Islamic funeral in different characters and have been taken up by other online magazines and social networks. In the concluding section, I provide some anthropological interpretations concerning the social and political dynamics of Tor Pignattara, considering as a reference the conflictual relations that emerged from Durgā Pūjā and the funeral.

2 Durgā Pūjā and the Municipal Council

One of the most important religious ceremonies for Hinduists of Bengal[17] is Durgā Puja[18]. The festival falls on the month of Āśvin on the Hindu calendar, which is between September and October. It consists of some commemorative and festive days, generally ten[19], remembering the victory of the Goddess Durgā against the demon Mahiṣa, who took the form of a buffalo. Durgā went back into the material world, grabbed Shiva's trident, stepped on him, and pierced him. The feast involves a peculiar gender issue: the "buffalo demon" defeated male gods, who invoked Durgā to

---

16. The initials with which the article is signed, and the subject matter would suggest that the author may also be Ginevra Nozzoli. However, I will stick to the official form of the source and report the contribution as G. N. 2017.
17. I consider "Bengal" as the geopolitical, cultural, and historical region facing the Bay of Bengal and the neighbouring regions such as West Bengal, Bihar, Orissa, Assam, and Tripura, as established before 1971, the date of the Liberation War that gave birth to Bangladesh, and before 1947, the year of the Indian Partition. We accept – with all the problems suggested by the anthropological perspective – Clark's consideration that this area is culturally connected and summarily homogeneous (Clark 1955, p. 37). The term "Bengali" refers to people from the area of Bengal thus defined, i.e., from both Bangladesh and the northeastern Indian States, predominantly of the Hindu religion.
18. I will limit myself here to a few indispensable notions to frame the festival, referring to Chapter 8 of this volume for a more in-depth analysis.
19. In 2019, Hindu temples of Tor Pignattara announced only five days.

aid them. To achieve this goal, everyone provided her with their "magical weapons". This event portrays the victory of good over evil[20].

The common reference for Bangladeshi Hinduists in Tor Pignattara – and other diasporic communities – is the feast in the metropole of Calcutta (Kolkata). Brahmins and worshippers venerate Durgā through rituals, which imply the edification of *paṇḍāls*, garnished and elaborate structures, even if they are temporary. At the end of the celebration, people should destroy them, while Roman Hinduists often recycle them secretly for the next year. Every *paṇḍāl* includes *mūrti*, a large sculpture of the Goddess Durga, or her paintings, both adorned with lights, flowers, and jewellery. Worshippers in Tor Pignattara told me that the Brahmin must monitor the *paṇḍāl* day and night because it cannot be left unattended.

The aesthetics in Durgā Pūjā celebration is central. It goes beyond the religious meaning and encompasses artistic and commercial ones, as a mass phenomenon. The festival provides the opportunity to exchange gifts, visit the most eye-catching *paṇḍāls*, and boast "traditional" dress[21]. Photographs, journalists, and broadcasters visit the aristocratic families' houses in Calcutta, intending to draw their expensive and majestic *paṇḍāls*, "wonderful and complex architectural works, with lightning and optical effects. The most famous Indian Artists projected them. They started from six to twelve months before the event"[22].

The Hindu community of Tor Pignattara experience the feast in a "suspended time" between "here" and the "original reference" to the Bengal[23], brokered by direct contact with relatives and friends, who send them photos and images via social networks. Furthermore, they shall inform through online newspapers and blogs, which provide them with new transformative issues and changes. In 2018, prostitutes managed their *paṇḍāl* in Sonagachi, a red-light district in Calcutta, where the transgender community also promoted activities[24].

Like the Islamic community of Tor Pignattara, the Hindu one is mainly composed of Bangladeshi citizens. It is not an accident, but a consequence of their peculiar concentration, as mentioned above. On the contrary,

20. Berkson 1995; Flood 1996; Giampietri et al. 2023; Simoncelli 2018.
21. Bandyopadyay 1987; Banerjee 2004; Banerji 2019; Bhattacharya 2007.
22. Simoncelli 2018.
23. Appadurai 2010.
24. Simoncelli 2018.

Indian people are a few minorities, to whom some Italian worshippers add. The Hindu community is pervaded by divisions, materialized by two different "temples" both hosted in two rooms on the ground floor: they are the Om Hindu Mandir in via Amedeo Cencelli 23A and the Puja Udjapon Parisad, which in 2019 changed its location from via Casilina 597 to a larger place in via Guido Cora 21. The first one only adheres to the Unione Induista Italiana (Italian Hinduist Union), thus it can benefit from the agreement, named *Intesa*, ratified with the Italian State[25].

Both temples are managed by Bangladeshi administrations. Every year, they organize two distinct ceremonies for Durgā Puja. In 2019, the Om Hindu Mandir community organized the festival at the Casa del Popolo (House of People) in Via Benedetto Bordoni 50[26], while the Puja Udjapon Parisad administration asked the Municipality to host their feast in a large hall on the ground floor in Via di Acqua Bullicante. Until about ten years ago, it was a councillor chamber used by Municipal Council meetings. During the last few years, it has been available for associations located in the district.

Puja Udjapon Parisad people presented the event with emphasis. The president and two secretaries wrote a message on social networks (in English and Italian), with which they encouraged all residents of Tor Pignattara and of other areas of the city to participate: "Ladies/Gentleman, we have the honour to cordially invite you and your family to our great festival 'Durgā Puja' which will be held on the 4, 5, 6, 7, and 8 October 2019. Your presence in our 'Puja Mondop' will give us great pleasure".

On 7 October, the day before the last and most important one for the ceremony, in which Durgā's victory against Mahiṣa is celebrated, Ylenia Sina wrote an article on "RomaToday online". The title dealt with municipal institutions' responsibilities: *Tor Pignattara, le foto di una consigliera*

---

25. The Constitution of the Italian Republic, adopted in 1948, declares that the Italian State has formally been secular, and it guarantees religious freedom beyond Christianity. Since 2012, the Italian Hinduist Union has obtained recognition from the Italian State through the *Intesa*, which is an agreement guaranteed by article n. 8 of the Italian Constitution. The leadership of the religious denomination that asks for it and the Italian government must sign the *Intesa* to start the legislative process which culminates with its implementation.
26. It was the Italian Communist Party headquarter in Tor Pignattara. In the last decades, Rifondazione Comunista (Communist Refoundation) managed the place, which has hosted cultural activities such as book launches and debates.

fanno chiudere la sala municipale: interrotti i festeggiamenti induisti (*Tor Pignattara, the photos took by a council member provide the closure of the council chamber: Hindu festival interrupted*):

> After days of celebrations, the Hindu community of Tor Pignattara cannot conclude the Durga Puja celebration in the former councillor chamber in Via di Acqua Bullicante. This morning the local police force got all the worshippers off, previously gathered inside. According to what RomaToday found out, the 5th Municipality urged the police intervention for a suspicious illegal occupation. The advisory has proved unfounded. The Hindu community obtained legal authorization from the competent municipal office and showed the necessary documents to the policemen[27].

Nevertheless, the municipal authority decided to close the hall, thus Hinduists moved to the temple in Via Cora. Some of them told me about their disapproval of the lack of deference for the *paṇḍāl*, especially for the *mūrti*. It was disassembled and quickly reassembled, with scant regard for its sacrality. Regarding this incident, Ylenia Sina interviewed the vice president of the 5th Municipality, Mario Podeschi. He stated as follows:

> The worship had nothing to do with it. Yesterday evening [6 October 2019], the Five Star Movement council member Roberta Francescone took pictures that witnessed some illegal activities committed by worshippers inside the hall on the ground floor. There was a gas cylinder, and some people were handing out food and beverage. They put a sign outside and a tray for free offers on the table. Because the hall is a public place, it is forbidden to ask for money and to hand out food […]. At the end of September, the Municipal Council approved a directive for hall regulations. The draft has already been ready. It will be approved by the [Municipal Council] competent committee and, after that, by the entire Council. I hope it will be ready within a month[28].

Thus, on 7 October, in the morning, law enforcement exhorted people who were in the hall for Durgā Pūjā festival to leave the place, as they rapidly did, without resistance.

27. Sina 2019a.
28. Ibid.

A delegation of Italian citizens went to the Municipal Council to ask for the reason for the hall closure and because the police did not spot infractions. In the meantime, on Facebook, many Tor Pignattara residents were showing their consternation against the Municipality for the prohibition of the use of the hall. They considered the Durgā Pūjā festival as a "community-building event". In their opinion, the former councillor chamber is "a symbolic place from which citizenship can benefit". Many of them disapproved of the municipal operation, which was perceived as dangerous for the relations among different national and religious communities in the district. The debate evolved online and offline, involving social networks and small groupings in the streets. Those who took sides against the municipal decision underlined the "unfair" conduct of the council member Francescone, who was accused of taking advantage of Hindu hospitality. Many people stressed that she entered the hall to participate in the festival, but "betrayed" the worshippers' trust by taking photographs that she took dishonestly: "The gas cylinder doesn't appear in the photos and even if Hindu people want to cook, it is not a problem". Inside the Hindu temples, as it is known, offering food – *prasāda* – complies with the ritual issue, as believers and visitors often give money to the temple (it is, as largely known, not only a Hindu trait but a very common question for many religions).

The issue of food surprised not only the municipal authorities but also "ordinary citizens". On 7 October, in the evening, I went to the Via Cora temple, where the ceremony was continuing, with some Tor Pignattara Italian residents, who "took to heart" the Hindu festival. Their intention was "to bring solidarity to the Indians". Probably they were not familiar with the iconographic, chromatic, bright richness of the Hindu symbolic apparatus. Above all, they were amazed at the food offered. While we sat on the floor and observed preparations – the feast was in an hour – a Bangladeshi boy came over to give us some fruits. Some of us took it and thanked him, but others were embarrassed and could not hide their feelings. They cordially refused, revealing suspicion. Nevertheless, all the comments were favourable: "They receive us by giving us fruit... the Hindu are so good!", "How can anybody want to hurt people so peaceful?", "We Italians treated them badly, and they respond to us with smiles on their faces!" I noticed that the endeavour to have a conversation focused on the incident of the morning with Hindu people collided with their disinterest: they avoided speaking about that theme and detracted from the problem.

After the article was published, council member Roberta Francescone asked for her right of reply and wrote a brief addition at the end of Ylenia Sina's paper, in a subsequent update:

> On October 7, RomaToday spread the news focused on the temporary former councillor chamber closure. The article was signed by Ylenia Sina and was titled *Tor Pignattara, le foto di una consigliera fanno chiudere la sala municipale: interrotti i festeggiamenti induisti* [*Tor Pignattara, the photos took by a council member provide the council chamber closure: Hindu festival interrupted*]. It is an oversimplification of the event. Starting with the article title, it seems that my photos provoked the hall closure. Instead, the reason is mainly the non-compliance with the safety rules. In the same article, the author reported the 5th Municipality vice-president claim, Mario Podeschi, and I fully agree with him.
>
> The irregularities I noted concern the delivery of food and beverage in a municipal and public building, the demand for money, in addition to the probable violation of the safety rules, such as the hall overcrowding, beyond its official capacity. In addition, it should be noted that the former councillor chamber borders the hospital "M. G. Vannini", and that it is located beside inhabited buildings. Furthermore, a banner outside the hall could be a violation of its intended use. The local police force removed it immediately. The hall closing was independent of my photographs, but it concerned the irregularities that have been committed. My work as a municipal councillor is legally recognized as a "public official" for the monitoring task of what happens in the municipal territory. It is good to remember that the Municipality intends to regulate the former municipal hall use (see Municipal guideline n. 24, 30 September, 2019).

The event mentioned above does not concern religious freedom, which is guaranteed by the Italian Constitution, even so it must be integrated with elementary safety rules in favour of all citizens, without distinction of race or religion. Grassroots citizens' initiatives are welcome, but in a safety and legal framework[29].

29. Ibid.

The municipal councillor was trying to avoid the charge of non-respect of religious freedom and that of menace against dialogue processes taking place in the district. She quoted legality as an instrument, even forcing the hand of "the demand of money" – anything but mandatory, such as the proximity of the hospital, and the banner outside the hall. Above all, the answer attempted to overturn the question: a meticulous "public official" should carry out her role "of municipal territory monitoring", according to a well-known rhetoric remarked by politicians, often related to peripheries.

Both Mario Podeschi and Roberta Francescone recalled the hall rules as a key for their "defence". The vice president stated: "I hope it will be ready within a month". The hall would remain closed, waiting for approval. Ylenia Sina continued to follow the incident. After only three days, on October 10, she wrote a new article: *Tor Pignattara, ex sala consiliare chiusa fino a regolamento. Boccuzzi ci ripensa*[30] [*Tor Pignattara, former councillor chamber closed until a new regulation will be approved. Boccuzzi changed his mind*]:

> The hall remains closed until a new regulation will be approved. The Municipal Council cancelled the decision not to grant citizenship, after 48 hours of its approval. "It takes more time in order to approve the regulation, in the meantime I believe citizens can use it", the 5th Municipality president Giovanni Boccuzzi explained. "The event that provoked the closure [the Durgā Puja] has not damaged the hall, thus we decided to revoke our decision. Also, we will ask citizens to better specify the use they might make for the place"[31].

Ylenia Sina noted the inconsistent behaviour of the Municipal Council. On 7 October, vice president Mario Podeschi stated that he signed a directive which suspended the hall usage until a new regulation will be approved[32], but on 9 October president Giovanni Boccuzzi immediately cancelled the directive and expressed in an unequivocal way: "Since today, the presidency will manage the hall, that is available for every citizen who will ask for it".

30. Sina 2019b.
31. Ibid.
32. Ibid.

In the meantime, people in the district were arguing towards the management of interreligious issues. A large debate involved Ecomuseo Casilino ad Duas Lauros and other associations to promote an interreligious roundtable inviting Tor Pignattara religious leaders. Twelve residents tended to concretize their displeasure against institutions' decisions and their support to confessional communities through an open letter. On 24 October they brought it to the two Hindu temples, the San Barnaba, Saints Marcellino and Pietro, and Santa Giulia Billiart parishes, to the three Muslim prayer halls Masjeed e Quba (Via della Marranella), Tor Pignattara Muslim Center (Via Carlo della Rocca), and another in via Alò Giovannoli. The letter text was also published on the Facebook page of the Centro Sviluppo Locale in Ambiti Metropolitani (Centre for the Local Development in Metropolitan Field).

> We are worried citizens of Tor Pignattara who found out from the press that the local police force unpleasantly interrupted the Durgā Pūjā ceremony in the former councillor's chamber. First, we want to inform you we strongly disapprove of that intervention. We consider it detrimental to the constitutional right of religious freedom. We turn to the Hindu believers and to the main religious communities of the area to express our solidarity. We are convinced that all of us are interested in the peaceful coexistence affirmation, mutual respect, knowledge, and dialogue among religions, cults, and worshippers.
>
> We believe that building shared citizenship is an antidote against violence, hatred, fear, clash, and fanatism. Consequently, we invite you to consider the opportunity to friendly meet each other, in order to promote shared initiatives for cooperation and dialogue. It will be advantageous that the Catholic community should host other religious groups for their ceremonies and festivals so that each religion can completely experience its faith.
>
> We consider this action as necessary and important, as an incitement for our territory citizens – believers, non-believers, and "differently believers" – associationism, and institutions to encourage a peaceful civil coexistence climate (twelve signatures).

3 A Muslim Funeral between Rights and Identitarian Emphasis

On 30 October 2017, a Muslim funeral took place in an apartment building courtyard in Tor Pignattara, bordering via Alò Giovannoli. The funeral generated a huge stir between "opposed factions" of citizens. RomaToday described the event on 2 November, as follows:

> The coexistence between the local Islamic community and the apartment building residents in Via Alò Giovannoli, a street of the multi-ethnic Tor Pignattara, is even more difficult. One month ago, local police sequestered a garage, used as a mosque. But worshippers moved to the adjacent one. On 30 October, they celebrated a funeral on the street, with the coffin on the sidewalk. Over a hundred silent Muslims, in neat rows, took part in the ritual. At the same time, astonished Italian residents looked out the window. They took pictures and videos of the scene. It was a moment: from the smartphones to the social network, to the indignant comments[33].

These lines seem to invoke the difficulty of an "impossible mediation" in the light of the well-known Samuel Huntington's "clash of civilizations"[34]. The American political analyst's theorization has benefited from a huge diffusion because of the extremely simplified representation of geopolitical relations. Similarly, the article's author wrote about the "local Islamic community", a vague misconception: although the four Islamic halls of prayer (five, adding the "mosque" in Via Alò Giovannoli, used occasionally) are all managed by Bangladeshi administrations, the statement reveals a lack of knowledge about fragmentation, rivalry, divisions that afflict Bangladeshi collective[35]. These dynamics also echo the relationships among the religious places' administrations[36]. On the other hand, Islam is not officially recognized as a religion by the Italian State, because no association has yet signed the *Intesa*.

The author wrote that "the coffin [was] on the sidewalk" and that "over a hundred silent Muslims, in neat rows, took part in the ritual": both

33. G. N. 2017.
34. Huntington 1996.
35. Priori 2014, 2017.
36. Russo 2017, p. 153; Russo 2018, pp. 333–345.

statements are not true. Firstly, the funeral took place in a confined space because the courtyard is located above the apartment building garages, some of which are designed as "mosques". Clarifications and explanations are needed regarding the connection between the building site confiscation and the Muslim presence in the location.

In 2003, the company BTS was granted the concession of the area between Via Alò Giovannoli and Via Cartaro. BTS erected several apartment buildings, with attached private garages. BTS did not fulfil compensation works, contrary to the agreement: the reclamation of an adjacent plot of land and the construction of a street to connect the building with Via della Marranella. "Meanwhile the residents wait for their rights, they don't tolerate third parties who use the building site for events, particularly religious ones. The October 30-funeral followed a series of rituals and prayers, which caused protests. The right-wing political forces ask for the requisition for a long time"[37].

In an article on 1 September 2017, Ginevra Nozzoli reaffirmed:

> For many years, the building site was dominated by neglect, waste, and abandonment. In the middle, a long series of vain events: the Municipal Council sent documents to the competent City Municipality office; Citizens reported the abuses to the police office; the Urbanistic Department provided an extension to BTS to complete the work, that expired in June 2013; and a dozen of garages designed as Islamic places [...]. The owner granted the use of some garages as cultural centres, mosques actually. In 2014, a judge provided for a confiscation order, later cancelled. A few months ago, work began on constructing a new mosque into six adjacent garages, where pillars and walls were slaughtered[38].

The rhetorical use of the terminology aspires to underscore the symbolic distinction between "our" – white civilized Italians – and "they" – uncivilized foreign bringers of disvalues[39] – : "a dozen of garages designed as Islamic places", "The owner granted the use of some garages", "a confiscation order", "where pillars and walls were slaughtered". On the contrary, the owner is a Bangladeshi Muslim group who regularly acquired

---

37. G. N. 2017.
38. Nozzoli 2017.
39. Dal Lago 2010, p. 11; Pitch 2016, p. 149.

the garages. They are the main victims of the abuses, requisitions, and disregard of the agreement of BTS.

The article is corroborated by some witnesses of "ordinary citizens". Antonella S. shares the images on the Facebook group Cittadini di Tor Pignattara [Citizens of Tor Pignattara] and writes that she "can never get over to these everyday scenes". Sandra N. uncertainly answers, "so they put a coffin with the body on the sidewalk?"[40]

The author rested on the opinion of the Chief of local police, Mario De Sclavis, who claimed that on 30 October police vehicles were there only for traffic management. The Chief would stress the Constitutional fundamentals concerning religious freedom. He assured people that Muslims would not need authorization, because the funeral did not concern public property. Article n. 8 of the Italian Constitution states the religious freedom for every believer. Article n. 19 claims the right to profess one's faith individually or collectively, to propagandize privately or publicly, providing the rituals are not in contrast with the principles of morality.

RomaToday continued the funeral description following two right-wing politicians' comments. The councillor of the 5th Municipality Fabio Sabbatani Schiuma[41] said:

> It is not the first time that they [the funerals] are celebrated on the street, in the squares or in an apartment building courtyard. At the beginning of the year [2017], some others were celebrated, with little funeral processions starting from the dwelling [of the dead] or from some cultural centres designed as mosques. We tried to understand if they asked for authorization, paid the stamp duties, and provided for all procedures, but it was useless[42].

The Municipal councillor Maurizio Politi, who was part of Fratelli d'Italia (Brothers of Italy) before he got into Lega stated:

---

40. Nozzoli 2017.
41. Fabio Sabbatani Schiuma was a candidate for the president of the 5th Municipal Council for the right-wing party Fratelli d'Italia (Brothers of Italy) and was the national leader of Riva Destra (Right Shore). From December 2014 to 2018, he became a member of Noi con Salvini (a movement at the side of the secretary of the Lega, Matteo Salvini). In 2018, Sabbatani Schiuma came back to Fratelli d'Italia.
42. G. N. 2017.

> The lack of attention from the Municipal Council and the willpower of the Bangladeshi community to continue acting off the books, into a part of the building site, which should not be accessible. They have caused tensions among residents [...]. My colleague Francesco Figliomeni and I verified the building company lacks common sense. We will continue to undertake every task to confiscate the entire building site. We must send out a vivid message on legality. We're breathing down on mayor Raggi's neck. It's time to stop![43]

We could note that, as it is drawn by RomaToday, the Muslim funeral was completely detached from its tragic and sacred meaning. It quoted two well-known exponents of early 20th century French ethnology and sociology from the *scandale de la mort* as collective representation and its *rite de passage*[44]. I collected testimonies during November 2017, which confirmed the compliance of some Italian residents to this attitude:

> We did not see the dead, we forgot the human pity, but we noted the broken rules. Thus, although we saw Muslims praying on the coffin, paying the last respect to the dead, we lost our good sense concerning a tragic issue and we called the police. Me too: I was looking out the window, I live right over there [...]. Their behaviour caused the failure to respect their religion. The struggle is between who respects civic rules and who does not. I can also park the car in my garage, so you can only do it: I don't care if you are French, Chinese, or whatever you are.

People I spoke with moved the focus from the funeral ceremony to compliance with the rules. This shifting fed on the supposed inferiority of Muslim people, calling into question, on one hand, their migrant character and, on the other, their alleged assimilation with the irregularities perpetrated by BTS:

> The problem, that conducts to racism, is the failure to observe the rules [...]. At the building site in Via Alò Giovanoli, the builder – who is Italian – broke the rules, thus these Islamic people followed him. They bought those garages, and rather than using them as car parking, they made an abusive mosque [...]. The builder is complicit

---

43. Ibid.
44. Hertz 1907; Van Gennep 1909.

with these Islamic people, which became the "master" of that area. They used it as a car park, they go in and out. The question isn't Islam, but the lack of rules.

In the previous subject, the language style is revealing: "these Islamic people", in which the demonstrative adjective underscores contempt and accentuates negativity. The Chief of the local police rises to a symbol of hostility. Oral sources that I investigated presented him on a par with "a traitor", a "defender of immigrants against the Italian people's interests":

When I looked out the window with my son, [...] I saw the coffin: I got angry! It wasn't the first time I saw a coffin: of course, somebody passes away in the district. It isn't a problem. The question is that they do as they please with us! It is true, they do as they please with us! I called the local police Chief, and he assured me they can have a funeral as they wish! But I'm not convinced I can have a funeral in a school!

The theme concerning Muslim people who "do as they please with us" is explicated by some residents through two stereotypical arguments: the lack of reciprocity in favour of "Western people" and Christians, and the "backwardness". A primary school teacher claims as follows:

You can't do like Christians of a million years ago, who prayed into the caverns. They were persecuted. On the contrary, they [Muslims] can freely worship: nobody persecutes them. I can't go to my garage because many shoes impede my path. They can't transfer their civilization – or uncivilization, I don't know what I can call it – to our country, in which there are other traditions [...].

I'm not born in Rome, I am from [she told me the name of her place of origin, in the South of Italy]. I often give this example: for Christmas Eve I can't adjust the traditions of my region to the Roman ones. But I don't force anyone in the apartment building to eat what I do. Thus, if you came here from Bangladesh, you now live in a country where children celebrate their birthdays at McDonald's: why do you not take part in the party? When we celebrate the Carnival parade, why do they not attend? It's an Italian tradition! Participate! You come to a new country: you must come on tiptoe! That's not fair. I should come back over fifty years!
[...]

> Little girls come to school with the veil: I feel suffocated! We tell them to wear comfortable clothes, also because of physical education: it's useless to insist. I am appalled at their traditions, which are in contrast with ours. We used to wear the veil, too: our grandmothers, when they went to church [...]. But we've evolved: if you go to church, nobody has a veil nowadays. You [Muslim people] must keep up with the times, and with the country which hosts you.

The ideas expressed above seem to legitimize supposed "fair" Italian supremacy. The words emerged from the opinion clearly distinguish between an advanced civilized Italian society and a retarded underdeveloped world of migration[45]. Only a short step brings to the parallelism between "contemporary Barbarians and primitive savages":

> What makes me angry is that they come here from countries where they lived under dictatorship. They know the lack of freedom. If I go to their countries and I want to open a church there, I can't. On the contrary, they come here and demand we have necessarily to adapt to their traditions. It's unfair! If you go to someone's house, you must go on tiptoe. You can't be the master! There are rules in Italy!

While Italian residents who opposed the Muslim funeral invoked coexistence rules as the basis for their complaint, a group of Italians took sides against the violent attitudes of their compatriots, inviting them to consider the event focusing on the feeling of sympathy at the death. As someone said, a fracture was created.

> There is a fracture. It doesn't concern the faith in Muhammad, Allah, or Jehovah's Witnesses. In my opinion, if the State regulates the relations and supervises on the abuses, we could live without conflict. Because we Italians live in constant conflict, between who of us tolerate, and who don't.

Who "tolerates" took the side of the freedom to celebrate the Islamic funeral and arranged a "counteroffensive" via Facebook. Its motto was the same as the Muslim people, who took part in the celebration, told me: "have mercy on the dead". An 18-year-old boy, a high school student of

---

45. Dal Lago 2010; Palidda 2019.

Bangladeshi descent who is waiting to obtain Italian citizenship, claimed as follows:

> I have known the dead; he is my friend's uncle. The funeral was surreal. I have lived in Tor Pignattara, and although I am used to conflicts, I didn't expect what I saw [...]. Shouts from the window, for a dead. I thought that people would respect death. No, they threw water and other objects out of their windows. I don't know what to say, also I can't expect this question.

I interviewed some Italians, some that were favourable and others that were unfavourable to the funeral, to know if they were interested in Bangladeshi Muslims' point of view. What emerged was their uninterest: although many Bangladeshi families have lived in the apartment buildings around the courtyard, no Italians asked for their opinions and feelings regarding the conflictual event. The only recurring element was the reference to a supposed unity of the "Bangladeshi community".

On the contrary, as mentioned above, Bangladeshi Muslims are diversified not only according to religious perspective and theological subject but also for political adherence, economic competition, and ability to take visibility inside their national community. The prayer room administrations are composed of "charismatic leaders" and "successful migrants". In other words, the opening of a prayer room involves a kind of power unnecessarily related to religious issues. As evidence, it is that the religious leaders of a Bangladeshi "mosque" are entrusted to "men of study" who are not involved in the steering of administration, which is attributable to "big men" who are committed to entrepreneurship. They manage local market stalls or informal trading, such as "street" stands. They send food, horticultural products, clothes, and various objects. Others are owners of restaurants, bars, and fast-food businesses that often boast the denomination "Indian" because of its appeal[46], or manage phone and internet offices, and money transfer ones. Bangladeshi entrepreneurs activate strong networks of fellow countrymen/women who aspire to have to do with their "sphere of influence", for work and/or economic reasons[47].

---

46. Vereni 2017.
47. Priori 2014, 2017; Russo 2018, pp. 344–345.

These questions became visible through large-scale social gatherings, such as festivals. Bangladeshi New Year's Day, Eid celebrations, and International Mother Language Day refracted into an increase of events in competition with each other. This dynamic is necessary to understand the novelty that the 2017 funeral has brought with it. Most of the Italian people missed the change of the event: Bangladeshi Muslims attempted to show a "united front" to go beyond the rivalry and fragmentations, to unanimously face some dangers, perceived as threats to the entire Bangladeshi community. It is a process that anthropologists have known since the beginning of the history of studies: Durkheim and Robertson Smith[48] theorized about the segment societies, focusing on peculiar North African and Arab populations, while Evans-Pritchard developed the theme by means of his research among the Nuer[49].

Although the funeral was promoted by the Bangladeshi leadership of the prayer room in Via Alò Giovannoli, it also involved other Bangladeshi administrations usually in rivalry. The political significance of the act was fundamental for the rhetorical communicative strategies toward fellow countrymen/women because it was the way to reply to the 5th Municipality intimidation, and to reaffirm their presence in the urban place and the public sphere. Since its 2016 assignment, the Five Star Municipal Council chaired by Giovanni Boccuzzi stood out for its policy against "illegality". Muslims perceived it as "aggressive" because they identified the Municipality as the guilty party of some prayer rooms' closure, justified by public safety issues. Between June 2016 and February 2017, seven prayer halls were closed in Rome, five of which were managed by Bangladeshi people. The reasons lie in the lack of an emergency exit, use change statement, and the authorization to demolish and build partition walls and toilets[50]. There were three "mosques" closed by the Authorities in the 5th Municipality[51]. Despite not being located in Tor Pignattara but in the adjacent district of Centocelle, some Bangladeshi Muslim leaders worked hard in favour of their reopening.

48. Durkheim 1893; Robertson Smith 1885.
49. Evans-Pritchard 1940.
50. Russo 2018, p. 363.
51. Over the last few years, the state of Bangladeshi Muslims in Tor Pignattara has further deteriorated. In May 2019 a prayer room in Via Serbelloni was closed and in June 2020 the via Capua one suffered the same fate.

In their opinion, the closures concerned religious freedom rights, considering the Italian Constitution. Some of them asked to be seen by the Municipal Council in September 2016. During September and October 2016, Muslim associations, mostly Bangladeshi and part of the CAIL (Coordination Islamic Associations of Lazio), organized a five-outdoor prayer series, to underline the right to collectively worship. The first three took place in the 5th Municipality: 16 September 2016, outside the Municipal Council headquarter (Via di Torre Annunziata); 23 September in piazza dei Mirti; 30 September in largo Preneste. In October, the other two demonstration-prayers were held in the 1st Municipality: on 7 October, in piazza Vittorio (Esquilino), and on 2 October near the Colosseum[52]. The last one had, predictably, a wide media echo.

To better understand the 30 October funeral, it is necessary to position it in contiguity with these events. It was a multidimensional affair, partially marked by the precarious persistence of Islamic places. Its prevalent meaning was the identity affirmation: that of conservative Italian people and the "opened to multiculturalism" ones; that of Bangladeshi leaders who aim at consolidating their power against the menace perpetrated by Municipal institutions and right-wing parties.

4   From Religious Super-diversity to Polarization

As noted at the beginning of this essay, statistics data reveals Tor Pignattara as a super-diverse place[53]. In recent years, religion is becoming increasingly central in the debate around the super-diversity category. Religious communities can establish in urban contexts and differently manage their relationship with the space[54]. Migrant religions and new religious movements emerge in superdiverse contexts. They interact among themselves and with the space, strongly contributing to reshaping it[55]. Consequently, many scholars have considered religion as a privileged lens to investigate super-diversity, focusing on religious phenomena as "super-diversity producers".

52. Russo 2018, pp. 363–364.
53. Vertovec 2007, 2019; Vertovec, Meissner 2015.
54. Becci et al. 2016; Kong 2010.
55. Becci, Burchardt 2016.

In Tor Pignattara, the geographical origin variety is intertwined with religious adherence. Three Catholic parishes and a long series of "other" religions shape a plural and complex religious landscape. It has changed over the last few years, because of its precarity. The Islamic prayer halls have been between three and five, the Evangelical ones between five and seven, in addition to two Hindu temples, a Buddhist one, and a prayer room for Jehovah's Witnesses. This variety struggles for its enhancement. In Tor Pignattara – not differently from Italy and Europe – rather than a richness it has been exploited by conservative people and right-wing politicians – and, as noted, by municipal institutions – to spread messages of exclusion from social rights for "undesirable people"[56] and, on the other side, to render an alleged majority on a likewise alleged cultural and religious homogeneity. Some scholars have moved critiques to Vertovec's theorization, focusing on his tendency to deny ethnic and religious conflict. On the contrary, since his first article Vertovec has already noted that the new super-diverse immigration has brought with it emergent forms of racism among citizens against newcomers, but also among longstanding minorities against immigrants, and newcomers themselves, directed against ethnic minorities[57]. Regarding segregation, Vertovec noted that several new immigrants have clustered in specific urban areas, thus new experiences of space, forms of cosmopolitanism, and creolization entail new patterns of social hierarchy and stratification[58]. Dynamics and relations engaging migrants, their religions and urban spaces are subordinate to social, political, and institutional inequalities and imbalance in power that implicate who really can choose to act, and who cannot[59].

According to these perspectives, most of the cities and towns, as Stringer stated, are not super-diverse but polarized[60], because migrants are not free to choose where they can set themselves up but are forced to settle for living in marginal areas, almost like in opposition to the housing developments. It is not possible to avoid the gap between centres and peripheries, and between rich neighbourhoods and degraded ones. The polarization is what mainly emerges from the Hindu festival and

56. Richmond, Valtonen 1994.
57. Vertovec 2007, p. 1045.
58. Ibid., p. 126.
59. Wolf 1982.
60. Stringer 2013.

the Islamic funeral. The relations between Italians and foreigners, citizenry and Municipality, and residents and law enforcement are respectively polarized. Every social group is, in turn, polarized and divided into shorter segments: the Muslim Bangladeshi community and the Hindu one, the Italian residents in Tor Pignattara, and the Municipal Council displays of conflict among its members.

Italian people in Tor Pignattara use the term "fracture" to describe opposite behaviours related to the two events. People who justify the festival and the funeral do it for a positive idea of alterity and respect for foreigners. On the contrary, those who oppose these events focus on legality and security, hiding migrants and non-Catholic religions' rights and the charge of racism. Both these positions denote simplified categories and topics. Regarding the first question, Ulrich Beck introduced the idea of banal cosmopolitanism[61] to underline shallow "global products" usage: exotic food, "ethnic" clothes, musical styles, television programs, and cinematographic products. Focusing on the second theme, "national values" are reduced to stereotypes: the flag, the identity emphasis, and its defence[62], the "tradition". The "national culture" interpreted as a huge and vague meaning that includes language, religion, cuisine, etc., is often considered in danger, because of its exposition to contact with the diversity[63].

Despite that they are ethically diverse, Piero Vereni stated that both perspectives are "two sides of the same coin", because both are strictly locally situated[64]. Completely untied by their inner meanings, the Durgā Pūjā sacrality and a Muslim's death become an arena for the competition between different social and political actors, into a circumscribed place, staging an immature dispute which removed the religious heritage from the debate. Rather than super-diverse, the context appears "super-conflictual". In both events, Bangladeshi people are the victims. Although their high statistical number in the 5th Municipality, and in particular in the Tor Pignattara district, Italian social and political players assimilated them to "people without history"[65], to the point that they are disinterested in Bangladeshi past and present, even disowning Bangladeshi

61. Beck 2002.
62. Gellner 1993, p. 409.
63. Billing 1995.
64. Vereni 2017, pp. 139–141.
65. Wolf 1982.

immigrants' feelings and opinions. Some Italian people in Tor Pignattara, however, consider them as strongly characterized, either positively as kind, good-natured, and tireless, or negatively, as retarded, male chauvinist, and introverted. Some others remove their national attribute, no less than confusing them with Indians or Arabs. Whether they are Muslim or Hindu, Bangladeshis are an easy target due to negative perceptions that prevent them from standing out in the global market's imagination[66]. The "opposite factions" reduce them to "good immigrants" or "bad barbarians". In Tor Pignattara, it seems that Italian people see Bangladeshi people through the same lenses, which simultaneously provide fascination for the alterity or xenophobic hatred. Both behaviours miss equal dignity and critical attitudes[67]. Avoiding examining Bangladeshis for their own "human nature" entails a lack of a serious non-ideological debate focused on the relationships between migrant people and "autochthonous" ones.

The will to aestheticize, if not to exoticize, the migrants has not been the objective of the "welcoming Italians", even though the idea of valuing Tor Pignattara diversities risks shaping stereotyped culturalized migrants' variations. Following an ethical perspective, this risk is less than those which can arise from conservative Italians' behaviour and statements. Behind arguments and complaints, a considerable part of politicians, municipal councillors, and citizens have hidden the obsession with concealment for indecorous, illegitimate, and degraded people. It is not accidental that they have focused on legality, decency, decorum, "civilian life", and "social order".

The inconvenience that emerged with the funeral and the feast concerns the management of contested spaces, caused by conflicting reasons among social groups. Yet, both cases have to do with the lack of rights for non-Catholic religions and their adherents. Consequently, the space is proposed as a condition of subtraction which touches the outcasts[68]. They are both consumers and victims in the capitalist and neoliberalist market, of which they are ambiguously part, experiencing the contradiction between the desire and the unavailability of goods, assets, necessities, and usages, that the capitalist system promises them[69]. It seems that

66. Vereni 2017, p. 142.
67. Squarcini 2019.
68. Wacquant 2007.
69. Vigh 2009.

Bangladeshi people in Tor Pignattara cannot free themselves from this yoke.

Author Biography

Carmelo Russo is Associate Professor at the Department of History, Anthropology, Religions, Arts, Performing Arts (SARAS) of Sapienza University, Rome (Italy) and has been Marie Skłodowska-Curie Actions Fellow. He teaches Cultural Anthropology, Anthropology of Religion, and Urban Anthropology. He has conducted fieldwork in Italy and Tunisia focusing on the migration process, religious dynamics, religious and spiritual minorities, and also considers super-diversity theories. He is the author of numerous journal articles and volume chapters. His monograph *Nostra Signora del limite* (*Our Lady of the Boundaries*), concerning the Marian worship in Tunisia, was published in September 2020.

References

Amescua, C. (2013), *Anthropology of Intangible Cultural Heritage and Migration: An Uncharted Field*, in L. Arizpe, C. Amescua (eds.), *Anthropological Perspectives on Intangible Cultural Heritage*, Springer, Cham, Heidelberg, New York, Dordrecht, and London, pp. 103–120.

Appadurai, A. (1996), *Modernity at Large: Cultural Dimensions of Globalization*, University of Minnesota Press, Minneapolis.

Appadurai, A. (2010), *How Histories make Geographies*, in "The Journal of Transcultural Studies", 1, 1, pp. 4–13. https://doi.org/10.11588/ts.2010.1.6129

Arizpe, L., Amescua, C. (eds.) (2013), *Anthropological Perspectives on Intangible Cultural Heritage*, Springer, Cham, Heidelberg, New York, Dordrecht, and London.

Bandyopadyay, P. (1987), *Mother Goddess Durga*, Image India, Kolkata.

Banerjee, S. G. (2004), *Durga Puja: Yesterday, Today, and Tomorrow*, Rupa, New Delhi.

Banerji, A. (2019), *The Social Drama of Durga Puja: Performing Bengali Identity in the Diaspora*, in "Ecumenica", 12, 1, pp. 1–13. https://doi.org/10.5325/ecumenica.12.1.0001

Becci, I., Burchardt, M. (2016), *Religion and Superdiversity: An Introduction*, in "New Diversities", 18, 1, pp. 1–7.

Becci, I., Burchardt, M., Giorda, M. C. (2017), *Religious Super-Diversity and Spatial Strategies in Two European Cities*, in "Current Sociology", 65, pp. 73–91. https://doi.org/10.1177/0011392116632030

Beck, U. (2002), *The Cosmopolitan Society and Its Enemies*, in "Theory, Culture and Society", 19, 1–2, pp. 17–44. https://doi.org/10.1177/026327640201900101

Beck, U. (2011), *Multiculturalism or Cosmopolitanism: How Can We Describe and Understand the Diversity of the World?*, in "Social Sciences in China", 32, 4, pp. 52–58. https://doi.org/10.1080/02529203.2011.625169

Berkson, C. (1995), *The Divine and the Demoniac: Mahisa's Heroic Struggle with Durga*, Oxford University Press, Delhi.

Bhattacharya, T. (2007), *Tracking the Goddess: Religion, Community, and Identity in the Durgā Pūjā Ceremonies of Nineteenth-Century Calcutta*, in "The Journal of Asian Studies", 66, 4, pp. 919–962. https://doi.org/10.1017/S0021911807001258

Billig, M. (1995), *Banal Nationalism*, Sage, London.

Bock, J.-J. (2021), *The Five Star Movement (M5S) in Rome: The Real Life of Utopian Politics*, in "Social Anthropology/Anthropologie Sociale", 29, 1, pp. 52–67. https://doi.org/10.1111/1469-8676.12976

Charrad, M. M., Adams, J. (2011), *Introduction: Patrimonialism, Past and Present*, in "The Annals of the American Academy of Political and Social Science", 636, *Patrimonial Power in the Modern World*, July, pp. 6–15. https://doi.org/10.1177/0002716211402286

Clark, T. W. (1955), *Evolution of Hinduism in Medieval Bengali Literature: Śiva, Caṇḍī, Manasā*, in "Bulletin of the School of Oriental and African Studies", 17, 3, pp. 503–518. https://doi.org/10.1017/S0041977X00112418

Dal Lago, A. (2010), *Note sul razzismo culturale in Italia*, in S. Palidda (ed.), *Il «discorso» ambiguo sulle migrazioni*, Mesogea, Messina, pp. 11–20.

Durkheim, É. (1893), *De la division du travail social*, F. Alcan, Paris.

Eade, J. (2012), *Religion, Home-making and Migration across a Globalising City: Responding to Mobility in London*, in "Culture and Religion", 13, 4, pp. 469–483. https://doi.org/10.1080/14755610.2012.728142

Evans-Pritchard, E. E. (1940), *The Nuer: A Description of the Modes of Livelihood and Political Institutions of a Nilotic People*, Clarendon Press, Oxford.

Flood, G. D. (1996), *An Introduction to Hinduism*, Cambridge University Press, Cambridge.

Gellner, E. (1983), *Nations and Nationalism*, Basil Blackwell, Oxford.

Giampietri, V., Khalil, R., Tozzi, L. (ed. C. Russo) (2023), *Una festa hindu in un quartiere di Roma. La Durgā Pūjā a Tor Pignattara durante il covid-19*, Carocci, Rome.

Hertz, R. (1907), *Contribution à une étude sur la représentation collective de la mort*, in "L'Année sociologique", 10, pp. 48–137.

Huntington, S. P. (1996), *The Clash of Civilizations and the Remaking of World Order*, Simon & Schuster, New York.

Kong, L. (2010), *Global Shifts, Theoretical Shifts: Changing Geographies of Religion*, in "Progress in Human Geography", 34, 6, pp. 755–776. https://doi.org/10.1177/0309132510362602

Machuca, J. A. (2013), *Challenges for Anthropological Research on Intangible Cultural Heritage*, in L. Arizpe, C. Amescua (eds.), *Anthropological Perspectives on Intangible Cultural Heritage*, Springer, Cham, Heidelberg, New York, Dordrecht, and London, pp. 57–70.

Nozzoli, G. (2017), *Via Giovannoli, la preghiera islamica nell'area di cantiere (abusiva): residenti in rivolta*, in "RomaToday", 1 September, available at: https://www.RomaToday.it/cronaca/preghiera-musulmani-via-giovannoli-1-settembre-2017.html#_ga=2.82096656.789378713.1597294621-1395363631.1597294621 (last accessed 3 June 2021).

N., G. (2017), *Tor Pignattara, il funerale islamico si fa per strada e i residenti insorgono*, in "RomaToday", 2 November, available at: https://www.romatoday.it/zone/pigneto/torpignattara/via-giovannoli-funerale-in-strada.html (last accessed 3 June 2021).

Palidda, S. (2019), *La guerra alle migrazioni: il fatto politico totale del XXI secolo*, in "Dialoghi Mediterranei", 36, available at: http://www.istitutoeuroarabo.it/DM/la-guerra-alle-migrazioni-il-fatto-politico-totale-del-xxi-secolo-2/ (last accessed 8 May 2021).

Pitch, T. (2016), *Politiche di sicurezza e cittadinanza nell'Unione Europea*, in S. Cingari, A. Simoncini (eds.), *Lessico Postdemocratico*, Perugia Stranieri University Press, Perugia, pp. 149–157.

Priori, A. (2014), *Il genius loci migratorio di Torpignattara*, in C. Cellamare (ed.), *Roma città autoprodotta. Ricerca urbana e linguaggi artistici*, ManifestoLibri, Rome, pp. 63–73.

Priori, A. (2017), *Bangladeshi Multi-Scalar Im/mobilities: Between Social Aspirations and Legal Obstacles*, in "New Diversities", 19, 3, pp. 29–42, available at: https://newdiversities.mmg.mpg.de/?page_id=3308 (last accessed 8 May 2021).

Richmond, A. H., Valtonen, K. (1994), *Global Apartheid: Refugees, Racism, and the New World Order*, in "Refugees: Canada's Journal on Refugees", 14, 6, pp. 25–28. https://doi.org/10.25071/1920-7336.21839

Robertson Smith, W. (1885), *Kinship and Marriage in Early Arabia*, Cambridge University Press, Cambridge.

Roma Capitale (2021), *Popolazione iscritta in anagrafe – Stranieri al 31 dicembre 2020 per municipio, genere e cittadinanza*, Tab. 12, available at: https://www.comune.roma.it/web/it/roma-statistica-popolazione1.page (last accessed 7 January 2022).

Russo, C. (2017), *Patrimonializzare il sacro. Tor Pignattara e i luoghi di culto dell'altro*, in A. Broccolini, V. Padiglione (ed.), *Ripensare i margini. L'Ecomuseo Casilino per la periferia di Roma*, Aracne, Rome, pp. 148–163.

Russo, C. (2018), *Musulmani di Roma. Spunti di riflessione da una etnografia*, in A. Saggioro, C. Russo (eds.), *Roma città plurale. Le religioni, il territorio, le ricerche*, Bulzoni, Rome, pp. 285–371.

Russo, C., Tamburrino F. (2015), *Luoghi comuni, luoghi in comune. Percorsi di dialogo e conoscenza a partire dai luoghi di culto della Provincia di Roma*, C. Peri (ed.), Centro Astalli, Rome.

Simoncelli, M. (2018), *Durga puja, luci e ombre della festività induista che per dieci giorni anima le vie di Calcutta*, in "Lifegate", 31 October, available at: https://www.lifegate.it/durga-puja-calcutta (last accessed 5 June 2021).

Sina, Y. (2019a), *Tor Pignattara, le foto di una consigliera fanno chiudere la sala municipale: interrotti i festeggiamenti induisti*, in "RomaToday", 7 October, available at: https://pigneto.RomaToday.it/torpignattara/ex-sala-consiliare--festa-induista-chiusa.html (last accessed 5 June 2021).

Sina, Y. (2019b), *Tor Pignattara, ex sala consiliare chiusa fino a regolamento. Boccuzzi ci ripensa*, in "RomaToday", 10 October, available at: https://pigneto.RomaToday.it/torpignattara/ex-sala-consiliare-via-acqua-bullicante-aperta.html (last accessed 5 June 2021).

Squarcini, F. (2019), *Selling Tolerance by the Pound: On Ideal Types' Fragility, Aśoka's Edicts and the Political Theology of Toleration in and Beyond South Asia*, in "Philosophy and Social Criticism", 45, 4, pp. 477–492. https://doi.org/10.1177/0191453719829852

Stringer, M. D. (2013), *Discourses on Religious Diversity: Explorations in an Urban Ecology*, Routledge, London-New York.

Ukah, A. (2012), *Religion and Globalization*, in E. K. Bongmba (ed.), *The Wiley-Blackwell Companion to African Religions*, Wiley-Blackwell, Hoboken, pp. 503–514.

Tozzi, L. (2023), *Lontana dagli occhi, vicina al cuore: la Madre del Bengala*, in V. Giampietri, R. Khalil, L. Tozzi (ed. C. Russo), *Una festa hindu in un quartiere di Roma. La Durgā Pūjā a Tor Pignattara durante il covid-19*, Carocci, Rome, pp. 17–49.

Van Gennep, A. (1909), *Les rites de passage*, Picard, Paris.

Vereni, P. (2017), *Uomini di strada. Rappresentazioni cosmopolite della violenza maschile nelle strade di Londra, Dacca e Roma*, in "Meridiana: Rivista di Storia e Scienze Sociali", 89, pp. 139–163.

Vertovec, S. (2007), *Super-diversity and its Implications*, in "Ethnic and Racial Studies", 30, 6, pp. 1024–1054. https://doi.org/10.1080/01419870701599465

Vertovec, S. (2019), *Talking around Super-diversity*, in "Ethnic and Racial Studies", 42, 1, pp. 125–139. https://doi.org/10.1080/01419870.2017.1406128

Vertovec, S., Meissner, F. (2015), *Comparing Super-diversity*, in "Ethnic and Racial Studies", 38, 4, pp. 541–555. https://doi.org/10.1080/01419870.2015.980295

Vigh, H. (2009), *Wayward Migration: On Imagined Futures and Technological Voids*, in "Ethnos", 74, 1, pp. 91–109. https://doi.org/10.1080/00141840902751220

Wacquant, L. (2007), *Urban Outcasts: A Comparative Sociology of Advanced Marginality*, Polity, Cambridge.

Wolf, E. R. (1982), *Europe and People Without History*, University of California Press, Berkeley.

Index of Names

'Abduh, Muḥammad 61–62, 64, 82
Abel 68, 69, 71
Abū Mūsā 69
Abu-Nimer, Mohammed 5, 14
Acharya, Tanka Prasad 93
Adam 66, 68–70, 190
Agnew, John 116, 136
al-Afġānī, Ğamāl al-Dīn 61–62, 64, 70, 82
Al-Ali, Nadje 252–253, 269
al-Bannā, Ḥassan 66
al-Hadā al-Ḥusaynī, Muḥammad 79
al-Ḫūrī, Adīb 68, 79–81, 84
Al-Maleh, Haitham (Hayṯam al-Mālih) 64–65
al-Nāṣir, ʿAbd 66
al-Nuqrāšī, Maḥmūd 66
al-Saqqā, ʿAbd al-Akram 65
al-Tilmisānī, ʿUmar 63
Albera, Dionigi 2, 5, 14, 16, 20, 42, 48–49, 135–136
Alietti, Alfredo 213, 239
Ambedkar, Bhimrao Ramji 103
Amiraux, Valérie 212, 237, 239–240
Ammerman, Nancy 146, 174
Anderson, Benedict 87, 109, 177, 265, 269
Appadurai, Arjun 11, 16, 263, 269, 278, 297
Appleby, R. Scott 9, 16
Aptekar, Sofya 3, 17
Ardener, Edwin 114, 136
Arendt, Hannah 218, 239

Arius 38
Arkoun, Mohammed (Arkūn, Muḥammad) 62, 82
Astuti, Putu Ayu Swandewi 119, 136

Bambang, Susilo 119
Ban Tuyên Giáo Quận Ủy (Propaganda Department Of The District Party Committee) 164, 174
Barter, Shane Joshua 118, 136
Barth, Fredrik 36, 49
Bayat, Asef 215, 239
Beatty, Andrew 126, 136
Becci, Irene 4, 8, 10, 17, 21, 25–26, 31, 47, 49–50, 58, 65, 82, 84, 115, 135–136, 139, 146, 174, 183, 188, 207, 255, 269, 276, 293, 297–298
Beck, Ulrich 24, 49, 276, 295, 298
Beckford, James A. 27–28, 47, 49
Bennabi, Malek (Malik b. Nabī) 62, 74, 82, 84
Berg, Eberhard 101
Berger, Peter L. 44, 50
Bhatia, Vijay K. 18
Bhattachan, Krishna B. 92, 110
Billig, Michael 276, 295, 298
Birendra, King of Nepal 95–96, 98
Blagov, Sergei Alexandrovich 142, 174
Blanes, Ruy L. 215, 218, 240
Bock, John-James 276, 298
Bosi, Lorenzo 213, 239
Bouma, Gary 146, 174
Bouta, Tsjeard 16

Bownas, Richard A. 98, 110
Breidbach, Stephan 18, 52
Broccolini, Alessandra 256, 269, 271, 300
Brown, Iem 121, 136
Brown, Peter 21, 39
Bùi, Đức Sinh 152, 174
Burchardt, Marian 2, 4, 8, 10, 17, 21, 25–26, 49–50, 58, 65, 82, 84, 115, 135–137, 139, 146, 183, 188, 207, 255, 269, 276, 293, 297–298
Burgat, François 218, 239
Burhanuddin, Jajat 127, 136
Butler, Judith 34–35, 50

Çağlar, Ayşe 139
Cain 69, 73–74
Campbell, Heidi 263, 269–271
Casanova, José 42, 50, 115, 136–137, 139, 215, 239
Cavalli-Sforza, Luigi Luca 12, 17
Celada Ballanti, Roberto 9–10, 17
Chakrabartee, Sumon 259
Chatterjee, Mohona 251, 270
Chaturvedy, Rajeev Ranjan 95, 110
Chia, Jack Meng-Tat 121, 137
Chu, Lan T. 143, 175
Clark, T. W. 277, 298
Couroucli, Maria 5, 16, 42, 48–49, 135–136
Cox, Harvey 5, 17
Cozma, Ioan 1, 5, 17
Cu, Chi Loi 166, 175
Cusack, Carole M. 247, 270
Czajka, Mathias 3, 17

D'Amato, Gianni 115, 137
Dall'Oglio, Paolo 79
Dang, Anh, et al. 164, 175
Davis, Carol C. 95, 110
Dayb, Muḥammad 79
de Haas, Hein 3, 17
de Sales, Anne 98, 110

Della Porta, Donatella 213, 239
Deumert, Ana 3, 17
Dipendra, King of Nepal 98
Do, Thien 151–152, 175
Doniger, Wendy 246, 270
Dreyer, Jaco S. 214, 239
Durkheim, Émile 264, 292, 298
Duyvendak, Jan Willem 10, 14, 17, 21, 24, 50, 137

Eck, Diana L. 27, 50
Eickelman, Dale F. 215, 239
Eriksen, Thomas Hylland 11, 17
Esposito, John 218, 239
Evans-Pritchard, Edward E. 292, 298

Farré, Lidia 134, 137
Fārūq, Ibn Fu'ād 66
Favole, Adriano 7, 17
Febriharjati, Sri 123, 137
Ferrara, Alessandro 43, 50
Ferrara, Marianna 1, 50
Fichte, Johann Gottlieb 33
Fisher, William F. 97, 110
Flood, Gavin D. 245–247, 270, 278, 298
Flores, Nelson 115, 137
Foner, Nancy 17, 50, 115, 137, 145, 175
Frankum, Ronald Bruce 141, 153, 175
Fraser, Nancy 221, 239
Frisina, Annalisa 213, 229, 239
Frykenberg, Robert Eric 109–110

Gaenszle, Martin 102, 110
Gallo, Ester 109, 207
Gandhi, Mohandas Karamchand 58, 80, 84, 103, 111
Gardner, Vika 231, 239
Geertz, Clifford 33, 51, 116–117, 126, 137–138, 215, 239
Gellner, David N. 92, 94, 107, 110–111, 295, 298
Geuss, Raymond 34, 51
Ghouse, Mohammad 103, 110

Ginzburg, Carlo 6, 17
Giorda, Maria Chiara 2, 5, 8, 14, 17, 20, 47–48, 51, 116, 136–137, 255, 269, 298
Giordan, Giuseppe 6, 17, 28–29, 51
Giorgi, Alberta 12, 17, 47, 51
Glick Schiller, Nina 182, 208–209, 270–271
Goebel, Zane 134, 137
Göle, Nilüfer 218, 237, 240
Goscha, Christopher 141, 175
Guldbrandsen, Thaddeus C. 270
Gunn, Geoffrey C. 154, 175
Gyanendra, King of Nepal 98

Habermas, Jürgen 215, 237, 239–240
Hachhethu, Krishna 94, 96, 110
Ḥāfiẓ, Yāsir 79
Hafner, Christoph A. 18
Hameed, Salman 231, 239
Hamid, Sadek 212, 240
Hannerz, Ulf 8, 17, 182, 208
Hansen, Peter 152–154, 157, 175
Hardjono, Joan 118, 137
Hasan, Mubashar 215, 240
Hasan, Noorhaidi 216, 240
Hausner, Sondra 110–111
Hayes, Louis D. 95, 110
Heck, Douglas 95, 110
Hefner, Robert William 120, 137
Hegel, Georg Wilhelm Friedrich 33
Hejazi, Hutan 219, 238, 240
Helland, Christopher 264–265, 270
Hertz, Robert 288, 298
Hewstone, Miles 6, 7, 17, 18
Hitler 68
Hodson, Gordon 6–7, 18
Hoey, Brian 118, 137
Hoftun, Martin 96, 112
Hollinger, David A. 24, 51
Holmberg, David 101–102, 107, 111
Honneth, Axel 33–35, 46, 50–51
Hsia, R. Po-chia 150, 175

Hudson, Wayne 219, 240
Hugo, Graeme 134, 137
Huntington, Samuel 285, 299
Huq, Samia 216, 240
Hutt, Michael 92, 96–97, 111

Iqbāl, Muḥammad 61–62, 67–68

Jacobs, Seth 142, 153, 175, 186
Jahanbegloo, Ramin 58, 84
Jesus 37–38, 80, 150, 202
Joas, Hans 215, 240
Johnson, Harry 117, 138
Jonker, Gerdien 212, 237, 239–240
Joseph, Siby K. 103, 111

Kadayifci-Orellana, S. Ayse 16
Karunakaran, Kotta 97, 111
Kasinitz, Philip 17, 50, 137
Katuwal, Rukmandag 109
Keane, Webb 169, 175
Keith, Charles 148–149, 151–152, 155, 175, 177
Kiftārū, Ṣalāḥ al-Dīn 79
Kivisto, Peter 25, 51, 115, 138
Klinkhammer, Gritt 10, 18
Knott, Kim 6, 18, 269, 271
Knowles, Caroline 116, 138
König, Anika 118, 138
Krauskopff, Gisèle 100–111
Kreager, Philip 134, 138
Kumar, Anup 258, 272
Küster, Lutz 18, 52

Lawoti, Mahendra 92, 97, 111
Lê Hữu Từ 156–157
Lecomte-Tilouine, Marie 98–99, 110–112
Lecours, André 100–111
Leone, Massimo 4, 18
Letizia, Chiara 100, 104, 106, 110–111
Levitt, Peggy 7, 18, 25, 51, 182–183, 188, 208–209

Lipner, Julius 92, 111
Little, David 16
Luce, Don 158, 176

Mahendra, King of Nepal, 93–96
Maḥmūd, Ibrāhīm 61, 66
Makoni, Sinfree B. 3, 18, 21, 51
Malik, Iftikhar H. 218, 240
Malone, David M. 95, 110
Manoussakis, John 237, 240
Mao, Zedong 95, 97
Mapril, José 215, 218, 240
Masud, Muhammad 218, 240
Matteucci, Ivana 263, 270
Mayall, James 11, 13, 18
McDermott, Rachel Fell 243, 245, 247–248, 250–252, 267, 270
McLeod, Mark W 171, 176
Meintel, Deirdre 42, 45, 51–52
Meissner, Fran 4, 18, 275–276, 293, 301
Menozzi, Paolo 17
Miller, Leslie 18
Mishra, Shree Govind 94, 111
Mongin, Olivier 218, 240
Monnot, Christophe 17, 49
Muḥammad 70, 78

Nath, Binita 265–266, 272
Ndhlovu, Finex 3, 18, 21, 52
Needham, Anuradha Dingwaney 102, 111
Neumaier, Anna 10, 18
Ngo, Lan Anh 147, 176
Ngô, T. T. Tam 141, 147, 169, 176
Nguyễn (dynasty) 149, 158, 176
Nugroho, Bayu Septiyan 125, 138

O'Leary, Stephen D. 265
Obeyesekere, Gananath 190, 203, 204, 208–209
Omer, Atalia 16
Onta, Pratyoush 111
Osman, Sulastri 138

Otten, Mariel 138

Pace, Enzo 17, 85
Padovan, Dario 239
Pahari, Anup K. 92, 97, 111
Pavlenko, Aneta 2, 3, 18, 21, 52
Pemberton, John 124, 138
Perceval, Landon 90, 111
Pettigrew, Judith 98–99, 111–112
Phạm Ngọc Chi 156
Piazza, Alberto 17
Pierret, Thomas 58, 64–65, 85
Pieterse, Hendrik J. C. 214, 239
Pradhan, Uma 95, 112
Priori, Andrea 14, 211, 213, 238, 240, 256, 271, 285, 291, 299
Prithvi Narayan Shah Dev, King of Nepal, 87–89, 92–93

Quṭb, Sayyid 66

Race, Richard 8, 18
Raeper, William 96, 112
Rajan, Rajeswari Sunder 102, 111
Rajasekhariah, A. M. 103, 112
Ramsay, Jacob 147, 176
Rashid, Sabina Faiz 216, 240
Rawls, John 6, 32, 241
Ray, Manas 250, 271
Regmi, Dilli Raman 89, 112
Repstad, Pål, 146, 176
Rivera, Annamaria 213, 240
Rizzo, Roberto 14, 113, 121, 124, 136, 138
Robertson Smith, William 292, 299
Rodrigues, Hillary 249, 251, 271
Rouméas, Elise 30, 52
Russo, Carmelo 1–2, 15–16, 18, 217, 241–242, 254–255, 270–271, 273, 276, 285, 292–293, 297–298, 300

Saggioro, Alessandro 1, 5, 15–16, 18, 37, 50, 52, 241, 271, 300

Sahlins, Marshall 7, 18
Said, Edward W. 215, 241
Said, Jawdat (Saʿīd, Ǧawdat) 14, 57, 58–83, 85
Salazar, Noel 18, 138
Salguero, Óscar 219, 238, 240
Salvatore, Armando 215, 239–240
Sarkar, Bihani 243, 245, 248, 271
Sassen, Saskia 5, 18
Sayad, Abdelmalek 216, 241
Saʿīd, Bišr 60, 63–64, 78–80
Scheifinger, Heinz 265, 271
Schielke, Samuli 215, 241
Schmenk, Barbara 18, 52
Schmidt, Garbi 212, 241
Scialdone, Marta 255, 271
Sciortino, Giuseppe 213, 241
Shneiderman, Sara 101, 112
Shrestha-Schipper, Satya 98, 112
Sigona, Nando 4, 18
Silvestri, Sara 11, 13, 18
Smith, Donald Eugene 102, 112
Sobary, Mohamad 119, 138
Socrates 69, 73
Song, Miri 215, 241
Sounaye, Abdoulaye 218, 241
Sparre, Sara Lei 215, 241
Spencer, Jonathan 189, 190–191, 193, 210
Steele, Liza 45, 52
Stirrat, Roderick 192, 194–196, 201, 210
Stringer, Martin D. 7, 13, 19, 294, 300
Subba, Tanka Bahadur 97, 112
Suryadinata, Leo 134, 138

Tambiah, Stanley J. 189
Taylor, Charles 68, 215, 241
Taylor, Keith Weller 141, 176
Taylor, Philip 142, 176
Telmissany, May 218, 241
Todd, James 89, 112
Torri, Davide 14, 86, 97, 101–102, 109, 112
Tran, Quang Anh 149, 160, 176
Tran, Thị Liên 153, 176
Trần, Tam Tỉnh 156
Tribhuvan, King of Nepal 93

Unsworth, Amy 231, 241

van Bruinessen, Martin 240
van der Veer, Peter 116, 139, 215, 241
van Dijk, Rijk 116, 127, 136, 139, 188, 210
Van Gennep, Arnold 288, 300
Van Schendel, Willem 103, 112
Vasantkumar, Chris 116, 139
Vasquez, Manuel 6, 18
Ventura, Marco 9, 19
Vereni, Pietro 276, 291, 295–296, 300
Vertovec, Steven 2, 4–5, 18–19, 21–25, 29, 31, 43, 52, 81, 85, 115, 134, 139, 144–145, 176–177, 182–183, 210, 251, 259, 271, 275–276, 293–294, 300–301
Vidyattama, Yogi 134, 139
Villa, Dana R. 218, 237–238, 241
Voci, Alberto 7, 17
Voirol, Olivier 17, 49

Wacquant, Loïc 296, 301
Wagner, Anne 18
Weber, Max 32
Weintraub, Andrew 130
Weiss, Sarah 124, 139
Werner, Jayne Susan 171, 177
Wessendorf, Susanne 24, 53, 117, 139
Whelpton, John 87, 94, 112
White, Sarah C. 216, 241
Williams, Raymond Brady 6, 19
Wolf, Eric R. 294–295, 301

Yuli Setyaningtyas, Bintang 118, 139

Zaman, Fahmida 219, 241
Zoetmulder, Petrus Josephus 125, 139

Index of Subjects

1954 Bắc di cư migration / Operation Passage to Freedom 140–141, 144, 151–153, 156, 162, 164–166, 173
2001 terrorist attacks 57–58, 83

Activism, Integrated 14, 79, 125, 212–213, 219, 223–224, 226, 236–237
Activism, Separatist 101, 122, 124, 186, 213–214, 217, 236–237
Adivasi / Janajati 91, 97, 99–101, 104–105, 112
Analytical Grid 14, 20, 31, 36, 42, 47
Angels 70–71
Animism 89, 100
Animal sacrifice 249
Anthropology of Christianity 174, 207
Anti-colonial movement 142–143, 155–156, 171
Arabic 59, 66–67, 72, 123, 130–131
Armed resistance 76
Asal Hindustan 89, 90
Assam 243, 265, 277
Atomic bomb 68
Āśvin 245, 249, 277

Bāṇa's Caṇḍīśataka 248
Bắc 54 / Bắc 75 / Người 75 161–162, 169
Bahun (Brahmins) 91
Bali 49, 119
Banal Cosmopolitanism 273, 295
Banal Nationalism 273, 276, 298
Banaras (Varanasi) 264, 268

Bangladeshi Community 13–15, 211–212, 214, 216–217, 220–221, 223, 225–226, 231–233, 236, 238, 240, 242, 250–252, 255–256, 259, 267, 275, 278–279, 281, 285, 288, 291–293, 295–297, 299
Bhārat Mātā 251
Bodhana 249
Border areas / regimes 3, 5, 27, 36, 42, 92, 207, 242, 282, 285
Brahmin 91, 93, 258–260, 264, 278
Broadcast 261, 264
Buddhism 13, 44, 89–90, 92, 99, 100, 108, 112–113, 117, 121–124, 130, 134–136, 149, 181–182, 189, 191, 193, 195, 198–199, 202–205, 208–210, 235
Bùi Chu diocese / Phát Diệm diocese 154–157, 159, 165–166
Butinage (Religious) 45, 50, 52

Cāmuṇḍā 243, 249
Caṇḍīmaṅgalakāvya 247
Cao Đài sect / Hòa Hảo sect 142, 150, 171–172
Caste System 90, 98
Catholic missionaries 90, 92, 147–148, 150–152, 155
Catholic morality 168–169, 170, 174
Catholic villages (làng đạo) 143, 151, 154–155, 162, 165–166, 173
Central Intelligence Agency (CIA) 153

Change (social and personal) 17, 27, 37, 40, 42, 44–46, 58, 73, 259
Chetri (Kshatriyas) 91
Christianity 6, 13, 37–41, 72, 90, 92, 108, 117, 121–122, 135, 149, 174, 181, 186, 192, 194, 200, 203, 206–207, 209, 229, 235, 279
Chronocentrism 37
Church/state relations 14, 39, 120, 140–141, 143, 147, 151, 155–157
Circassian ethnicity 59–60
Citizenship 12, 40, 51, 165, 184, 219, 239–240, 270, 275–276, 281, 283–284, 291
Coercion 66, 77
Cohabitation 1, 113, 181, 187–189, 192, 204
Cohabitation and conflict 11, 13, 15–16, 39, 46, 48–49, 140, 147, 150–151, 168, 192, 207, 274–275, 277, 290–291, 295–296
Cold War 153, 176
Collective memory / historical narrative 14, 140–141, 158
Colonialism 62, 82, 147, 191
Colonizability 62
Communist Party of Nepal-Maoist (CPN-M) 88, 91, 97
Communist Party of Nepal Unified Marxist-Leninist (UML) 91
Compulsion 7, 71, 75, 77, 80, 82
Conflict resolution 49, 83, 207
Constitution 8, 93–94, 96–97, 100, 102, 104–106, 108, 111, 254, 279, 282, 284, 287, 293
Constriction 76
Conviviality 10, 22, 48, 51
Corruption 65, 70, 71
Cosmopolitan identities 5
Covid-19 11, 184, 242, 244, 253, 258, 260–262, 265–266, 268, 270, 298, 300

Dalits (menial castes) 98–99, 110

Darśana 242, 248, 261, 265–266
Defensive war 77, 79, 155
Delhi Sultanate 89
Democracy 49, 63, 74, 87, 93–95, 97, 99, 100, 102–103, 110–111, 210, 239, 276
Deshification 246, 249
Devī / Mahā Devī 244–247, 249
Devī Māhātmya 246
Devībhāgavata Purāṇa 246
Dhaka 268
Dharma Nirapeksha Rajya 100, 103
Dharmaśāstra 247, 271
Dialogue 5, 8–10, 13, 15, 18, 38–39, 57–59, 69, 72, 78–81, 83, 103, 145, 172, 174, 176, 220, 229–232, 238, 245, 283–284
Diaspora / Diasporic community 2, 13–15, 18, 44, 52–53, 186, 205, 208, 210, 242–244, 250–253, 255–256, 258–260, 263–264, 266–271, 278, 297
Digital Religion 261–263, 269–271
Disbeliever 60
Discrimination 3, 10–11, 25, 98, 161, 192, 230
Discursive traditions 60, 82
Diversity 2–4, 6, 11–12, 14, 20, 23–24, 26, 28–33, 36–40, 42, 44, 52, 60, 65, 70, 73, 75, 78, 81, 149, 183, 188, 204, 231, 298
Diversity (Religious) 20, 29, 30, 32, 35, 42–43, 47, 57, 59, 78, 101, 141, 172, 174, 190, 198, 300
Djinn 133, 135
Đổi Mới (economic reform) 168–169, 173
Durgā 266–267, 277, 279, 284
Durgā Pūjā / Navarātrī 15, 242–244, 248–254, 256–258, 260–262, 265–268, 270–271, 273, 275, 277–278, 280–281, 298, 300
Durgāpūjātattva 247, 271

Index of Subjects   309

Enemy 64, 81
Ethnic Revival 101, 107
Ethnocentrism 72
Eurocentrism 37
Everyday religion / lived religion 174, 176, 188
Exegetical approach 58

Facebook 128, 261, 264, 266, 272, 281, 284, 287, 290
Federalism 100, 111
Fragmentation 38–39, 139, 285, 292
Freedom 8, 12, 30, 41, 45, 65, 71, 77, 90, 101, 104, 141, 175, 279, 282–284, 287, 290, 293
French colonialism/Indochina War 141–143, 147, 154–155
French mandate 59

Gaṇeśa 248
Generational differences 236, 240, 258–259
Generative Model 36
Geneva Accords / Geneva Conference 141, 152, 156
Ghaṭ 248, 260
Global cities 5, 50, 113, 115, 136
Global village 6
Gospels 80–81, 151

Ḥadīṯ 69
Ḫalīfa 70
Hiǧra 78
Hindu Community of Tor Pignattara 278, 280
Hindu Rastra Swabhiman Jagran Abhiyan 109
Hinduism 13, 44, 86, 88–93, 98–101, 103, 106–107, 110–111, 117, 181, 193, 203, 242, 246, 255, 265, 270, 299
Hindutva (Hindu nationalist ideology) 109–110

Ho Chi Minh City / Saigon 141–142, 156, 158–159, 162, 164, 165, 167, 172–173, 175–176
Home-making processes 183
Ḥudaybiyya agreement 78
Hyper-diversity (Religious) 43
Hyper-pluralism (Religious) 43
Hyper-plurality (Religious) 43

Imagined Communities 109, 265, 269
Inequality 3, 4, 22, 25
Instagram 128, 261
Institutional/Normative Recognition 26, 28, 33–36, 45–46, 48, 101
Integration 4, 12, 40, 46, 142, 149, 161, 187, 212–213, 219, 237
Integration vs. Separation 103, 229, 232–234
Intercultural conviviality 10
Interfaith and interreligious marriage 170
Interfaith dialogue 78, 229, 230, 232
Interfaith dialogue events 220–231
Interreligious dialogue 5, 10, 58, 78–79, 83, 172
Interreligious dynamics 143, 149, 171–173
Interreligious pluralism/plurality 36, 39, 41
Interrituality 188
Intuitive recognition 35
Islam 13, 14, 41, 44, 57, 60–62, 72, 80–81, 92, 107, 116, 121–122, 126–127, 135, 192, 203, 206, 211–212, 214–215, 218–221, 223–224, 227, 229–230, 235–236, 238, 285
Islamic modernism 61, 82
Islamic State 76, 119
Islamic theology 83
Islamic-Christian dialogue 79
Islamist 64
Islamophobia 192, 214, 225–226
Italian Hindu Union (UII) 262, 255

Italian Residents of Tor Pignattara 275, 281, 295
Izzat (prestige/family honor) 216

Jakarta 122, 133
Jana Andolan 87, 88, 98, 109
Judaism 72
Justice 71, 73

Kailāsa 249
Kālī 243
Kārtikeya 248
Killing 62, 64, 66, 72, 75, 77, 82, 93, 105–106
Kirat 97, 108
Kolkata 268, 278
Knowledge 9–10, 61, 67, 69–71, 75, 106, 143–144, 147, 149, 167, 170, 172, 199, 216, 222–223, 229, 231, 237, 284–285
Kṛttibās's Bengali Rāmāyaṇa 245
Kumārī 243, 246, 249

Law of the jungle 69, 71
Laws of change 69
Legality vs. Religious Freedom 283
Lived religion 188
Love 75, 80–81, 250

Madhab 60, 66, 68
Mahābhārata 245
Mahiṣa 243, 246–247, 249, 277, 279
Mahiṣāsura 246–247
Mandala model 87, 89
Mārkaṇḍeya Purāṇa 245–246
Migrant / Migration 2–4, 6, 21, 23, 25, 29, 42–44, 61, 82, 88, 134, 137–38, 141, 143, 145–146, 151–154, 161, 162, 164–166, 173, 175, 183–185, 187, 199, 203, 205–208, 213, 216, 251, 254–255, 259, 267, 274, 294
Mobility 42, 82, 114, 116, 117, 134

Modernity 14, 61, 103, 169, 218, 220, 227–229, 235–236, 238
Monotheism 235, 237–238
Moral cultivation/Moral subjectification 169–170, 172
Mosque closures and protests 213, 226, 231–233, 293
Movement for the Restoration of Democracy (MRD) 95
Mughal Empire 89
Multiculturalism 185
Multiethnic 96
Muluki Ain 91
Mūrti 248, 250, 252, 260, 278, 280
Muslim Brotherhood 64, 66
Muslim Brothers 63–64
Muslim Funeral 16, 273, 275, 285, 288, 290

Nation-building 141–142, 147
Negotiation 35, 188, 203
Nenek Moyang 126, 132–133, 135
Neoliberalism 114
Nepal Federation of Indigenous Nationalities (NEFIN) 97
Nepalese Civil War 88, 91, 96–97
Nepali Congress 93–94
New religious pluralism 5
Newar people 89
Newari Buddhism 100
Northern Catholic migrants 153–154, 161, 165
Nyadran 113–114, 117, 120, 122, 125–131, 133–135

Onlife 45
Oppression 14, 76
Orissa 243, 277
Oslo Accords 64
Otherness 59, 74, 82

Paṇḍāl 250, 252, 278, 280

Panchayat System 94–95
Parish community 143, 160, 165, 167, 170–171
Pārvatī/Umā 247
Peacebuilding 1, 2, 5, 12–15, 59, 81, 83, 120, 134–135
Peaceful coexistence 5, 11, 14, 16, 142, 171–172, 274, 284
Persecution 11, 148, 151
Persuasion 69, 76–77, 82
Philip Morris International 119
Pilgrimage 185, 196–197, 199–201, 206
Place-Making 255
Plurality 14, 20, 29, 30–33, 35, 37, 41, 44–47, 182, 193, 204, 259
Plurality (religious) 30, 32–33, 35–36, 38, 42
Polarization 293–294
Positivist sociologists 57
Power asymmetries 3
Praja Parishad 92
Prāṇa 248
Prasāda 257, 281
Prophets 37, 67, 69, 70–73, 80
Public space 32, 102, 193–194, 218–219, 228–229, 237, 244, 250
Public Sphere 13–14, 32, 57, 213–215, 218, 221, 227, 230, 236–238, 292

Quranic exegesis 58

Racialization 186
Racism 4, 22, 63, 72, 275, 288, 294–295
Rana 87, 92, 93
Ranarchy 90, 92
Rationality 69, 237
Reformism 82
Refugee camps 143, 157–159
Reification 34, 46
Religious conflict 88, 273
Religious education 104, 168, 170, 174, 216–217
Religious identification 143–144

Religious freedom 6, 12, 90, 104, 154, 279, 283, 293
Religious leadership 13, 37, 142, 184, 284
Religious pluralism 5, 14, 29–30, 40–41, 46, 90–91, 94, 101, 107, 210
Religious super-diversity 1, 2, 5, 25–26, 30, 42, 49, 52, 58–60, 82, 114, 116, 120, 135, 146, 150, 183, 189, 212, 269, 276, 298
Religious super-diversity's place building 5
Remote areas 114, 117, 136
Republic of Vietnam 141, 152, 157, 164
Resettlement 119, 142–144, 153, 156–159, 166, 173, 251
Responsibility 69, 71, 73, 74, 168, 196, 225
Ritual online 265
Ritual practices 168, 171, 191, 202, 264, 269

Salafism/Salafists 61, 64, 241
Sanatana Dharma 92, 272
Sanskritization 246
Saranam 263
Śākta Purāṇas 245
Sāṛī 259
Secularism 4, 5, 17, 44, 46, 50, 62–63, 86–87, 97, 99–104, 106, 110–112, 156, 176, 215–216, 218, 229, 231–232, 236, 240–241, 279
Self-defence 76, 155
Semarang 114, 123–124, 130, 139
Shah 86–89, 92–93, 111
Shamanism 45, 89, 100, 109–110
Shared places / spaces of sharing 49, 188, 197, 200, 207–208
Śiva 249, 298
Social change 58, 67, 69, 71, 73–74, 81, 83, 225–226, 257, 292
Social media 123, 132–133, 231, 244, 262, 264–266

Social Recognition 45, 216
Socialist government 162, 216
Society of Jesus (Jesuits) 79, 150–151
Stigma 11, 36, 39, 45, 155, 162, 169, 238
Sumatra 118
Sunna 69
Sunni 41, 60, 64, 66, 82
Superconflict 15, 273
Super-diversity 3–4, 10, 14–16, 19, 21–25, 29, 31, 43, 82, 85, 115–116, 120, 134, 137, 139, 143, 145–146, 175, 182, 185, 189, 206, 251, 259, 293, 301
Surabaya 119
Sustainability (of peaceful societies) 11–12
Syncretism (Beyond Syncretism) 189–190
Systemic oppression 14

Tantrism / Tantric context 245–247
Technology 150, 169, 244, 263–264, 268
Territory / Territorialization 2, 7–8, 12, 33, 51, 116, 151, 183, 200, 255–256, 274, 282–284
Theology 14, 59–60, 81, 83, 208, 239–240, 300
Theravada Buddhism 121, 124, 209
Tibetan Buddhism 89, 100
Tolerance 39–41, 74, 77, 83, 90, 150, 226, 300

Tor Pignattara 16, 243–244, 253–254, 256, 259–261, 265, 267, 270–271, 273–285, 287, 291–300
Transmigration 137
Transnationalism 42, 182
Truth 34, 60–62, 66–68, 75, 83, 225
Tyranny 74, 76–77

Unification of Nepal 87, 95–96, 104–105, 108
Unthinkable 62
Urban Spaces 164, 170, 172, 229, 238, 255, 294

Vernacular Cosmopolitanism 193
Viceroys 74
Việt Minh 159, 174
Vietnamese Catholicism 143, 151, 154
Vietnamese nationalist movement 149, 171
Vijayā Daśamī 243
Visarjana 248–249, 252
Vishwanath Temple (Varanasi) 264

War 11, 68, 76–78, 88–89, 91, 97, 110, 143, 160, 162, 175, 189–192, 226, 229, 277
West Bengal 243, 253, 258, 277

Yogyakarta 114, 130, 132

Zoom 262, 266, 272

www.ingramcontent.com/pod-product-compliance
Lightning Source LLC
Chambersburg PA
CBHW070336240426
43665CB00045B/2046